The Spirit of
Modern Philosophy

The Spirit of Modern Philosophy

AN ESSAY IN THE FORM OF LECTURES

Josiah Royce

Dover Publications, Inc.
New York

TO MY FRIEND

𝕸𝖆𝖗𝖞 𝕲𝖗𝖆𝖞 𝖂𝖆𝖗𝖉 𝕯𝖔𝖗𝖗

I GRATEFULLY DEDICATE THIS BOOK
AS A TOKEN OF AFFECTION AND VENERATION
IN RECOGNITION OF THE WISE COUNSEL
THAT SUGGESTED ITS PREPARATION
AND OF THE THOUGHTFUL ADVICE
THAT ACCOMPANIED AND AIDED
ITS GROWTH

Published in Canada by General Publishing Company, Ltd., 30 Lesmill Road, Don Mills, Toronto, Ontario.
Published in the United Kingdom by Constable and Company, Ltd., 10 Orange Street, London WC2H 7EG.

This Dover edition, first published in 1983, is an unabridged republication of the work originally published by Houghton, Mifflin and Company, Boston, in 1892.

Manufactured in the United States of America
Dover Publications, Inc., 180 Varick Street, New York, N.Y. 10014

Library of Congress Cataloging in Publication Data

Royce, Josiah, 1855-1916.
The spirit of modern philosophy.

Reprint. Originally published: Boston: Houghton, Mifflin, 1892.
1. Philosophy, Modern. I. Title.
B791.R8   1983   190   82-17724
ISBN 0-486-24432-6

PREFACE.

———◆———

THE friend to whom I have dedicated this book asked me, a little more than two years ago, for some account of the more significant spiritual possessions of a few prominent modern thinkers. I was to tell what I could about these possessions in comparatively brief and un-technical fashion. With some misgivings as to my right and many misgivings as to my power to set forth any portion of the content of modern philosophy in the com-pass of a few short lectures, I still undertook the task, and soon found it unexpectedly absorbing. The com-pany of friends for whom I was to prepare my lectures proved to be more numerous than I had foreseen; the undertaking became more elaborate and thorough-going than I had any way intended; and the exceeding kindli-ness and earnestness of my hearers called erelong for a response that taxed all my poor wit to the utmost. My lectures once finished in their first form, under the general title "Representative Modern Thinkers and Problems," I was asked to read them yet again, before another equally cordial and stimulating company in another city. The re-reading suggested, of course, much revision. In the following year I again offered my papers, partly rewritten and much enlarged, to the members of Harvard University, as public evening lectures.   Still other opportunities to present all or part of the same material to various audiences caused me to get considerable critical aid.   I then resolved to give the whole discussion a final form.

This volume contains, therefore, an essay, in the shape of a series of lectures, and with a twofold object.   On the one hand my essay deals not so much with the minuter details as with the connections, the linkages, the general growth, of modern philosophical thought since the seventeenth century.   On the other hand my purpose is constructive as well as expository.   I have my own philosophical creed, — a growing and still elementary one, indeed; and this creed has been strongly suggested to me by what I know of the progress and outcome of modern thought.   What I have seen I delight to try to suggest.   And the book is the product of my delight, and the embodiment of my efforts at suggestion.

On the other hand, these studies are not *mere* fragments, but are bound together by a single principal idea, this idea being the one that seems to me to embody the true spirit of modern philosophy, — the doctrine concerning the world which, amidst all our vast ignorance of nature and of destiny, we still have a right to call, in its main and simple outlines, a sure possession of human thought.   What this doctrine is I have already had occasion to suggest in the more positive chapters of my book called " The Religious Aspect of Philosophy."   To the arguments of that work, particularly to the chapters therein entitled " The Possibility of Error " and " The Religious Insight " (the first containing a metaphysical discussion of the proof of the main thesis of Objective Idealism, the other a general sketch of certain conse-

quences of this thesis), I must refer such readers as may
desire a fuller acquaintance with some matters of fundamental importance which the present study, in view of its
limitations, will leave more or less incomplete. But these
lectures have their own unity, are intended to be understood by themselves, represent, I hope, a considerable
advance in the organization of the philosophical doctrine
which was set forth in the former book, and meanwhile
have the decided advantage which the historical fashion
of philosophizing always possesses as against the dialectical fashion.

Our common dependence upon the history of thought
for all our reflective undertakings is unquestionable.
Our best originality, if we ever get any originality, must
spring from this very dependence. Doctrines of genuinely revolutionary significance are rare indeed in the
history of speculation, and they ought to be so. Of
lesser surprises, of marvels, of beautifully novel insights,
all the greater highways of speculation are full; and
yet most of the marvels are only such in so far as they
are set off upon a very large background of the historically familiar. Only a very few times in the history of
thought is the continuity of the evolution distinctly
broken. The novelties are elsewhere only relative, and
get their very value from the fact that they are so.

For us to-day, after so many centuries of philosophy,
the necessity of keeping in mind our relation to earlier
thought is peculiarly pressing, and the neglect (or misunderstanding) of those historical relations is peculiarly
disastrous. Mere eclecticism in philosophy is of course
worthless. But to condemn the past, as full of error and
delusion, and then to set forth what we imagine to be our

own fundamentally significant and wholly new methods in philosophy, is a procedure that in general can have but one ending. We, then, but unwittingly transplant old growths to new soil, seeing not how old the growths are, and considering only the newness of the garden that we have planned. But the new soil is of necessity lacking in the ancient wealth and depth, and the transplanted doctrines take little root. Synthesis and critical re-organization of the truths furnished us by the past, in the light of present science, is not mere eclecticism, and leaves ample room for healthy originality. On the other hand, it is so easy to feel a train of philosophical thought to be wholly new, merely because we have eagerly thought it out, and have been all the while unaware of our actual philosophical environment and atmosphere. And yet this subjective sensation of originality, — to what unnecessary cares, to what disappointments may it not in the end lead us!

Such misadventures, I, for my part, am minded to avoid by remaining fully aware of my historical relations. Faithfulness to history is the beginning of creative wisdom. I love the latter, and want to get it. To that end, however, I cultivate the former.

The present philosophical situation in this country seems to be peculiarly favorable to such efforts. Two philosophical branches are especially prospering to-day in our Universities, the study of Empirical Psychology, and the study of the History of Philosophy. I believe for my own part that these two pursuits ought to flourish and will flourish together, and that they will lead to very important constructive work. I see no just opposition of spirit between them.

A student of philosophy, who is also occasionally a critic of his living fellow-students, is of necessity glad to have applied to his own work the same tests that he would apply to the work of others, and severer tests, too, than he would have wit to apply. Where grave errors of scholarship or profound misunderstandings of my historical relations mar my work, I desire to have the fact pointed out with the utmost definiteness of speech. For I bring no gold with me unless some portion of my work can bear the test of the most fiery trial. Let the dross suffer. I shall never regret the loss of it, nor feel aggrieved at the flames. I distinguish very easily between a student's person and his teaching. Let the man be respected according as he has meant well, and has labored with sincere devotion. I myself have never had occasion to criticise any philosophical writer of whom this could not be sincerely said. But let the teaching be tried wholly without mercy, whether meant well or not. Were we, indeed, as negative critics in philosophy, assuming the right to be judges of the hearts and of the inner and personal merits of our living philosophical opponents instead of estimating, as we do in such cases, their published work, I, for my part, remembering my own weakness and personal unworthiness, should be the first to echo, just as even now I do in the presence of God and man, the words of my departed friend, whose verses entitled "The Fool's Prayer" I have quoted in my closing lecture. But the criticism of the public deeds of scholarship, offered in the public service, is wholly independent of our personal fondness for a man, and involves no desire for other than intellectual contest with him. Therefore, such criticism,

whenever its wholly objective motive is understood, does
well to be merciless.

It is perhaps tedious, I am sure that I wish it were
quite needless, to set forth here such obvious truisms as
these. Most readers, indeed, will have them already in
mind. For such they are not intended.

However severe or kindly our critics, it is all the while
true that a book must be judged by what it undertakes,
and that this essay must, of course, have and confess
the defects of its qualities. I have tried, accordingly,
throughout my text, to avoid raising false expectations.
The reader will, indeed, find here many things that at the
outset he does *not* expect. I hope that some of these
things will be a pleasing surprise to him. But in no case
will he either expect or find technical completeness. To
be sure, the later papers are more elaborate than the earlier ones; partly because I have added to my text many
passages which were not read at all in my original lectures; partly because I have expected my hearers and
readers to grow a little in reflective patience as they became used to the argument.

I may add a few special observations on various of
the individual lectures. The traditional beginning of the
story of modern thought with the Cartesian *cogito ergo
sum* I have not employed, because it is almost universal
 in the text-books, and because, meanwhile, in its usual
context, it produces, despite its literal accuracy, a very
misleading impression. The seventeenth century was not
on the whole a period of subjectivism, but the very reverse. Descartes was himself best known to his contemporaries, not for his theory of knowledge, but for his
physical and metaphysical system. Of the philosophical

Absolutism of the century Spinoza is meanwhile the best, because the extremest representative. Interested as I here am in the broad outlines and not in the details, I have, therefore, chosen to illustrate the general attitude of the time towards the deepest problems of the spirit by this extreme but still typical case of Spinoza, and to leave the rest to a brief general sketch. In the superficial glance over the period from Spinoza to Kant I have omitted Leibnitz altogether, and I feel this to be the most serious error of mere omission in my whole book. Yet the defect proved to be inevitable, in view of my space and time limitations.

With the lecture on Kant begins a more careful study of doctrine. The modern Kant-philology has here been of indispensable service to me, so far as I have been able to follow it. Yet I have tried to write my own personal impression of Kant himself as plainly as I could. To Professors Vaihinger and Benno Erdmann every student of Kant owes a debt which, as I hope, I have not obscured for my readers by my playful remarks on pages 104–105. In the later historical lectures I have been unable to make sufficient acknowledgement of numerous literary obligations. I feel such most of all to Julian Schmidt, to Professor Haym, to Dr. Hutchinson Stirling, to Professors Windelband, Falckenberg, and J. E. Erdmann, to Professor Edward Caird, and to Principal Caird. Of footnotes I have been permitted by my plan to make only very scanty use. In case of my exposition of Hegel I have felt it needful to show by rather more frequent notes, as well as by appendix C, that between my very untechnical phraseology and Hegel's elaborate processes there is a pretty deliberately planned relation, which the professional student can verify. Schopenhauer, on the other hand, very readily lends himself to the method of these lectures, and footnotes could in his case, although unwillingly, be wholly spared. Both the Hegel and the Schopenhauer papers have appeared in the "Atlantic Monthly." Both are here considerably enlarged.

That the modern philosophical doctrine of Evolution, in its wholeness is, historically speaking, an outcome, and not a very remote one, of the Romantic movement, is an obvious observation for a student of the history of thought; and yet I am not aware that this observation has hitherto been frequently made in a form easily accessible to English readers. So important and doubtless permanent an acquisition of modern thought as is the theory of evolution deserves to be itself understood as a product of a genuine and continuous growth, and not as a special creation of Mr. Spencer, or as the result of any single catastrophic change such as even the appearance of Darwin's wonderful "Origin of Species." These things played their great part; but the historical motives of the whole movement were very deep-lying and manifold.

Two of my constructive papers in Part II, the *tenth* and the *twelfth* of the series of lectures, have been entirely rewritten, and have never been read at all as lectures in their present form. In the eleventh lecture, on Idealism, and elsewhere throughout my book I have given prominence to the strictly "metaphysical" rather than to what is technically called the "epistemological" meaning of the word *idealism* itself. The technical reader is familiar with the numerous meanings which this well-known word has come to possess. In its "epistemological" sense idealism involves a theory of the *nature of our human knowledge;* and various decidedly different theories are called by this name in view of one common feature, namely, the stress that they lay upon the " subjectivity " of a larger or smaller portion of what pretends to be our knowledge of things. In this sense Kant's theory of the subjectivity of space and time was called by himself a " Transcendental Idealism." But in its " metaphysical " sense, idealism is a theory as to *the nature of the real world*, however we may come to know that nature. Falckenberg, in his " Geschichte der neueren Philosophie," p. 476, defines one very prominent form of metaphysical idealism as the " belief in a spiritual principle at the basis of the world, without the reduction of the physical world to a mere illusion." In *this* sense, as he goes on to say, namely in the sense " that matter is an expression (*Produkt*) of the world-spirit, Fichte, Schelling, Hegel, and their allies are together named the idealistic school." As Vaihinger has well remarked, in his admirable essay on Kant's " Widerlegung des Idealismus " (p. 95), it is the metaphysical and not the epistemological meaning of the term " idealism " that has been customary in the literature since Hegel. This fact every well-informed student will have in mind whenever he uses the word without express definition.

The problems of the theory of knowledge exist of course in some form for every serious philosopher. The analyses suggested by the various forms of " epistemological " idealism will have, moreover, permanent value for the investigator of our knowledge. Every " metaphysical " idealism will have been affected in one way or another by such analyses. But to imagine that a " metaphysical " idealist is as such a person whose principles con-

sistently involve the doubt or denial of the existence of
everything and every one excepting his own finite self, is
an old and trivial misunderstanding, unworthy of an historical student.   A metaphysical idealist will of course
deal with the problem of the relation of knowledge and
its object, and will try to get at the nature of the real
world by means of a solution of this very problem.   How
he may do this I have tried to show in the proper
place.   None the less, a doctrine remains, in the metaphysical sense, idealistic, if it maintains that the world
is, in its wholeness, and in all of its real constituent
parts, a world of mind or of spirit.   The *opposite* of
an idealist, in this sense, is one who maintains the ultimate existence of wholly unspiritual realities at the basis
of experience and as the genuine truth of the world —
such unspiritual realities for instance as an absolute
"Unknowable," or, again, as what Hobbes meant by
"Body."   The "epistemological" problem, that is, the
question as to how we "transcend" the "subjective" in
our knowledge, exists at the outset of philosophy, in precisely the same sense for metaphysical realists and for
their opponents, the metaphysical idealists.   Whether and
how they are to solve this problem depends upon their
seriousness of philosophical reflection, as well as upon
what the true solution may turn out to be.   My own view
is that only the metaphysical idealist is in possession of
a successful solution for the epistemological problem (see
text, page 382).

These last remarks are meant mainly for the technical
reader, to whom, also, appendices B and C are exclusively
addressed.

But Lecture XII, on "The World of Description and

the World of Appreciation," attempts a statement of certain general speculations in a form which I feel to have its own degree of relative novelty, despite the fact that the problems are of the oldest, and that the paper is only one effort more to define a "double-aspect" theory of the relations of the physical and the moral and æsthetic worlds. I hope that the argument of this paper will be on the whole accessible to every reader. Despite the rapid flight there taken through a very wide region, what I present may have for some fellow-students a genuine and not wholly momentary suggestiveness.

My thanks are due for the constant stimulation and frequent kindly criticism received from my colleagues Professors Palmer and James. In previous publications I have more than once had occasion to acknowledge their aid, without which all my work would have been impossible. To repeat such acknowledgment is only to confess that the debt to my elder colleagues is as enduring as is my wish to make some return.

Dr. Benjamin Rand, Assistant of the Philosophical Department at Harvard, is responsible for the careful index.

JOSIAH ROYCE.

CAMBRIDGE, MASSACHUSETTS, *Jan.* 1, 1892.

CONTENTS.

The Spirit of
Modern Philosophy

THE SPIRIT OF MODERN PHILOSOPHY.

LECTURE I.

GENERAL INTRODUCTION.

IN the following course of lectures I shall try to suggest, in a fashion suited to the general student, something about the men, the problems, and the issues that seem to me most interesting in a limited, but highly representative portion of the history of modern philosophy. I undertake this work with a keen sense of the limitations of my time and my powers. I plead as excuse only my desire to interest some of my fellow-students in the great concerns of philosophy.

I.

The assumption upon which these lectures are based is one that I may as well set forth at the very beginning. It is the assumption that Philosophy, in the proper sense of the term, is not a presumptuous effort to explain the mysteries of the world by means of any superhuman insight or extraordinary cunning, but has its origin and value in an attempt to give a reasonable account of our own personal attitude towards the more serious business of life. You philosophize when you reflect critically upon what you are actually doing in your world. What you are doing is of course, in the first place, living. And life involves passions, faiths, doubts, and courage. The critical inquiry into what all these things mean and imply is philosophy. We have our faith in life; we want reflectively to estimate this faith. We feel ourselves in a world of law and of significance. Yet why we feel this homelike sense of the reality and the worth of our world is a matter for criticism. Such a criticism of life, made elaborate and thorough-going, is a philosophy.

If this assumption of mine be well-founded, it follows that healthy philosophizing, or thorough-going self-criticism, is a very human and natural business, in which you are all occasionally, if not frequently engaged, and for which you will therefore from the start have a certain sympathy. Whether we will it or no, we all of us do philosophize. The difference between the temperament which loves technical philosophy and the temperament which can make nothing of so-called metaphysics is rather one of degree than of kind. The moral order, the evils of life, the authority of conscience, the intentions of God, how often have I not heard them discussed, and with a wise and critical skepticism, too, by men who seldom looked into books. The professional student of philosophy does, as his constant business, precisely what all other people do at moments. In the life of non-metaphysical people, reflection on destiny and the deepest truths of life occupies much the same place as music occupies in the lives of appreciative, but much distracted amateurs. The constant student of philosophy is merely the professional musician of reflective thought. He daily plays his scales in the form of what the scoffers call "chopping logic." He takes, in short, a delight in the technical subtleties of his art which makes his enthusiasm often incomprehensible to less devoted analysts of life. But his love for speculation is merely their own natural taste somewhat specialized. He is a sort of miser, secretly hoarding up the treasures of reflection which other people wear as the occasional ornaments of intercourse, or use as a part of the heavier coinage of conversation. If, as non-professional philosophers, you confine your reflections to moments, the result is perhaps a serious talk with a friend, or nothing more noteworthy than an occasional hour of meditation, a dreamy glance of wonder, as it were, at this whole great and deep universe before you, with its countless worlds and its wayward hearts. Such chance heart searchings, such momentary communings with the universal, such ungrown germs of reflection, would under other circumstances develop into systems of philosophy. If you let them pass from your attention you soon forget them, and may then even fancy that you have small fondness for metaphysics. But, none the less, all intelligent people, even including the haters of metaphysics, are despite themselves occasionally metaphysicians.

II.

All this, however, by way of mere opening suggestion. What you wish to know further, through this introductory lecture, is, how this natural tendency to reflect critically upon life leads men to frame elaborate systems of philosophy, why it is that these systems have been so numerous and so varied in the past, and whether or no it seems to be true, as many hold, that the outcome of all this long and arduous labor of the philosophers has so far been nothing but doubtful speculation and hopeless variety of opinion. I suppose that a student who knows little as yet of the details of philosophic study feels as his greatest difficulty, when he approaches the topic for the first time, the confusing variety of the doctrines of the philosophers, joined as it is with the elaborateness and the obscurity that seem so characteristic of technical speculation. So much labor, you say, and all thus far in vain! For if the thinkers really aimed to bring to pass an agreement amongst enlightened persons about the great truths that are to be at the basis of human life, how sadly, you will say, they seemed to have failed! How monstrous on the one hand their toils! Hegel's eighteen

volumes of published books and of posthumously edited
lecture notes are but a specimen of what such men have
produced. A prominent English philosopher was flip-
pantly accused, a few years since, in a gay and irrespon-
sible volume of reminiscences, of having been the writer
of books that, as the scoffing author in substance said,
"fill several yards on the shelves of our libraries." The
prominent philosopher indignantly responded, in a letter
addressed to a literary weekly. "His critic," said he,
"was recklessly inaccurate." As a fact his own collected
works, set side by side on a shelf, cover a little less than
two feet! How vast the toil, then, and on the other hand,
to what end? A distinguished German student of the
history of philosophy, Friedrich Albert Lange, upon one
occasion, wrote these words: "Once for all we must definitely set aside the claim of the metaphysicians, of whatever school and tendency, that their deductions are such
as forbid any possible strife, or that if you only first thoroughly come into possession of every detail of some system
six fat volumes long, then, and not till then, you will recognize with wonder how each and every individual conclusion was sound and clear." Does not this assertion of
Lange's, this definitive setting aside of the claim of the
metaphysicians, seem warranted by the facts? What one
of these systems, six fat volumes long, has ever satisfied in
its entirety any one but the master who wrote it, and the
least original and thoughtful of his pupils? What so
pathetic, then, in this history of scholarly production, as
this voluminous and systematic unpersuasiveness of the
philosophers? They aimed, each one in his own private
way, at the absolute, and so, if they failed, they must,
you will think, have failed utterly. Each one raised, all
alone, his own temple to his own god, declared that he, the
first of men, possessed the long-sought truth, and undertook to initiate the world into his own mysteries. Hence
it is that so many temples lie in ruins and so many images

of false gods are shattered to fragments. I put the case thus strongly against the philosophers, because I am anxious to have you comprehend from the start how we are to face this significant preliminary difficulty of our topic. It may be true that the philosophers deal with life, and that, too, after a fashion known and occasionally tried by all of us. But is not their dealing founded upon vain pretense? How much better, you may say, to live nobly than to inquire thus learnedly and ineffectually into the mysteries of life? As the "Imitation of Christ" so skillfully states the case against philosophy, speaking indeed from the point of view of simple faith, but using words that doubters, too, can understand, "What doth it profit thee to enter into deep discussion concerning the Holy Trinity, if thou lack humility, and be thus displeasing to the Trinity? For verily it is not deep words that make a man holy and upright. I had rather feel contrition than be skillful in the definition thereof." And again, "Tell me now where are all those masters and teachers, whom thou knewest well, when they were yet with you, and flourished in learning? Their stalls are now filled by others, who perhaps never have one thought concerning them. Whilst they lived they seemed to be somewhat, but now no one speaks of them. Oh, how quickly passeth the glory of the world away! Would that their life and knowledge had agreed together! For then would they have read and inquired unto good purpose." Or once again, and this time in the well-known words of Fitzgerald's "Omar Khayyám" stanzas : —

> "Why all the Saints and Sages who discussed
> Of the two worlds so learnedly are thrust
> Like foolish prophets forth. Their words to Scorn
> Are scattered, and their mouths are stopt with dust."

Well, if such is the somewhat portentous case against philosophy, what can we say for philosophy? I answer first, that the irony of fate treats all human enterprises in precisely this way, if one has regard to the immediate intent of the men engaged in them. Philosophy is not alone in missing her directly sought aim. But true success lies often in serving ends that were higher than the ones we intended to serve. Surely no statesman ever founded an enduring social order; nay, one may add that no statesman ever produced even temporarily the precise social order that he meant to found. No poet ever gave us just the song that in his best moments he had meant and hoped to sing. No human life ever attained the fulfillment of the glorious dreams of its youth. And as for passing away, and being forgotten, and having one's mouth stopped with dust, surely one is not obliged to be either a saint or a sage to have that fate awaiting one. But still the saints and sages are not total failures, even if they are forgotten. There was an enduring element about them. They did not wholly die.

In view of all this, what we need to learn concerning philosophy is, not whether its leaders have in any sense failed or not, but whether its enterprise has been essentially a worthy one, one through which the human spirit has gained; whether the dark tower before which these Rolands have ended their pilgrimage has contained treasures in any way worthy of their quest. For a worthy quest always leaves good traces behind it, and more treasures are won by heroes than they visibly bring home in their own day. A more careful examination of the true office of philosophy may serve to show us, in fact, both why final success in it has been unattainable and why the partial successes have been worth the cost. Let such an examination be our next business.

III.

The task of humanity, to wit, the task of organizing here on earth a worthy social life, is in one sense a hopelessly complex one. There are our endlessly numerous

material foes, our environment, our diseases, our weaknesses. There are amongst us men ourselves, our rival-
ries, our selfish passions, our anarchical impulses, our
blindness, our weak wills, our short and careful lives.
These things all stand in the way of progress. For progress, for organization, for life, for spirituality, stand, as
the best forces, our healthier social instincts, our courage, our endurance, and our insight. Civilization depends
upon these. How hopeless every task of humanity, were
not instinct often on the side of order and of spirituality.
How quick would come our failure, were not courage and
endurance ours. How blindly chance would drive us, did
we not love insight for its own sake, and cultivate contemplation even when we know not yet what use we can
make of it. And so, these three, if you will, to wit,
healthy instinct, enduring courage, and contemplative insight, rule the civilized world. He who wants life to pros-
per longs to have these things alike honored and cultivated.
They are brethren, these forces of human spirituality; they
cannot do without one another; they are all needed.

Well, what I have called contemplative insight, that
disposition and power of our minds whereby we study
and enjoy truth, expresses itself early and late, as you
know, in the form of a searching curiosity about our world
and about life, a curiosity to which you in vain endeavor
to set bounds. As the infant that studies its fist in the
field of vision does not know as yet why this curiosity
about space and about its own movements will be of service to it, so throughout life there is something unpractical, wayward, if so you choose to call it, in all our curious
questionings concerning our world. The value of higher
insight is seldom immediate. Science has an element
of noble play about it. It is not the activity, it is the
often remote outcome of science, that is of practical service. Insight is an ally of the moral nature of man, an
ally of our higher social instincts, of our loyalty, of our

courage, of our devotion ; but the alliance is not always
one intended directly by the spirit of curious inquiry
itself. A singular craft of our nature links the most
theoretical sorts of inquiry by unexpected ties with men's
daily business. One plays with silk and glass and amber,
with kites that one flies beneath thunder clouds, with
frogs' legs and with acids. The play is a mere expression
of a curiosity that former centuries might have called idle.
But the result of this play recreates an industrial world.
And so it is everywhere with our deeper curiosity. There
is a sense in which it is all superfluous. Its immediate
results seem but vanity. One could surely live without
them ; yet for the future, and for the spiritual life of mankind, these results are destined to become of vast import.
Without this cunning contrivance of our busy brains,
with their tireless curiosity and their unpractical wonder-
ings, what could even sound instinct and the enduring
heart have done to create the world of the civilized man ?

Of all sorts of curiosity one of the most human and
the most singular is the reflective curiosity whose highest
expression is philosophy itself. This form of curiosity
scrutinizes our own lives, our deepest instincts, our most
characteristic responses to the world in which we live, our
typical " reflex actions." It tries to bring us to a self-
consciousness as to our temperaments. Our temperaments, our instincts, are in one sense fatal. We cannot
directly alter them. What philosophy does is to find
them out, to bring them to the light, to speak in words
the very essence of them. And so the historical office of
the greatest philosophers has always been to reword, as it
were, the meaning and the form of the most significant
life, temperaments, and instincts of their own age. As
man is social, as no man lives alone, as your temperament
is simply the sum total of your social " reflex actions," is
just your typical bearing towards your fellows, the great
philosopher, in reflecting on his own deepest instincts and

faiths, inevitably describes, in the terms of his system, the characteristic attitude of his age and people. So, for instance, Plato and Aristotle, taken together, express for us, in their philosophical writings, the essence of the highest Greek faith and life. The Greek love of the beautiful and reverence for the state, the Greek union of intellectual freedom with conventional bondage to the forms of politics and of religion, the whole Greek attitude towards the universe, in so far as the Athens of that age could embody it, are made articulate in enduring form in the speculations of these representative men. They consciously interpret this Hellenic life, — they do also more : they criticise it. Plato especially is in some of his work a fairly destructive analyst of his nation's faith. And yet it is just this faith, incorporated as it was into his own temperament, bred into his every fibre, that he must needs somehow express in his doctrine. And now perhaps you may already see why there is of necessity nothing absolute, nothing final, about much that a Plato himself may have looked upon as absolute and as final in his work. Greek life was not all of human life ; Greek life was doomed to pass away ; Greek instincts and limitations could not be eternal. The crystal heavens that the Greek saw above him were indeed doomed to be rolled up like a scroll, and the elements of his life were certain to pass away in fervent heat. But then, into all nobler future humanity, Greek life was certain to enter, as a factor, as a part of its civilized instincts, as an ennobling passion in its artistic production, as a moment of its spirituality. And therefore, too, Plato's philosophy, doomed in one sense not to be absolute or final, has its part, as a fact, in your own reflection to-day, and would have its part in the absolute philosophical estimate of the highest human life if ever we attained that estimate. If philosophy criticises, estimates, and to that end rewords life, if the great philosopher expresses in his system the most

characteristic faiths and passions of his age, then indeed
the limitation of the age will be in a sense the limitation
of the philosophy; and with the life whose temperament
it reflectively embodied the philosophy will pass away.
It will pass away, but it will not be lost. A future humanity will, if civilization healthily progresses, inherit the
old kingdom, and reëmbody the truly essential and immortal soul of its old life. This new humanity, including in
itself the spirit of the old, will need something, at least,
of the old philosophy to express in reflective fashion its
own attitude towards the universe. This something that
it needs of the old philosophy may not be that which the
philosopher had himself imagined to be his most absolute
possession. Like the statesman, he will have builded
better than he knew. As Cæsar's Roman empire had for
its destiny not to exclude the Germans, as Cæsar had
driven out Ariovistus, but to civilize and to Christianize
them, and finally to pass in great part over to their keeping, so Plato's philosophy had for its office to suggest
thoughts that Christianity afterwards made the common
treasure of the very humanity that his mind would have
regarded as hopelessly barbarian. No, the philosopher's
work is not lost when, in one sense, his system seems to
have been refuted by death, and when time seems to have
scattered to scorn the words of his dust-filled mouth.
His immediate end may have been unattained; but thousands of years may not be long enough to develop for
humanity the full significance of his reflective thought.

Insight, this curious scrutiny of ours into the truth,
keeps here, as you will see, its immediately unpractical,
its ultimately significant character. There is indeed a
sense in which life has no need of the philosopher. He
does not invent life, nor does he lead in its race; he
follows after; he looks on; he is no prophet to inspire
men; he has a certain air of the playful about him.
Plato, in a famous passage, makes sport of the men of the

world, who are driven by business, who are oppressed by the law courts, whose only amusement is evil gossip about their neighbors. The philosopher, on the contrary, according to Plato, has infinite leisure, and accordingly thinks of the infinite, but does not know who his next neighbor is, and never dreams of the law courts, or of finishing his business at any fixed hour. His life is a sort of artistic game ; his are not the passions of the world ; his is the reflection that comprehends the world. The Thracian servant maids laugh at him, as the one in the story laughed at Thales, because he stares at the heavens, and hence occasionally falls into wells. But what is he in the sight of the gods, and what are the servant maids ? When *they* are some day asked to look into the heavens, and to answer concerning the truth, what scorn will not be their lot ? After some such fashion does Plato seek to glorify the contemplative separation from the pettiness of life which shall give to the philosopher his freedom. And yet, as we know, this freedom, this sublime playfulness, of even a Plato, does not suggest the real justification of his work. This game of reflection is like all the rest of our insight, indirectly valuable because from it all there is a return to life possible, and in case of a great thinker like Plato, certain to occur. The coming humanity shall learn from the critic who, standing indeed outside of life, embodied in his reflection the meaning of it.

Thus far, then, my thought has been simply this. Humanity depends, for its spirituality and its whole civilization, upon faiths and passions that are in the first place instinctive, inarticulate, and in part unconscious. The philosopher tries to formulate and to criticise these instincts. What he does will always have a two-fold limitation. It will, on the one hand, be criticism from the point of view of a single man, of a single age, of a single group of ideals, as Plato or Aristotle embodied the faith of but one great age of Greek life, and did that from a somewhat private and personal point of view. This first necessary limitation of the philosopher's work makes his system less absolute, less truthful, less final than he had meant it to be. Another humanity will have a new faith, a new temperament, and in so far will need a new philosophy. Only the final and absolute humanity, only the ultimate and perfect civilization, would possess, were such a civilization possible on earth, the final and absolute philosophy. But this limitation, as we have seen, while it dooms a philosopher to one kind of defeat, does n't deprive his work of worth. His philosophy is capable of becoming and remaining just as permanently significant as is his civilization and its temperament; his reflective work will enter into future thought in just the same fashion as the deeper passions of his age will beget the spiritual temper of those who are to come after.

There remains as second limitation, so we have seen, the always seemingly unfruitful critical attitude of the philosopher. He speculates, but does not prophesy; he criticises, but does not create. Yet this limitation he shares with all theory, with all insight; and the limitation is itself only partial and in great measure illusory. Criticism means self-consciousness, and self-consciousness means renewed activity on a higher plane. The reflective play of one age becomes the passion of another. Plato creates Utopias, and the Christian faith of Europe afterwards gives them meaning. Contemplation gives birth to future conduct, and so the philosopher also becomes, in his own fashion, a world-builder.

IV.

But now, having said so much for the philosopher, I may venture to say yet more, that if his work is not lost in so far as it enters into the life of the humanity which comes after him, there is yet another and a deeper sense in which his labor is not in vain. For truth is once for

all manifold, and especially is the truth about man's relation to the universe manifold. The most fleeting passion, if so be it is only deep and humane, may reveal to
us some aspect of truth which no other moment of life
can fully express. I know how difficult it is to comprehend that seemingly opposing assertions about the world
may, in a deeper sense, turn out to be equally true. I
must leave to later discussions a fuller illustration of how,
for instance, the optimist, who declares this world to be
divine and good, and the pessimist, who finds in our finite
world everywhere struggle and sorrow, and who calls it
all evil, may be, and in fact are, alike right, each in his
own sense ; or of how the constructive idealist, who declares all reality to be the expression of divine ideals, and
the materialist, who sees in nature only matter in motion
and law absolute, may be but viewing the same truth from
different sides. All this, I say, will be touched upon
hereafter. What I here want to suggest is that the truth
about this world is certainly so manifold, so paradoxical,
so capable of equally truthful and yet seemingly opposed
descriptions, as to forbid us to declare a philosopher
wrong in his doctrine merely because we find it easy to
make plausible a doctrine that at first sight appears to
conflict with his own. Young thinkers always find refutation easy, and old doctrines not hard to transcend ; and
yet what if the soul of the old doctrines should be true
just because the new doctrines seemingly oppose, but
actually complete them ? Our reflective insights, in following our life, will find now this, now that aspect of
things prominent. What if all the aspects should contain truth ? What if our failure thus far to find and to
state the absolute philosophy were due to the fact, not
that all the philosophies thus far have been essentially
false, but that the truth is so wealthy as to need not only
these, but yet other and future expressions to exhaust its
treasury? I speak thus far tentatively and vaguely. I

must illustrate a little, although at best I can thus far only suggest.

Some people have a fashion of recording their reflective moments just as they happen to come. If such persons chance to be poets, the form of the record is often the thoughtful lyric. And the thoughtful lyric poem usually possesses the very quality which made Aristotle call poetry a "more philosophical" portrayal of human life than history. It is indeed marvelous how metaphysical a great poem of passion almost always is. The passion of the moment makes its own universe, flashes back like a jewel the light of the far-off sun of truth, but colors this reflected light with its own mysterious glow. "You are, you shall be mine," cries the strong emotion to the earth and to the whole choir of heaven, and the briefest poem may contain a sort of philosophic scheme of the entire creation. The scheme is sometimes as false as the passion portrayed is transient; but it is also often as true as the passion is deep, and whoever has once seen how variously and yet how significantly the moods expressed in great poems interpret both our life and the reality of which our life forms part, will not be likely to find that philosophical systems are vain merely because the philosophers, like the poets, differ. In fact the reason why there is as yet no one final philosophy may be very closely allied to the reason why there is no final and complete poem. Life is throughout a complicated thing; the truth of the spirit remains an inexhaustible treasure house of experience; and hence no individual experience, whether it be the momentary insight of genius recorded in the lyric poem, or the patient accumulation of years of professional plodding through the problems of philosophy, will ever fully tell all the secrets which life has to reveal.

It is for just this reason, so I now suggest, that when you study philosophy, you have to be tolerant, receptive,

willing to look at the world from many sides, fearless as
to the examination of what seem to be even dangerous
doctrines, patient in listening to views that look even ab-
horrent to common sense. It is useless to expect a simple
and easy account of so paradoxical an affair as this our
universe and our life. When you first look into philosophy you are puzzled and perhaps frightened by those
manifold opinions of the philosophers of which we have
thus far had so much to say. " If they, who have thought
so deeply, differ so much," you say, " then what hope is
there that the truth can ever be known?" But if you
examine further you find that this variety, better studied,
is on its more human side largely an expression of the
liveliness and individuality of the spiritual temperaments
of strong men. The truth is not in this case "in the
middle." The truth is rather " the whole." Let me
speak at once in the terminology of a special philosophical
doctrine, and say that the world spirit chose these men
as his voices, — these men and others like them, and that
in fact he did so because he had all these things to voice.
Pardon this fashion of speech; I shall try to make it
clearer hereafter. Their experience then, let me say, is,
in its apparently confusing variety, not so much a seeing
of one dead reality from many places, but rather a critical
rewording of fragments of the one life which it is the destiny of man to possess and to comprehend. These warring musicians strike mutually discordant tones. But let
each sing his song by himself, and the whole group of
Meistersänger shall discourse to you most excellent music.
For grant that the philosophers are all in fact expressing
not dead truth, but the essence of human life, then because this life is many-sided, the individual expressions
cannot perfectly agree. It is the union of many such
insights that will be the one true view of life. Or again,
using the bolder phrases, let us say that all these thinkers
are trying to comprehend a little of the life of the one

World Spirit who lives and moves in all things. Then surely this life, which in our world needs both the antelopes and the tigers to embody its endless vigor, that life which the frost and cold, the ice and snow, do bless and magnify, is not a life which any one experience can exhaust. All the philosophers are needed, not merely to make jarring assertions about it, but to give us embodiments now of this, now of that fragment of its wealth and its eternity. And in saying this I don't counsel you in your study of philosophy merely to jumble together all sorts of sayings of this thinker and of that, and then to declare, as makers of eclectic essays and of books of extracts love to say, " This is all somehow great and true." What I mean is that, apart from the private whims and the non-essential accidents of each great philosopher, his doctrine will contain for the critical student an element of permanent truth about life, a truth which in its isolation may indeed contradict the view of his equally worthy co-workers, but which, in union, in synthesis, in vital connection with its very bitterest opposing doctrines, may turn out to be an organic portion of the genuine treasure of humanity. Nobody hates more than I do mere eclecticism, mere piecing together of this fragment and that for the bare love of producing fraudulent monuments of philosophic art. But the fact is that, frauds aside, the god-like form of truth exists for us men, as it were, in statuesque but scattered remnants of the once perfect marble. Through the whole ruined world, made desolate by the Turks of prejudice and delusion, the philosophers wander, finding here and there one of these bits of the eternal and genuine form of the goddess. Though I hate fraudulent restorations of a divine antiquity, still I know that, notwithstanding all, these fragments do somehow belong together, and that the real truth is no one of the bits, but *is* the whole goddess. What we who love philosophy long for is no piece-work, but that matchless whole itself.

The kind of philosophical breadth of view for which I am now pleading is not, I assure you, the same as mere vagueness, merely lazy toleration, of all sorts of conflicting opinions. Nobody is more aware than I am that the errors and false theories of the philosophers are facts as real as are the manifold expressions which they give to truth. I am not pleading for inexactness or undecisiveness of thought. What I am really pleading for, as you will see in the sequel, is a form of philosophic reflection that leads to a very definite and positive theory of the universe itself, the theory, namely, which I have just suggested, a theory not at all mystical in its methods, nor yet, in its results, really opposed to the postulates of science, or to the deeper meaning at the heart of common sense. This theory is that the whole universe, including the physical world also, is essentially one live thing, a mind, one great Spirit, infinitely wealthier in his experiences than we are, but for that very reason to be comprehended by us only in terms of our own wealthiest experience. I don't assume the existence of such a life in the universe because I want to be vague or to seem imaginative. The whole matter appears to me, as you will hereafter see, to be one of exact thought. The result, whatever it shall be, must be reached in strict accord with the actual facts of experience and the actual assumptions of human science. The truth, whenever we get it, must be as hard and fast as it is manifold. But the point is that *if* the universe is a live thing, a spiritual reality, we, in progressing towards a comprehension of its nature, must needs first comprehend our own life. And in doing this we shall pass through all sorts of conflicting moods, theories, doctrines ; and these doctrines, in the midst of their conflict and variety, will express, in fragmentary ways, aspects of the final doctrine, so that, as I said, the truth will be the whole.

V.

Thus far I have spoken of the various opinions and of the general human significance of the philosophers. I called attention, also, a little while since, to the apparently unpractical attitude that they assume towards life. In this connection I have already suggested that their criticism of life has often its destructive side. In these present days, when philosophy is frequently so negative, it is precisely this destructive, this skeptically critical character of philosophy, that to the minds of many constitutes its best-known character, and its most obvious danger. It is not mine to defend recent philosophy from the charge of being often cruelly critical. To many of us it might, indeed, in pity be said: "Mayest thou never know what thou art." I have myself more than once felt the pang, as I have studied philosophy, of finding out to my sorrow what I am. I have, therefore, many times lamented that philosophy is indeed often so sternly and so negatively critical of many things that our hearts have loved and prized. If any one fears the pangs of self-consciousness, it is not my office to counsel him to get it. But I must, indeed, point out here that when a wise philosophy is destructive, the true fault lies not with the critic who finds the wound in our faith, but with the faith that has secretly nursed its own wounds in unconsciousness. Philosophy, in the true sense of that word, never destroys an ideal that is worth preserving. Coming to consciousness of yourself can only bring to light weakness in case the weakness already exists in you. If you fear, I say, the pang of such a discovery, — and, as I can assure you, the pang is often keen, — then do not try philosophy. For the rest, however, this relation of philosophy to positive faith is one whereof I may speak in yet a very few words before I leave it. Let me point out in what sense philosophy is critical, but in what sense also it can hope to be constructive.

Of course philosophy, as thus far described, is sure to begin at once, if it can, with inquiries into the largest and most significant instincts, the deepest faiths of humanity. These, when it discovers them, it will single out and criticise. Hence, indeed, the philosophers are always talking of such problems as duty and God. Hence they inquire how we can come to know whether there is any external world at all, and, if so, whether this world is to be treated as dead matter, or as live mind. Hence they are curious to study our ideas of natural law, of moral freedom, of time, of space, of causation, of self. They pry into the concerns of faith as if these were theirs by divine right. They are not only prying, they are on one side of their activity merciless, skeptical, paradoxical, inconsiderate. They don't ask, it would seem, how dear your faith is to you; they analyze it, as they would the reflex action of a starfish, or the behavior of a pigeon; and then they try to estimate faith objectively, as an editor looks critically at a love-sonnet which somebody has sent him (a sonnet written with the author's heart's blood), and weighs it coolly and cruelly before he will consent to find it available. Even so the philosopher has his standard of the availability of human faiths. You have to satisfy this with your creed before he will approve you. All this sometimes seems cynical, just as the editor's coolness may become provoking. But then, as you know, the editor, with all his apparent cruelty, is a man of sympathy and of more than negative aims. He has to consider what he calls availability, because he has his critical public to please. And the philosopher — he, too, has to be critical and to seem cruel, because he also has a public to please with his estimate; and his chosen public ought to be no less than the absolute judge, the world spirit himself, in whose eyes the philosopher can find favor only if he be able to sift the truth from the error. That is why he is rigid. Nothing but an absolute critical standard ought to satisfy

him, because he wants nothing short of the truth itself.
He will fail to get it, but then, as I have said, we all of us
fail more or less in some career or other; and the metaphysician, with his one talent of critical estimate, must do
what he can.

Yet I hasten to correct this seemingly too lifeless a
picture of the philosopher's cruel analysis of passion, by
a reference to the thoughts upon which I have already
dwelt. From the often disheartening difficulties and incompleteness of the human search for absolute truth, we
who read philosophy continually find ourselves returning,
hand to hand with the author himself, to the world of the
concrete passions which he criticises. We find this world
at each return more fair and yet more serious, because we
know it better. The sacred tears that were shed in it are
none the less sacred because we have been trying to find
out from the critic what they meant. Their mystery,
long pried into, becomes even the dearer for that. The
criticised passions become like old letters, treasured up by
a lover after his dear friend's death, — often read and reread, until the reader has looked at every curve to know
why it was traced in just this way. He has found out, or
not, — still the search was consoling. So, too, we have
analyzed our long past life; and now the more confidently
may we henceforth live in the new life before us. We
have criticised, so much the more cheerfully may we enjoy. I once saw something of a pair of literary lovers,
friends of mine, who, being a trifle reflective, were prone
to amuse themselves by affecting to treat each other's productions with a certain editorial coldness and severity of
critical estimate. They wrote poems to each other, sup-
pressing or changing of course the names, and then each,
wholly ignoring whom this poem might be intended to
mean, used to pick the other's work to pieces with an air
of gentle and pathetic disdain. " Here the sentiment
somehow failed to justify its object, being expressed un-

musically. There the experiment was a clever one, but the lines were such as a dispassionate observer (like either of us who should happen not to be the author) could not approve, might even smile at." These people never precisely quarreled, to my knowledge, at least over their literary criticism. I was not able to make out altogether why they did this sort of thing, but, so far as I could discover, they both liked it, and were the better lovers for it. I conjecture that their delight must have resembled the kind of joy that philosophical students take in analyzing life. Let me admit frankly: it is indeed the joy, if you like, of playing cat and mouse with your dearest other self. It is even somewhat like the joy, if so you choose to declare, which infants take in that primitive form of hide and seek that is suited to their months. " Where is my truth, my life, my faith, my temperament? " says the philosopher. And if, some volumes further on in the exposition of his system, he says, " Oh! *there* it is," the healthy babies will be on his side in declaring that such reflections are not wholly without their rational value. But why do I thus apparently degrade speculation by again deliberately comparing it with a game? Because, I answer, in one sense, all consciousness is a game, a series of longings and of reflections which it is easy to call superfluous if witnessed from without. The justification of consciousness is the having of it. And this magnificent play of the spirit with itself, this infantile love of rewinning its own wealth ever anew through deliberate loss, through seeking, and through joyous recognition, what is this, indeed, but the pastime of the divine life itself? We enter into the world of the spirit just when even the tragedy of life becomes for our sight as much a divine game as a divine tragedy, when we know that the world is not only serious, terrible, cruel, but is also a world where a certain grim humor of the gods is at home ; when we see in it a world, too, where a serene and childlike confidence is justified, a world where courage is in place as well as reverence, and sport as well as seriousness; where, above all, the genius of reflection, expressing at once vast experience of life and a certain infantile cheerfulness or even sportiveness of mood, rightfully lets itself loose in the freest form, now assuming a stern and critical air, now demurely analyzing, as if there were nothing else to do, now prying into men's hearts like a roguish boy playing with precious jewels, now pretending that all faith is dead, now serenely demonstrating unexpected truths, and, last of all, plunging back again into life with the shout of them that triumph.

VI.

It now behooves me, in conclusion, to say something of the relation of a course of lectures like the one herewith begun to the technicalities of philosophical study. There is a great deal in every noteworthy metaphysical treatise which can be grasped only by special study. I shall make little attempt to transgress into this more technical field during these lectures. I must, indeed, discuss topics which only a rare kindliness on your part can make clearly comprehensible, for they are, once for all, serious and difficult, but I do not understand it to be the purpose of our present discourse to give what in the University would be called an Introduction to the literature of metaphysics proper. The only question that can arise about such a proceeding as I here propose is, of course, a question as to whether it is worth while to separate the general consideration of philosophical tendencies from a more minute study of the works of the philosophers. Such a question only the outcome can decide. I am aware that it is hard to be historically accurate in what I have to say without being much more specific than I shall have time to be. I must warn you at the outset that a full and fair understanding of any great thinker demands a knowledge, both of the history of thought in general, and of his own period in particular, which it is very hard, even for the professional student, after years of study, to attain. All fragmentary views, meanwhile, have something of the misleading about them. Yet, on the other hand, the necessary imperfections of a partial expression of the truth never ought to discourage us from expressing all the truth that we can. The purpose of the subsequent lectures will in any case be sufficiently accomplished, if they bring you nearer to the throbbing heart of this intense modern speculative interest, so that you shall better know that warm blood flows in philosophic veins.

For the rest, I confess to you that, although I myself often take a certain personal delight in the mere subtleties of speculation, although I also enjoy at times that miserliness which makes the professional student hoard up the jewels of reflection for the sake of gloating over their mere hardness and glitter, I find always that when I come to think of the thing fairly, there is, after all, no beauty in a metaphysical system, which does not spring from its value as a record of a spiritual experience. I love the variety of the philosophers, as I love the variety of the thoughtful looks which light up earnest young faces. I love all these because they express passion, wonder, truth. But alas for me if ever I have for professional reasons to study a book behind whose technical subtleties I can catch no glimpse of the manly heart of its author. His conclusions may be sound. I shall then hate him only the more for that. Error may be dull if it chooses ; but there is no artistic blasphemy equal to so placing the harp of truth as to make it sound harsh and wooden when you strike it fairly. Philosophical books I have read, with whose doctrines, as doctrines, I have even been forced in great measure to agree ; and yet, so lifeless, so bloodless, were their authors, so reptilian were the cold and slowly writhing sentences in which their thought was expressed, that I have laid down such volumes with a sense of disgrace and rebellion, " bitterly ashamed," as a friend of mine has expressed the same feeling in my hearing, " bitterly ashamed to find myself living in a universe whose truth could possibly be made so inefficacious and uninteresting." To be sure, in saying all this I am far from desiring to make technical metaphysics easy, for the study is a laborious one ; and there are many topics in logic, in the theory of the sciences, and in ethics, to whose comprehension there is no royal road. But then, once your eyes opened, and you will indeed find subjects that at first seemed dry and inhuman full of life and even of passion ; as, for instance, few sciences are in their elementary truths more enticing to the initiated, more coy and baffling to the reflective philosophical student, in fact, more romantic, than is the Differential Calculus. But if such matters lie far beyond our present field, I mention them only to show that even the hardest and least popular reflective researches are to be justified, in the long run, by their bearings upon life.

PART I.

STUDIES OF THINKERS AND PROBLEMS.

LECTURE II.

OUR general purpose in these lectures has now been
defined. As we pass to the study of certain representative modern thinkers and problems, the difference between
our method and that of a text-book, or of a regular course
of academic lectures on the history of modern thought,
must be well borne in mind. We wish to select certain
tendencies especially characteristic of the spirit of modern
philosophy. We shall therefore lay most stress upon
what happened in the culminating period of modern
thought, — that from Kant to Schopenhauer, — and upon
the problems that seem to me most permanent and significant in that period itself. In earlier periods our method
will be one of the briefest sketching. Later we shall
become more specific. Of no thinker before Kant shall
we give any extended account. Several thinkers of first
rank, such as Descartes, Malebranche, Leibnitz, we shall
barely mention or wholly ignore. Always, even where we
are fullest in statement, we shall select those aspects of
the thinker in question that concern our own undertaking. What this undertaking will lead to will not become
manifest until, in the second part of our course, we have
suggested in outline a certain philosophical creed to which
I wish to direct your attention.

It is in vain that one seeks, in the history of thought,
to choose any perfectly satisfactory place of beginning for

the purpose of a course of lectures like this. Always one must run a risk of producing the illusion in your minds that the point where he chances to begin is somehow peculiarly significant as a beginning. But always, of course, if you should ever hereafter come to look deeper, you would find this point of beginning very arbitrary, and what immediately preceded it vastly important for the true understanding of the whole matter. My beginning, therefore, as I must warn you, will be indeed very arbitrary, just as my methods will have to be very different from those of a text-book.

I.

As to the general scope of our course, modern philosophy, our topic in what follows, is as wealthy and complex an evolution in its way as is the life which it depicts. What we call modern thought, in these matters, is a very recent affair, dating back only to the seventeenth century. Since then, however, philosophy has lived through several great periods, which for our purpose we may reduce to three.

The first period was one of what we may call naturalism, pure and simple. It belongs almost wholly to the seventeenth century. The philosophy of this first age lived in a world where two things seemed clear: first, that nature is full of facts which conform fatally to exact and irreversible law, and second, that man lives best under a strong, a benevolently despotic civil government. The philosophers of this time had left off contemplating the heaven of mediæval piety, and were disposed to deify nature. They adored the rigidity of geometrical methods; they loved the study of the new physical science, which had begun with Galileo. Man they conceived as a mechanism. Human emotions, even the loftiest, they delighted in explaining by very simple and fundamental natural passions. There is often something merciless and cynical about their analysis of many things

sacred in human life. They are cold, formal, systematic,
at least as to the outward shape of their doctrines. At
heart, however, they are not without a deep piety of their
own. The nature which they deify has its magnificent
dignity. It is no respecter of our sentimentalities ; but
it does embody a certain awful justice. You would pray
to it in vain ; but you may interrogate it fearlessly, for it
hides no charmed and magical secrets in its breast which
an unlucky word might render dangerous to the inquirer.
It notices no insult ; it blasts no curious questioner for
his irreverence. This nature is a wise nature. Her best
children are those who labor most patiently to comprehend
her laws. The weak she crushes ; but the thoughtful she
honors. She knows no miracles ; but her laws are an inexhaustible treasure house of resources to the knowing.
In fact, knowledge of such laws is the chief end of man's
life. God is n't any longer what he had often seemed in
more clerical ages, — a God that hides himself from the
natural and unassisted intellect of man. He showed himself of old to the Greek geometers, to Euclid, to Archi-
medes. In these days of the seventeenth century he
unveils new mysteries to the students of physics. In the
world of such a ruler, fear is out of place ; you may even
doubt if you will. The incredulous are no longer public
enemies ; they are merely the learners. Descartes, a representative thinker of the century, and the one from whom
our period is often dated, begins his reflection by doubting everything. As for the method of escaping from
doubt, that consists in the use of reason and in the study
of the facts of experience ; nothing else serves. Revelation you treat with such respect as political and social
considerations require ; but for philosophy, in this age of
the seventeenth century, the supernatural has only a secondary interest, if it has any interest at all. Religious
conformity is a matter of policy ; a noisy atheist would
be, of course, a cause of scandal, and might even bring

philosophy into discredit. Besides, almost every serious philosopher of this our first period believes in God as in some sense the source of nature. It is, however, not well to tell the unlearned too much about what sort of God you believe in. The unlearned are gross, still dread witches, carry amulets, know nothing of geometry; best be cautious of speech to them. Philosophy makes no propaganda, appeals to philosophers, lets faith alone. Besides, loyalty to the state counsels some measure of religious conformity. Hobbes, the great Englishman, himself a speculative materialist, and, as I fancy, the most well-knit and highly organized thinker in the whole history of English philosophy, was clear that whatever a man's opinion might be, it was his duty to submit all matters of religious conformity to the judgment of the state. " I submit," he says in effect somewhere, "to the Church of England, because that is the church ordained for me by the will of my sovereign, the king of England." And this confession of Hobbes involves no hypocrisy. It is the frankest confession in the world. His conformity is openly a conformity to civil laws. Philosophy and religion are once for all separated. It is a matter of accident whether the philosopher has or has not a traditional creed left him by his philosophy. His thought is no longer the handmaid of his faith, as had generally been the case with the thinkers of the Middle Ages. But as for his faith itself, social and political considerations must decide how and in what way he shall give evidence of it to his fellows. His very loyalty, his good citizenship, his frank benevolence, counsel prudence of speech.

And here appears again another side of the philosophy of this first period. It is a loyal philosophy, a philosophy of good citizenship; it has a great respect for the highest political interests of man; it studies jurisprudence, state-craft, international law, natural justice; it founds its loyalty, indeed, upon reason, makes little of the divine right

of kings, loves to declare all men equal, despises tradition in social matters, throws contempt on the mere customs of mankind, looks for the sanction of law in the
eternal and just order of the world, in short seeks most
distinctly not in the clouds, but here upon earth, for an
abiding city.   Hence, it generally opposes clerical interference in political matters ; it gives to the kingdom of
God a naturalistic interpretation, takes no interest in the
jeweled walls and the pearl gates of a scriptural new
Jerusalem, but undertakes to build a terrestrial one of its
own on a geometrical plan of modern devising, a city
not without foundations, but very sober as to ornamenta-
tion.   Better a rational constitution than golden streets.

Does this first period of modern philosophy, thus very
rudely outlined as to its most general interests, seem to
some of you dishearteningly unspiritual?   Then reflect,
it surely has not pleased God to save his people by an-
archy ; and these who in this recent century, in the age
when science first grew lusty in its young strength, and
when the sanctions of mediævalism were already partly
obsolete, spoke the word for the freedom of human reason,
and the reasonableness of good order, served the spiritual
necessities of mankind no whit the less because they told
only part of the truth.   What they bequeathed to us was
a faith in sober realities, a reverence for the dignity of
the world of law, a love of lucidity, for which we cannot
thank them too much.   As to their deification of nature,
it was surely the beginning of modern wisdom, an insight
that whatever God is, he is not far from every one of us,
a turning away from the mere gazing up into heaven
after a distant and ascended divine ruler, a sense that if
the spirit is indeed poured out on earth, you have a right
to look upon the simplest facts as containing it.   These
men may be cold ; for my part I find a clearness about
the snowy mountain summits amongst which they live,
which goes far to compensate for the hardness of the out-

lines of their world. That they, too, have a genuine and lofty piety to proclaim to us, I shall try to exemplify in the case of Spinoza. For nature, also, has its divine side; the hard, clear outlines of the mountains stand out, after all, against the heavens of God. He who reflects upon our human love of clear reason and of sound order reflects upon certain of the deepest, though surely not upon the hottest, passions of man. And Spinoza, as we shall find, knew how to give to this eternal order of nature a mystical and almost romantic glamor. Under the gently glowing evening twilight of his peaceful reflection, these mountain peaks, if we may yet again strain our figure, gleam with an almost ghostly dignity, and seem no longer sharp or cruel. Spinoza, like other mystical souls, knows of a peace which the world of sense can neither give nor take away. This peace he finds in an absorbing contemplation of the divine order as eternal and necessary. It is of the nature of reason, he says, to regard all things under the form of eternity. So regarded, even this passionate, struggling life of ours seems an apparition of the changeless. God is everywhere. The wise man asks no happy fortune; his unalterable fortune it is to love God with the same love wherewith God loves himself.

But the second age of modern philosophy, rejecting this sublime indifference to the concerns of the individual human being, turned curiously back to the study of the wondrous inner world of man's soul. To deify nature is not enough. Man is the most interesting thing in nature, and he is not yet deified; nor can he be until we have won a true knowledge of his wayward heart. He may be a part of nature's mechanism, or he may not; still, if he be a mechanism, he is that most paradoxical of things, a knowing mechanism. His knowledge itself, what it is, how it comes about, whence he gets it, how it grows, what it signifies, how it can be defended against skepticism, what it implies, both as to moral truth and as to theoretical truth, — these problems are foremost in the interests of the second period of modern thought, whose beginnings we can see in Locke, and whose culmination was in the philosophic movement that expressed itself, towards the close of the eighteenth century, in Kant's "Critique of Pure Reason." The early thinkers of this period, Locke, the early English moralists, Leibnitz, belong in part to the first period, as is always likely to be the case in such orderly evolutions. Gradually, attention is turned more and more from the outer world to the mind of man. The first period had been one of naturalism; the second is one of a sort of new humanism. In the first half of the eighteenth century this humanism developed the works of the great classical representatives of English ethics, as well as the idealism of Berkeley. Reflection is now more an inner study, an analysis of the mind, than an examination of the business of physical science. Human reason is still the trusted instrument, but it soon turns its criticism upon itself. It distinguishes prejudices from axioms, fears dogmatism, scrutinizes the evidences of faith, suspects, or at best has consciously to defend, even the apparently irresistible authority of conscience, and so comes at length, in the person of the greatest of the British eighteenth century thinkers, David Hume, to a questioning even of its own capacity to know truth, a doubting attitude which brings philosophy into a sharp and admitted opposition to common sense. At this point, however, a new interest begins in Europe. If the age was already disposed to self-analysis, Rousseau, with his paradoxes and his even pathological love of limitless self-scrutiny, introduced into this man-loving period a sentimental tendency, from which, erelong, came a revival of passion, of poetry, and of enthusiasm, whose influence we shall never outgrow. Contemporaneous with this influence was the appearance of the modern romance in its early forms. Not much later came the "Storm and

Stress " period of German literature, and by the time this
had run its course, the French Revolution, overthrowing
all the mechanical restraints of civilization, demonstrated
afresh to the world's outer sense the central importance of
passion in the whole life of humanity.

The philosophy of Kant, developing in the quiet solitudes of his professorial studies at Königsberg, in far
eastern Prussia, reflected with a most wonderful ingenuity
the essential interests of the time when all this transformation was preparing. In 1781, he published his " Critique of Pure Reason," nearly, if not quite, the most
important philosophical treatise ever written. The essential doctrine of this book is the thought that man's nature
is the real creator of man's world. It is n't the external
world, as such, that is the deepest truth for us at all ; it
is the inner structure of the human spirit which merely
expresses itself in the visible nature about us. The interest of Kant's presentation of this paradoxical thought
lay not so much in the originality of the conception, for
philosophers never invent fundamental beliefs, and this
idea of Kant's is as old as deeper spiritual faith itself ;
but rather in the cool, reflective, mercilessly critical ingenuity with which he carries it out. Issued several
years before the French Revolution, the book seems a sort
of deliberate justification of the proud consciousness of
man's own absolute rights with which, in that mighty
struggle, the human spirit rose against all external restraints, and declared, as we in America had already
showed men how to do, that the true world for humanity
is the world which the freeman makes, and that the genu-
uinely natural order is one which is not external until
reason decrees that it shall exist.

And herewith begins what I have ventured to call in
its wholeness the third period of modern philosophy, a
period not yet ended. The great thoughts of Kant ruled
the philosophic reflection of the next fifty years after the

appearance of the " Critique," with what extravagancies
and with what excellencies of result we shall in a measure see hereafter.   There is a sense in which this doctrine of Kant's is the very soul of all our modern life,
not, I repeat, as if the philosopher had invented it, but
because once for all this is the essentially humane view of
reality.   You can easily make wild and romantic misuse
of it.   But when rightly interpreted, Kant's world, where
the inner reason is lord over the outer sense, will prove to
be as hard and fast a world of fact, of law, and of eternal majesty, as ever the seventeenth century had conceived.   At all events, whether we will it or no, in this
universe of Kant's philosophy we all still live.

But the outcome of these fifty years of post-Kantian
speculation was, after all, an unfinished organization of
philosophic thought.   The undertaking was too vast for
one generation.   After a period of speculative quiescence,
a period when attention was directed away from philosophy by other human concerns, this, our third period of
modern thought, has come to see a revival of philosophic
activity, a revival in the midst of which we now live.   To
the legacy of Kant has been added the wealth of problems offered to us by recent advances in natural science
and in the study of the history of humanity.   The doctrine of evolution, itself no novelty in opinion, has received a wholly unlooked-for empirical formulation and
confirmation.   The sciences have grown until no one can
even remotely hope to overlook their whole field.   In consequence, however, external nature has once more gained
for us an imposing authority which makes us in many
ways sympathize afresh with the pure naturalism of the
seventeenth century.   Man we once more see to be, not
merely the sentimental rebel and creative hero of Rousseau and the romanticists, not merely the organ of the
world-forming reason of the Kantian schools, but also,
and just as truly, the mechanism which the seventeenth

century declared him to be. How can he be both these things, that is, both natural and spiritual? How can he have sprung from an animal ancestry, yes, ultimately from dead matter, and yet be the embodiment, the organ of the absolute reason? How can he at once be part of the spirit whose live thinking dreams out this whole frame of things, and yet he himself the slave of the very order of nature which this dream creates? How can he, this mere mechanism, this creature of nerves, this mortal thing whose brain secretes thought, be also, as Kant made him, the very source of the laws of nature themselves? How comprehend this paradox? Well, I answer, after all, it is the ancient paradox of the double nature of man. It would be unpardonably absurd even to mention such a strange problem, were it not so real, so pertinacious, so every day a matter, were it not absolutely forced on us afresh by every new word of modern science, as by every old word of the devotional books. And this problem, I insist, is now in the forefront of speculation as it never was before : in what sense, with what prospect of solution, with what beauty of statement, with what depth of significance, with what manifold illustration in facts, with what passionate longing of inquiry, I should be glad, indeed, if I could hope to express in the subsequent lectures of this course. And so, for the first, our rude sketch is before us. How much I desire to suggest its significance, let one brief illustration suffice to show ere I go further.

There is a certain earlier and idealistic drama of Ibsen's which the current public interest in that remarkable poet seems still disposed to neglect altogether. I mean the drama entitled "Emperor and Galilean." In this play the author introduces the apostate Emperor Julian, struggling to replace the kingdom whose authority is not of this world, by an imperial power whose aims and sanctions shall be earthly, naturalistic, human, and whose

ideals shall not look beyond any man's sepulchre.   When
the power of the romantic apostate is already on the
wane, he converses, in one scene, with his confidential adviser, the heathen seer and mystic, Maximos.   The emperor is by this time weary of the strife, fearful of the
end.   " Will the Galilean conquer ? " he cries.   And he
calls upon Maximos, as reader of portents, to prophesy.
Who shall win, he says, in this struggle?   Is the kingdom that is from above to destroy the kingdom of this
earth?   Or will the legions and the natural order be able
to withstand the unearthly power of this wondrous and
unseen world of spiritual influences ?   Maximos answers
darkly.   *Neither* can succeed, he declares.   *Both* powers,
both kingdoms, the earthly and the unearthly, shall fall.
That is fate.   " But what, then, shall take their place ? "
cries Julian.   " Who is, then, the right ruler ? "   " He,"
answers Maximos, " in whom both Emperor and Galilean "
shall be joined.   There is to come, he prophesies, the third
realm, neither of earth alone, nor yet of heaven alone, —
" God-Cæsar, Cæsar-God, Cæsar in the kingdom of the
Spirit, God in the realm of the flesh."   " This, Julian,"
declares Maximos, " is the third realm, for in it alone can
be fulfilled the word, ' Render unto Cæsar the things that
are Cæsar's, and unto God the things that are God's.' "
For only in such a realm, runs the thought of Maximos,
will the earthly and the supernatural, once wholly in unity,
cease to have conflicting and irreconcilable claims.   Fate,
holds Maximos, will yet bring this thing to pass, but not,
indeed, in these times of Julian.

I do not feel these words of Ibsen's to be more than
merely suggestive.   I do not pretend to find in them anything final.   But I cannot do better, as I try to give here
some faint notion of the vast historical process whereof
all this reflective philosophy forms so subordinate a part,
than to point out that the third realm, of which Ibsen
so mystically speaks, the realm where a rigid order of

nature shall be one with the most miraculously significant divine truth, where Cæsar shall become a spiritual, and God an earthly ruler, is precisely the realm which not so much our philosophy, but our age, whose echo this philosophy is, is even now seeking to comprehend, and with prophetic voice to proclaim.

II.

Let us return to our first period. A long course of lectures would be needed to give you any full account of its significance. Let me dwell a moment once more upon three things of importance concerning its representative thinkers.

As to the first matter: I have already suggested that philosophy, in those days of the seventeenth century, was much *influenced by the example of physical science.* The modern method of what is called induction, that is, the method of finding the laws of nature from a careful collection and study of facts, won its first great triumphs in the work of Galileo and of his contemporaries and immediate successors in physical science. The Galilean method of studying nature was for that age one of wonderful novelty and fruitfulness. Galileo, as you know, introduced the fashion of making exact experiments under artificially simplified physical conditions. Such experiments showed in intelligible form how natural things really behave. Nature, as you see her in gross, is too complex for our simple minds. She hides her secrets from our untrained reason, by revealing them all at once. Experiment separates out particular groups of facts, and examines them alone. Thus experiment aids the weakness of our reason, in its effort to find nature reasonable. Experiment so stands for a sort of cross-questioning of nature. The answers to our questions show us the rationality of things. But Galileo did not make such experiments at random. He thought out well what questions to ask nature. That is, by acute observation of what one might call the general trend of things in some part of nature, Galileo made exact and mathematically stateable hypotheses as to the true laws at work. So he did, for instance, in case of the facts about falling bodies, and in case of the facts about bodies rolling down inclines. When he had made his scientific guess, his hypothesis, he applied, if necessary, mathematics to this guess, and computed what ought to happen, if it were true, in certain definite cases, such as an experiment could artificially bring to pass. Then, and not till then, he tested the hypothesis by the experiment itself. He asked nature, " Is it so and so with you, as my hypothesis demands, in this special case, that it shall be? " If nature, questioned through experiment, responded " Yes," then the hypothesis was verified, and the law was regarded as in its own proper measure established. Thus reason triumphed over brute fact.

The brilliant successes of this Galilean method during his own and the following generations were, as I have said, immensely impressive to that whole century. Nature had at last been made to answer multitudinous sharp questions. And the noteworthy thing was that her answers were so exact, and that her laws, when you found them, were so rigid, so capable of mathematical precision of statement, so general. Mechanical science, thus early and very rapidly progressing, soon suggested of itself the thought that nature was all one vast mechanism. The philosophers, with their love of grand generalizations, easily seized upon this idea. They tried to expound it, to reflect upon it, to defend it, to develop its meaning. Just imagine it for a moment : could one only seize upon the genuine and all-embracing hypothesis, could one but guess by good luck at the one absolute law of laws, as Galileo had guessed at the law of the falling bodies ! Would not one then have an hypothesis whereof every fact of physical nature would be a case, a verification, an experimental justification? Such a law, if you found it, — would it not be mechanical, like Galileo's special laws? So, at least, the century declared. But there was the other side to this idea, a side which suggests my *second* point. If this was so, if these exact laws, which so perfectly answer the demands of our reason, are true of things, then *is n't this world about us one that clear thinking, exact definition, is especially fitted to comprehend?* Previous ages had found the world mysterious, and had appealed to faith, which reason could only supplement. This new age *is sure of reason*, makes it lord, reveres it as the one revealer of mysteries, and as capable of discovering absolute truth. But this once more brings me yet a step further, namely, to my *third* point. Clear thinking about nature needs a good model. Galileo and all the other men of the new time had such a model before them in the *geometrical science* that had come down from the Greeks. The hypotheses that Galileo made were of a sort long since known in geometry, namely, mathematically exact statements, from which sharp conclusions could be drawn for verification or refutation. He showed how to apply such hypotheses to nature, namely, by means of crucial experiments. But the idea of the clearly thought hypothesis was old. Very well, then, Galileo's successes suggested that geometry is indeed the model science, that nature, being reasonable, geometrizes, so to speak, throughout all her world of things, so that if you could once get her laws in mind, as Euclid got his axioms, then all the facts of nature down to the least would become as clear, as certain, as demonstrable to you as Euclid's theorems are to the student of mathematics. Such a notion it is which is the common property of the seventeenth century. It was the presupposition of that time, the cold but deep passion of exact rationality, upon which the philosophers reflected, and in terms of which they taught. Hence it was that they loved mathematical methods in philosophy.

These three ideas, then, that nature is a mechanism, that human reason is competent to grasp the truth of nature, and that, since nature's truth is essentially mathematical, geometry is the model science, whose precision and necessity philosophy, too, must imitate, — these are the ideas of our first period. Descartes shares them with Hobbes. The widest divergence of opinion does not exclude them anywhere, in the representative men of that day. Human nature also is interpreted in terms of them.

But how, you may ask, can such an age as this grasp the whole breadth and depth of the deeper passions of humanity? Man is n't merely a computer, nor yet a geometer. He estimates, he appreciates his world; he does n't merely long to describe it in mathematical terms; he has religious interests, too; and what have Galilean physics and Euclidean geometry to say of these? Well, I have already observed that our seventeenth century knew of such a thing as a philosophical religion, and my illustration of that fact is the man who was in many respects the deepest speculator of that whole age, namely, Spinoza, to whom I may now pass.

III.

Every one has heard something of the marvelous and lonely Jewish philosopher, who, separated from the world of European cultivation by his race, and from his own people by his heresy, devoted himself to peaceful and fearless reflection, and died early, not without leaving an immortal treatise behind him. And every one must have noticed how singularly varied is the view of Spinoza that one gets from those who know him more or less superficially. In his own age he was denounced as atheist, profane person, monster. Long afterwards, however, his works were re-discovered, greedily read, admired by great poets like Goethe, and by ardent and even romantic philosophers like Schelling; and now he has become an authority for all students of philosophy, a necessary part of the knowledge of every one who would comprehend modern thought. This great thinker himself was, to be sure, no universal genius in philosophy. His doctrine, compared with those that have come since, is comparatively simple, clear cut, crystalline in its hardness and isolation, and yet, how many-sided even this crystal, how varied the impressions that it has produced on those who have seen it in different lights! Judging by some of the commentators of Spinoza, you would regard him as merely a lover of mathematical clearness and coldness of statement, as a believer in the hard and fast, eternal, but purely natural order of things. Others, on the contrary, have called him, in a phrase that has been too often repeated, " a God-intoxicated man," so that, far from being an atheist, it was the existence of nature that he in truth denied. Others have named him a mystic, a seer, a prophet; have taken, as the young Goethe took, an almost sentimental interest in him; have found his doctrine poetical and romantic. Others still have prized in him the gentle humility of life. He won, as we learn, not only the respect of certain great men in his own time (who knew him mainly from afar and by letter), but also the love of the few homely and obscure people with whom he daily and personally associated; and this has led one of his eulogizers, Ernst Renan, to remind us enthusiastically that " nothing is worth so much as the judgment of the little ones, for it is almost always the judgment of God."

What, then, was Spinoza? The cold and merciless mathematical thinker, the remorseless fatalist that some call him; or the romantic and poetic soul, the mystic, the seer; or, finally, the saint of gracious and gentle life that others find him? In fact, Spinoza had something of all these traits in his character and in his thought. Were I expounding his system in full I should make you feel this fact. It is already a satisfaction to be able to say that

the least wealthy of the systems which we are to consider
expressed so wide an experience of life, reflected upon so
varied a group of human attitudes in the presence of the
divine order.   But still it is not for the purpose of a
panegyric of Spinoza that I now ask your attention to
him.   His personal character cannot detain us very long.
Nor yet, on the other hand, can we give much time to examining the technical details of his system.   It was indeed a many-sided doctrine, and in some of its aspects
highly problematic.   Its sources, its growth, and its meaning have in recent times been the topic of elaborate
researches, of which I can give you no fair notion here.
I shall dwell upon but a single aspect of the whole, and
this is the religious aspect; for Spinoza had a religion.
There is, then, this one thing in his teaching that I wish to
illustrate, and, if possible, to explain.   This is the deep
piety which in Spinoza's mind is not only consistent with
the belief in a rigid, mechanical order of nature, but
which is even involved, according to him, in the very
expression of such a doctrine concerning nature.

Had Spinoza been any one but himself, he would have
been a materialist, a cynic, and, indeed, the cold and
merciless thinker that many, misled by one-sided views,
have declared him to be.   Because he was a man of
profound character, he looked upon the whole order of
things, and said, " While it is necessary, while it is rigid,
while it is in one sense merciless, it is also divine, and the
value of our knowledge of this order is that thereby we
are led to a love of God, to a peace which the world can=
not give or take away."

It is surely the office of philosophic reflection to bring
out the deeper problems of our nature.   And nowhere else
can one find a more significant problem than this, that he
who looks upon the world solely with the eye of reason
finds himself, when once possessed of Spinoza's wisdom,
forced to adore.   Listen, then, in Spinoza's case, to the

tale of the religious experience of a great heretic, whom many men used to denounce as atheist.

The external facts of Spinoza's life, so far as they concern us, must be very briefly summarized. A colony of Spanish and Portuguese Jews, refugees from persecution, was, in the second quarter of the seventeenth century, resident in Amsterdam, in the enjoyment of the freedom of the Dutch republic. A son of a poor family, members of this Jewish community, Spinoza was born in the year 1632. He was early distinguished as a studious boy for his learning in the mediæval literature of the Jews; he was an enthusiastic reader of Talmudic interpreters and commentators; but he was also not without a wide curiosity that led him to the study of the learned language of the day, namely, Latin, and to an early acquaintance with thought that lay far beyond the circle of the intolerant interests of his fellows. These studies of profane learning led to suspicions of his orthodoxy, and a series of events followed of which we have only extremely untrustworthy accounts from two of his early biographers. What happened we do not precisely know. Report says that companions and fellow-students of Spinoza, having drawn from him heretical views concerning the interpretation of the Scriptures, revealed the facts to the authorities of the synagogue; and that Spinoza was called to account, and was urged in more ways than one, namely, by bribes as well as by threats, to abandon his heresy or to remain silent. The affair, whatever it was, seems to have extended over several years; it ended in the excommunication of Spinoza, in the year 1656. Thenceforth he was alone and free. To most other men this loneliness would have meant destruction. Even for Spinoza it led to certain defects of thought and expression which are not without significance for his system as a whole. Spinoza had thenceforth no reason to appeal in the least to the prejudices and learning of his former co-religionists. He seems rather anxious in all his philosophical writings to say little of his relation to Jewish philosophy, and considerable difference of opinion exists among competent inquirers as to the actual relation between his own philosophical doctrines and those which, from time to time, had been put in form by Jewish mediæval writers. At all events, however, he was rather a man of his time than a Jew. His system has a closer connection with that of Descartes and with those of other prominent European thinkers than with any Jewish doctrines. One of his books, indeed, has a special relation to the studies of his early youth. It is a book on freedom of opinion, called the " Theologico-Political Tractate." The essence of the doctrine is that both the formation and the expression of opinion should be entirely unhindered by legal interference. In the course of the book, Spinoza enters upon an elaborate historical criticism of the Old Testament literature, and, in many respects, curiously suggests analogies to the results of modern critical study of the Bible. But in all his other writings Spinoza is simply the speculative thinker. His life in his exclusion from the Jewish community is as simple and uneventful as ever the experience of a philosopher has been. It is, in fact, the peculiar privilege of the philosopher to live in a certain separation from human responsibility, which leaves him free to criticise the life that no longer enchains him. It is at once his privilege and his danger, for freedom from the bondage of life may easily mean disorganization or morbidness of life. Spinoza, however, was not only forced to live apart from the world, but was able to win spiritual health in his isolation; and the result of such separation from the passions of humanity shows itself all the more plainly in a power of dispassionate criticism which is the very life of philosophy. One limitation remains, however, especially noteworthy in Spinoza's case. His form of isolation renders him a poor critic of the deeper social relationships. In fact, had Spinoza lived in an age of great poetical production, this dispassionate loneliness of experience would have rendered him much less competent than he was to reword the meaning of his time. But in an age of investigation he was enabled to be a model critic, for the interest of humanity then lay in comprehending the natural order of things, and one does not need a rich experience of social life to give expression to the inner meaning of an undertaking like this.

IV.

If one turns, however, from the thinker himself to his thought, it is next necessary for us to see what drove Spinoza to his patient and life-long business of reflection upon so dry and apparently lifeless a thing as the mathematical and rigid laws of external nature. And here meets us the most noteworthy fact of all about our philosopher. I have already said that the outcome of Spinoza's reflection is an adoration, an immovably peaceful reverence, for God's eternal order. What I have not yet said is, that the longing for such an object of adoration is the beginning as well as the end of his whole work. Spinoza has left us, in an essay on "The Improvement of the Understanding," a sort of confession of the course of thinking which led him to his final faith. This confession brings us at once upon ground that is familiar to every one who knows well the religious passion of humanity.

The higher religious consciousness has its origin in the human heart in two interests. One is the interest of the moral being in finding some authority that may guide him in the conduct of his life. The other is the interest of the baffled and disappointed soul in coming into the presence of some external truth, some reality that is perfect, that lacks our weakness, that is victorious even though we fail, that is good even though we are worthless. I must pause a moment to define and illustrate these two interests. They are both of them well known to all of you, whether you have succeeded in satisfying either of them or not. What you do not always see, until you reflect, is that they are really two interests, that they are often very hard to reconcile, that they lead you by two very different roads to faith, and are likely to lead to two sharply contrasted sorts of faith. Spinoza, I am going to show you, had one of these interests very deeply, the other hardly at all.

The religious interest of the first sort, I say, seeks an authoritative guide. If it finds one in some conceived deity, it rejoices. This deity is, in this case, above all a moral one. He directs me, and I follow. My delight, if I am devout, is then in the " law of the Lord." The law may be a ceremonial one ; then I build altars, offer sacrifices, hold solemn feasts. Or again, his law may be a law of righteousness of heart and life ; then, commanded by God, sure that he knows the right way and has shown it, I order my life as well as I can according to this righteousness. I become just, merciful, charitable, strenuous. I don't ask so much who the Lord is, as what his will is. I may philosophize, but in that case my philosophy will be principally a moral philosophy. The subtleties of theology, the origin of evil, the nature of the divine plan, will concern me little. God wants me to work ; he asks service of me, not comprehension. As for the evils of life, I see that they are mostly the just punishment of my sins ; I endure hardness as a good soldier. I know meanwhile that my will is free, that I can serve the law of God if I want to, that there is one who does not serve this law, to wit, the devil, and that I must fight this devil and all his works wherever I see them. My philosophy consists in clear thinking about my duty ; my faith is an assurance that the right will somehow conquer ; my love is for all who desire God's kingdom to come ; my hope is for the victory that is near at hand, and for the

word, "Well done, good and faithful servant!" The
crown of life is beyond, the sword is in hand, the Lord
directs the fight, and, best of all, he *needs me* to help
him against the mighty, — *needs* me, for he says so. In
fact his saying so is just what constitutes his law and my
moral comfort. If he did not need me, my life would be
vain; in his need is my consolation. The world thus
viewed is so simple, so directly present to you, so majestic,
so inspiring! Love the Lord, love all his friends, and
hate Satan. What could be plainer? Here, you see, is
the fine and sinewy religion of St. Christopher. The
Lord is the strongest, fight on his side. He grants you
a place in his service, how great is this reward! This
love of him and of his servants, how perfect and plain a
doctrine!

> "Love-making, how simple a matter! No depths to explore,
>   No heights in a life to ascend! No disheartening before,
>   No affrighting hereafter, — Love now will be love evermore."

And true love will be the fulfilling of the law, — love
of the good, warfare with ill. Here, then, says the active
soul, is peace at length, the only true peace, — the peace
of endless service, the rest of a glorious activity, the joy of
life amongst the sons of God. After this fashion, then,
the religion of duty meets the first of the two interests
which I have been distinguishing. You all well know
what religious faiths express this interest.

Were I just now a practical teacher, I should leave you
to enjoy the thrill of this sort of energetic devotion, and
should not trouble you with the critical observation that
there is quite another sort of religious interest in the
world, which is not only very different from the foregoing,
but which is, in the first place and naturally, opposed
thereto. Yet this other interest, this second source of
religion, does exist in the human heart, and gives birth
to some of the deepest forms of piety. I am here, not as
a practical teacher, but as an observer of life, and it is

my duty, therefore, to call your attention to the variety
of these two great interests, and then to show you that
Spinoza's religious interest, profound, saintly, mystical as
it was, belongs to the second sort.

Life has its wounds as well as its weapons. Your
moral hero occasionally sees not only the discomfiture of
Satan, but also the warm blood of his own mortal veins
oozing forth as well. Or again, he finds himself an outcast, as Spinoza was, who knows no army that will accept
him, and who hears all human voices call him traitor.
And then, indeed, he knows an experience that even the
weaklings may aspire to share. He knows, namely, what
it is to feel faint and sick at heart, and to see his own
worthlessness. Then it occurs to him that perhaps the
divine order, if haply it does really exist, may possibly
need just his right arm a little less than he had thought.
The idea is so commonplace a suggestion, after all. What
more natural? thinks the injured soul. Here I am, a
mere writhing worm, *ein trüber Gast auf der dunkelen
Erde*, alone in infinite space, and I pretended to ask for
guidance as to my petty conduct! I pretended that the
divine order needed just me! Why did I pretend this?
Because of my pride, was it not? I called this sort of
thing piety, and then kindly offered my services to God,
on the ground that he could do worse than to accept them,
and with the observation that the rolls of his army were,
before my accession, noteworthily incomplete. This, I
called religion; and now, what happens? Fate moves on
its own way; I am wounded, cast down, weak, worthless.
All his billows are gone over me. My righteousness,
what worth was it in his sight? Shall mortal man be
just before God? After all, if there is a moral order, is
it not complete unto itself? Did God wait all the eternities until I was ripened before He should triumph?
Either he exists not at all,— and then, how shall I create
him? — or he exists, and then from eternity to eternity

he has triumphed. His holiness I cannot create. Let me, if haply I may, see it, worship it, enjoy it as wondering, contemplative, adoring, helpless onlooker, consoled, if at all, by the knowledge that though I fail and am lost, he is from everlasting to everlasting.

I do not fear to seem unmindful of the dignity of the genuine religious consciousness when I thus present to you the curious and, in fact, paradoxical opposition between its two typical moods and their interests. The affair is so vital and familiar an experience that nobody can have failed to pass through this change of mood or to come close upon the problem involved in it.· For ourselves, as critics of life, we have just now only to look on while this second form of the religious consciousness develops itself before our eyes into the form in which it becomes immediately characteristic of Spinoza. The problem involved is, as a general philosophical question, one that will concern us much later on in our course, when I shall ask how we are really to solve, if at all, the paradoxical opposition between the active and the submissive forms of piety. For the time being I shall simply let the helpless mood of the defeated soul find its own form of religious faith. This form is the one embodied in many kinds of what is called mystical religion. Forgive me if I dwell upon it a little. The digression will in the end aid us to comprehend Spinoza.

This second mood, you have seen, began just now with a somewhat cynical despair, which looked at first sight rather unheroic, not to say immoral. Well, relatively *un*moral this form of the religious consciousness remains to the end. It is not its office to inspire the warriors so much as to comfort the downcast and to succor the wounded. The honors and consolations of a noble office it has not to offer you. It finds you despairing, and it teaches you to despise even your despair, and to rejoice even in your failure. After all, look about you, and see what you have learned. Is not the lesson of your defeat the lesson of the universal vanity of every individual undertaking of man? And what more comforting than this lesson, if only you become wise enough to see that above all these failures of ours there is the strong and divine order that never strives or is weary, but that is eternally fresh in the youth of its perfection? If you can but once see that God reigns, you will also see, says this mood, not only that mortals must fail, but that they deserve to fail, so idle is their trust in themselves, so sinful is their pride, so weak is everything in which they put their hope.

If you want further illustration of this mood, you might, if you choose, take up that permanently charming record of experience, the old and thoroughly orthodox devotional book called "Imitation of Christ," and let it put into words this new feeling. Spinoza, very probably, never read this book, but, I call your special attention to it, we shall find him saying much the same thing, *nur mit ein Bischen andern Worten.* The burden of the "Imitation" is the old story of human defeat. Who could say worse things of life than these? "How can the life of man be loved, seeing that it hath so many bitter things, that it is subjected to so many calamities and miseries? How can it be even called life when it produces so many deaths and plagues?" "I resolve that I will act bravely, but when a little temptation cometh, immediately I am in a great strait. Wonderfully small sometimes is the matter whence a grievous temptation cometh, and whilst I imagine myself safe for a little space, when I am not considering, I find myself often almost overcome by a little puff of wind." "Thou shalt lamentably fall away, if thou set a value upon any worldly thing." "To-day thou confest thy sins, and to-morrow thou committest again the sins thou didst confess." "What canst thou see anywhere which can continue long under the sun? Thou believest, perchance, that thou shalt be satisfied, but thou

wilt never be able to attain unto this. If thou shouldst
see all things before thee at once, what would it be but a
vain vision?" "Trust not thy feeling, for that which is
now will be quickly changed into somewhat else." In
brief, then, to sum up this whole pessimism of the devout
author of the "Imitation," we, and all finite things about
us, are utterly vain, and so, not only is our life a plague,
but it ought to be a plague; its miseries, its sins, its failures, are not only inevitable, but they are somehow justified by our fatal worthlessness. Yet consider how just this
pessimism about the finite is used, in the "Imitation," to
produce and to sustain that exalted rapture in the contemplation of the eternal which makes the "Imitation" so
curiously consoling a book. The marvel of this contrast
between the utter corruption of the finite and the glory of
God, the singular effect of it all upon the reader, is one of
the most marvelous psychological puzzles about this fascinating and, I may even add, dangerous work of genius.
Herein lies the wiliness of that melancholy and yet inspiring old work: it condemns your vanities until you
are fairly ashamed of having even once tried to be actively righteous with this weak will and this worthless
nature of yours. The sword of your moral heroism turns
to rust, and your whole warlike harness fairly rots away
into nothingness as you read. Life is dust and ashes.
Death, yes, annihilation, would be a relief to your hopeless self-condemnation. And yet, above all, glittering in
the icy glories of its eternal frost, rises before you the
sacred mountain of God's unapproachable grandeur. You
look upwards to that, and lo! like a shadow every trace
of your misery has vanished. "When a man cometh to
this, that he seeketh comfort from no created being, then
doth he perfectly begin to enjoy God; then also will he
be well contented with whatsoever shall happen to him.
He committeth himself altogether and with full trust unto
God, who is all in all to him, to whom nothing perisheth

or dieth, but all things live to him and obey his word
without delay." "Let therefore nothing which thou doest
seem to thee great; let nothing be grand, nothing of value
or beauty, nothing worthy of honor, nothing lofty, nothing praiseworthy or desirable, save what is eternal.
Let the eternal truth please thee above all things; let
thine own great vileness displease thee continually."
Thus, then, as all readers of the "Imitation" know, the
author, turning steadfastly from the finite, comes at last to
a new life of contemplative freedom, a life where indeed
positive action, service of the Lord with a sense that the
Lord needs one, has small place, but where once more
something called love inspires afresh the heart.   This
"love" of the "Imitation" is no longer the naïve, childlike, warmly vital love of the optimistic warrior who in
this world cheerfully serves God, like a St. Christopher,
because God is the strongest.   This new sort of love is a
mystical adoration.   It produces acts, but they are done
in a dream-like sort of somnambulistic ecstasy; they are
the acts of one hypnotized, so to speak, by a long look
heavenwards.   Strength this love has, but it is the
strength of gazing; movement it has, but it is an anæs-
thetic, unconscious sort of movement.   "Love feeleth no
burden, reckoneth not labors."   This anæsthesia is not
the willing work of the faithful servant so much as an
incident of the rapturous wandering of one lost in God.
"Nothing is sweeter than love, nothing stronger, nothing
loftier, nothing broader, nothing pleasanter, nothing fuller
or better in heaven or earth; for love was born of God
and cannot rest save in God, above all created things.
He who loveth, flyeth, runneth, and is glad; he is free
and not hindered; he giveth all things for all things, and
hath all things in all things, because he resteth in One
who is high above all, from whom every good floweth
and proceedeth.   He looketh not for gifts, but turneth
himself to the Giver above all good things. . . . Love is

watchful, and whilst sleeping still keeps watch; though
fatigued it is not weary, though pressed it is not forced,
though alarmed it is not terrified; but like the living
flame and the burning torch, it breaketh forth on high,
and securely triumpheth. If a man loveth, he knoweth
what this voice crieth. For the ardent affection of the
soul is a great clamor in the ears of God, and it saith, My
God, my Beloved! Thou art all mine, and I am all
thine."

v.

I have dwelt upon the expressions of this kind of religious interest as we find them in such orthodox books as
the " Imitation," because I want to remind you of the
peculiarities of the well-known mood of the mystics, in
order to make the attitude of Spinoza, the heretic, more
easily comprehensible. Spinoza's religious concern, I
insist, is of this latter sort. He is n't a man of action;
his heroism, such as it is, is the heroism of contemplation.
He is not always, let me tell you, in his religious mood;
and when he is not, he appears as a cynical observer of
the vanity of mortal passions. But as religious thinker,
he is no cynic. Unswervingly he turns from the world of
finite hopes and joys; patiently he renounces every sort
of worldly comfort; even the virtue that he seeks is not
the virtue of the active man. There is one good thing,
and that is the Infinite; there is one wisdom, and that is
to know God; there is one sort of true love, and that is
the submissive love of the saintly onlooker, who in the
solitude of reflection sees everywhere an all-pervading
law, an all-conquering truth, a supreme and irresistible
perfection. Sin is merely foolishness; insight is the only
virtue; evil is nothing positive, but merely the depriva-
tion of good; there is nothing to lament in human affairs,
except the foolishness itself of every lamentation. The
wise man transcends lamentation, ceases to love finite
things, ceases therefore to long and to be weary, ceases

to strive and to grow faint, offers no foolish service to God as a gift of his own, but possesses his own soul in knowing God, and therefore enters into the divine freedom, by reason of a clear vision of the supreme and necessary laws of the eternal world.

This, then, is the essence of Spinoza's religion. He begins his essay on the "Improvement of the Understanding" with words that we now are prepared to comprehend. This essay and the fifth part of the ethics show us Spinoza's religious attitude and experience, elsewhere much veiled in his works. "After experience had taught me," says the essay, "that all the usual surroundings of social life are vain and futile, seeing that none of the objects of my fears contained in themselves anything either good or bad, except in so far as the mind is affected by them, I finally resolved to inquire whether there might be some real good which would affect the mind singly, to the exclusion of all else, whether there might be anything of which the discovery and attainment would enable me to enjoy continuous, supreme, and unending happiness." Here is the starting-point. Life for Spinoza is in the ordinary world a vain life, because, for the first, it is our thinking that makes the things about us good or bad to us, and not any real value of the things themselves, whilst the transiency, the uncertainty of these finite things brings it about that, if we put our trust in them, they will erelong disappoint us. Rapidly, from this beginning, Spinoza rehearses the familiar tale of the emptiness of the life of sense and worldliness, the same tale that all the mystics repeat. The reader, who has never felt this experience of Spinoza and of the other mystics, always feels indeed as if such seeming pessimism must be largely mere sour-heartedness, or else as if the expression of it must be pure cant. But after all, in the world of spiritual experiences, this, too, is a valuable one to pass through and to record. Whoever has not sometime fully felt what

it is to have his whole world of finite ambitions and affec-
tions through and through poisoned, will indeed not easily
comprehend the gentle disdain with which Spinoza, in this
essay, lightly brushes aside pleasure, wealth, fame, as
equally and utterly worthless. We know, indeed, little of
Spinoza's private life, but if we should judge from his
words we should say that as exile he has felt just this bitterness, and has conquered it, so that when he talks of
vanity he knows whereof he speaks. People who have
never walked in the gloomy outlying wastes of spiritual
darkness have never had the chance to find just the sort
of divine light which he finally discovered there. These
mystics, too, have their wealth of experience; don't
doubt their sincerity because they tell a strange tale.
Don't doubt it even if, like Spinoza, they join with their
mysticism other traits of the wonderful Jewish character,
— shrewd cynicism, for instance. When they call pleasure and wealth and fame all dust and ashes, they possibly
know whereof they speak, at least as far as concerns themselves alone. Spinoza, at any rate, twice in his life, refused, if his biographers are right, the offered chance to
attain a competency. He declined these chances because,
once for all, worldly means would prove an entanglement
to him. He preferred his handicraft, and earned his living by polishing lenses. Steadfastly, moreover, as we
know, he refused opportunities to get a popular fame, and
even to make a worthily great name. The chief instance
is his refusal of the professorship which the Elector Pala-
tine offered him in 1673 at Heidelberg, under promise of
complete freedom of teaching, and with the obvious chance
of an European reputation. So Spinoza did not merely
call the finite world names, as many do; he meant his
word, and he kept it. He was no sentimentalist, no emotional mystic. He was cool-headed, a lover of formulas
and of mathematics; but still he was none the less a true
mystic.

Well, he finds the finite vain, because you have to pursue it, and then it deceives you, corrupts you, degrades you, and in the end fails you, being but a fleeting shadow after all. " I thus perceived," he says, " that I was in a state of great peril, and I compelled myself to seek with all my strength for a remedy, however uncertain it might be, as a sick man struggling with a deadly disease, when he sees that death will surely be upon him unless a remedy be found, is compelled to seek such a remedy with all his strength, inasmuch as his whole hope lies therein. All the objects pursued by the multitude not only bring no remedy that tends to preserve our being, but even act as hindrances, causing the death not seldom of those who possess them, and always of those who are possessed by them." " All these evils," he continues, " seem to have arisen from the fact that our happiness or unhappiness has been made the mere creature of the thing that we happen to be loving. When a thing is not loved, no strife arises about it; there is no pang if it perishes, no envy if another bears it away, no fear, no hate ; yes, in a word, no tumult of soul. These things all come from loving that which perishes, such as the objects of which I have spoken. But love towards a thing eternal feasts the mind with joy alone, nor hath sadness any part therein. Hence this is to be prized above all, and to be sought for with all our might. I have used the words not at random, — ' If only I could be thorough in my seeking ; ' for I found that though I already saw all this in mind, I could not yet lay aside avarice and pleasure and ambition. Yet one thing I found, that as long as I was revolving these thoughts, so long those desires were always behind my back, whilst I strenuously sought the new light; and herein I found great comfort, for I saw that my disease was not beyond hope of physic. And although at first such times were rare, and endured but for a little space, yet as more and more the true good lighted up my mind, such times came quicker and endured longer."

VI.

This, then, the beginning of Spinoza's Pilgrim's Progress. But now for what distinguishes him from other mystics, and makes him a philosopher, not a mere exhorter. He has his religious passion, he must reflect upon it. The passion any one might have who had passed through the dark experience of which we spoke a moment since. The philosopher must justify his faith. And how hard to justify such a faith it would seem in this cold and severe seventeenth century. It was an age, you remember, when everything held to be at all occult was banished from the thoughts of the wise, and when clear thinking alone was believed in, when man, too, was held to be a mechanism, a curiously complicated natural machine, when Hobbes, greatest amongst the English speculative thinkers of the age — a writer much read by Spinoza — could declare that the word " spirit " was a meaningless sound, and that nothing exists but bodies and movements. How defend a mystical religious faith at such a moment? Spinoza's defense is so ingenious, so profound, so simple, as to give us one of the most noteworthy and dramatic systems ever constructed. Once more I assure you that I here expound only one aspect of his thought. I ignore his peculiar methods; I ignore his technicalities; I give you but the kernel of his doctrine concerning religious truth.

Technicalities aside, this doctrine is essentially founded upon what Spinoza regards as the axiom that everything in the world must be either explained by its own nature, or by some higher nature.[1] You explain a thing when you comprehend why it *must be* what it *is*. Thus, for instance, in geometry you know that all the diameters of any one circle must be precisely equal, and you know *that* this is so, because you see *why* it must be so.[2] The diam-

---

[1] See *Eth.* I. Axioms i. and ii.
[2] See examples in the *Tractat. de Emendat. Int.* under the head of rules for definition.

eters are all drawn in the circle and through the centre of it, and the circle has a certain nature, a structure, a make, a build, whereby, for instance, you distinguish it from an oval or a square. This build, this make of the circle, it is that *forces* the diameters to be equal. They can't help being equal, being drawn through the centre of a curve which has no elongation, no bulge outwards in one direction more than another, but which is evenly curved all around. The nature of the circle, then, at once forces the diameters to be equal, — pins them down to equality, hems in any rebellious diameter that should try to stretch out farther than the others, — and also explains to the reason of a geometer just *why* this result follows. My example is extremely dry and simple, but it will serve to show what Spinoza is thinking of. He says now, as something self-evident, that anything in the world which does n't directly contain its own explanation must be a part of some larger nature of things which does explain it, and which, accordingly, forces it to be just what it is. For instance, to use my own illustration, if two mountains had precisely the same height, as the diameters of a circle have precisely the same length, we should surely have to suppose something in the nature of the physical universe which forced just these two mountains to have the same height. But, even so, as things actually are, we must suppose that whatever is or happens, in case it is not a self-evident and necessary thing, must have its explanation in some higher and larger nature of things. Thus, once more, you yourself are either what you are by virtue of your own self-evident and self-made nature, or else, as is the view of Spinoza, you are forced to be what you are by the causes that have produced you, and that have brought you here. Cause and explanation mean for Spinoza the same thing. He knows only rigidly mathematical necessity. Yet more, not only you, but every act, every thought of yours, each quiver of your eyelashes, each least shadow of feeling in your mind, must be just as much a result of the nature of things as your existence itself. Nothing comes by chance; everything must be what it is. Could you see the world at one glance, "under the form of eternity," you would see everything as a necessary result of the whole nature of things. It would be as plain to you that you must now have this quiver of eyelash or this shade of feeling; it would be also as plain to you *why* you must have these seemingly accidental experiences, as it is plain to the geometer why the evenly curved circle must forbid its diameters to be unequal. It is of the nature of reason to view things as necessary, as explicable, as results either of their own nature, or, if this is n't the case, then of the higher nature of things whereof they form a part.

From this axiom, Spinoza proceeds, by a very short but thorny road, to the thought that, if this is so, there must be some one highest nature of things, which explains all reality. That such highest nature exists, he regards as self-evident. The self-explaining must, of course, explain, and so make sure, its own existence. Spinoza shows by devices which I cannot here follow that there could n't be numerous self-explained and separate natures of things.[1] The world is one, and so all the things in it must be parts of one self-evident, self-producing order, one nature. Spinoza conceives this order, describes its self-explaining and all-producing character, as well as he can, and then gives it a name elsewhere well known to philosophers, but used by him in his own sense. He calls the supreme nature of things the universal " Substance " of all the world. In it are we all; it makes us what we are; it does what its own nature determines; it explains itself and all of us; it is n't produced, it produces; it is uncreate, supreme, overruling, omnipresent, absolute,

[1] *Eth.* I. prop. v. ; prop. viii. schol. ii. ; props. xi. and xiv. ; *Epist.* xxxiv. (Hague edition).

rational, irreversible, unchangeable, the law of laws, the nature of natures ; and we — we, with all our acts, thoughts, feelings, life, relations, experiences — are just the result of it, the consequences of it, as the diameters are results of the nature of a circle. Feel, hope, desire, choose, strive, as you will, all is in you because this universal " substance " makes you what you are, forces you into this place in the nature of things, rules you as the higher truth rules the lower, as the wheel rules the spoke, as the storm rules the raindrop, as the tide rules the wavelet, as autumn rules the dead leaves, as the snowdrift rules the fallen snowflake ; and this substance is what Spinoza calls God.

If you ask what sort of thing this substance is, the first answer is, it is something eternal; and that means, not that it lasts a good while, but that no possible temporal view of it could exhaust its nature.[1] All things that happen result from the one substance. This surely means that what happens now and what happened millions of years ago are, for the substance, equally present and necessary results. To illustrate once more in my own way : A spider creeping back and forth across a circle could, if she were geometrically disposed, measure out in temporal succession first this diameter and then that. Crawling first over one diameter, she would say, " I now find this so long." Afterwards examining another diameter, she would say, " It has now happened that what I have just measured proves to be precisely as long as what I measured some time since, and no longer." The toil of such a spider might last many hours, and be full of such successive measurements, each marked by a spun thread of web. But the true circle itself within which the web was spun, the circle in actual space as the geometer knows it, would its nature be thus a mere series of events, a mere succession of spun threads?[2] No, the true circle

---

[1] *Eth.* I. def. viii. and *Explicatio.*

[2] This illustration will easily be recognized as an effort at a **para-**

would be timeless, a truth founded in the nature of space,
outlasting, preceding, determining all the weary web-spinning of this time-worn spider.   Even so we, spinning our
web of experience in all its dreary complication in the
midst of the eternal nature of the world-embracing substance, imagine that our lives somehow contain true novelty, discover for the substance what it never knew before,
invent new forms of being.   We fancy our past wholly
past, and our future wholly unmade.   We think that
where we have as yet spun no web there is nothing, and
that what we long ago spun has vanished, broken by the
winds of time, into nothingness.   It is not so.   For the
eternal substance there is no before and after ; all truth is
truth.   " Far and forgot to me is near," it says.   In the
unvarying precision of its mathematical universe, all is
eternally written.

> " Not all your piety nor wit
> Can lure it back to cancel half a line,
> Nor all your tears wash out one word of it."

What will be for endless ages, what has been since time
began, is in the one substance completely present, as in
one scroll may be written the joys and sorrows of many
lives, as one earth contains the dead of countless generations, as one space enfolds all the limitless wealth of
figured curves and of bodily forms.

This substance, then, this eternal, is Spinoza's God.   In
describing it I have used terms, comparisons, and illustrations largely my own.   I hope that I have been true to
the spirit of Spinoza's thought.   Remember, then, of the
substance that it is absolutely infinite and self-determined ; that it exists completely and once for all ; that
all the events of the world follow from it as the nature

phrase of *Eth.* II. prop. viii. coroll. and schol., a passage where, as
in the illustration above used, one finds presented, but not solved, the
whole problem of the true relation of finite and infinite, temporal
and eternal.

of the diameter follows from the nature of the circle, and
that as for yourself, it enfolds, overpowers, determines,
produces both you and your destiny, as the storm embraces the raindrop, and as the nature of a number determines the value of its factors. Yet now you will ask one
question more. This substance, so awful in its fatal perfection, is it, you will say, something living and intelligent
that I can revere, or is it something dead, a mere blind
force? Spinoza answers this question in a very original
way. The substance, he says, must have infinitely numerous ways of expressing itself, each complete, rounded,
self-determined. It is like an infinite sacred scripture,
translated into endlessly numerous tongues, but complete
in each tongue. Of these self-expressions of the substance, we mortals know only two. One is the material
world, — Spinoza calls it body or bodily substance. The
other is the inner world of thought, — Spinoza calls it
thinking substance, or mind. These two worlds, Spinoza
holds, are equally real, equally revelations of the one
absolute truth, equally divine, equally full of God, equally
expressions of the supreme order. But, for the rest, they
are, as they exist here about us, mutually independent.
The substance expresses itself in matter; very well, then,
all material nature is full of rigid and mathematical law:
body moves body; line determines line in space; everything, including this bodily frame of ours, is an expression of the extended or corporeal aspect or attribute of
the substance. In stars and in clouds, in dust and in
animals, in figures and in their geometrical properties,
the eternal writes its nature, as in a vast hieroglyphic.
Equally, however, the substance writes itself in the events
and the laws of mental life. And that it does so, the
very existence of our own minds proves. Thought produces thought, just as body moves body, while on the
other hand it is inconceivable that mind should act on
body, or body explain mind. And so these two orders,

mental and corporeal, are precisely parallel. For neither
belongs to, or is part of, or is explained by, the other.
Both, then, must be equally and independently expressions of God the substance. Hence, as each of the two
orders expresses God's nature, each must be as omnipresent as the other. Wherever there is a body, God, says
Spinoza, has a thought corresponding to that body. All
nature is full of thought. Nothing exists but has its own
mind, just as you have your mind. The more perfect
body has, indeed, the more perfect mind ; a crowbar is n't
as thoughtful as a man, because in the simplicity of its
metallic hardness it finds less food for thought.[1] But, all
the same, the meanest of God's creatures has some sort
of thought attached to it, not indeed produced or affected
in any wise by the corporeal nature of this thing, but
simply parallel thereto; an expression, in cogitative or
sentient terms, of the nature of the facts here present.
Well, this thought is just as real an expression of the
divine nature as is matter. There is just as much necessity, connection, completeness, mutual interdependence,
rationality, eternity, in mind as in body. Of God's thought
your thought is a part, just as your body is a part of the
embodied substance. His thinking nature produces your
ideas, as his corporeal nature produces your nerves.
There is, however, no real influence of body over mind,
or the reverse. The two are just parallel. The order
and connection of ideas is the same as the order and connection of things. Just so far as your bodily life extends,
so far and no further, in the mental world, extends your
thought. You make nothing by your thinking but your
own thoughts; but as your body is a part of nature, so
also is your mind a part of the infinite mind. "I declare,"
says Spinoza, in a letter to a friend, "I declare the human
mind to be a part of nature, namely, because I hold that

[1] The illustration is my own. The thought is that of *Eth*. II.
prop. xiii. and the scholium thereto.

in nature there exists an infinite power of thinking, which
power, so far as it is infinite, contains ideally the whole
of nature, in such wise that its thoughts proceed in the
same fashion as nature herself, being, in fact, the ideal
mirror thereof.[1] Hence follows that I hold the human
mind to be simply this same power (of divine thought),
not so far as it is infinite and perceives the whole of
nature, but as far as it perceives alone the human body;
and thus I hold our human mind to be part of this infinite intellect."

VII.

I have thus led you a tedious way through this thorny
path of Spinoza's thought. I have had no hope to make
their connections all clear; I shall be content if you bear
in mind this as the outcome : our reason perceives the
world to be one being, whose law is everywhere and eternally expressed. Only this eternal point of view shows
us the truth. But if we are rational, we can assume such
an eternal point of view, can see God everywhere, and can
so enter, not merely with mystical longings, but with a
clear insight into an immediate communion with the Lord
of all being. And this Lord, he is indeed the author of
matter. The earth, the sea, yes, the very geometrical
figures themselves write his truth in inanimate outward
forms. But meanwhile (and herein lies the hope of our
mystical religion) this substance, this deity, possesses and
of its nature determines also and equally an infinite mind,
of whose supreme perfection our minds are fragments.
We are thus not only the sons of God ; so far as we are
wise our lives are hid in God, we are in Him, of Him ;
we recognize this indwelling, we lose our finiteness in
Him, we become filled with the peace which the eternal
brings ; we calm the thirst of our helpless finite passion
by entering consciously into his eternal self-possession

---

[1] *Nimirum ejus ideatum*, the corrected reading of the Hague edition of Van Vloten and Land. See *Epist.* xxxii. p. 130.

and freedom. For the true mind, like the true natural order, knows nothing of the bondage of time, thinks of no before and after, has no fortune, dreads nothing, laments nothing; but enjoys its own endlessness, its own completeness, has all things in all things, and so cries, like the lover of the " Imitation," " My Beloved, I am all thine, and thou art all mine."

In the fifth part of Spinoza's " Ethics," his own description of the wise man's love of God closes his wonderful exposition. This love is superior to fortune, renounces all hopes and escapes all fears, feeds alone on the thought that God's mind is the only mind, loves God with a fragment of " that very love wherewith God loves himself." The wise man thus wanders on earth in whatever state you will, — poor, an outcast, weak, near to bodily death; but " his meditation is not of death, but of life; " of the eternal life whereof he is a part, and has ever been and ever will be a part. You may bound him in a nut-shell, but he counts himself king of infinite space; and rightly, for the bad dreams of this phantom life have ceased to trouble him. " His blessedness," says Spinoza, " is not the reward of his virtue, but his virtue itself. He rejoices therein, not because he has controlled his lusts; contrariwise, because he rejoices therein, the lusts of the finite have no power over him." " Thus appears how potent, then, is the wise man, and how much he surpasses the ignorant man, who is driven only by his lusts. For the ignorant man is not only distracted in various ways by external causes, without ever gaining true acquiescence of mind, but moreover lives, as it were, unwitting of himself and of God and of things, and, as soon as he ceases to suffer, ceases also to be. Whereas the wise man, in so far as he is regarded as such, is scarcely at all disturbed in spirit, but being conscious of himself and of God and of things, by a certain eternal necessity, never ceases to be, but always possesses true acquiescence of his spirit.

If the way which I have pointed out as leading to this result seems exceedingly hard, it may, nevertheless, be discovered. Needs must it be hard since it is so seldom found. How would it be possible if salvation were ready to our hand, and could without great labor be found, that it should be by almost all men neglected? But all things excellent are as difficult as they are rare."

With these words closes the book of Spinoza's experience.

LECTURE III.

In the lecture of to-day, as I must frankly assure you
at the outset, our path lies for the most part in far less
inspiring regions than those into which, at the last time,
Spinoza guided us. You are well acquainted with a fact
of life to which I may as well call your attention forthwith,
the fact, namely, that certain stages of growing intelligence,
and even of growing spiritual knowledge, are marked by
an inevitable, and, at first sight, lamentable decline, in
apparent depth and vitality of spiritual experience. The
greatest concerns of our lives are, in such stages of our
growth, somehow for a while hidden, even forgotten. We
become more knowing, more clever, more critical, more
wary, more skeptical, but we seemingly do not grow more
profound or more reverent. We find in the world much
that engages our curious attention ; we find little that is
sublime. Our world becomes clearer ; a brilliant, hard,
mid-morning light shines upon everything ; but this light
does not seem to us any longer divine. The deeper
beauty of the universe fades out; only facts and problems are left.

Such a stage in human experience is represented, in
great part, by the philosophical thinkers who flourish
between the time of Spinoza's death, in 1677, and the
appearance of Kant's chief philosophical work, "The Critique of Pure Reason," in 1781. It is the period which

has been especially associated, in historical tradition, with the eighteenth century, so that when one speaks of the spirit of the eighteenth century, he is likely to be referring to this skeptical and critical mood, to this hard, mid-morning light of the bare understanding, beneath which most of these thinkers of our period saw all their world lying. When I undertake to describe such a time, I therefore feel in its spirit a strong contrast to that curious but profound sort of piety which we were describing in the last lecture in the case of Spinoza. Spinoza, indeed, was in respect of his piety a man of marked limitations. His world had but one sublime feature in it, one element of religious significance, namely, the perfection of the divine substance. But then this one element was enough, from his point of view, to insure an elevated and untroubled repose of faith and love, which justified us in drawing a parallel between his religious consciousness and that of the author of the "Imitation of Christ." This sort of piety almost disappears from the popular philosophy of the early eighteenth century. What the people of that time want is more light and fewer unproved assumptions.

As against the earlier seventeenth-century thinkers, who, as you remember, also abhorred the occult, and trusted in reason, the thinkers of this new age are characterized by the fact that on the whole they have a great and increasing suspicion of even that rigid mathematical method of research itself upon which men like Spinoza had relied. In other words, whereas the men of the middle of the seventeenth century had trusted to reason alone, the men of the subsequent period began, first hesitatingly, and then more and more seriously, to distrust even human reason itself. After all, can you spin a world, as Spinoza did, out of a few axioms? Can you permanently revere a divine order that is perhaps the mere creature of the assumptions with which your system happened to start? The men of the new age are not ready to answer " Yes " to such questions. They must reflect, they must peer into reason itself. They must ask, Whence arise these axioms, how come we by our knowledge, of what account are our mathematical demonstrations, and of what, after all, does our limited human nature permit us to be sure? Once started upon this career, the thought of the time is driven more and more, as we have already said, to the study of human nature, as opposed to the exclusive study of the physical universe. The whole range of human passion, so far as the eighteenth century knew about it, is criticised, but for a good while in a cautious, analytical, cruelly scrutinizing way, as if it were all something suspicious, misleading, superstitious. The coldness of the seventeenth century is still in the air; but Spinoza's sense of sublimity is gone. Spinoza himself, you remember, had altogether rejected, as occult, everything miraculous, marvelous, extra-natural. Not the thunder or the earthquake or the fire could for him contain God; God was in the still small voice that the wise man alone heard. Now the popular philosophy of the eighteenth century more and more approached a position which unconsciously agreed with Spinoza's in a number of respects. It cordially recognized, for instance, that the earthquake, say the great Lisbon earthquake of 1758, was a fearful thing, but that God was very certainly not in that earthquake. It could readily make out the same thing concerning any amount of thunder, fire, or wind that you might produce for inspection. But it went one step further than Spinoza's wise man, and was forced to observe, that, after considerable scrutiny, it had as yet been able to detect in the world of reason and experience no still, small voice whatsoever. That at least, as I say, was the outcome of a considerable portion of the thought of the time. It was indeed not the outcome of all the thinking of this age. In Leibnitz, who was a younger contemporary of Spinoza, and who flourished in the closing decades of the seventeenth century, and at the beginning of the new period, philosophical theology found an expositor of the greatest speculative ingenuity and of the most positive tendency. Later, in the ever-fascinating Bishop Berkeley, not merely theological doctrine, but a profoundly spiritual idealism got voice. In Rousseau, a new era of sentimental piety found its beginning, and all this movement led erelong to Kant himself. But for the moment I am speaking of tendencies in a most general way, and this negative, this cautious, skeptical attitude, is the one most observable in the philosophy of our period.

I.

Those of us who look to philosophy for positive experiences, rather than for technical instruction, will at first sight regard such a period as this with some natural indifference. The skeptic is not always an interesting person; but then, you must remember, as skeptic he does n't want to be interesting. He only wishes to be honest. He is meanwhile not only to be tolerated; he is also indispensable. Philosophical thought that has never been skeptical is sure not to be deep. The soul that never has doubted does not know whether it believes; and at all events the thinker who has not dwelt long in doubt has no rights to high rank as a reflective person. In fact, a study of history shows that if there is anything that human thought and cultivation have to be deeply thankful for, it is an occasional but truly great and fearless age of doubt. You may rightly say that doubt has no value in itself. Its value is in what it leads to. But then consider what ages of doubt have led to. Such an age in Greece produced that father of every humane sort of philosophizing, Socrates. The same age nourished with doubts the divine thought of Plato. Another and yet sterner age of doubt brought about the beginnings of Christian thought, prepared the Roman empire for the new faith, and saved

the world from being ruined by the multitudinous fanati-
cal rivals of Christianity. Yet a third great age of doubt
began, at the Renaissance, the history of modern literature,
and made the way plain for whatever was soundest about
the Reformation. And a fourth age of doubt, the one
under our consideration in this present lecture, proved
more fruitful for good to humanity than a half dozen
centuries of faith had done at another time. For, as we
shall see, this eighteenth-century doubting drove thinkers
from the study of nature to the study first of human
reason, then of human conscience, then of all the human
heart and soul, and meanwhile cleared the way for those
triumphs of the spirit over great evils which have taken
place from the moment of the French Revolution until
now. Despise not doubting; it is often the best service
thinking men can render to their age. Condemn it not;
it is often the truest piety. And when I say this I do
not mean merely to repeat cant phrases. I speak with
reason. Doubt is never the proper end of thinking, but
it is a good beginning. The wealth of truth which our
life, our age, our civilization, our religion, our own hearts
may contain, is not quite our property until we have won
it. And we can win it only when we have first doubted
the superficial forms in which at the outset it presents
itself to our apprehension. Every true lover has in the
beginning of his love grave doubts of his beloved's affection
for him. And such doubts often take on bitter and even
cynical forms in his soul in the various bad quarters of an
hour that fall to his lot. Doubt, however, is not the foe,
but the very inspirer of his love. It means that the beloved is yet to be won. It means that the simple warmth
of his aspiration is n't enough, and that, if the beloved is
worth winning, she is worth wooing through doubt and
uncertainty for a good while. Moreover, it is not the
fashion of the beloved, in the typical case, to be especially
forward in quelling such doubts, by making clear her atti-

tude too soon. If it were, love-making might be a simpler
affair, but would not be so significant an experience as it
is. Doubt is the cloud that is needed as a background for
love's rainbow. Even so it is, however, in the world of
abstracter thought. The more serious faiths of humanity
can only be won, if at all, by virtue of much doubting.
The divine truth is essentially coy. You woo her, you
toil for her, you reflect upon her by night and by day, you
search through books, study nature, make experiments,
dissect brains, hold learned disputations, take counsel of
the wise; in fine, you prepare your own ripest thought, and
lay it before your heavenly mistress when you have done
your best. Will she be pleased? Will she reward you
with a glance of approval? Will she say, Thou hast well
spoken concerning me? Who can tell? Her eyes have
their own beautiful fashion of looking far off when you
want them to be turned upon you; and, after all, perhaps
she prefers other suitors for her favor. The knowledge
that she is of sufficiently exalted dignity to be indifferent
to you, if she chooses, is what constitutes the mood known
as philosophical skepticism. You see that, in sound-
hearted thinkers, it is like the true lover's doubt whether
his unwon mistress regards him kindly or no. It is not,
then, a deadening and weakening mood; it is the very soul
of philosophical earnestness.

Meanwhile, in describing the skepticism of our period
I am far from wishing to trouble you with its endlessly
varied technical subtleties. These lectures are throughout
selective, and they sacrifice numberless intrinsically important aspects of our various subjects, in order to be able
to seize upon a few significant features, and to hold these
up to your view. I cannot warn you too much that there
is no chance of completeness of treatment anywhere in the
course of our brief work together. I spared you, in the
last lecture, whole cargoes of problems which are consigned
to every special student of Spinoza. I shall omit in this

every mention of innumerable significant features in the philosophy of our present period. All this is a matter of course. I remind you of it only to excuse an immediate and somewhat dry statement of the few features of this eighteenth-century skepticism to which I intend to confine myself in what follows.

II.

There are certain philosophic problems of which you are sure, sooner or later, to have heard something in general literature, and for which the time from Spinoza to Kant is at least partially responsible. I want to set forth a little of the growth of these problems, never forgetting, I hope, that they interest us here in their human rather than in their technical aspects, and that we are above all concerned in them as leading to Kant himself, and to those who came after him. And my selection is as follows : —

You have all heard about the controversy as to whether man's knowledge of more significant truth is innate, or whether it comes to him from without, through his senses; or, otherwise, as to whether the mind at birth is a *tabula rasa*, a blank white piece of innocent paper, upon which experience writes whatever it will, or whether the soul is endowed from the start with certain inborn rational possessions, — a divine law, for instance, written on the tablets of the heart, a divine wisdom about number and space, registered in some imperishable form in our very structures. You may have met with more or less elaborate arguments upon this topic. I do not know whether it has ever had more than the interest of a curious problem to many of us. I do know that in many styles of treatment it must appear as a sort of hackneyed debating-club question, an apparently excellent one of its sort, but a rather dry bone of contention, after all.

But you now know that philosophic research is no affair of the debating clubs, but a struggle of humanity to make its own deepest interests articulate, and therefore you will not expect me to deal with this question after the forensic fashion. What I want to do is this : —

I want to suggest summarily the origin of the controversy about the innate ideas, and to show you what interest first led men to the question. Then, I want to indicate the value of the controversy as bringing about that study of man's inner life which, at the close of the century, bore fruit in the great Romantic movement itself. Finally, I want to narrate how the problems erelong took form, what skeptical outcome the discussion, upon one side, seemed to have, and what solution, what re-winning of the great spiritual faiths of humanity, it suggested on the other. In this way I shall try to prepare you for that stupendous revolution of philosophic thought which is associated with the name of Kant.

For the first, then, as to the origin of the controversy about the innate ideas. I shall not go back farther in the history of thought than to Descartes, 1596-1650, a predecessor of Spinoza, and the man whose name usually begins the lists of modern philosophers proper, as they are set forth in the text-books of the history of philosophy. Had I been engaged in technical teaching, it would have been my duty, in the last lecture, to describe the highly interesting relation in which Spinoza's doctrine stands to that of his predecessor. As it is, I have so far passed Descartes over. At present I must mention, in a word, one or two features of his doctrine. Descartes had early become dissatisfied with the scholastic philosophy which he had learned at Jesuit hands, and decided to think out a system for himself. He began his reasoning by a formal philosophical doubt about everything that could conceivably be doubted, and then proceeded to examine whether any unassailable certainty was still left him. He found such an absolutely unassailable assurance in his own existence as a thinking being, and accordingly began

his positive doctrine with the famous principle, " *Cogito,
ergo sum,* " " I think, and so I exist. " He proceeded
from this beginning to prove the existence of God, and
then the existence of two so-called substances, mind and
matter, as comprising the whole world of which we mortals
know anything. The laws of matter he found to be those of
mathematics, and of the elementary physics of his time.
Of mind he also studied the constitution as well as he
could, and the result appeared in several elaborate works.
Now the principle on which Descartes proceeded throughout his investigations was this: " My own existence
is the standard assurance of my thought. I know
that *I* at least am. But surely, if, on examining some
principle, say an axiom in geometry, I perceive that it is
as plain to me, as clear, as distinct, as is my own existence,
then indeed it must be as certain a truth as my existence."
This, I say, was his way of procedure, whenever he was
puzzled about a principle. " Is it as clear to me as my own
existence ; or can I somehow make it as clear and distinct? Well, then, it is true. Is it less clear? Then I
must examine it still further, or lay it aside as doubtful."
By this fashion of procedure, which Descartes regarded
as the typically rational one, he managed to collect after
a time a very goodly stock of sure and clear principles.
Others have n't always found them all as clear and sure
as did Descartes, but that concerns us not now. Well,
Descartes had a name, or in fact a brace of names, for
these principles of his. He called them " eternal truths,"
and he also called them " innate " ideas or truths. We
know them because it is of the nature of our reason to know
them. We know them whenever we come to look at them
squarely, whether we ever saw them in this light before or
not. That $2 + 2 = 4$, that things equal to the same thing
are equal to each other, these are examples of such truths.
They are as clear to me as that I myself exist. They are
clear to me because my reason makes them so, and that is

the sort of reason I have. They are innate in me. I don't see them with my bodily eyes. I just know them, because I do know them, and I know them also to be eternal.

Innate truths then, for Descartes, are of this sort. He is n't so much interested in finding out how so many truths could be innate in one poor little human soul all at once, as he is interested in singling them out and writing down bookfuls of them. The seventeenth century, you remember, was not much interested in man himself, but was very much interested in eternal truth. Hence Descartes makes light of the problem *how* all this thought-stuff could somehow be innate in a soul without the poor soul's ever even guessing the fact until it had studied philosophy. Yet of course if one becomes strongly interested in human nature for its own sake, this problem which Descartes ignored must come to the front.

The true interest of this problem, then, lies in the fact that by reflecting upon it philosophers have been led to some of the deepest undertakings of modern thought. For the moment it comes up as a question of mere idle curiosity. As such, however, the question was rather tauntingly suggested to Descartes himself by certain of his opponents. "How can so many ideas be innate?" they said. "Observe, children don't know these truths of yours, and could n't even grasp them. Much less could infants. And yet you call them innate." Descartes, thus challenged, replied curtly, but not unskillfully. They may be innate, he said (in substance), as predispositions, which in infants have n't yet grown to conscious rank. The thing is simple enough. In certain families, so Descartes further explains (I do not quote his words but give their sense), good-breeding and the gout are innate. Yet of course, as he implies, the children of such families have to be instructed in deportment, and the infants just learning to walk seem happily quite free from gout. Even so, geometry is innate in us, but it does n't come to our

consciousness without much trouble. With the taunting
questions put to Descartes, and his example about the
heredity of good-breeding and the gout, the question of
the innate ideas enters modern philosophy. It was later
to grow much more important.

III.

In Locke's famous "Essay on the Human Understanding," published in 1689–90, the investigation may be said to
have been fairly opened. Locke was born in the same year
as Spinoza. Had he died when Spinoza died, the English
thinker would never have been heard of in the history of
thought. In Locke's patient devotion to a detailed investigation, we find a quality that reminds us of the most
marked characteristic of another great Englishman, the
scientific hero of our own day, Darwin. Locke was early
busy with philosophy, natural science, and medicine.
Later, he was for a short time abroad, in diplomatic service, and then lived long as the intimate friend of Lord
Anthony Ashley, afterwards Earl of Shaftesbury, whose
political fortunes he followed. His whole life was a mingling of study, private teaching, writing and practical politics. His character is thoroughly English. There is
that typical clearness in seizing and developing his own
chief ideas, and that manly, almost classically finished
stubbornness as against all foreign, mystical, and especially
Continental ideas, which usually mark the elder English
thinkers. Give Locke a profound problem like that of the
freedom of the will, and he flounders helplessly. Ask
him to look at things from a novel point of view, and he
cannot imagine what fancy you can be dreaming of. But
leave him to himself, and he shows you within his own
range a fine, sensible, wholesome man at work, a thorough
man, who has seen the world of business as well as the
world of study, and who believes in business-like methods in his philosophy. His style, to be sure, is endlessly

diffuse, yet without being precisely wearisome, because, after all, it is itself the diffuseness of a man of business, whose accounts cover many and various transactions, and who has to set down all the items. Nobody can fail to respect Locke, unless, to be sure, his work is employed as a text-book for classes that are too immature to grapple with him. It has too frequently been thus abused, to the great injury of the excellent man's popular fame.

Locke made, as everybody knows, short work of all innate ideas. He found none. Infants, with their rattles, show no sign of being aware that things which are equal to the same things are equal to each other. Locke himself, to be sure, is a poor expert concerning infants, as is evident from many things that he says about them, in the course of his book, but as to this matter he is not only confident but right. As for the hereditary predispositions, similar to good-breeding and the gout, Locke in one or two passages recognizes that there may, indeed must be, such things. But he does not see of what service they could be in forming knowledge, were it not for our senses.

What interests us most in Locke, however, is not this negative part of his argument, but his general view of the nature, powers and scope of human reason, a view which introduces a whole century of research into man's inner life. In the preface to his Essay, Locke describes to us the history of his book. "Were it fit," he says, addressing the reader, "to trouble thee with the history of this essay, I should tell thee that five or six friends meeting at my chamber, and discoursing on a subject very remote from this, found themselves quickly at a stand by the difficulties that rose on every side. After we had awhile puzzled ourselves, without coming any nearer a resolution of those doubts which perplexed us, it came into my thoughts that we took a wrong course, and that before we set ourselves upon inquiries of that nature, it was necessary to examine our own abilities, and see what objects our understandings were, or were not, fitted to deal with. This I proposed to the company, who all readily assented ; and thereupon it was agreed that this should be our first inquiry. Some hasty and undigested thoughts on a subject I had never before considered, which I set down against our next meeting, gave the first entrance into this discourse ; which, having been thus begun by chance, was continued by entreaty ; written by incoherent parcels ; and, after long intervals of neglect, resumed again, as my humor or occasions permitted, and at last, in a retirement, where an attendance on my health gave me leisure, it was brought into that order thou now seest it."

In this modest way Locke introduces a book whose historical value lies precisely in this insistence upon the importance of knowing our own understandings, as a preliminary to every sort of research. And how great this historical value of the book ! Locke and his five or six friends fall to discussing, in club fashion, certain unnamed problems. They find themselves in a quandary. Locke proposes that they go back on their own track a little and study the structure and powers of the understanding itself. He himself begins the analysis, the entreaty of his friends leads him to continue the research. The result is a big book, sensible, many-sided, influential. It arouses a great controversy, and herefrom springs, first the philosophic movement from Locke through Leibnitz, through the wonderful Berkeley, through the ingenious, fearless, and doubting Hume, to Kant himself, and European thought is transformed. Meanwhile, from the same root grow other inquiries into the mind of man. The great English moralists of the eighteenth century, a stately row, Shaftesbury, Hutcheson, Butler, Adam Smith, and Hume once more, set forth the mysteries of the moral consciousness. The general public is aroused. A subjective, a humane mode of inquiry becomes everywhere prominent. Much of all this is cold and skeptical in tone. In France it gives us the encyclopedists, such as Diderot. But the same movement also gives us Rousseau. The modern novel, too, that great analyst of the mind and the heart of every man, takes its rise. I think I am not wrong in attributing the novel largely to that interest in analysis for which Locke stood. Yonder mere outer nature is no longer everything. And erelong, lo! almost before they know it, the nations of Europe themselves are once more plunged into the very midst of the great problems of the spirit. For at length the inquiry loses its negative and skeptical air altogether. The world glows afresh. Passion, brought by all this out of its hiding-places, grows hot; men have once more found something to die for; and what they learn to die for in the revolutionary period is the inner life. They die for the freedom of the subject; for the sacred rights of humanity; for the destruction of inhuman and despotic restraints. They make, indeed, vast blunders in all this, behead an innocent queen, set up a new despot merely because his rule is n't traditional, die amid the snows of Russia for a bare whim, in short sin atrociously, but meanwhile they cleanse Europe of a whole dead world of irrationalisms; they glorify the human nature that can endure and suffer so much for the sake of coming to possess itself; they create our modern world. And all this, I say, because they had rediscovered the inner life.

Do I seem to exaggerate the significance of the mere thinker and his work? I assure you that I do not. My idea of the mission of the philosopher is, I insist, a very moderate one. As I have several times said, he does n't create the passions of men; he makes no new ideals. His only mission is to direct the attention of man to the passions and ideals which they already possess. He doubts, analyzes, pries into this and that; and men say, How dry, how repellent, how unpractical, how remote from life. But, after all, he is prying into the secret places of the lightning of Jove; for these thoughts and passions upon which he reflects move the world. He says to his time: This and this hast thou, — this sense of the rights of man, a sword of the spirit, fashioned to slay tyrants ; — this love of liberty, an ideal banner bequeathed thee by a sacred past to cherish, as the soldiers of old cherished the standard beneath which they conquered the world. Such things he says always, to be sure, in his own technical way, and for a time nobody finds it out at all or even reads his books. But at length discussion begins to spread, the word of wisdom flies from one book to another, and finally the people hear. They look at the sword and at the banner. No philosopher made these. They are simply humanity's own treasures. The philosopher had the sole service of calling attention to them, because, in the course of his critical research, he found them. But the rediscovery, how great its significance ! I suppose that you have frequently heard it said that the philosophers had much to do with making the French Revolution, and you have wondered how this was. You may also have wondered how this was consistent with our view that philosophers are the mere critics of life. I show you the solution. The critic creates nothing, he only points out. But his pointing may show you powers that were indeed always there, and that were even effective, but that, once afresh seen, suggest to active passion a thousand devices whereby the world is revolutionized.

We return to Locke. By an inquiry of the sort which he has described to us, he had sought to comprehend the nature and the limits of our understanding. He had, as we saw, decided that innate ideas cannot do anything for knowledge. And the force of this notion of Locke's really was that, according to him, it is useless to assume, as the basis of our human reason, anything occult, mysterious, opaque, hidden away in the recesses of the mind. The real cause of Locke's hatred of innate ideas is his horror of anything mystical. If thought is not to be clear, what shall be clear ? Hence, if you pretend to have any knowledge, you must be prepared to tell where it comes from. It won't do to appeal, as Descartes did, to a certain impression of the clearness and distinctness of your ideas. Their origin will decide their value. And what is this origin ? Locke puts the question plainly, at the beginning of the second book of his Essay, and answers it in a general way. I quote the whole passage : —

" Let us, then, suppose the mind to be, as we say, white paper, void of all characters, without any ideas ; how comes it to be furnished? Whence comes it by that vast store which the busy and boundless fancy of man has painted on it with an almost endless variety ? Whence has it all the materials of reason and knowledge ? To this I answer, in one word, From Experience ; in that all our knowledge is founded, and from that it ultimately derives itself. Our observation, employed either about external sensible objects, or about the internal operations of our minds, perceived and reflected on by ourselves, is that which supplies our understandings with all the materials of thinking. These two are the fountains of knowledge from whence all the ideas we have or can naturally have do spring." " First," he continues, " our senses, conversant about particular sensible objects, do convey into the mind several distinct perceptions of things, according to those various ways wherein those objects do affect them ; and thus we come by those ideas we have of yellow, white, heat, cold, soft, hard, bitter, sweet, and all those which we call sensible qualities ; which when I say that the senses convey into the mind, I mean, that they from external objects convey into the mind what produces there those perceptions. This great source of most of the ideas we have, depending wholly upon our senses, and derived by them to the understanding, I call Sensation.

" Secondly, the other fountain, from which experience

furnisheth the understanding with ideas, is the perception
of the operations of our mind within us, as it is employed
about the ideas it has got; which operations, when the soul
comes to reflect on and consider, do furnish the understanding with another set of ideas, which could not be had
from things without; and such are perception, thinking,
doubting, believing, reasoning, knowing, willing, and all
the different actings of our own minds. . . . This source
of ideas every man has wholly in himself; and though it
be not sense, . . . yet it is very like it, and might properly
enough be called internal sense. But as I call the other
sensation, so I call this Reflection, the ideas it affords
being such only as the mind gets by reflecting on its own
operations within itself. . . . These two, I say, namely,
external material things, as the objects of sensation, and
the operations of our own minds within, as the objects of
reflection, are to me the only originals from whence all
our ideas take their beginnings."

So much, then, for Locke's notion of how we come by
knowledge. I quote him at this length, because his view
was of such critical importance in what followed in all
European thought.

You will ask at once, What sort of a real world did
Locke manage to make out of this material of bare sensations and reflections? We see, touch, smell, taste this
our world, and then we reflectively observe of ourselves
that we are doubting, willing, hoping, loving, hating, thinking, and thus we get all our knowledge. That is all the
mind we have. That is the human understanding. Such
at least is Locke's view. But what does it all come to?
Is the result a materialism pure and simple, or is it a skepticism? Not so. Locke was an Englishman; he saw,
heard, smelt, tasted, what his fellow-countrymen also did;
and he reflected upon all this after much their fashion.
His world, therefore, is the world of the liberal English
thinker of his day. He believes in matter and its laws,

in God also, and in revelation, in duty and in the human
rights of the British freeman, and in the Essay he tries
to show how just such things can be known to us through
bare seeing, hearing, tasting, and the rest, coupled with
reflection upon what we are doing. There is nothing
revolutionary about Locke's own view of his world, great
as was the revolution that he prepared. By touch we
learn that there are substances about us, solid, space-oc-
cupying, numerous, movable. By all our senses we learn
that these substances have many curious properties, how
or why brought about, we cannot discover. Sugar is
sweet; gold is yellow ; various drugs have specific effects
in curing diseases; water flows; iron is rigid ; every substance is as God wills it to be. These things are so,
because we find them so. Meanwhile, being reflective
Englishmen, we can't help observing that all these things
require God to create them what they are, because, as
one sees, things always have adequate causes; and our
minds, too, being realities, must have been made by a
thinker. Moreover, a fair study of the evidence of revelation will convince any reasonable person of the essential
truths of the Christian religion, and that is enough.

You will not find this world of Locke an exciting one.
But remember, after all, what it is that he has done for us.
He has tried hard to remove every mystery from the nature
of human reason. Because innate ideas, the eternal truths
of Descartes, were mysterious, he has thrown them over-
board. Experience it is that writes everything on the
blank tablet of the mind. But thus viewing things, Locke
has only given us a new mystery. Can experience, mere
smelling, tasting, seeing, together with bare reflection, do
all this for us, — give us God, religion, reality, our whole
English world ? Then surely what a marvelous treasure-
house is this experience itself ! Surely ages will be needed
to comprehend it. Locke cannot have finished it off thus
in one essay.

And indeed he has not done so. His book is the mere beginning both of the psychology of experience, and of discussions about the nature and limit of consciousness. The truly important argument over Locke's problems was opened by Leibnitz, the great Continental thinker, whose views I must entirely pass over, vastly important as they are, and that the less unwillingly just now because his answer to Locke, written about 1700, was not published until many years after his own death. I must, however, ask you to examine the next step forward in English philosophical reflection, the one taken by the admirable and fascinating Berkeley.

IV.

The world that Locke found with his senses is at once too poor and too much encumbered for Berkeley's young enthusiasm. Berkeley is a born child of Plato, a lineal descendant of a race whose origin is never very far off, and is divine. Men of Berkeley's type are born to see God face to face ; and when they see him, they do so without fear, without mystical trembling, without being driven to dark and lofty speech. They take the whole thing as a matter of course. They tell you of it frankly, gently, simply, and with a beautiful childlike surprise that your eyes are not always as open as their own. Meanwhile, they are true philosophers, keen in dialectic, skillful in the thrust and parry of debate, a little loquacious, but never wearisome. Of the physical world they know comparatively little, but what they know they love very much. A very few lines of philosophical research they pursue eagerly, minutely, fruitfully; concerning others they can make nothing but the most superficial remarks. They produce books young, and with marvelous facility. They have a full-fledged system ready by the time they are twenty-five. They will write an immortal work, as it were, over night. They are, for the rest, through

and through poetical.   Each one of their essays will be as
crisp and delicate as a good sonnet.   Yet what they lack
is elaboration, wiliness, and architectural massiveness of
research.   They take after Plato, their father, as to grace
and ingenuity.   His life-long patience and mature productiveness they never reach.   The world finds them paradoxical; refutes them again and again with a certain
Philistine ferocity; makes naught of them in hundreds of
learned volumes ; but returns ever afresh to the hopeless
task of keeping them permanently naught.   In the heaven
of reflection, amongst the philosophical angels who contemplate the beatific vision of the divine essence, such
spirits occupy neither the place of the archangels, nor of
those who speed o'er land and sea, nor yet of those who
only stand and wait.   Their office is a less serious one.
They cast glances now and then at this inspiring aspect
or at that of the divine essence, sing quite their own song
in its praise, find little in most of the other angels that can
entertain them, and spend their time for the most part in
gentle private musings, many of which (for so Berkeley's
own portrait suggests to me) they apparently find far too
pretty to be uttered at all.   We admire them, we may even
love them; yet no one would call them precisely heroes of
contemplation.   They themselves shed no tears, but they
also begin no revolutions, are apostles of no world-wide
movements.

Berkeley's grandly simple accomplishment, as you
know, lay in his observation that in the world of the senses,
in the world of experience, as Locke knew it, there was
properly no such thing as material substance discoverable
at all.   The world of sense-experience, said Berkeley, is a
world of ideas.   I have an idea, say of this fruit.   It is a
complex idea.   The fruit is round, soft, pleasant to the
taste, orange-colored, and the rest.   But then, as you see,
all these things that I know about the fruit are just my
ideas.   Were I in the dark, the fruit would have no color.

Do I refuse to bite it, the taste of it remains a bare possibility, not a fact. And so as to all the other properties of the fruit. All these exist for me in so far as I have ideas of them. Have I no idea of a thing, then it exists not for me. This is Berkeley's fundamental thought, but he does not leave it in such absolute and crude simplicity as this.

His deeper significance lies in the fact that he carries out in a new field an analysis of our inner life, namely, of a portion of the process of knowledge. His grandly simple idea, here applied, leads to very engaging results; but they are results which no other philosopher would be likely to accept without at once carrying them further than did Berkeley. The young student of Trinity College early became fascinated with the problem of the theory of vision. We seem to see objects about us in a space of three dimensions. These objects look solid, move about, stand in space relations to one another. But now, after all, how can we possibly see distance? Distance runs directly outward from my eyes; my eyes are at the surface of my body, and a distant object is not; my eyes are affected where they are, and, for the rest, not the distance of the opposite wall as such affects me, but the wall in so far as rays of light come from it. All this even Locke's man of plain sense has to admit. How, then, if distance itself is not one of my visual sensations, if distance is n't itself color or light, how can I still *see* distance? For all that I see is after all not even the object, but only the color and light of the object. This is Berkeley's problem about vision. His answer was early this: I don't really see distance. What I see is something about the color or shape of the distant object, or better still about the feelings that accompany in me the act of sight, — something which is to me a *sign* of distance. A distant orange is n't as big as a near one. That is *one* sign of distance then, namely, the size for me of my idea of a patch of color which I see when I look at the orange. Again, very distant objects, such as mountains, are known to be distant because they look to me blue. In short, to sum up, my apparent seeing of distance is n't any direct seeing of distance at all. It is a reading of the language of sight, as this is exhibited to my eyes by the colors and forms of things. A certain look of things, a certain group of signs, which I have learned, by long experience, to interpret, tells me how far off these things about me are. Distance is n't known directly. It is read as we read a language, read by interpreting the signs of the sense of sight. And as with distance, so with solidity. I don't really see things as solid. The solid things don't wander in through my eyes to my soul. But there are signs of solidity about the look of the things, signs that you learn to copy when you learn to draw in perspective, and to imitate the relief of objects ; these signs are the language of the sense of sight. You learn, when you come to comprehend this language, that if a thing looks in a certain way, has a certain relief of colors, a certain perspective arrangement of its outlines, that then, I say, it will feel solid if you go up to it and touch it. Infants don't know all this until they have learned to read the language of vision. Hence they don't see things as solid for a good while, don't judge distances accurately, have no eye for a space of three dimensions.

Seeing, then, is reading, is interpreting a world-language, is anticipating how things will feel to your touch by virtue of the signs given by the color, light, relief, perspective, of things. Such is Berkeley's view, and as far as it goes, it is obviously true. But he is not content to leave his thought here. He goes further. What is all my life of experience, my seeing, feeling, touching, moving about, examining my world? Is n't it from first to last a learning to read the language of things? Is n't it a learning to anticipate one thing by virtue of the signs that are given of its presence by another? Yes, all experience is after all learning to read. And this reading, what is it? It is merely rightly and rationally putting together the ideas which my world gives me. These ideas come in certain orders, follow certain laws. I learn these laws, and thus I read my world. I have one idea, say the glow of a fire. It suggests to me another idea, namely, that in case I go near the fire I shall feel warm. All experience, then, is a learning how my ideas ought to go together; it is a learning that upon one idea another will follow under certain circumstances. What, then, is this world of my experience? Is it anything but the world of ideas and of their laws? What existence has my world for me apart from my ideas of it? What existence can any world have apart from the thought of some thinker for whom it exists? Whose language, then, am I reading in this world before me? Whose ideas are these that experience impresses upon me? Are they not God's ideas? Is it not his language that I read in nature? Is not all my life a talking with God?

"Some truths there are," says Berkeley, " so near and obvious to the mind, that a man need only open his eyes to see them. Such I take this important one to be, to wit, that all the choir of heaven and furniture of the earth, in a word, all those bodies which compose the mighty frame of the world, have not any subsistence without mind; that their being is, to be perceived or known; that consequently so long as they are not actually perceived by me, or do not exist in my mind, or that of any other created spirit, they must either have no existence at all, or else subsist in the mind of some eternal spirit."

This is Berkeley's interpretation and extension of Locke's thought. I don't ask you to accept or to reject it, I only ask you to see once more how it holds together. Let us review it. My experience is a learning to read my world. What is my world? Merely the sum total of my ideas, of my thoughts, feelings, sights, sounds, colors,

tastes. I read these when one of them becomes sign to
me of another, when the idea of a glow tells me of the yet
unfelt warmth that a fire will arouse in me if I approach
it, when the ideas of forms and shadows warn me how a
solid thing will feel if I touch it. My ideas and their
laws, this is all my reality. But then surely I am not the
only existence there is. No, indeed. The things about
me are indeed only my ideas; but I am not the author
of these ideas. This language of experience, those signs
of the senses, which I decipher — I did not produce them.
Who writes, then, this language? Who forces on my
mind the succession of my ideas? Who spreads out
the scroll of those experiences before me which in their
totality constitute the choir of heaven and the furniture
of earth? Berkeley responds readily. The sources of
my ideas are two: my fellow-beings, who speak to me
with the natural voice, and God, who talks to me in the
language of the sense. "When," says Berkeley, "I
deny sensible things an existence out of the mind, I do
not mean my mind in particular, but all minds. Now
it is plain they have an existence exterior to my mind,
since I find them by experience to be independent of
it. There is some other mind wherein they exist, during the intervals between the time of my perceiving them,
as likewise they did before my birth, and would do after
my supposed annihilation. And as the same is true with
regard to all other finite created spirits, it necessarily follows, there is an *omnipresent eternal mind*, which
knows and comprehends all things, and exhibits them to
our view in such a manner, and according to such rules,
as He himself hath ordained, and are by us termed the
laws of nature."

Here is the famous idealism of Berkeley. Never was
philosophical idealism more simply stated. Nowhere is
there a better introduction to a doctrine at once paradoxical and plausible, namely, the idealistic scheme of things,

than in Berkeley's early essays.   They are favorites —
these essays — of all young students of philosophy.   As
you read them, unprepared, you first say, How wild a
paradox !   How absurdly opposed to common sense !
Then you read further and say, How plausible this Berkeley is !   How charming his style !   How clear he makes
his paradoxes !   Perhaps, after all, they are n't paradoxes,
but mere rewordings of what we all mean.   He knows a
real world of facts, too.   Nobody is surer of the truths
of experience, nobody is firmer in his convictions of an
outer reality, than Berkeley.   Only this outer reality —
what is it but God directly talking to us, directly impress-
ing upon us these ideas of the " choir of heaven and furniture of earth ? "   In sense, in experience, we have God.
He is in matter.   Matter, in fact, is a part of his own
self : it is his manifested will, his plan for our education,
his voice speaking to us, warning, instructing, guiding,
amusing, disciplining, blessing us, with a series of orderly
and significant experiences.   Well, I say, as you read
further, the beauty of Berkeley's statement impresses you,
you are half persuaded that you might come to believe
this ; and lo !   suddenly, as you read, you *do* believe it, if
only for an hour, and then, in a curious fashion, the
whole thing comes to look almost commonplace.   It is so
obvious, you say, this notion that we only know our own
ideas, so obvious that it was hardly worth while to write
it down.   After all, everybody believes that !   As for the
notion of God talking to us, through all our senses, that
is very pretty and poetical, but is there anything very
novel about the notion ?   It is the old design argument
over again.

So I say, your mood alters as you read Berkeley.   The
value of his doctrine, for our present purposes, lies in its
place in this history of the rediscovery of the inner life
which we are following in this lecture.   Of the truth of
Berkeley's doctrine I have just now nothing to say.   I am

simply narrating to you Berkeley's experience of spiritual things. And his experience was this : that our consciousness of outer reality is a more subtle and complex thing than the previous age had suspected, so that the real world must be very different from the assumed substantial and mathematical world of the seventeenth century, and so that our inner life of sense and of reason needs yet a new and a deeper analysis. Everything in this whole period makes, you see, for the study of this inner life. It is no matter whether you are a philosopher, and write essays on the " Principles of Human Knowledge," or whether you are a heroine in an eighteenth-century novel, and write sentimental letters to a friend; you are part of the same movement. The spirit is dissatisfied with the mathematical order, and feels friendless among the eternities of the seventeenth-century thought. The spirit wants to be at home with itself, well-friended in the comprehension of its inner processes. It loves to be confidential in its heart outpourings, keen in its analysis, humane in its attitude towards life. And to be part of this new process is Berkeley's significance.

V.

But now, if you are to enjoy the inner life, you must bear also its burdens and its doubts. To become sure of yourself, you must first doubt yourself. And this doubt, this skepticism, which self-analysis always involves, who could express it better than the great Scotchman, David Hume ? Hume is, I think, next to Hobbes, the greatest of British speculative thinkers, Berkeley occupying the third place in order of rank. I cannot undertake to describe to you in this place the real historical significance of Hume, his subtlety, his fearlessness, his fine analysis of certain of the deepest problems, his place as the inspirer of Kant's thought, his whole value as metaphysical teacher of his time. What you will see in him is merely the merciless skeptic, and, in this superficial sketch of the rediscovery of the inner consciousness, I don't ask you to see more. Hume accepted Locke's belief that reason is merely the recorder of experience. He carries out this view to its remotest consequences. Our minds consist, as he says, of impressions and ideas. By impressions he means the experiences of sense; by ideas he means the remembered copies of these experiences. You see, feel, smell, taste; and you remember having seen, felt, tasted or smelt. That is all. You have no other knowledge. Upon some of your ideas, namely those of quantity and number, you can reason, and can even discover novel and necessary truth about them. This is owing to the peculiarity of these ideas and of the impressions on which they are founded. For these ideas, also, even all the subtleties of mathematical science, are faded and blurred impressions of sense. And, as it chances, on just these faded impressions you can reason. But Berkeley was wrong in thinking that you can by searching find out God, or anything else supersensual. Science concerns matters of fact, as the senses give them, and ends with these.

With this general view in mind, let us examine, in Hume's fashion, certain of the most familiar conceptions of human reason. Hume is afraid of nothing, not even of the presumptions at the basis of physical science. Matters of fact he respects, but not universal principles. "There are," says Hume, "no ideas . . . more obscure than those of power, force, or necessary connection." Let us look a little more closely at these ideas. Let us clear them up if we can. How useful they seem. How much we hear in exact science about something called the law of causation, which says that there is a necessary connection between causes and effects, that given natural conditions have a "power" to bring to pass certain results, that the forces of nature *must* work as they do. Well, apply to such sublime and far-reaching ideas, — just such

ideas, you will remember, as seemed to Spinoza so significant, — apply to them Hume's simple criterion. Ideas, in
order to have a good basis, must, Hume declares, stand
for matters of fact, given to us in the senses. "It is
impossible for us to *think* of anything which we have not
antecedently *felt*, either by our external or internal senses."
"By what invention, then," says Hume, "can we throw
light" upon ideas that, being simple, still pretend to be
authoritative, "and render them altogether precise and
determinate to our intellectual view?"   Answer: "Produce the impressions or original sentiments from which
the ideas are copied." These impressions will "admit of
no ambiguity."   So, then, let us produce the original impression from which the idea of causation, of necessary
connection, or of power is derived.   You say that in
nature there is and must be *necessity*. Very well, let us
ask ourselves afresh the questions that we asked of Locke.
Did you ever see necessity? Did you ever hear or touch
causation? Did you ever taste or smell necessary connection? Name us the original impression whence comes
your idea.   "When," says Hume, "we look about us
towards external objects, and consider the operation of
causes, we are never able, in any single instance, to discover any power or necessary connection, any quality
which binds the effect to the cause, and renders the one
an infallible consequence of the other. We only find that
the one does actually in fact follow the other.   The impulse of one billiard ball is attended with motion in the
second. That is the whole that appears to the outward
senses." "In reality, there is no part of matter that does
ever by its sensible qualities discover any power or energy,
or give us ground to imagine that it could produce anything," until we have found out by experience what happens in consequence of its presence. Thus outer sense
gives us facts, but no necessary laws, no true causation,
no real connection of events.

We must, then, get our idea of power, of necessary connection, from within. And so, in fact, many have thought
that we do. If in outer nature I am only impressed by
matters of fact about billiard balls and other such things,
and if there I never learn of causation, do I not, perchance, directly feel my own true power, my own causal
efficacy, my own will, making acts result in a necessary
way from my purposes? No, answers Hume. If I examine carefully I find that my own deeds also are merely
matters of fact, with nothing causally efficacious about my
own conscious nature to make them obviously necessary.
After all, " is there any principle in nature more mysterious than the union of soul with body? " " Were we
empowered," adds Hume, " to remove mountains, or control the planets in their orbit, this extensive authority
would not be more extraordinary, or more beyond our
comprehension," than is the bare matter of fact that we
now can control our bodies by our will. In inner experience, then, just as in outer, we get no direct impression
of *how* causes produce effects. We only see *that* things
do often happen in regular ways. In experience, then,
" all events seem entirely loose and separate. One event
follows another ; but we can never observe any tie between them. They seem *conjoined*, but never *connected*.
But as we can have no idea of anything which never appeared to our outward sense or inward sentiment, the
necessary conclusion *seems* to be, that we have no idea of
connection or power at all, and that these words are absolutely without any meaning." From this seeming conclusion, Hume makes, indeed, an escape, but one that is, in
fact, not less skeptical than his result as first reached.
The true original of our idea of power, and so of causation, he says, is simply this, that " after a repetition of
similar instances, the mind is carried, by habit, upon the
appearance of one event, to expect its usual attendant,
and to believe that it will exist." " The first time a

man saw the communication of motion by impulse, as by
the shock of the two billiard balls, he could not pronounce
that the one event was *connected*, but only that it was
conjoined, with the other. After he has observed several
instances of this nature, he then pronounces them to be
connected. What alteration has happened to give rise to
this new idea of *connection?* Nothing but that now he
feels these two events to be *connected* in his imagination."
Custom, then, mere habit of mind, is the origin of the idea
of causation. We see no necessity in the world. We
only *feel* it there, because that is our habit of mind, our
fashion of mentally regarding an often-repeated experience of similar successions.

The importance of all this skepticism lies, as you of
course see, in its removal from our fact-world of just the
principles that the seventeenth century had found so inspiring. "It is of the nature of reason," Spinoza had
said, "to regard things as necessary." Upon that rock
he had built his faith. His wisdom had reposed secure
in God, in whom were all things, just because God's
nature was the highest form of necessity, the law of laws.
And now comes Hume, and calls this "nature of reason"
a mere feeling, founded on habit, a product of our imagination, no matter of fact at all. What becomes, then, of
Spinoza's divine order? Has philosophy fallen by its
own hands? Is the eternal in which we had trusted
really, after all, but the mass of the flying and disconnected impressions of sense? All crumbles at the touch of
this criticism of Hume's. All becomes but the aggregate
of the disconnected sense-impressions. Nay, if we find
the Holy Grail itself, it, too, will fade and crumble into
dust. Hume is aware of some such result. He skillfully
and playfully veils the extreme consequences at times by
the arts of his beautiful dialectic. But he none the less
rejoices in it, with all the fine joy of the merciless foe of
delusions : — *matters of fact, relations of ideas*, — these

are all that his doctrine leaves us. "When," he once says, "we run through libraries, persuaded of these principles, what havoc must we make? If we take in our hand any volume of divinity or school metaphysics, for instance, let us ask, *Does it contain any abstract reasoning concerning quantity or number? No. Does it contain any experimental reasoning concerning matter of fact and existence?* No. Commit it then to the flames, for it can contain nothing but sophistry and illusion."

VI.

Hume represents thus, indeed, the extreme of purely philosophical skepticism in the eighteenth century. Others, to be sure, outside of the ranks of the philosophers, went further in many ways, and were rebels or scoffers in their own fashion, far more aggressive than his. But Hume's thought is in its result as fruitful as in its content it is negative. The spirit, you see, has become anxious to know its own nature. After all, can we live by merely assuming the innate ideas? Can even Spinoza's wisdom save us from doubt? And yet this doubt does n't mean mere waywardness. It means longing for self-consciousness. And in the last third of the century this longing took, as we shall next time learn, new and positive forms. The inner life, to be sure, has appeared so far as a very capricious thing, after all. Study it by mere analysis of its experiences, as Hume did, and in this its capriciousness it will seem to shrivel to nothing under your hands. Where you expected it to be wealthiest, it turns out to be poorest. It is mere sense, mere feeling, mere sophistry and illusion. But is this the end? No, it is rather but the beginning of a new and a higher philosophy. The spirit is more than mere experience. Locke's account of the inner life is only half the truth. And what the other half is, Kant and his successors shall teach us. The age of poetry and of history — of a new

natural science, also, yes, even this our own century —
shall take up afresh the task that Hume rejected as impossible.   The revolutionary period shall first rediscover
passion, shall produce Goethe's " Faust," and shall regen-
erate Europe.   Historical research, reviving, shall prove
to the spirit the significance of his own earthly past.
Science, entering upon new realms, shall formulate the
idea of cosmical evolution.   No longer Spinoza's world,
but a changing, a glowingly passionate and tragic world,
of moral endeavor, of strife, of growth, and of freedom,
shall be conceived by men ; and meanwhile, in Kant and
in his successors, as we shall find, a more fitting philosophy will arise to formulate with all of Hume's keen dialectic, with all of Locke's love of human nature, and still
with all of Spinoza's reverence for an absolute rationality
in things, something of the significance of our modern
life.

Remember, however, finally, that if the skepticism of
the eighteenth century is to be gotten rid of, this will only
be by transcending it, living through and beyond it, not
by neglecting or by simply refuting it, from without.   Philosophical insight, however partial, is never to be refuted.
You can transcend it, you can make it part of a larger
life, but it always remains as such a part.   The genuine
spirit includes all that was true and earnest in the doubting spirit.   The only way to get rid of a philosophic
doubt, in its discouraging aspect, is to see that, such as it
is, it already implies a larger truth.   The great spirit
says to us, like Emerson's " Brahma," —

> " They reckon ill who leave me out ;
> When me they fly, I am the wings ;
> I am the doubter and the doubt."

And this, namely, the inevitableness and the true spirituality of genuine doubting, is the great lesson that the
eighteenth century, in its transition to Kant, teaches us.
It is a lesson well to be remembered in our own day,

when, notwithstanding the vast accomplishments of recent
research, there is a sense in which we, too, live in a world
of doubt, but live there only that we may learn to conquer and possess it, all its doubts and its certainties, all
its truth.   In doubt we come to see our illusion; the
phantoms of the night of thought vanish; but the new
light comes.   The old world dies, but only to rise again
to the immortality of a higher existence.   The spirit destroys its former creations, shatters its idols, and laments
their loss.   But, as in "Faust," the chorus still sings : —

> " Thou hast it destroyed,
>   The beautiful world,
>   With powerful fist :
>   In ruin 't is hurled,
>   By the blow of a demigod shattered !
>   The scattered
>   Fragments into the Void we carry,
>   Deploring
>   The beauty perished beyond restoring.
>   Mightier
>   For the children of men,
>   Brightlier
>   Build it again,
>   In thine own bosom build it anew !
>   Bid the new career
>   Commence,
>   With clearer sense,
>   And the new songs of cheer
>   Be sung thereto ! "

Such a building anew of the lost universe in the bosom of
the human spirit, it was the mission of Kant to begin.

LECTURE IV.

KANT.

WE saw in the last lecture how the self-analysis of the eighteenth century inevitably tended towards the rediscovery of passion, and finally towards the great revolutionary movement, in life and in literature, with which the century closed. But we also found that the same Lockean tendency was bound to produce a philosophical skepticism whereof Hume was our chief example. Hume stated the essence of Locke's theory with an almost brutal simplicity of formulation. We know, he said, impressions, which come to us through sense, and ideas, which are the copies of impressions. About some ideas we can reason. These form the subject-matter of our only demonstrative science, mathematics. All our other science concerns matters of fact, that is, recorded impressions of our experience, with such rational observations as we can make upon them. Does the inner life pretend to more than this, to more than a knowledge of impressions and ideas, — then what is this pretense but sophistry and illusion? The inner life, under this merciless analysis, shrivels up, as it were, into a mere series of chance experiences. The sacred faiths of humanity, do they record seen and felt matters of fact? The moral law, is it more than a feeling in the mind of the sympathetic subject? Hume is indeed merciless; but his mercilessness is, after all, the clear insight of a reflective man. Bare experience of the Lockean sort does indeed contain no such supreme rationality as earlier thinkers had found there. What Hume showed was that unless there is more in experience than Locke's view permitted it to contain, the hope of any transcendent knowledge or faith for humanity is indeed gone. That Hume showed this is his great merit, for hereby he led the way to Kant.

I.

When I mention the name of Kant, who forms our special topic to-day, I introduce to you one whose thought arouses more suggestions in the mind of a philosophical student than cluster about any other modern thinker. One despairs of telling you all or any great part of what Kant has meant to one in the course of a number of years of metaphysical study; but let me still try to suggest a little of Kant's place in such a line of work. One hears of Kant early in one's life as a student of philosophy. He is said to be hard, perhaps a little dangerous (a thing which of course attracts one hugely!). He is said to be also certainly typical of German speculation, and always worthy of one's efforts if one means to philosophize at all. Perhaps one, therefore, first tries him in translation, with a sense that, even if one's German is not yet free, something must already be done to win him. The "Critique of Pure Reason," how attractive the name! How wise one will be after criticising the pure reason through the reading of five or six hundred pages of close print! There is an old translation of Kant, in Bohn's Library, by a certain Meiklejohn. One begins with that. The English is heavy, not to say shocking; but the first effect of the reading is soon a splendid sense of power, a feeling of the exhaustiveness of the treatment, of the skill and subtlety and fearlessness of this Kant. What seems to be a good deal of the book — not the chief part, indeed — one can even fairly grasp at the first reading. In fact, so persuasive, to certain minds, is the general external appearance of Kant's method of work, that there are students who, on their first superficial acquaintance with

him, really fancy that they have actually comprehended
the whole thing at one stroke. I myself have heard this
feeling expressed by diligent young readers, who have
assured me, after their first trial of the "Critique," that,
as they supposed, it must be that they had somehow failed
to understand Kant, for whereas people said he was hard,
they themselves had n't found anything very difficult in
the book at all. To their great alarm, as it were, they
had n't even been puzzled. Yet when such persons come
to read Kant a second time, I fear that they usually find
themselves considerably puzzled; or rather, I should say
that I hope so. Puzzle is a sensation that soon comes,
when one begins to examine Kant more cautiously and
worthily. The first superficial joy in his power, in his
skill, in his subtlety, in his fearlessness, fades away. One
sees his actual doctrine looming afar off, a mountain yet
to be climbed. On nearer approach, one finds the mountain well wooded; and the woods have thick underbrush.
The paths lose themselves in the dark valleys, leading
this way and that, with most contradictory windings.
Kant is a pedantic creature after all, one says. He loves
hard words. He takes a mass of them, — as one of
his critics fiercely says, he takes a mass of Latin terms
ending in *tion*, and translates them into so many equivalent vernacular terms, ending in the German in *heit* and
keit, and he calls this sort of thing philosophy! Getting
such things through the medium of an English translation does n't improve them. One begins to anathematize
the poor translator, Meiklejohn, in fear lest one should
blaspheme instead the sacred name of the immortal Kant.
One finally concludes that this is a book full of great
insights and of noble passages, but that the real connections are n't to be made out until one shall have fought
the good fight in German. And so one drops the subject
until one's German shall be free.

That happy time comes. One has first read Schopenhauer, whose German, to use a comparison of Jean Paul Richter's, is as limpid as a mountain lake that lies beneath gloomy cliffs, under a clear and frosty sky. One has even plunged down the tumultuous streams of Fichte's eloquence, where the frail bark of a student's understanding is indeed occasionally rather near to destruction, but whence a man still usually escapes with his wits. Now it is time to return to Kant. One hereupon falls upon the " Critique " with new zest, and finds that, as reading goes in a studious but rather busy and distracted life, one can at length read the book through in about three years, and can feel that thereafter he might do well to begin and read it again. After doing so, one lays it aside for a spell, and so returns afresh, from year to year, for a longer or shorter season, to the fascinating but baffling task. In Germany, where there has been a revival of interest in Kant, during the past twenty years, reading the " Critique " has come to take rank, so to speak, as one of the liberal professions. There are learned men who, in all appearance, do nothing else. The habit is dangerously fascinating. The Kant devotee never knows when to stop. When I studied in Germany as a young college graduate, some fifteen years ago, it was my fortune to meet one of the most learned and many-sided of the new philosophical doctors of the day, who was just then preparing for a docentship. He was a man who promised, as one might say, almost everything ; who wrote and published essays of remarkable breadth and skill, and who was especially noticeable for his wide range of work. Some years later, it unhappily occurred to him to begin printing a commentary on Kant's " Critique of Pure Reason." He planned the commentary for completion in four volumes octavo. Of these four he published, not long afterwards, the first, a volume of several hundred large pages, wherein he deals — with Kant's introductory chapter. Since then my former acquaintance is lost.

The final volumes of the commentary have never appeared, although he has now been at work upon them more than ten years. How many volumes will really be needed to complete the task, only the " destroyer of delights and terminator of felicities," whom the Arabian Nights' tales always love to mention as they close, to wit, Death himself, can ever determine. The thorough student of Kant is, so to speak, a Tannhäuser, close shut in his Venusberg. You hunt for him fruitlesssly in all the outer world. Worse than Tannhäuser he is, for you can never get him out. Pilgrims' choruses chant, and waiting Elizabeths mourn for him, in vain. As for me, I, as you perceive, am no reader of Kant, in the strict sense, at all. I won a doctor's degree, years since, in part by writing a course of lectures upon the " Critique." I have since come to see that those lectures were founded upon a serious, I might say an entire, misinterpretation of Kant's meaning. Since then I have repented, as you also observe, of this misinterpretation, and, as I might add, of several others. I love still to lecture to my college classes on Kant. I think that possibly I know a little about him. But then, after all, Kant, you see, is Kant ; and the Lord made him, and many other wondrous works besides ; and it takes time to find such things out.

You will understand therefore, at once, that I can have no intention of making clear, within the limits of a single lecture, a doctrine so subtle and involved as this. But then the justification of my undertaking in these lectures is wholly that I attempt, not to describe the philosophers and their opinions as the monuments of technical skill and of exhaustive research which they are, but to set forth to you something of the temperament which they embody. Kant shall be for us a character in a story, an attitude towards the spiritual concerns of humanity. As such you want to know him ; as such only can I attempt here to describe him.

II.

The man Kant is an old subject for literary portraiture.
It is hard to say anything in the least new about him.
He was born in 1724, in the city of Königsberg, in the
province of East Prussia, and never once in his life traveled beyond that province. His family was poor; his
father was of Scotch descent, and was a saddler, and in
religion a pietist. Both Kant's parents lived a narrow
and glowing religious life, cheerful, harmonious, and, in a
worldly sense, dispassionate. At school Kant attracted
such attention that a university course of study followed,
in Königsberg, of course, and this led him to an academic
career. At the outset of his literary work Kant is a curious mixture of the pedant, the many-sided student, the
young man of literary skill, and the independent investigator. His earliest essay was in philosophical physics,
and was in more senses than one a failure. In 1755, he
published, however, a remarkable paper on the "General
Natural History and Theory of the Heavens," wherein he
anticipated the essential features of the nebular hypothesis which Laplace afterwards developed. Up to this
time he had been a private tutor. Thenceforth he lectured as privat-docent at the university until his appointment as professor in 1770. Promotion, as one sees, was
thereabouts slow, and Kant was perhaps at first over-
looked by higher officials, whom he never sought to
please. During these earlier years he was a man of
considerable literary skill, but in philosophy was still
under the influence of the reigning dogmatic school.
The poet Herder, who heard him as docent, speaks very
highly of his power in those days as a lecturer. Of Kant
in his young prime we have a portrait, showing him
at the age of forty-four. More common is the portrait
taken much later in life. Both show us the spare, small,
insignificant-appearing man. He was of frail health, but

seldom or never ill. His height was barely beyond five feet; as he grew older he became more and more an almost fleshless but very cheerful shadow of a man, all mind and no body, genial, gossiping, a lover of a small but very clever circle of friends, a great reader of books of travel, a passionate student, strange to say, of the manners and customs of various and distant lands and peoples, topics upon which he loved to lecture. His bachelor life grew, meanwhile, more and more methodical. As he grew older, thought absorbed him more and more. For more than a decade, namely, from 1770 to 1781, he published very little, and meditated solely his " Critique of Pure Reason," gladly free, as he once says, from the obligation of defending early and hastily written essays in philosophy. Now he became indeed an original thinker. His loneliness of thought grew almost oppressive. To his friends he apparently said only a little of the new doctrine that was forming in his mind. His lectures became less eloquent; his inner life grew ever deeper, stiller, — not melancholy, but hidden away, involved, problematic. Henceforth, moreover, his style gravely suffers. The genial soul shows itself again and again in the great " Critique," in chance figures, in brilliant but too brief passages. Yet on the whole Kant's writing is henceforth burdened, as it were, with the weight of his whole new world. His sentences groan beneath their treasures. He works beneath the earth, in the mines of humanity's gold.[1] Great thoughts glitter in the rich quartz of his meditation, but only with toil and suffering is this gold to be extracted. From the first issue of the " Critique " men

---

[1] In a remarkable note, published in Benno Erdmann's edition of Kant's *Reflexionen* (vol. ii. p. 6), Kant himself says, of his own style, " Es scheint zwar nichts geschmackswidriger zu sein als die Metaphysik, aber die Zierrate die an der Schönheit glänzen, lagen erstlich in dunkeln Grüften, wenigstens sah man sie zuerst durch die finstere Werkstatt des Künstlers."

complained of Kant's obscurity; years later Herder lamented bitterly the lost instructor of his youth, the man
whom he used to be able to comprehend, but of whom
now he could make almost nothing, and whose doctrine
he sternly opposed. The first impression that the great
" Critique " produced was of wonder and of a sort of
puzzled dread. Some said, " This man has destroyed all
faith. He doubts everything. It is a dangerous book;
it is terrible." Others said, " This is Berkeley's idealism over again." Many said, " Whatever it is, it is
quite unreadable." But erelong the thought came home
to people that all this was not only novel, but vastly en-
lightening. The universities took up the book. The
great literary men read it. Schiller himself was in many
respects almost revolutionized by it, and by the Kantian
works that followed it. The age of the revolution was
ripe for it. Young men became fascinated by it, and
within twenty-five years the " Critique " had converted a
people decidedly unproductive in philosophy into the typically metaphysical nation of Europe, so that, as Jean
Paul said, while God had given to the French the land
and to the English the sea, he had granted to the Germans the empire of the air.

Meanwhile, Kant, gradually wasting away in body, ate
his one meal daily, walked over his regular path every
afternoon, lectured genially but intricately to his classes,
and wrote book after book until some years later than
1790. Old age was now approaching fast. This frail
body could not very well endure the coming enemy. Kant
grew less productive and more methodical. There is a
well-known passage by Heine,[1] wherein this daily life of
Kant is sketched : —

" The life of Immanuel Kant," says Heine, " is hard to
describe ; he had indeed neither life nor history in the

[1] Quoted, also, by Professor Edward Caird, in his *Philosophy of
Immanuel Kant*, 2d ed. vol. i. p. 63.

proper sense of the words. He lived an abstract, mechanical, old-bachelor existence, in a quiet, remote street
of Königsberg, an old city at the northeastern boundary
of Germany. I do not believe that the great cathedral-
clock of that city accomplished its day's work in a less
passionate and more regular way than its countryman,
Immanuel Kant. Rising from bed, coffee-drinking, writing, lecturing, eating, walking, everything had its fixed
time; and the neighbors knew that it must be exactly
half past four when they saw Professor Kant, in his gray
coat, with his cane in his hand, step out of his house-door,
and move towards the little lime-tree avenue, which is
named, after him, the Philosopher's Walk. Eight times
he walked up and down that walk at every season of the
year, and when the weather was bad, or the gray clouds
threatened rain, his servant, old Lampe, was seen anx-
iously following him with a large umbrella under his
arm, like an image of Providence.

" Strange contrast between the outer life of the man
and his world-destroying thought. Of a truth, if the citizens of Königsberg had had any inkling of the meaning
of that thought, they would have shuddered before him
as before an executioner. But the good people saw nothing in him but a professor of philosophy, and when he
passed at the appointed hour, they gave him friendly
greetings — and set their watches."

III.

To this characterization of Heine's, which has become
almost classic, it is hard to add anything besides what
every reader of literary gossip also knows, unless one
enters into details that would detain us here too long.
Still, we must go yet a little farther. This odd and
gentle little man was, as you already see, a singular combination of the keen-witted analyst and the humane lover
of all things human. Give him an old problem, or a

well-known abstract conception, such as the idea of wisdom or of justice, and he would quickly show you his
analytic skill by mentioning a long series of distinctions,
of aspects, of possible ways of defining or of stating the
thing, — so long a series, and often so dry, that you would
at first be likely to suspect him of genuine pedantry.
And yet this seeming pedant — what a lover he is of
books of travel, of descriptions of live men, and of concrete affairs! He has indeed never traveled beyond his
simple and quiet little province; but yet, as we just saw,
he loves to lecture, and with a wide knowledge, too, upon
geography and upon anthropology. Physical science also,
after the fashions of his day, he knows very fairly. In
that early essay he has anticipated Laplace's nebular
hypothesis. Moreover, he has published a long paper on
the sentiments of the sublime and beautiful. When he
speculates, he shows himself as many-sided as he is keen.
His systematic plans are vast. When, in his old age, he
has published half a dozen important and varied treatises
upon different and fundamental departments of philosophy, he still laments the fragmentariness of his work, and
still promises himself a chance to complete his system by
one great book. Before he can do much upon this, old
age takes away first his noble powers of mind, and then
his life. This life itself had been as beautiful in its simple humanity as it had been rigid in its routine. Kant
was above all a *good* man, strictly honorable, unalterably
loyal to his tasks, pleasant and even charming to his few
near friends, and in his fashion very deeply pious. As
for the form of his piety, you must know what that was
before you can be prepared for his reflective doctrines.

Some people, including, for instance, Heine himself,
have imagined that there were, in Kant's religious life,
two or even three distinct periods, — an early period, say,
of faith; then a revolutionary and destructive period,
when, in a sort of secret but none the less Titanic rebel-

liousness, this terrible professor revolted against theology, and wrote books that make an end once for all of every positive religious belief; then, finally, a third period of cowardly, or at all events of weakly timid, withdrawal from conflict, when Kant, the old man, fearing the government, and perhaps taking compassion upon common folk, reconstructed, in an inconsistent fashion, the beliefs that his "Critique of Pure Reason" had shattered, and so taught God, freedom, and immortality, solely for the sake of his own peace. Upon what facts this disgraceful myth about Kant's inconsistency in his old age was founded, I will not pause to explain here. You will soon see in what sense his great "Critique" was destructive. You will also soon see in what sense his later writings were constructive as to religious faith. I mention, however, the often-repeated tale just to warn you that it *is* a myth, and that Kant's attitude towards the affairs of the religious consciousness changed very little at any time, and not at all after once the critical doctrine was in his hands.

But as to the real form of his piety, it was never akin to Spinoza's mysticism; it belonged rather to that other, to that active form of the religious consciousness, of which I spoke, by way of contrast, when I was describing Spinoza to you. And yet there was something so simple and direct about Kant's attitude towards divine things that when he talks of God to you, you feel in as direct a relation with one important fact of the eternal world as, in Spinoza's case, you felt in relation to another fact. Spinoza says to you: Look upon the seeming chaos of nature. For sense it is a disheartening whirlwind of vain and fragmentary facts; yet for reason an infinite law dwells in it. This law is supreme, all-compelling. It is the law of the divine mind, which reveals one attribute of God's substance, and of which your mind is a part. In the presence of this infinite majesty are you every moment. Enter consciously into it, and dwell there,

and to you, as wise man, God's infinite perfection will be
present as a religious consolation, and you will be unalterably at peace. Of such mystical comfort Kant knows
nothing. He hates mysticism with a shrewd and sternly
analytical keenness of critical ill-will, suggestive, in his
case, of the attitude of the very deliberate and economical
old bachelor, who dreads nothing more than falling in
love, or than wasting his hoarded energies upon any
similar vain and expensive sentimentalities. Mysticism
and what he would call lovers' *Narrheit* are, in Kant's
simple and honest mind, closely associated and mercilessly
scorned. They are both called by him by his favorite
term of reproach. They are *Schwärmerei*, vain and
vague enthusiasm, mere fancy, by gazing fed. Kant,
this genial and bloodless old hero of contemplation, wasting away in his cheerful asceticism, reverences, as everybody knows, duty and the stars, but has no time for romance. The God whom he worships is indeed stern and
majestic, cares not even to have you demonstrate his existence, and eludes the cleverness of your theoretic reason
as loftily as he rejects the loverlike importunities of your
weak and sentimental moments. He reveals himself,
indeed, but to your conscience.

Conscience, for the first, shows you the moral law, —
shows it as something overwhelmingly rational, absolute,
universal, indifferent to your private wishes, independent
of your present happiness, sublime as the heavens are,
but as directly known to you as is the very existence of
your will and of your reason. Conscience shows you this
absolute law, and says sternly, unwaveringly, uncompro-
misingly, "Do thy duty." And because conscience shows
you this, it demands of you that you labor henceforth and
forever as if you were an instrument, a minister, of a
divine law that moves in all things. It orders you, then,
to live as if God were present here all about you in this
world of sense. He is not to be seen here, indeed, with

the eye of sense. In vain, for the critical Kant of the
days after 1780, does even weak theoretic reason try to
prove to our poor wits that he is here. Sense and speculation alike fail you. But none the less must you *act as
if God were* your constant and visible companion, as if
the moral law, which you must regard as his only direct
revelation, were spoken in your ear by him as by your
next friend at this moment. And to know that thus you
ought to act, that thus you ought to live, to wit, as if the
unsearchable God whom the heavens cannot contain were
as familiar to you as your daily walk, as visible to you as
the town-clock, — to know this is to do what Kant calls
postulating God's existence. It is n't sentimental faith
that you have in God. You don't believe in him because
you long to, or because life would be blank if you did n't,
or because you fear the charge of atheism. You believe
in God in one sense and for one reason only, — because a
man sure of his duty is sure that the right ought to win,
that in the sense-world it does n't win, and that in the
universe it can win only if God is at the helm, — God
as the absolute and all-powerful well-wisher of the whole
visible and invisible world-order. This notion of God's
existence, a mere hypothesis to your theoretic speculation,
is for your active consciousness just in such sense a certainty as you propose to behave as if it were one.

For the rest, Kant, in his later years, has no hope of
even illustrating anything about God's providence by
appealing, as so many do, to our experience of justice in
this world, or by any other theoretical means. Kant
is no optimist, just as he is no sentimentalist, about the
world of experience. The divine justice does n't very obviously show itself here below. Kant sees much evil all
about him ; condemns, in one passage, the people who find
our present life happy ; declares that not one of us would
willingly lead his own life over again, if he had the free
choice and were not bound by some sort of duty to do

so; in short, speaks almost cynically of those earthly joys
whereof, with all his cheeriness and his open-heartedness,
he tasted so little. The few good things of life are such
things as healthy friendships and successful toils, the
sober routine of business, of conversation, and of thinking. And yet even these are all of them only relatively
good. The only absolutely good thing in our world is a
good will, in a being who does his duty. Thus, then, our
sense-world, if coldly cheerful for the brave and resolute,
is still no place of rewards; nor does God's benevolence
manifest itself except to the moral consciousness. But
there, indeed, in our conscience, despite all the mystery,
we know the mind of God. This is what he wants of us,
namely, our duty. And that he wants this, and will see
to the absolute success of the right, this is the whole content of our moral faith.

Such was Kant's piety. It has been much misunderstood. Especially are people at fault in fancying it a late
thing in Kant's life, a product of his old age. He expresses substantially the same thoughts as early as 1766,
when he is still hoping for theoretical proofs of God's
existence. Such proofs, he says, whether we ever get
them or no, we do not need. The moral consciousness
reveals God in its own way. Early, then, Kant had
reached his main assurance. Very late in his career he
declares, in one passage, that this assurance is no matter
of subtle philosophy at all. "The progress of metaphysics in theology is," he observes, " the easiest " [and therefore the least] " of all " her achievements, and, " although
concerned with the remote above sense, is not itself at all
recondite, but is as clear to common sense as to the philosophers, so much so, in fact, that the thinkers have here
to find their way by the very light of common sense, lest
they be lost in the mazes of the recondite."

Notice here, if you will, at once the novel aspect of
Kant's insight, and at the same time the simplicity and

familiarity of the thing. Novel is his insight into the
relations of religion and of reason, — novel, namely, just in
so far as it is a philosophical insight. The seventeenth
century had regarded God as first of all an object of
theory, as the demonstrable source and principle of the
visible world, and so as a being whose existence we had to
accept, as it were, submissively, helplessly, because of the
dogmas of reason. To this dogmatic faith in reason,
skepticism had later opposed its cruel objections. And
now comes Kant, whom a long experience of problems
makes skeptical above all men, cautious, critical, resigned to doubts, a hater of mystical faith, a destroyer of
dogmas; and yet he gives us back our faith, not as a
dogma, but as an active postulate, as a free spiritual construction, as a determination to live in the presence of the
unseen and eternal. New are some of his philosophic
doubts; new in an uncommon sense will be his fashions
of theorizing in philosophy; old is his appeal to that
courage and that loyalty upon which our very civilization
is founded. For, I insist, this notion of Kant's about the
spiritual world, this appeal, not to sentiment, but to conscience as the warrant of faith, is it not indeed the very
soul of all instinctive civilization? Consider this same
fashion of looking not only at the problems about God, but
at the affairs of worldly experience. Consider the attitude
of a soldier going into battle against a foe whom he knows
to be nearly his match in force and arms. He possesses,
if he is a brave man, some sort of confidence that he will
win. Well, it is much like Kant's faith in God. In what
is this confidence founded? In experience? No, this battle has n't yet been fought, so that experience is not his
guide as to this fight, and, as to the past, any old soldier
is likely to know from experience a good deal about
defeat, as well as about victory, perhaps even more of lost
than of won battles. Does he know, then, that he will
win by any rational intuition? Is it an innate idea in

him that he is going to win? No; to say so would be mere trifling. Neither intuition nor experience assures him of victory. No merely sentimental faith is this his assurance; no datum is it of sense. His belief that he will win is identical with his active, manly resolve that he is minded to win, that his teeth are set to win, that this sword is sharpened, that this bayonet has been pointed, that this bullet will soon be winged, with the determination of victory. Each army knows that, other things equal, the force which is thus *most* minded to win is the force destined to conquer, that here is a case where faith can *create* its own object, that the unseen victory will be fashioned precisely by and for the side which most fully takes hold of that unseen, and which actively creates what it believes in. Well, then, there is in active life this way of vindicating your faith. It is by creating the very idea of the world wherein your faith is to come true. You all know, furthermore, to take an example from everyday life, how it is largely our own choice whether our lives, in certain aspects of them, say in their cares and responsibilities, their routine and their disappoint- ments, are tolerable or not. Evil besets us, pain op- presses us, chagrin or calamity overwhelms us. We cry out bitterly, "Prove to me that such a life is good. Ex- perience does n't show it to be good. And as for faith, as for intuitive trust that it is good, this I have lost. My noble sentiments fade out; my natural love of life for- sakes me. Is it all tolerable? Prove that to me." The answer of the active temperament, the answer which seems so stern to us in our moments of weakness and cowardice, so inspiring to us in our moments of spiritual dignity and courage, is the answer: " Your world is toler- able, yes, is even glorious, if, and only if, you actively make it so. Its spirituality is your own creation, or else is nothing. Awake, arise, be willing, endure, struggle, defy evil, cleave to good, strive, be strenuous, be devoted, throw

into the face of evil and depression your brave cry of hatred and of resistance, and then this dark universe of destiny will glow with a divine light. Then you will commune with the eternal. For you have no relations with
the eternal world save such as you make for yourself."
My illustrations are here inadequate to the full expression
of Kant's notion of the postulate, but that is because of
the difference of the objects treated.

In describing thus the answer of spiritual courage to
our despair, I am, as you see, once more stating a mood,
an attitude of life. You see all along the contrast
between this way of viewing the deepest truths and the
way which Spinoza suggested to us. I am not here concerned with the final rights of the controversy. I am
only trying to introduce you to Kant's notion of our relation to spiritual truth ; and Kant's piety, Kant's attitude
towards religious problems, Kant's notion of faith in God,
is in essence this heroic notion. He conceives here, as
later in the theoretical part of his philosophy, that truth,
so far as we mortals can know it, is neither from innate
ideas, nor from our experience. It comes to us because
we make it. This determination of ours it is that seizes
hold upon God, then, just as the courage of the manly soul
makes life good, introduces into life something that is
there only for the activity of the hero, finds God because
the soul has wrestled for his blessing, and then has found
after all that the wrestling *is* the blessing. God is with
us only because we choose to serve our ideal of him as if
he were present to our senses. His kingdom exists
because we are resolved that, so far as in us lies, it shall
come. In this sign we conquer. This is the victory that
overcometh the world, not our intuition, not our sentimental faith, but our live, our moral, our creative faith.

You see thus more fully how highly common-sense is
this core of Kant's doctrine. This is, if you will, the wisdom of modern practical men of high mind everywhere.

" I don't know much about God himself, or about the
world," says such an one, " but I can know something of
my own nature, and I propose to behave as if God were
now looking at me." Well, Kant took this doctrine of
what one might call the higher common sense, and, as we
shall also see in his theoretical philosophy, he applied
it to everything from geometry to theology. So applied
the thing becomes vastly involved, prodigiously technical,
the work of a life-time. But the hearty and humane
Kant stirred his age so profoundly because in his quiet
way he carried, deep in his pious soul, a doctrine of
life so simple, so stern, so heroic, and yet so universally
manly and sensible, that all modern men were touched by
it. This is, indeed, the wonder of Kant, that, born and
reared in the midst of pedantry, a mere man of books, a
system-maker, a metaphysician, he should still express the
very heart of the high-minded man of the world. " I am
very ignorant of the nature of things," — so far Kant and
the man of the world are together; " but I do know my
duty, and I am determined to live as under God's eye," —
this is the other, the practically positive side of Kant's
doctrine, and, as you see, once more the high-minded man
is with Kant. This doctrine, however, means, of course,
in the reflective thinker, far more in one sense than it
means in the man of the world. It leads him to an
exhaustive research into the foundations of human reason,
it means decades of philosophical experience, of wandering from hypothesis to hypothesis, of criticism, of resignation to the truth, combined with fearless constructive
research. And that, again, is why it finally takes in
Kant's case so elaborate a form.

To this form itself we now proceed. If Kant's religious consciousness underwent little change with years, his
theoretical opinions were subjected between 1755, when
he entered upon his docentship at the university, and
1781, when he published his " Critique of Pure Reason,"

to a course of discipline such as few men have ever borne
and lived. In matters of theory, Kant was, after all,
by nature a very conservative person. Some men are
born rebels, and some men have the reformer's office
thrust upon them. Kant was of the latter class. He was
as rigidly economical of his faiths as he was of all his other
possessions. He never gave up an idea until his self-criticism forced him to do so. Skeptical, I have called him,
above all men ; but his skepticism meant at the start mere
considerateness, mere thoroughness and honesty of reflection. He had no wish to make his reflections negative.
If fortune forced negative results upon him, he could not
help that.[1] Against change he, to be sure, never blindly
struggled, just as he never hastened towards the revolution that he was destined to bring to pass. Shall I weary
you too much if I sketch to you a little of Kant's reflective fortunes?

He began, in his youth, where the traditional university
philosophy of his time had placed him, with the traditions
of the philosophy of the seventeenth century in his mind.
The world where he found himself was the world that
reason comprehends, where all is to be clear, distinct, logical, formal. We know a real world of law, where God
reigns, and where everything is rational. The philosopher is to make plain the logic of things. But alas for
the fixity of this formalism ! Kant is unfortunately more
than a mere philosopher. He loves to study science and
man. And in the world of science there are so many surprising things, so many strange facts, that logic can't construct, — yes, there are more things in heaven and earth
than are dreamt of in your *philosophy*. And not mere

---

[1] See the valuable note, No. 3, in Benno Erdmann's *Reflexionen
Kant's*, vol. ii. p. 4, where Kant states very finely his relations to
skepticism and to dogmatism. My own immediately following paragraph is an effort to summarize the much discussed and rather obscure period from 1755 to 1766.

magic, not only superstition shows you such things, as they were shown to Hamlet. It is just science that proves how, amidst all the longings of our reason for the clear and distinct truth of nature, we are continually in the presence of opaque and ultimate facts, — yes, even of principles that our pure reason could n't have predicted — such principles, for instance, as the law of gravitation. And as for man, how mysterious and often how illogical is his wayward inner nature. Kant meditates upon these things. Can logic, after all, give you a world? As Kant thus examines the littleness of our powers, he grows, as it were, an ascetic in the enjoyment of his logic. He is n't so sure that you can spin the world out of reason. He doubts whether the secret of things can ever be made open to even the highest finite intelligence. Perhaps the lesson of philosophy will prove to be resignation. At all events the lesson of every failure of reflective thought is sure to be caution.

So far Kant went in the first ten years of his university life as docent. The results of his work were poor. They almost discouraged him. Often he imagined himself on the very verge of discovering a great and new method of thinking. As often he seemed to be disappointed. "I have the fortune," he says, in 1766, "to be a lover of Metaphysics; but my mistress has shown me few favors so far." In those days, and later, Kant as a student had odd fashions of work. He jotted down numberless notes, chaotic-seeming dead leaves of fallen reflection that lay, as it were, forgotten amidst the dark forest of his secret thought. He cared little for such notes; he let the dead leaves moulder into the soil, if we may say so, to fertilize it for the coming springtime; and now, indeed, it was the autumn of his silent meditations. Since his death, Kant's lovers have busily hunted for such of the autumn leaves as did not moulder, and to-day there are Kant archives in the Königsberg library, and elsewhere, where such things are kept and prized. Singular bits of paper they are, these notes! The poor and thrifty Kant wasted nothing. Here, say, is an old invitation to dinner, or to a visit at Herr So and So's country-house. Kant has refolded the letter, and has written, not only on its back, but perchance all about and through its text, such memoranda as that Mr. Charisius Stockheim has paid his fees for the course this term, and that in a capillary tube of such a diameter water rises so high. He adds, perhaps, some quoted Latin verses, the title of a book or two, and then a paragraph of metaphysics. Reality can only be given to us through sensation, but perception adds thereto the construction of the idea of quantity; then there are, moreover, just three functions of apperception; but the mind itself gives us the only idea of what synthesis means. Thereupon, perhaps Kant jots down a triangle or two, makes a computation, and lets his note-making degenerate into illegible marks. What one wonders at is the vast numbers of such scraps. Kant never let a thought go by. The margins and interleavings of his books, especially of his lecture text-books, were also full of such things. So unwearied was Kant. The years fly on and he notes and notes — so fruitlessly, one would think! He is so faithful to his thoughts, and yet so merciless, — so faithful, for they all go down; so merciless, for he takes no pain to give them permanent form or fair shape and organization. Later jottings seem to have forgotten the earlier ones. The children of his reflection are never spared. He loves them not; he flies from them to new thoughts. On and on his life of meditation grows, so slowly, so patiently, once more just like the forest. What is the meaning, what will be the outcome of this endless bearing and casting down of thoughts? [1]

Yet there is indeed method in it all. About 1768, Kant

[1] The illustrations of Kant's notes above are brought together from several places in Reicke's *Lose Blätter aus Kant's Nachlass*.

shows traces of a wholly new fashion of thinking. The world undergoes a change for him, whose significance, at first, he himself can hardly estimate. He observes, in a fresh fashion, and with a novel accent, how all truth about the physical world is dependent upon the truth concerning time and space. I reword some of his thoughts about space in my own way. Whatever matter there were in the outer world, there would in any case have to be space to put the matter in, and so the laws of matter have to conform to the laws of space. Nature must perforce obey geometry; else could she get no room for her things, and even so with time. The laws of space come first in order. The laws of physics come, as it were, logically later, and must be congruent with the space laws. But space, on the other hand, is not obliged to conform to the laws of matter. Just as the principle that what is done can't be undone, even so the principle that a straight line is the shortest distance between two points, or that you can't put the left glove on the right hand, illustrates formal laws of the world, prior in nature to the laws of matter. Moving bodies may fly as they will in accordance with laws of physics. They cannot fly in accordance with any possible law so as to move through the shortest distances and yet not fly in straight lines. The matter of your hands may have what laws or nature it will; nothing could permit the left glove to go on to the right hand but a change in the necessary laws of geometry. Geometrical laws, then, like the laws of time, go together to make nature possible. Know what space and time are, and you will know something about the truths that condition the world's very existence.[1]

Well, then, what are space and time? About 1769, it

[1] The importance here given to the well-known essay of 1768 is in agreement so far with Riehl's view (*Der Philosophische Kriticismus*, vol. i. p. 262). See also Caird, *op. cit.* vol. i. p. 164. From this point on, I follow partly the views of Benno Erdmann.

occurred to Kant to observe that both space and time are, when regarded as real things, thoroughly and hopelessly paradoxical, self-contradictory in their nature. Kant was fond in those days [1] of setting over against one another opposing assertions about fundamental truths, and giving a fair chance to both sides in the controversy. He elaborated this old method of research very carefully and in an original fashion, and in consequence he called it by special names of his own choosing. He used it to bring out the paradoxical character that after all lies so deeply imbedded in the very heart of all human thinking. Applying this fashion of analysis to space and time, Kant found that, if you once regard them as realities, as facts existent outside your own mind, you can make diametrically opposed assertions about them, and yet prove both of a pair of such assertions to be true. The result so far is puzzling; but look at it an instant. Of space you can say that it is infinitely divisible, that is, that cut it up as small as you like, the parts will still have size, and so can be cut again, so that you could never reach the end of your cutting. This you can say, and you can prove it too, *if*, namely, space is a real thing that stays there to be cut, apart from your ideas of it. Equally certain it is, however, in case space is real, and is made up of parts, that then, if you let it in conception crumble away like a heap of sand, to find what in the last analysis it is made of, there must be found somewhere ultimate parts, real space-atoms, which you could reach by this process of ideal analysis, and which you couldn't divide. For if there is a heap of manifold parts, like a heap of sand, and you conceive it to fall into bits for the sake of analysis, then surely where there are many units there must be units. Therefore, if space is a reality, you can prove, thinks Kant, that it is infinitely divisible and that it isn't infi-

[1] See the introduction to Benno Erdmann's *Reflexionen Kant's zur Kritischen Philosophie*, vol. ii. p. xxxv.

nitely divisible. That seems absurd, but what does such
an absurd result prove? It proves, so Kant holds, that
space is n't real at all, but just an idea of yours, a universal but inner condition of your consciousness of outer
objects. This result is revolutionary for him. Space and
time, he had already said, are the conditions prior of all
physical nature. And now space and time can be thus
proved to be unreal outside of our minds. What follows?
The whole of this seeming outer nature is no outer fact at
all. It is a mere phenomenon in us. That doctrine is
the first half of Kant's critical philosophy.

IV.

In 1770, he stated this theory of the subjectivity of
time and space, as he called his notion, in a dissertation
that he wrote on his assumption of a professor's chair at
Königsberg. In this dissertation he gives yet another
proof of his new doctrine. Space and time can't be real,
Kant now says, for we know too much about them, know
them, not by bare observation, but with a mathematical
completeness such as we could n't possess with regard to
outer facts, know more than we could have found out if
they existed really beyond ourselves. We know, for instance, of time and space as they are for our minds, that
they are infinite wholes, prior to any of their own parts as
well as to the things that exist in them. Furthermore, as
you can easily see, space and time don't seem to us to be
properties of things, as color and taste are; nor yet are
they separate things of nature. Rather are they just conditions of our sense-knowledge of things. So, then, they
can't be real at all, except as facts of our consciousness.
Kant therefore calls space and time forms of perception,
or sense-forms. Our world seems to be in space and time
because it is our own nature to view it as spatial and temporal. Space and time appear to us to belong outside
us, merely because they are conditions in us of our seeing

and feeling things, forms of our sense. It is with them as with colored spectacles. If one always wore green goggles, all his world would seem green to him. Even so, because we always perceive under these forms of sense, space and time, which are just our forms of perceiving things, cannot but seem real to us. In fact they aren't revelations of truth outside us at all. They are our own fashions of receiving the things that we perceive. It was largely in consequence of this doctrine, which I state now, after all, in its outcome, rather than in its full proof, that Kant later came to declare that the things themselves outside of us, which arouse our sensations, the things as they are in themselves, since they can't be spatial, nor temporal, are in fact utterly unknowable. Nobody can prove the least thing about what the real world is. We know first of all only our own sense impressions, which are whatever they happen to be. We know also that there are things beyond us which we view through our sense-forms. But what those things are, how should we ever find out? We are cut off from them by the illusions of sense. We know our seeming world in space and in time. It has law and order in it, such law and order as science finds there. Astronomy is true for the seeming world, although in the absolute world there is no space, and although what the stars and the atoms are is unknowable. But thus, you see, we have found a limit to science. It can never know things in themselves. And so Kant's critical doctrine ultimately came to be one of the necessary limits of all theoretical thought.

That, at least, was the idea that Kant in his later works reached. In 1770, he still hoped to find by some device of logic a way to a knowledge of things in themselves beyond our private and human sense-forms of space and time. But from this hopeful "dogmatic slumber" (as he once calls it) Hume's skepticism finally awoke him in the years immediately following 1772.[1]

[1] Of several hypotheses current in the literature of the topic I

V.

Hume it was who gave the final touch to Kant's reflection by his stern assertion that in the world of experience facts are only conjoined, and never connected. Impressions we know, says Hume, and ideas we know; but who ever yet saw causation, or experienced necessity? In the world of sense there are facts, but there are no links. You see things happen; you can't see why they must happen. This criticism of Hume's deeply affected Kant. Kant had already almost given up finding out the nature of outer things by logic. He was ready very soon to give it up altogether. He was content with the narrow limits of our sense-forms; if only the seeming space-and-time-world, the seeming world which science looks upon and examines, could be shown to have order in it. The astronomer does n't care whether space and time are sense-forms, or whether he knows or not the stars as they are in themselves. What he wants to be sure of is that nature, seeming or real, in show-space or in itself, has discoverable law and order in it, uniformity, causal fixity, genuine reasonableness, about it. Well, Kant wanted to make out this thing, too. He thought it over in silence for some years. The result of his reflection was expressed in the great "Critique." And that new result, the second and greater half of his doctrine, was something like the following : —

In so far as the world is seen by us in our sense-forms of space and time, it is bound to appear to us as conformable to their laws. Nature, then, is forced to obey geometry, because nature, after all, is just a show-nature, our

choose the most probable. Here as before I largely follow Benno Erdmann. The awakening influence of Hume was formerly referred to the years from 1762 to 1766. Professor Paulsen of Berlin first called in question this view, and suggested 1769 as a more likely date.

own experience, and so conformable to our own fundamentally geometrical ways of viewing it. Well, even so,
when we *think* of natural events, there are certain conditions governing our thinking process. And to these
conditions the products of our thought, the objects of our
experience, must needs conform. For the objects of
our experience are n't the things in themselves, but are
just our thoughts. If our thought, as a process of comprehending our experience, is obliged to treat the facts
before it as conforming to rational laws, in order to think
of them at all, well, then, the facts of experience, being
once for all facts of inner life, will have to conform to
law, and that will be the end of it. To be sure, *if* we
knew by sight the things as they are in themselves, we
should indeed have to conform wholly to *their* ways ; and,
as Hume's criticism implied, unless we then saw causation and necessary connection amongst the matters of
fact, we could n't be sure of such connections at all. But,
you see, we don't know by sight any things in themselves.
We see only the show-world in the sense-forms. Its matters of fact are then just our own matters of fact. In
knowing nature we are but learning to know ourselves.
If it is the fundamental fashion of our thinking to become
conscious of objects as orderly, then orderly they will be
for us. Then *our* world will have in it not only conjunc-
tion, but connection of facts. Our understanding will
think the linkages into our show-world. The dutifully
bound seeming universe of our experience will obey the
law of the inner life, whose thought it is. This obedience
will control all things, however remote, in these phantom-
forms of space and time, — yes, as it were, will preserve
the stars from wrong, and the most ancient heavens
through this be fresh and strong. Is such a conception a
paradox ? Then look at it once more.[1]

[1] The immediately following free paraphrase of one central
thought of the " deduction " is more fully discussed in Supplement

A sane man differs from a man with a maniacal flight
of ideas, or from a patient in delirium, most in this, that
the sane man, at every moment, looks, as it were, out of
this moment to his larger self, and links this moment with
the past and future, while the other's soul, as Kant would
say (although he does not use this, my own illustration),
is filled with a *Gewühl von Erscheinungen*, with a mass
of flighty seemings. The sane man continually *collects
himself*, as we ordinarily express it, binds this to that,
and *thereby*, — and this is Kant's central thought, —
thereby sees links in his seeming outer world just because he does collect himself, just because it is of the
essence of his sanity to think connections there yonder in
his show-world. Kant has a technical name for what I
have just named sanity. He himself does not use the
latter word; he calls this process and condition of all
rational consciousness *Transcendental Unity of apperception*. It depends upon and involves self-recognition; but
self-recognition, if you look at it carefully, is indeed seen
to include the binding of fact to fact in your experience.
If I be I, as I think I be, says the little old woman of
the song, *then will my little dog know me*. The poor
woman is striving, you remember, to recover the unity of
her apperception, of which a sad and recent incident has
deprived her. She seeks it, and how? By striving to
link fact to fact in her sleepy experience. Well, even so,
Kant holds, that if I be I, as I think I be, then will the
phenomena of my sense-world in a certain deeper just
sense know me, that is, recognize the authority of my
thought-forms, or categories. The little woman, then, had,
in her way, grasped the idea of that most puzzling part of
Kant's "Critique," the so-called transcendental deduction
of the categories. For once more, if I am to be at this

B. The illustration of the " Unity of Apperception " by the idea of
" sanity " is, I think, justified by many aspects of Kant's phraseology,
remote as it is from his own wording.

moment sane, then I must regard myself as much more than this momentary self. I must communicate, as it were, with my past and my future, which are n't now here at all. And in doing this, causation, and the other ideas of connection in nature, are the tools of my understanding. They give to my objects a communicable, a typical, a universal character. By connecting facts in my mind, I connect my mind in itself. This desk before me, to take yet another example, this desk, as a fact in my sense form of space and time, is the product of my natural sanity, which simply makes coherent a mass of feelings, holds together in some sort of unity what I see and touch. In so far as I am a sensible person I say to myself, " All these feelings of mine just at this point of space must somehow belong together. Hereby only can I make an object out of them, having a permanent type that I can recognize again. This object must also somehow cohere with what I have seen before, because I am one self, and my experience must somehow hold together. Therefore I say that the object has substantiality, that it persists in time, that whenever it came into being something produced it as its cause, and so on." Thus, you see, I bring the table into my world, into the one coherent experience which constitutes my larger self. To my larger self, to my whole actual and possible coherent experience, always I look up; to this I make my active appeal. The moment is *my* moment so far only as it conforms to the universal and orderly types of my whole self-consciousness.

In large part, however, this process of constructively making my world coherent, is, on its theoretical side indeed unconscious, just as the inventions of an artistic mind are often unconsciously made. There is in me a blind application of my forms of thought, a reasonable but not necessarily self-conscious defense of my sanity. Kant calls this busy and half-blind application of the forms of thought to the facts of sense, whereby we make everything, from pictures in the firelight to the sublimest constructions of science, whereby we get our great world of tables and people and houses and suns and star-systems and atoms and laws of nature, — he calls, I say, this busy inner world-building power of our minds the "constructive imagination." It builds solely on the basis of our experienced sensations; it produces purely in the forms of space and time; it has as theoretical power nothing to say of God, nor yet of the moral law; it builds our world as a great genius makes a poem, how, he knows not; it is involuntary, hidden away in the mind, the servant of our understanding, the minister of the forms of thought; but it gives us this bright and solid world that is all about us; and, in the way of theoretical knowledge, we have nothing better than what it gives us. Without continual support from sense, this poetical faculty of ours could do nothing. As sensations, unformed, would be a mere flight of ideas, unreal and insane, so these notions of the understanding, causation, substantiality, and the rest, have no meaning except as applied by our constructive imagination to rendering coherent our world of sense. That is just why we do not know at all that these forms of thought apply to the things in themselves.

And it is thus that so much the more, when we come to those other objects of pure and constructively voluntary faith, namely, God and the rest, we have a right to trust "the truths that never can be proved." For by this theoretical doctrine we have shown that nothing *but* the clear and unmistakable demands of the moral law, which requires of us a submission to an eternally significant order, could ever by any possibility carry us beyond sense. We have no theoretical power whereby we can escape from the prison of the inner life, or from the purely phenomenal reality, the show-world, which our constructive imagination builds up. Theoretically speaking, our show-world is only the poem which the inner life makes. Hence only

our homage to the absolute imperative of our practical
reason, which categorically demands of us that we act as
if we were in an eternal world, — only this, and our free
choice to obey, can put us into relations with the unknown
beyond sense. The theoretical view of things, this work
of art of the inner life, is morally insufficient. Hence we
have to postulate God beyond it. Such, then, in sum, is the
content of my world. The understanding creates the laws
of phenomenal nature, creates them, indeed, not without
the most close and constant reference to the facts of sense,
creates them, in truth, merely by actively uniting together
these facts of sense, but still creates the whole organization, the coherence, the unity, the sanity, of our world of
business, of society, and of science. The stars, too, just
because they are our stars, experienced by us, must be
orderly, as our understanding is orderly. That you and I
see the same world depends merely upon the fact that
we all work upon similar ideas of sense with similar
powers of understanding. We all have part, as it were,
in the one ideal self of humanity's experience. For us all
alike this world is an inner creation. To state the case
finally, in a general formula : The unknown things in
themselves give us sense experiences. These we first perceive in the forms of space and time, because that is our
way of perceiving. Then, being coherent creatures, we
order this our world of sense according to the laws of
causation and the other " categories " which are forms
of thought. Thus we all alike get a world, which, while
it is in all its sanity and order an inner world, is still for
each of us apparently an outer world, — a world of fact,
a world of life. The unity of our personality demands
the unity of our experience ; this demands that our show-
world of nature should conform to the laws of thought ;
and thus causality, necessity, and all the other categories
of the understanding are realized in the world through
our constructive imagination, which working in the ser-

vice of the understanding actively puts them into the world.

VI.

By this marvelously subtle thought Kant at once destroys and builds up. The world of Locke's bare experience vanishes. The world of the Cartesian innate ideas is nothing any more. Even for Spinoza's eternal order, as an outward fact, Kant's theory has no place. He devotes long sections of the "Critique" to an elaborate undermining of every form of speculative dogmatism. As the freeman hates tyrants, so Kant hates submission to an outward and absolute order invented by the pretensions of a thought that would transcend our limited powers. And yet he does n't assert all this for the mere sake of destructive skepticism. *One* certainty remains to him which is indeed absolute enough. It is that certainty of the moral law, which in Kant's system takes the place that the adoration of the eternal order took in Spinoza's doctrine. To the moral law and its consequences, Kant devoted three of the most important of his later works. You know theoretically only that rigid order of the world of show which is indeed enough for empirical science, but which gives you no warrant to talk about things as they are in themselves. But you do know one practical certainty which sends you far beyond sense. You know that you ought to do right, and doing right for Kant is something very simple, rigid, and absolute. There is no compromise in his case between the moral law and the desires of sense. Inclination and duty are no friends for Kant. To do right, thinks Kant, is to act at any time as you could wish that a whole world full of moral agents should act, to act after a fashion worthy to be made a public and universal law of life. The moral law admits of no exceptions. It is reasonableness in action. Kant loves to dwell on its simple and awful sublimity. Universality of the method or principle of your conduct is its aim. Absolute truthfulness, absolute respect for the rights and freedom of every one of your fellow-men, utter devotion to the cause of high-mindedness, of honesty, of justice, of simplicity, of honor, — such is Kant's ideal, and so far as in him lay he was always true to it. It is a stern and rigid ideal, very rare in philosophy, and even infrequent in the life of the world ; but it is Kant's ideal. And now he further says : In this show-world of your limitation and ignorance, you are bound to behave thus reasonably and sublimely, and there is necessarily associated with your behavior a determination to trust faithfully and absolutely that the right, thus acted out, will triumph, and that there is a God who will see that it triumphs. You are moved so to trust in God, because that is simply the wise and honorable thing to do. And this world of yours, as one sees, is not a world of absolute insight, but first of sane and active unification of your personal experience, and then of honorable doing, a world whose highest wisdom is the service of the ideal that reason conceives.

This hasty sketch has now put before you, not Kant's whole doctrine, but something of the fine and manly attitude which, amidst all his subtlety and his skepticism, he always maintained. I know not how wearisome this subtlety itself has been to you, even in my utterly fragmentary suggestion of its quality. The professional student often forgets how these things used to seem to him when he began his work, and wonders now how such long pursuit of the inner life, even into the recesses of its dimmest and most sacred temples of faith, may appear to those who do not spend their lives in such wanderings. Well, be that all what it may, my duty is done if I have suggested to you anything of a doctrine which has created the philosophy of the present century ; and as for the present obscurity of the whole to you, remember that all the rest of these lectures will be of necessity, in one aspect, an exposition of the consequences of this theory of Kant, so that we shall know it better hereafter.

What, then, is our outcome? We have reached almost
the opposite pole of reflection from that which Spinoza's
system occupied. Spinoza saw the substance with the eye
of an undoubting reason. He was sure, dogmatic, absolute in his pretensions; and being thus too sure of himself, he lost himself in contemplating the eternal. We
have seen how the study of the inner life drew men away
from this confidence of reason, even as far as the skepticism of Hume. Now we have seen how Kant, in the
midst of this wilderness of skepticism, built once more
the fair spiritual world. Strongly contrasted as are these
two systems, that of Spinoza and that of Kant, both
stand, I think, for moments, for elements, in the higher
thought of humanity. Whether any synthesis of the
two is possible, we have yet to see. Both are for us,
thus far, experiences of humanity, stages of fortune
through which man's spirit passes; and as for Kant's
stage, he shows, as you see, how, amidst the ruins of
sense and of doubt, the triumphant reason still builds its
world of law and of ideal truth, builds because it is
minded to do so, builds by virtue of its natural coherence
and its moral courage. Kant's thought, then, is, in one
aspect, the thought which Tennyson has made so familiar
to our time: —

> "O living will that shalt endure
>   When all that seems shall suffer shock,
>   Rise in the spiritual rock,
> Flow thro' our deeds and make them pure,
>
> "That we may lift from out of dust
>   A voice as unto him that hears,
>   A cry above the conquer'd years
> To one that with us works, and trust,
>
> "With faith that comes of self-control,
>   The truths that never can be proved
>   Until we close with all we loved,
> And all we flow from, soul in soul."

LECTURE V.

FICHTE.

Now that we have reached and passed for the first time in our study the thinker upon whom, more than upon any other centre, modern thought turns, as upon a fulcrum, I am tempted to pause, at the beginning of this lecture, until I have suggested still more of what Kant means to modern thought. It is not, I suppose, merely historical sketches of the philosophers that you desire from me. You want to get from these philosophers such help as this brief study can suggest towards a comprehension of the spiritual problems of our own day. So, after suggesting at the last lecture what manner of man the historical Kant was, and what was the essence of his doctrine, I shall now try to draw afresh the moral from this part of our story.

I.

The movement from Spinoza to Kant has taught us a lesson which human thought everywhere has to learn, namely, that deeper truth is too valuable to be won by any short and easy process, and that spiritual history has everywhere a decidedly tragic element. We begin with our world simply, in a childlike faith that nature and God are ours by right of our birth. Our first lesson is that they are both of them at all events far deeper realities than we had supposed. Nature for Spinoza, as for all other great thinkers, is n't the nature that you see with your eyes. It is the nature that you think with your reason; and to think it with your reason you have to go behind sense to the law, to the substance of things. Even so, in your relations with God, you have, according to Spinoza, to forsake the naive and joyous trust in life through which you first see him. " When," says Spinoza, " I had learned that all the surroundings of life are vain and futile," — so his pilgrimage began. A long training, he tells us, was needed ere he became at home in those solitudes where he ultimately found God. It was, he declares, through a contempt for all the things which the multitude seek that he came to learn the true good, beyond all that they seek, namely, the peace which the world can neither give nor take away. Encouraging to us about Spinoza was, then, that his tale ended joyously, in a wisdom whereby he was exalted beyond all the phantom world of sense; but grave and stern about him was his teaching that the way to this wisdom is so toilsome ; " for all things excellent," he says, " are as difficult as they are rare."

This lesson, that the true joy of the spirit is indeed *res severa*, a stern thing, is still further deepened in our minds by the struggle of thought in the eighteenth century. It was not the mere waywardness of the eighteenth-century thinkers that forbade them to accept as final the guidance of even the intuitive reason to which Spinoza and his fellows had all trusted so implicitly. It was a necessary progress in reflection that drove these men to their scrutiny of the inner life, a scrutiny whose tragedy we found exemplified by Hume's lightly and cheerfully spoken, but weighty and gloomy words, " sophistry and illusion." But this, at all events, still seems to me sure : Whoever has not wandered that Via Dolorosa of the eighteenth century's doubt of both reason and sense alike, will never be able to knock at the door at the end of that way, the door which Kant first of all men found opened to him. It has opened before us now in the last discussion. We have entered, and what do we find? We find, not what, in the childlike simplicity of our first love

of truth we should have desired, a God revealed direct to
sense, or a divine order manifest even to our intuitive
reason; but something very different. We read, when we
enter the new door, as it were a mysterious writing, prepared by unseen and unknown hands, a letter, left for our
guidance by a remote and even unknowable guide. The
letter contains only the moral law, and the word, " Serve
the unseen God as if he were present with you." That is
in the first place all. Upon this and this only, according
to Kant, our faith must build. For this, as the inner
voice now tells us, is the call that, with all our better nature, we are henceforth minded to obey. Our *will* is the
solution. "Work out the divine," says the new philosophy. "Build anew the lost spiritual world, which skepticism shattered; " such is the command of Kant's practical reason. All this is unquestionably a hard doctrine.
It is not what we sought. We sought peace, and the philosopher has brought us not peace, but a sword. We
sought the joy of God's presence, and Kant has sent us
to work out a divine mission in a wilderness far remote
from all absolute insight. And yet, stern as this doctrine
is, you must feel its courage and its wisdom. After all,
here is at least a part of the truth. Life is not an easy
thing; the spiritual life is the hardest of all lives; and of
all spiritual gifts, next perhaps to charity itself, insight is
surely the most difficult to win. As long as these things
are so, Kant's doctrine will retain its profound ethical and
religious significance. But, you will ask, is this, then, wisdom's last word, " *der Weisheit letzter Schluss ?* " Well,
for my part I do not think so. I warn you indeed that
in philosophy, if you will go beyond Kant, you must
meet new dangers, and must attempt new and venture-
some wandering. But for my part I love to wander, far
and long, and I hold that there are indeed heights yet to
climb that cleave the heavens far above and beyond this
dwelling-place of Kant. If you will go with me, we will try

also these new adventures; but meanwhile I want to point out to you, ere we bid farewell to our greatest modern thinker, how there are more senses than one in which henceforth, wherever our feet carry us, his wisdom will go with us and direct us. After all, the spiritual world that Kant bade us build is the modern world; and Kant is the true hero of all modern thought. If in one sense it is only by transcending him and even by forgetting some of his limitations that we are to triumph, he is none the less forever our guide. Kant is, if you like, the homely and somewhat incongruous figure, a sort of John Brown of our century of speculative warfare. Derided as a rebel and an enemy of the faith by many of his own time, he dies before the modern conflict is fairly begun, but his soul goes marching on through the whole of it. Or to take another more suggestive, but similarly inadequate comparison, he resembles the hero of the Heroic Symphony, who is dead and buried in the second movement, but who is none the less spiritually and obviously present in the romantic and fairy-like outburst of new life in the scherzo, and the joyous apotheosis of the triumphant warriors that, in the fourth movement, crowns the symphony. Both these figures, I grant you, are somewhat imperfect; but still, I insist, in some such sense Kant will henceforth be our companion, — the leader who inspires us while we no longer see him at the head, the man whose precise system we no longer hold, but who still is the creator of our thought.

I must indeed have failed entirely in my summary of Kant's own theoretical views, in the last lecture, if I did not suggest to you how full Kant's cautious and skeptical doctrine is of motives that will lead us beyond him. Remember how, for the first, he declared the world of the things in themselves to be wholly inaccessible to our intellect, just because the world for our intellect is *our own* world. The search for accessible truth, thinks Kant, is then the search for one's own personal larger self. Be cause I am sane, because I have what Kant calls unity of apperception in me, because I need an orderly conscious- ness, therefore it is that the world of sense and of expe- rience has an outwardly visible good order about it. My understanding, working upon sense, gives laws to nature, because if there were no such laws given by my under- standing I should have no true inner experience at all. The show world of experience is the poem of our construc- tive imagination, the product, then, of our deepest nature, of our largest selves. Moreover, even Kant, with all his caution, has to speak of that true self, to which you and I alike appeal, whenever we discourse about the things of space and time, as if it were something that we all shared in, a certain universal self, whose offspring are we all, with our flying moments of sense, our weak efforts at truth, our study of experience, our common trust in understanding. The world that we know is, according to Kant, the world, not of dead outer things, but of human thoughts; and when we try to get at truth we are trying to find how the world in space and time would seem to the experience of a perfectly sane and rational and far- seeing onlooker; in other words, we are trying, all of us alike, as we think, to find out the mind of the ideal man. Well, I say, that is the essence of Kant's thought, re- stated in one word.

II.

And now for a very natural extension of this view. I suggest this extension here first merely as a possible view, then as the one that we shall find history developing. You will think it at first fantastic, but I shall not try as yet to defend or to attack it. I am so far only chronicler.

Grant, if you will, the existence of such a universe as Kant describes, a universe of numerous, free, but ignorant moral agents, each naturally engaged in imaginatively building up, with an unconscious but thoughtful art, an inner personal world, in the sense-forms of space and

time, and through numerous forms of thought, applied
to experience by their various constructive imaginations.
Each one of these moral agents is bound, by his manhood
and by his rationality, to serve an unseen and eternal
moral law, and to believe in a divine order that supports
this law. Such a universe as this of Kant, viewed as it
were from without, suggests irresistibly an interpretation
which at first sight may seem as romantic as indemonstra-
ble, but which is at all events not excluded by the facts.
Let us look at them dispassionately, — these moral agents,
blind to absolute truth, but each and all properly destined
to be willing servants of an unseen order; world-creators,
meanwhile, each and all of them, but creators solely of
their inner worlds, communing somehow with one another,
by virtue of their common rationality, but cut off from
things in themselves. How does such a state of things
appear? Does it not suggest at once a plan of reality
which might not yet demonstrably, but just possibly, stand
for the true divine order itself? Might not this whole
universe of the apparently separate and sense-encom-
passed creatures be an organized spiritual community? —
where, like bees working each in his own part of the cell-
wax, but all combining to build the honey-laden comb,
these creatures, in the very isolation and darkness of each
life, labored together for the realization, — yes, I mean it
literally, — for the very expressing and constituting of
God's life; a divine life, I repeat, of infinite complexity,
whose purposes were so manifold that an endless number
of agents might be needed to embody them; whose ideals
were so lofty that only such courage and fidelity and devotion as finite beings, in this ignorance and isolation,
would have opportunity to develop, could serve the stern
and noble ends of the divine decrees. Suppose, in a
word, that the infinite whole made up of these finite lives
were itself the divine life. From such a point of view,
which I now suggest only by way of a pure hypothesis,

could not this Kantian universe be both interpreted, and, after a fashion, even justified? To be sure, by such an interpretation it would be indeed transformed. In my opening lecture I ventured to suggest to you the doctrine that the universe, despite its seemingly stubborn physical fixity, is a live thing, an infinite spirit. According to Kant, the world of the natural order, in space and in time, cannot be thus alive, simply because, apart from our sense and our constructive imagination, this natural order has no existence. Spinoza's substance, then, would be for Kant a mere mirage; but now, as you see, the true universe for Kant consists of perceiving moral agents, and of the dim and shadowy things in themselves, and of what the practical reason postulates; and that is all. If this be so, however, do we care much for those shadowy things in themselves? Perhaps they are n't worth knowing. Perhaps they even do not exist at all. Our inner world does n't contain them. They are no object of natural science. You can't weigh them or measure them, much less see them. Perhaps they are, as Hume would say, "sophistry and illusion." What, then, remains to us? Why, precisely this: the world of the natural order, which, mirage though it be, is the very mirror of our sanity, and is therefore useful enough; this, and the world of our fellow-men, the world of practical and therefore of spiritual relationships, the world of live beings, ignorant, but rational like ourselves. With these we live, we act; we seek to realize through them the moral order; we respect their rights, we love them, we treat them as God's children. But see: perhaps, in dealing with them, *we touch the divine order itself.* Perhaps, to use a more modern phrase, God simply differentiates himself into the forms of all these live beings, who may be, for all we know, as numerous, and as various in their degrees of loftiness, as the stars and the atoms of physics. Perhaps in the very depths of their finite ignorance he does n't quite lose himself; perhaps his transcendent wisdom consists simply in knowing, in establishing, in harmonizing their relationships, so that, as Schiller says, " while no one of them is his equal, his own endlessness foams up to him from out this beaker of the infinite world of spirits." Then, indeed, their lonely heroism is his triumph ; their seeming isolation is simply the manner in which he realizes, through them, the organization of his own life ; their diversity and ignorance are merely his way of expressing the unity in variety, the completeness in differentiation, of his own manifold nature. If so, then God is n't somewhere far off there, outside the world, so that we feel in vain for him amongst the dead and dismal things in themselves. God is in you, just in so far as you are alive and hearty and humane ; in your human relationships, just so far as they are devoted, loyal, organic ; in your very ignorance, in so far as it enables you to be heroic ; in your very finiteness, in so far as it is a condition for your accomplishment of a definite task. God, outside of such a world of finite agents, would rejoice only in his empty infinity ; he would be, as Schiller also said, in the poem from which I have just quoted,—he would be " friendless," he would " suffer lack." To be the God in reality, he would have to enter into finite form, and preserve his infinity merely through the unity, the organization, the conscious spiritual form of his universe of active creatures. We were wrong then, when we sought him as it were afar off, in the mirage of space and time, or even in the laws of outer nature as Spinoza did. We were even wrong to say, as Kant said : We never take hold of his real self, we only postulate him. The fact is that, in our spiritual life, we already possess him, are flesh of his flesh, are one with him, just in so far as we have vitality, courage, loyalty, wealth, strength, sanity, of will and of understanding. We know of him just so much as we *are*. And we are of him just so much as we are morally worthy to be.

This is the interpretation which dawns upon us when we reflect awhile upon Kant's universe. Mystery enshrouds his world. The curtain of sense is " so thick ! " Such darkness is for us beyond it ! We know so little. We have nothing left us but morality ; and that is just a postulate. But no, is this so little, after all ? Suppose that the curtain itself *were* the picture, that the dark mystery lay simply in this, that we have refused to recognize as divine so much of God's own essence as we ourselves possess, and have failed to see how our life, just in so far as it is spiritual, is, not a postulating, but a realizing of the divine life. Suppose all this to be no mere hypothesis, but a certainty. Would it not transform our philosophy? Well, I suggest here this transformation, because, as an idea, it was precisely the transformation of the Kantian doctrine which was the common undertaking of the great post-Kantian German idealists, Fichte, Schelling, and Hegel.

Philosophy is full of surprises. Just when you think that the road is ended against a dark and impassable wall, the door opens, as it opened to Kant. And just when you think again that Kant's discovery is the end, a new life for the first time begins. This is the new life of modern idealism. It accepts in one sense Kant's result. Yes, it goes further in negation than even he went. He held fast by the things in themselves, whose existence he acknowledged, although he could know nothing about them. The later German idealists say frankly that they care nothing for the things in themselves, and either doubt or deny whether there are any such things at all. Kant, however, paused at the threshold of the show-world. Beyond, he said, dwells, as we must faithfully believe, a God whom we serve, but who is forever the unknown God. The later idealists say : Indeed, the deepest truth is the truth of the manly will to act morally ; but then this will itself embodies in each of us a portion of the divine per sonality. This is, so to speak, the real presence of God in us, to wit, just as much of our own nature as is holy. Our holiness, if we have any rag of holiness about us, much more if we are filled with heroism and with reasonable service, is, in its own inner quality, divine. As for God, his life is just this eternal sacrifice of his infinity by entering into the rational lives of a world of limited, but moral beings. For in this sacrifice he wins himself. He enjoys his peace, not apart from the world,

> " Where never creeps a cloud nor moves a wind,
> Nor ever falls the least white star of snow
> Nor ever lowest moan of thunder rolls,
> Nor sound of human sorrow mounts."

No, his peace is the peace of triumphing in the midst of *our* world of agony and of passion, as the tragic poet triumphs even while losing himself in the sufferings of his own creations. God's life is simply *all* life, and it is not concealed, but revealed by our own lives. God lives in every kindly friendship, in every noble deed, in every well-ordered society, in every united people, in every sound law, in every wise thought. He has no life beyond such rationality. His personality is just this, the communion, the intercourse, the organization of all finite persons. Here, you see, is in one sense indeed a new notion of personality. A person beyond our whole world, even of morality, was what we had hoped for. The new doctrine declares that the infinite one pervades the whole finite world of spirits, and simply lives by constituting, by unifying, and by enjoying, this very life of ours and of all our brethren, the rational beings, wherever and whatever they may be. Thus indeed we are limited, and may be even transient embodiments of God's life; but we ourselves, in so far as we make for unity and for righteousness, are in nature one with him. New is the doctrine, I say, namely, as a reflective speculation in modern thought. But in one sense, as these idealists are never weary of pointing out, it is a very old doctrine; it is the very core of Christian faith. When Paul said to the faithful, "Ye are dead, and your life is hid with Christ in God;" when the fourth Gospel makes the Logos say, "I am the vine, ye are the branches;" when the whole doctrine of the church rested upon the idea of a God revealed in the flesh; when even a simpler and more primitive Christian tradition, that of the first synoptic Gospel, represents the final judgment as dependent upon the principle, "Inasmuch as ye did it unto the least of these, ye did it unto me;" when, finally, the deep mysticism of the historical church represented the faithful as actually feeding upon God's very essence and living thereby, — what doctrine was this but the very teaching upon which rests the new philosophy which now undertakes to transform Kant's dark world of faithful and isolated beings into the world of God's own realization and presence? These moral agents of Kant's world are *not* isolated, for, ignorant as they are, they work together. And what better revelation of a divine order than a world where spirits *can* commune and *can* work together?

Once more, as you see, the philosopher invents nothing; he only reflects. In reflection he has cast down the dogmas of a blind faith; in reflection he builds anew their rational and eternal significance. So, at least, these German idealists hold. As for me, I am so far, as I just observed, a mere chronicler. This doctrine, too, may be an imperfect speculation. I am not now defending it, but only expounding it. As expositor I present it now before you. So far we find it as an hypothesis. It needs proof. Perhaps it will need further alteration and adjustment. At all events, here is for us a new experience in philosophy, namely, the very essence of Christianity embodied in a speculative theory.

III.

Meanwhile, the form which this doctrine takes in German thought is one dependent upon the special conditions of a very charming and a very wayward age, the age of German classical and romantic literature. Whether or no you find this sort of speculation in itself satisfactory, you will at all events be interested in watching with me, during the rest of this lecture and during the next, some of the more obvious and immediately human aspects of a time so full of fire, of imagination, of productiveness, of faults, of wanderings, and of glory. But let us proceed at once to the man who first embodied this new idealistic doctrine in a series of writings wherein the spontaneity, the eloquence, the confidence, the complexity, and the fragmentariness of the work done reflect very well the character of this period. I refer to Fichte.

Johann Gottlieb Fichte is the first of the great successors of Kant. He was a man three years younger than Schiller, thirteen years younger than Goethe, and thirty-eight years younger than Kant himself. The story of his life is one of ardor, poverty, high aims, brilliant literary success, bitter conflicts, and an untimely death in his country's service. For at the close of his career, during the great war of liberation, in 1813, he and his devoted wife busied themselves in the encouragement of the warriors and in the care of the wounded. Fichte, as you see, had just passed the age of fifty. His wife, while nursing wounded soldiers, was stricken with typhus fever. She recovered, but the contagion had already passed to Fichte, to whom it proved fatal, in January, 1814. A nobler death, in a more heroic time, was scarcely possible to a professor of philosophy and a patriot. Fichte was spared the pain of seeing the darker years of national stagnation and of illiberalism in Germany, that followed the triumph over Napoleon. And for the rest, his work was in one sense already done. He had influenced younger men who by that time had already transcended him.

This work had been, however, manifold and exacting. Fichte had a temperament at once logical and enthusiastic. The struggle between a keen and subtle intellect and a warm and imaginative emotional nature, had joined itself with outer hindrances to make his early years eventful and arduous. The son of a poor weaver, and one of a large family of children, Fichte chanced to attract, while yet a boy, the kindly attention of a nobleman, who adopted him, showed him a little of the great world, and then, suddenly dying, left him a penniless youth, only the more keenly ashamed, under such circumstances, of his poverty. At the university he supported himself by private teaching, was more than once near to despair in his neediness, and at length, after graduation, became a *Hofmeister* in a Zürich family. While here, in 1788, he met his future wife, a certain Johanna Rahn, a niece of the poet Klopstock. They were soon betrothed, but were too poor to marry until 1793.

Fichte's since published love-letters to his betrothed are described, by those who have read them through (I have not), as somewhat pedantic — the natural product of a mind conscientious, learned, but impulsive, and so far at once flighty and even a little despondent. He is fond of accusing himself of many faults, laments his restlessness and unsteadiness of ideas and plans, knows no guiding star but her love, and wonders what Providence can be meaning with him. Meanwhile, during this period of his betrothal, he changed his position often and traveled much, looking for a permanent occupation, — a project-maker and an unpromising wanderer. In philosophy he was so far a sort of amateur Spinozist, and occupied a position to which he later looked back as one of darkness and of the gall of bitterness. Suddenly a change came. It was 1790, and he was now twenty-eight years old.

While in Leipzig he undertook to give a young man private lessons in philosophy, and to that end took up for the first time the study of Kant. Very soon he wrote to Fräulein Rahn in an entirely new vein. It is a wonderful philosophy, this of Kant, he asserts. It tames a man's wild imagination; it gives one "an indescribable elevation above all earthly affairs." "I have obtained from it," he continues, "a nobler ideal. I don't concern myself so much now with outward things; I am busied within myself. Thence has come to me a peace that I have never before known. In the midst of my perplexing material situation, I have been enjoying the most blessed days of my experience. I mean to devote to this philosophy at least some years of my life. It is above all conception a difficult doctrine, and it deserves to be made easier. Its basis, to be sure, is a mass of head-splitting speculations that have no immediate bearing on human life, but the consequences are vastly important to an age which, like ours, is morally corrupt to the very source; and one would deserve well of his time if he made these consequences luminous to the world. Tell your dear father that he and I used to err in our investigations about the necessity of all man's acts. . . . I have found out now that man's will is free, and that not happiness, but worthiness is the end of our being. And I ask your pardon, too, that I used to teach you false doctrine about these things. Henceforth believe your own feeling, even if you can't refute a sophist."

One might wonder whether this confession to Johanna Rahn, of the superlative blessedness of days passed out of her company, and alone with the "Critique of Pure Reason," might not have made her a trifle jealous of Kant; but in fact, as she was a person of both maturity and discretion, being four years the senior of Fichte himself, she wrote him that, since after all he appeared unable to earn his living, and since her father's means were now apparently

sufficient, he might return to Zürich and marry her, and
then devote himself to philosophy at his leisure. A curious wavering followed in the mind and conduct of Kant's
new disciple. He wrote to his brother that Fräulein
Rahn was indeed the noblest soul in the world, but that
for one thing he himself was a wanderer, an independent
creature, and that for the rest something new had just
come into his life, which seemed to drive him out to conquer the whole world afresh. Marriage would clip a
man's wings, would imprison him yonder in Switzerland,
would perhaps hinder his philosophizing in this wondrous
and novel way. He felt restless; he was even often disposed to flee altogether and never write to her again.

To Johanna herself, Fichte's letters expressed of course
nothing of these rebellious sentiments, and I mention
them only to suggest a little of the ferment which in this
needy young tutor's soul was then under way. He
must do everything, — teach Johanna the new insight,
marry, cease this wavering that had made him like a
wave of the sea; and yet, he must also convert the whole
world to the Kantian doctrine, in all its spirituality and
earnestness; he must save his countrymen in this time of
revolution and of corruption; he must wander, work,
think incessantly. One has here, you see, something of
the typical erudite German of the story-books, crude and
elevated in one — lover, world-stormer, sentimentalist, and
cynic, all at the same time. For Fichte, too, was occasionally a bit of a cynic. "When I met Johanna," he once
writes to his brother, "my heart was empty. I just let
her love me. I did n't care much about it." "Dear
one," he writes to her in all sincerity, at about the same
time, "take me with all my faults. What a creature I am!
Men have attributed to me fixity of character, but I have
always been merely the creature of circumstances. You
have the stronger soul. Give fixity to my waverings." [1]

[1] The present sketch is dependent largely upon that of Julian

In this state of mind Fichte journeyed, in the way of business, to accept a tutor's position at Warsaw. He failed there to give satisfaction, because his French pronunciation was poor, and on his way back he called upon Kant at Königsberg, in July, 1791. The aged, prudent, and, as you will remember, highly economical philosopher regarded this reverent, fiery, but obviously impecunious young disciple with a certain suspicion, and received his confidences coolly. The rebuff only heated Fichte the more. He tarried in Königsberg two months, in order during that time to write, for presentation to Kant, a work on religious philosophy, which, once finished, proved to be so thoroughly in Kant's spirit that, when in the spring of the next year the book was published anonymously, it was very generally hailed by Kant's admirers as a new production of the master's own genius. Kant himself had to correct this misapprehension, and in doing so named, and now with warm praise, the real author. Thus at one stroke, as it were, Fichte's career was made. He had won the great philosopher's approval and the ear of the public at the same time. Within another year he returned to Zürich. He was at length famous, and, as his beloved was now, by chance, even more obviously in comfortable circumstances than she had been at the time when she wrote the aforementioned highly practical letter, there was nothing further to hinder his marriage, which took place in October, 1793, and remained to the end a very happy one. In 1794 came the call to the University of Jena, which was then at the centre of the mental life of Germany.

IV.

Fichte's career has thus been suggested to you through a sketch of its first important crisis. There is the same interesting union of the great, the ardent, the thoughtful,

Schmidt, as given in the fifth edition of his *Geschichte d. deutschen Literatur seit Lessing's Tod,* vol. i. p. 347 sqq.

and, if one wants to be frank, of the petty also, in the rest of his life. Accused of atheism in 1799, the heroic, but lamentably indiscreet man replied to an unjust charge in so violent and unhappy a fashion as to make him thenceforth impossible at Jena, so that even the chief patron of liberal culture and free thought in Germany, Goethe's own duke at Weimar, had regretfully, and by Goethe's personal advice, to dismiss him from his chair. Then followed, however, the Berlin career, with its noble ending. Later years, indeed, in some respects mellowed Fichte; but to the end he was always a fighter, and a man of books as well, with all the faults of both these species, with a temperament whose lofty heroism and true piety could not save it from an appearance of polemical narrowness and furious self-assertion whenever he was in an actual conflict with any man or party. In argument Fichte is, so to speak, *all* temperament. His dialectic is indeed keen, his analysis is deep and searching, his sense of the unity of all science is profoundly rational; but deeper than all is the strong sense of his own personality, the love of making articulate his own character, which led him to say with truth, but with a peculiar and individual strength of accent: "What system of philosophy you hold depends wholly upon what manner of man you are." Hence, in all his lengthy and frequently very technical writings, he after all never merely argues; he appeals to more than your understanding; he appeals to your honor, to your dignity of soul, to agree with his system. He would not merely convince you; he would convert you from an error which, as he feels, shows in you a defect of character. Goethe used to say that, by way of amusement, he occasionally read Fichte, "just to let myself be abused by him for a little while." Meanwhile, Fichte abused frankly his own early blindness, before Kant came into his soul, with all the ardor of the ransomed convert. What Kant had ransomed him from was Spinozism, and

the dread bondage of the outer world. What Fichte conceived himself to have learned from Kant was therefore
this : *The rational subject builds its own world, and the
dead external world is naught.* What Fichte added to
Kant, as he went on, was however somewhat elaborate,
and constitutes, along with the strictly Kantian elements,
his own system, which is almost universally but rather
inaptly named "Subjective idealism."

Let me state it, too, first in rough outline, then a little
more systematically. As everybody knows, Fichte accepted Kant's result in so far as Kant said that space and
time are facts only for our consciousness, and that we
can't know any things in themselves beyond us. Only
Fichte went further. He denied that there can exist any
things in themselves beyond consciousness at all. The
world that we spiritual beings know, however hard and
fast it may seem, however helplessly we ourselves may
individually be subjected to its facts, is still, in the last
analysis, there only *in so far* as we recognize it as there
for us. The world, then, is the world that the self makes.
So Fichte's chief principles are these: (1) All philosophy
has its source in one primal truth, namely, the truth that
living and voluntary selves *freely* choose to assert themselves, and so to build up their whole organized world ;
(2) The moral law is, in consequence of this, really prior
to all other knowledge, and conditions all that we theoretically know. For as you see, knowing a world is for
Fichte making a world, consciously recognizing the truth,
acting then in this way or in that. But the law of action,
the moral law, thus becomes for Fichte the basis of all
theoretical knowing ; (3) The apparently fatal outer
world about us is simply, in Fichte's bold and stirringly
fantastic words, "the stuff, the material (the opportunity), for our duty, made manifest to our senses ('*das versinnlichte Material unserer Pflicht*')." Beyond all this,
however, in the fourth place, Fichte went later, when he

developed more clearly a doctrine obviously latent and implied in his earlier works, namely, the doctrine that the universe of the self-asserting and world-creating selves, each of whom sees about him in daily life simply the very stuff and fibre of his moral law made manifest to his senses as an opportunity for his moral work, — that this universe of selves, I say, constitutes the life and embodiment of the one true and infinite Reason, God's will, which, itself supreme and far above the level of our finite personality, uses even our conscious lives and wills as part of its own life. This doctrine Fichte himself, in one of his later works ("The Way to the Blessed Life"), identifies with the teaching of the fourth Gospel. According to this view, you see, God, in so far as he reveals himself, is indeed the vine, and we, in so far as we truly live, are the sap-laden and fruitful branches. The only real world is the world of conscious activity, and so of spiritual relationships, of society, of serious business, of friendship, of love, of law, of national existence, — in a word, of work; as for matter, that is the mere show stuff that is needed to embody, to express, to give form, stability, outline, as it were, to our moral work.

I may put Fichte's theory of the external world in yet another fashion, thus: In company with another spirit, so Fichte thinks, I can only work in case he and I have a sense world in common. Hence our common devotion, our social enthusiasm, our duty, *requires* of us all that we try to embody our ideals in the same sense forms. If we succeed, we all see the same houses and streets, the same people moving, the same flags waving. Seeing thus in common, we can work in common. If we did not find out how to work in common, we should express the vagueness of our immoral isolation in the separateness of our various sense worlds; in other words, we should dream or be delirious. I dream when I am not at work. When I am strenuously active I am awake; and therefore, in so far as I am effectively righteous, I see the same stuff that my fellow-workers see. Matter is thus the mere condition of our common tasks. Each one of us creates it for himself. We create together and in agreement, in so far as we want to toil for a common purpose. And the rationality of the divine plan secures to us a power thus to create and to work together. Meanwhile, good and bad men, noble and base men, strong and weak men, really do not see precisely the same sense world. The seeming outer world for any man actually varies with his moral perceptions. The sense world is saner and more orderly for the cultivated man than for the savage, for the good man than for the man absorbed in the pleasure of the moment, for the wise man than for the fool. And thus the doctrine conforms, thinks Fichte, to the actual facts. "The necessity," says the philosopher, "with which the belief in the reality of phenomena forces itself upon us is a moral necessity, the only one that is possible for a moral being ; herein our duty reveals itself." And thus we have, in the barest outline, the famous " subjective idealism " of Fichte. One might better call it " ethical idealism " in its extremest expression. So much, then, for my first rough summary. And now what shall we say of this sort of idealism ?

A bold, yes, an extravagant doctrine ! you will say. Kant's things in themselves have gone out of this world of Fichte. Yet somehow we at first scarcely miss them. Kant, to be sure, felt quite out of place in Fichte's fantastic universe, and publicly expressed his repentance, ere he died, that he had ever encouraged this young disciple so freely. " Save me from my friends," cried Kant, very sincerely, in a printed note of explanation. The transformation lay of course in Fichte's determination not merely to do away with Kant's things in themselves, but to see at once into the very heart of the moral order, whose supremacy Kant had only postulated. If you now ask

me, however, whether, as modern idealist, I myself accept
Fichte's statement as the final truth of the doctrine, I
respond of course at once that I do not. This is n't the
idealism that has, as idealism ought to have, a deep and
genuine respect for the natural order and for experience.
Fichte's easy disposal of the whole external and natural
order is, indeed, not only bold, but quite unwarranted.
The modern student of nervous physiology, of the facts
of evolution, and of the interdependence of the physical
and moral worlds generally, is not likely to find Fichte's
"ethical idealism" anywhere near to the last word.
More philosophical surprises await us hereafter; upon
newer insights the thought of to-day is based; and in
some, not in all respects, the whole later German idealistic movement, which Fichte began, represents to my
mind, as you will later see, a circuit to one side of the
main stream of modern thought. Only, as we shall learn,
from this circuit thought returns enriched. This experience also will have its part in the outcome; and he who
has not once fairly viewed Fichte's universe will see less
than he ought to see in the universe of to-day.

As an experience, then, as one more of the many ways
of looking at truth, I want you to consider this doctrine.
Think of Fichte, when you read or hear of him, as one
embodiment only of that beautiful, that profoundly wise
and instructive, waywardness of German thought and
sentiment, which we all know so well to-day in song, in
story, and in the drama, as well as in the other arts. It
is this same waywardness that has given us "Faust," and
Heine's "Buch der Lieder;" that instantaneously trans-
forms the whole universe for us in any song of Schubert's
or of Schumann's; that builds worlds and casts them
down in fiery despair in a Wagnerian trilogy. In presence of this waywardness, not, indeed, of the Germany
of Bismarck and of the two Williams, but of the now
almost dead romantic Germany, whose empire, as Jean

Paul said, was of the air, — in presence of this wayward-ness, the world is once for all plastic, changeable ; a world of divine or of diabolical ideas, but of ideas that are not so much eternal as capricious. Fichte makes this ideal world a moral one. Others, as we shall see, will find this universe of the selves a universe of romance, of senti-mentality, of anything but hard fact. Yet think not that this capricious world utterly lacks truth. The real world, too, once for all flows ; flows and changes throughout its whole existence, as Heraclitus long ago said ; and pre-serves, too, its sacred and permanent *logos* just by chan-ging. Well, it is the office of the wayward to note the various aspects of just this change, this plasticity, this seemingly hopeless variety, under which the eternal truth presents itself to us. In the world of the wayward, no-thing seems fast. View follows view, romantic theory chases romantic theory, until we begin to fear that no-thing is true, and that here, even as in Hume's skeptical world also, if we find the Holy Grail itself, " it, too, will fade, and crumble into dust." But, if we watch patiently, we shall see that, from this very wealth of forms, the true form which is present through all the changes will in some fashion ultimately come to light. Fichte's moral universe, where matter is only our duty made manifest to our senses, and the universe of the romantic school, where all is sentiment, are, after all, fragments of the true faith. That thought is the thread which is to guide us through the labyrinth. The truth is the whole. Even the fantastic has its part therein.

v.

But let us look a second time and more closely at Fichte's view. The only perfectly clear thing, he says, at the outset of philosophy, is that there is a self. Any self will of course do, but some self one must start with, namely, of course, his own. Now a self asserts, " I am."

It also equally asserts, "Something exists beside me; there is a not-self." If you don't believe that this is always asserted, Fichte invites you to try it and see.[1] Well, here forthwith is a puzzle. I assert that I exist; and then I assert that something exists beside me. Now I can of course know myself, it would seem, but how can I get outside myself to see what is not myself? How come I to guess at the existence of something other than I am? Fichte's solution is simple. I *don't* guess at it; nor is it a fact forced upon me from without, in any fashion. My true self freely *chooses* to recognize the existence of something beside myself as a fact. To be sure, I, in my private, empirical, momentary capacity, seem *not* to choose, but helplessly to *find* this outer existence. Really, however, it is my own, my deeper self, whose choice is at each moment shown to me. But, then, observe, *unless* I thus chose to recognize something beyond myself, I should have nothing to do, I should have nothing to resist, to fight, to win, to love, — in short, to act upon, in any way. The deepest truth, then, is a practical truth. I *need* something not myself, in order to be active, that is, in order to exist. My very existence is practical; it is self-assertion. I exist, so to speak, by hurling the fact of my existence at another than myself. I limit myself thus, by a foreign somewhat, opaque, external, my own opposite; but my limitation is the free choice of my true self. By thus limiting myself I give myself something to do, and thus win my own very existence. Yet this opposition, upon which my life is based, is an opposition within my deepest nature. I have a foreign world as the theatre of my activity; I exist only to conquer and win that apparently foreign world to my-

---

[1] Cf. the noteworthy passage in the *Grundlage* of 1794, Fichte's *Werke*, vol. i. p. 253 : " Dass es ein solches Setzen gebe [namely, of the *Nicht-Ich*] kann jeder nur durch seine eigene Erfahrung sich darthun."

self; I must come to possess it; I must prove that it is mine. In the process of thus asserting a foreign world, and then actively identifying it as not foreign and external, but as our own, our life itself consists. This is what is meant by work, by love, by duty.

But this process, thinks Fichte, is essentially an endless one. The more of a self I am, the more of a world outside me I need, to develop and to express my energies. A busy man needs, and therefore posits, a world full of the objects of his business. Without this asserted world of objects, he, as busy man, would cease to exist; he would, so to speak, retire from business; he and his busy world would stagnate together. This, then, is Fichte's central thought: Your outer world, your not-self, is just as large as your own spiritual activity makes it. Fichte tries to show in detail how the various forms of our recognition of outer reality, such as perception, imagination, space, time, causality, and the rest, arise. Into such details I have no time to follow him; but the essence of his doctrine consists in identifying Kant's theoretical and practical reason, and in saying that all our assertion of a world beyond, of a world of things and of people, merely expresses, in practical form, our assertion of our own wealthy and varied determination to be busy with things and with people. Thus, then, each of us builds his own world. He builds it in part unconsciously; and therefore he seems to his ordinary thought not to have built it at all, but merely to find it. Each of us sees, at any moment, not only the world that we are now making by this act, but the world that we have made by all our past acts. And hence our whole life is thus consolidated before our eyes; our world is the world of our conscious and unconscious deeds. Thus we often regard it as our fate, and talk of an external substance, as Spinoza did. In this we are wrong. No activity, no world; no self, no not-self; no self-assertion, no facts to assert ourselves upon. So, at least, Fichte teaches.

But, you will say, is not the outcome of all this a sort
of solitary self-existence, where each one of us is shut up
to his own life? Has the *spiritual* world no absolute
reality? Is it, too, the mere dream of our activity? No,
thinks Fichte, not so; and here comes a part of his doctrine that was to himself the hardest part. He never
made it perfectly clear, although he tried again and again.
To you I can only suggest it. When we reflect upon our
inner activity we find it, after all, not an individual self-
will, but a deep longing for universal life. The true self,
therefore (and so far the thing is indeed clear enough),
the true self is n't the private person, the individual called
Johann Gottlieb Fichte, the impecunious tutor, the wavering lover of Johanna Rahn, the professor in Jena, falsely
accused of atheism. This true self, thinks Fichte, is something infinite. It needs a whole endless world of life to
express itself in. Its moral law could n't be expressed in
full on any one planet. Johann Gottlieb may be one of
its prophets; but the heavens could not contain its glory
and its eternal business. No one of us ever finally gets
at the true Reason which is the whole of him. Each one
of us is a partial embodiment, an instrument of the moral
law, and our very consciousness tells us that this law is
the expression of an infinite world life. The true self
is the will, which is everywhere present in things. This
will is, indeed, the vine, whereof our wills are the branches.
Fichte has innumerable ways of trying to tell finally and
clearly the story of what the infinite will is and does. It
is eternally asserting itself afresh, through countless finite
wills. Each one of these finite wills, as moral agent,
builds its sense world, and finds, in this sense world, the
manifestations of other agents. For all the agents, as
ministers of the divine, work together. The moral consciousness says to each, " If I am real, so also are these.
Work with them; respect their rights; honor their freedom; join with them to build a higher and freer world

than any of us now see." In this organization of life, even here on earth, in this kindliness, this honorable conduct, this social unity, which constitutes our better life, something of the divine will is thus realized. But the problem of its complete realization is an endless one. Nowhere, in all the infinity of countless worlds of moral struggle, can the divine will be fully realized. As I myself seek to assert myself all my life long, but never succeed fully in my task, am always struggling with obstacles, casting aside all that I have won, in order to pursue new triumphs, even so the divine will is restless through all its worlds, and pulses from self to self, from attainment to attainment, in an everlasting search for a complete self-realization. The true God is, therefore, as Fichte holds, existent in our universe as the pulse of its moral order, as the life of lives, the eternal spiritual self-creator, whose work is never done, who rests never, and who is no one individual being anywhere, but who is the live and organic unity of all beings. Even herein, however, thinks Fichte, he finds his highest peace, that in endless toil he shall reassert himself, and shall win the world which is his embodiment.

VI.

The completest popular statement possible of Fichte's system is given in his own words in his book on the "Vocation of Man." This work was first published in 1800, shortly after Fichte left Jena, and was no doubt meant to justify him, in the eyes of the general public, against the charge of atheism. The argument of the work falls into three parts, denominated respectively, "Doubt," "Knowledge," and "Faith." Under the first head Fichte describes the views and problems of his own pre-Kantian period. Under the second head he sets forth the revolution produced in his thought by the influence of Kant. In the third part he explains the conceptions of the moral order and of the infinite will. The style is eloquent, tireless, too full of explanation and of illustrations ; the work as a whole is profound and inspiring. Let us hear yet a word of Fichte's own from this book, in a fine passage where he appeals direct to this infinite itself. " Supreme and living will," he says, " whom no name names, to thee may I lift up my soul, for thou and I are not parted. Thy voice sounds in me, and mine again in thee ; and all my thoughts, if only they be true, are thought in thee. I comprehend thee not, yet in thee I comprehend myself and the world. . . . Best fitted to know thee is childlike and submissive simplicity. . . . I know not what thou art for thyself, . . . and after thousand lives lived through, my spirit will comprehend thee as little as now, in this house of clay. For what I have once won to my comprehension becomes even thereby finite. . . . Nay, I wish not to know of thee what thou art in thyself. I know thy bearings on my life. . . . Thou producest in me the knowledge of my duty. . . . Thou knowest what I think and will ; . . . thou choosest that my free obedience shall be effective to all eternity ; . . . thou doest, for thy will is itself Deed. Thou livest and art, for thou dost know, will, and do, and art ever present to my insight ; but *what* thou art I shall never wholly know through all the eternities."

This, you see, is Fichte's theism. The essence of it is, with all the analogies between the two, something very different from Kant's postulating of a God beyond the world of sense. The fact is that, for Fichte, my own vocation is the central fact of consciousness. But what my vocation is, is a matter for deeper consideration. And, if I duly consider my vocation, I find that there is a measureless strength of restless will about me, which demands an infinity of time in which to work out my vocation, and an infinite business to meet, with its magnitude, the endlessly significant office that I choose for myself. Plainly, then, I, the true self, am not the mere self of the world of sense, the self who eats and talks, and has this name. It might be truer to say that I, the real, the deeper, the relatively impersonal, or, rather, if you like, the genuinely and essentially personal self, need, and so express myself in, the world of social business. All we human selves are thus one true organic self, in so far as we work together. And this organic self we all of us experience just in so far as we do toil together. But not even this larger self of society can fully express the vocation which constitutes me in my true, in my deeper personality. No, my true vocation is endless, is eternal. By it I am linked, not through a mere postulate, but through all my deeper self-consciousness, to the very essence of the divine personality. When I reflect upon this truth, lo! my earthly existence, in its darkness and limitations, vanishes from before my eyes. With you I stand in presence of the divinest of mysteries, the communion of all the spirits in the one self whose free act is the very heart's blood of our spiritual being. Nay, must it not, then, thinks Fichte, must not this be true of us? We are dead, and our life is hid in God. He is the only self. His will is the only will; his self-assertion lives in our every deed and love; his restlessness trembles in every throb of our hearts; his joy thrills in every triumph of our courage.

Well, in this thought, thus eloquently suggested by the restless and unsatisfying Fichte, you have the beginnings of the post-Kantian German idealism. The question, " Who is the true self ? " thus becomes central in thought. Kant had really made it so, when he made all reasonable experience a continual appeal of my momentary to my larger self. Fichte merely universalizes the problem. The world is the poem thus dreamed out by the inner life. Who, then, is the dreamer? That is the question of the romantic period of German speculation. If you remember this as the central problem in all that is to follow in the two succeeding lectures, you will have in hand the thread that will guide us through this labyrinth of German speculation. Do not tremble, I beg you, before the mysterious seeming of the region into which we enter. The thread, firmly held, will soon lead us back again to the study of the natural order, back again to the kingdom of modern science, to the region where the facts are indeed stubborn, but where the deepest problems, as the idealists will meanwhile have taught us, must needs be spiritual. To teach, indeed, just this lesson, the spirituality of the stubborn world of outer fact, was the true mission of these idealists, who so often despised facts.

LECTURE VI.

THE ROMANTIC SCHOOL IN PHILOSOPHY.

FICHTE, as we have seen, had begun by setting aside Kant's things in themselves. What, after all, thinks he, is the use of even mentioning such mysteries as the dead things in themselves, whereof you only declare that they are unknowable? What if they *are* said to exist? Unless we can know them, they are to us as good as nought. But now, for others besides Fichte, Kant's things in themselves used at that time to be objects of no little sport, — sport which took, of course, a rather heavy and German form, but which was very well warranted by the situation. The things in themselves of Kant's theoretical philosophy, the sources of all our experience, but themselves never experienced, were too dim and distant to seem to a further reflection anything but chimeras. An epigram, usually attributed to Schiller, compared them to useless household furniture, once the pride of that very form of metaphysic which Kant's " Critique " had undertaken to slay. For this old metaphysic had pretended to know them. Now that the pretentious doctrine is dead, what is the use of the abandoned furniture?

> " Da die Metaphysik vor Kurzem unbeerbt abging
> Werden die Dinge an sich morgen *sub hasta* verkauft." [1]

But the house of our philosophy thus once emptied of cumbersome furniture, Fichte had found himself able to

---

[1] That is, freely translated : —

" Notice : The late metaphysic is dead without heirs, and to-morrow
All the things in themselves shall under the hammer be sold."

fill it in his own fashion with the rarest treasures of truth. The real thing in itself, according to Fichte, is the active I, the Ego, the subject of self-consciousness. This each of us knows in his own person. To watch the activity of this great source of our being, to sound the depths of its endless nature, is to come to the true knowledge of God and of things which Spinoza already demanded for the wise man, and which Kant sought in vain in the external world. We and our world exist together. Our world is the expression of our character. As a man thinketh, so is he; but with equal truth, according to Fichte, as a man is, so thinks he. He sees himself in all he sees. And this self that a man sees crystallized in all his world of sense, of society, and of philosophy, is simply his own fashion of conduct, his busy world-building temperament. At the outset of life each personal self says, "I must exist, I *will* exist." But no one can exist unless he is ready to act. My life, my existence, is in work. I toil for self-consciousness, and without toil no consciousness. But once more, also, I can only work if I have a task, something foreign to me, a not-self to influence and finally to conquer. Therefore it is, thinks Fichte, that I stand from the beginning in the presence of a world which seems external. My deeper self unconsciously produces this foreign world, and then bids me win my place therein. The material things yonder are therefore just the products of my unconscious activity. Their office it is to give me something to do; they are the outer embodiment of my duty; they are my moral law made manifest to sense. You and I see the same world about us merely because we, as moral beings, need and choose common tasks. And, in a deeper sense, the reason why you and I see the same world is that we are actually fragmentary manifestations of one infinite self, whose ultimate nature we can never fathom, but whose world is through and through a world of common tasks, — a world of a moral order. whereof we are all instruments.

I.

In the present lecture we have to follow the further story of German idealism as exemplified in the views and experiences of a number of persons who, for lack of a better name, are usually classed together as constituting the German Romantic School. The peculiar character of our undertaking in this course bids us attend as much as possible to the relations between philosophy and life. Where, as in the case of the German romantic school, a group of writers tried to embody a philosophy in a literary movement, and to translate their own lives directly into philosophy, such a phenomenon cannot but be of great service to our purpose. And therefore I shall spend time upon matter that will indeed lack the technicality inseparable from even the most general account of Kant's philosophy, but that will still have its bearing on our general task. In fact, my discussion will for the time leave the field of technical philosophy almost altogether, and for the rest of this lecture I shall speak of thoughts that will have their more metaphysical bearings shown only in later lectures.

I mentioned in the last lecture how Fichte's philosophy is an example of that beautiful waywardness which is everywhere characteristic of the Germany of the classical and romantic periods. For the rest, to particularize concerning this waywardness as it shows itself in Fichte, he is, after all, a very arbitrary thinker. His system has vast gaps in it. You in vain seek to get from Fichte, for instance, any precise deduction of *how* the world of our senses, down to its very details, is an embodiment of the moral law. We, in this age, whose world is so full of material facts, whose science has delved so deeply into physical nature, whose industrial art is so multiform in its inventions, whose whole view of man makes him so dependent for his health, his fortune, and his very reason, upon physiological conditions, feel at once the great gulf that divides Fichte's ethical idealism from the world of the natural order. We honor the stern enthusiasm of this idealist, but we find in his system the record of a distinctly individual experience. That he has a hold upon a very genuine truth we ought to recognize; but we cannot read his fearless and often intolerant essays without becoming aware that it has not pleased God to create any perfectly orthodox Fichtean, save Fichte himself. Many of us will no doubt call ourselves, with Fichte, ethical idealists, since we indeed hold that the world is through and through a moral order; but his way of showing *how* it is a moral order will not content us. I, the active being, shall create this sense-world of mine unconsciously, for the sake of having my task, the material of my duty, made manifest to my senses. Very good, but why, then, do I create a world that has a belt of asteroids in it between the orbits of Mars and Jupiter? What portion of my personal and private duty do the comets, or the jelly-fishes, or the volcanoes, or the mosquitoes, make manifest to my senses? What part has the Silurian period in the scheme of my moral order? And of what ethical value to me are the properties of the roots of algebraic equations, or the asymptotes of an hyperbola? In the world of this moral order, you see, there is a great deal that will not easily submit to my ethical interpretation. But if we say, with Fichte, that the real world is after all not the world of just *my* private and individual moral order, but the world of God's infinite ethical activity, so much the more is it incumbent upon us to be industrious in our efforts to comprehend the spirituality of the truths of nature by means of formulæ that are more submissive to facts, more widely sensitive to the varied aspects of reality, less impatient of mystery, than were Fichte's impetuous undertakings. If God's world is through and through moral, it is *also* through and through complicated, profound and physical.

Well, the story of the romantic school is the story of the enlargement of Fichte's onesidedness through the appearance, in the first place, of other not less arbitrary doctrines, which sought to interpret the whole world in terms of our spiritual interests, but which expressed other interests than those that he made central. And, for the rest, this story is also the tale of the gradual fixing of all such waywardness into the directions that have proved so fruitful in the recent decades of modern research. We are too frequently disposed to fancy that the philosophy of the period of Fichte, Schelling, and Hegel is something very remote from the philosophy of our own day. That philosophy, we say, was above all just wayward, fantastic, regardless of the limits of human knowledge, indifferent to science, unwisely imaginative. Nowadays we have changed all that, have abandoned romantic wanderings, have come to respect the facts of science, and to let the mysteries alone. But such a view of our relations to the age of the romantic school is not precisely historical; and wherein it is not precisely historical I want to make plain to you. Deeper than the contrast between that age and ours is, as we shall soon see, the relationship between the two. Our age, as we shall learn, contains merely what was implicit in the very waywardness of that revolutionary period. Their youthful enthusiasms, at first vague, wandering, conflicting, took form at length through growth, and produced, in their maturity, our modern doctrine of evolution, our modern efforts to bring into close relation the natural and the spiritual, our whole modern many-sidedness of interest and experience. The romantic period was the time of bloom and of flowers. Our period, if you will, is, in its matter-of-fact and apparently prosaic realism, the time of the ripened seeds, a time which the warm-hearted usually scorn as a bleak and autumnal period of dry seed-pods and chilly night airs. But the wise love such ages of ripening and of harvest; for they know that a richer growth is erelong to spring from all these barren-seeming seed-kernels of truth. But such metaphors apart, what I want to insist upon is the essential unity of recent philosophy amidst all its transformations. Properly viewed, the lesson of the most fantastic speculations of the later German metaphysic is precisely the lesson which the thought of to-day is trying to express and to utilize. To understand the meaning of contemporary thought, say concerning evolution, apart from a comprehension of the period from Kant to Hegel, is therefore, indeed, like trying to appreciate the mature and prosaic, but successful man, without some reference to the splendid dreams of his youth. We have never wholly broken with the romantic period. We have only grown older, and possibly a little more saddened; but those earlier ideals live still in our breasts, only I should be glad if we were better aware of the fact than sometimes we are.

Our immediate task in the coming lectures is thus twofold. We want first to show how the romantic school, far outdoing the waywardness of Fichte, supplemented his one-sided interpretation of things by other, equally idealistic and much more fantastic, interpretations of reality. And, secondly, we want to show how our own more realistic age expresses, after all, not so much an abandonment of the true spirit of this idealistic period, as a fixation and a maturing of some of its deepest interests.

And now, as to the romantic school itself, what, first of all, is the meaning of the word?

II.

German literature, in its great modern outgrowth, began, as you know, with Lessing's early works, just after the middle of the eighteenth century, and ended with the death of its last prominent representative, Heine, in 1856. But the principal productions of this century of literary activity belong to a very much briefer period.

Lessing was a sort of forerunner of the classical age. Long as was Goethe's literary life, his best years are those between 1770 and Schiller's death in 1805. And to the credit of these thirty-five years may be reckoned much the larger half of the literary and a decidedly large fraction of the philosophical work of the whole great century of German mental life. Not only was this most productive period decidedly brief, but the geographical limitations of the intenser literary interest, at any rate, in view of the fact that Germany had no natural literary capital, are decidedly noteworthy. Two circles, the court at Weimar and the university a few miles distant at Jena, were, between 1775 and 1805, far and away the chief influences in German literature and philosophy. At Weimar, Goethe and Schiller were for a time together. In Jena, Schiller himself taught for some years, while Fichte, Schelling, and Hegel all began their academic activity there. After 1800, indeed, Berlin became a centre second in importance only to Weimar, while the university at Jena sadly declined. But not until still later was intellectual activity of high rank observable all over Germany from Berlin to Heidelberg, and from Munich to the Rhine. However, as the streams spread they lost their swiftness, and erelong, for the intense life of the great years, there was substituted more and more of that fruitful but quiet industry of minute German scholarship, to which we all owe so much.

The years from 1770 to 1805, and the circles of Weimar, of Jena, and, in a less degree, of Berlin, are therefore central in importance in the history of German thought. But now, as must be pointed out, even here there are to be specially mentioned, as of most critical significance, ten years out of these thirty-five. They were the flower of the flower for German life. These were the last ten years of Schiller's career, when his friendship with Goethe was most intimate, and when also, in addition

to the great classical poets, a new generation of ambitious
young men began to appear upon the scene. You must
remember that, in 1800, Goethe was fifty-one and Schiller
forty-one years old; and at such an age men who have
become early famous are certain to find themselves sur-
rounded by circles of eager and often envious youth,
whose hearts have been set on fire by the example of the
elder geniuses, and who themselves are minded to do even
better than their betters. So it was with Goethe and
Schiller. The young generation already swarmed all
about them in Jena and in Weimar. It was a matter of
course, in that day and region, that if you were young,
and were anybody at all, you were a genius. The only
question was what sort of a genius, in your lordly spiritual freedom, you had chosen to be. Four sorts of
geniuses were especially popular, and all four sorts were
as plenty as blackberries. There was the romancer of
genius, who was plotting to outdo Wilhelm Meister.
There was the dramatist of genius, who was disposed to
banish Schiller's plays into oblivion, so soon as he himself
had learned his trade. There was the critic of genius,
who had grasped the meaning and lesson of the literature
of the ages, and who was especially fond of contrasting
the Greek tragedy with Shakespeare, and of laying down
poetical laws for all future time. And finally there was
the philosopher of genius, whose business it was first of all
to transcend Kant, and secondly to transcend everybody
else. Best indeed was your lot in case you chose to
exemplify in your person all four sorts of genius at once,
as, for instance, the young Friedrich Schlegel for a while
delighted to do. Your inner experiences were then simply inimitable. In brief, " Bliss was it in that dawn to
be alive, but to be young was very heaven."

We may smile a little at all this ferment of ambitious
hopes, but we can never be too grateful for what that
brief period accomplished for us. It gave us philosophi-

cal ideas that, fragmentary though they were, will never
be forgotten, and it produced some enduring poetry and
romance, in addition to what Goethe and Schiller wrote,
and of no small merit at that. Now from these circles of
the younger geniuses, one especially stands out in interesting prominence. It is the circle which delighted to
call itself the Romantic School. From its often crude
efforts sprang a movement, the romantic movement in a
wider sense, which lasted far on into our own century.
It is this romantic movement in the wider sense that has
proved the most characteristic outcome of modern German
life as it was before 1848. To the romantic movement
must be credited the whole wealth of German tales and
songs that we love best after the greatest works of Goethe
and of Schiller. The same general movement had its
part in nourishing and in inspiring the music of modern
Germany from Beethoven to Wagner. In brief, without
this movement, German thought and German emotion
would have no such meaning as they have for us to-day.

But in the narrower sense, the name Romantic School
was originally applied only to the little company of young
men, all born somewhere between 1765 and 1775, of
whom the most prominent were the two Schlegels, Augustus and his brother Friedrich, Ludwig Tieck, romancer
and dramatist, Novalis (whose real name was Friedrich
v. Hardenberg), the philosopher Schelling, and the theo-
logian Schleiermacher. The Schlegels were the critics of
the school, and were also men of considerable metaphysical interest. Novalis, who died very young, touches, in
his fragmentary remains, upon all the characteristic interests of the romanticists; he is philosophical, poetical, critical; but he is everywhere and always the born dreamer.
Schelling was intimately associated in a personal sense
with all his fellow romanticists. If his intense metaphysical tastes kept him from attempting very seriously
either dramas or romances, his early speculations bear

everywhere the mark of his friendships; they are the
work of a restless and artistic soul, who loved the universe
with a sort of tender passion, and whose philosophy is,
even in its most technical subtleties, as much the confession of a fiery heart as it is the outcome of a brilliant
imagination and a wonderfully skillful wit. I have preferred rather to discuss the philosophy of the romantic
school under this name than to confine my title or my
survey to Schelling, the representative philosopher of the
little group, because it is here the movement that expresses itself in the man, not the man who masters the
movement. Schelling was himself, always, even as philosopher, a creature of the moment. His moments were
indeed often very great ones and might need each a whole
volume to express itself. But Schelling is not, like Kant,
a systematic and long-plotting thinker; nor yet, like
Fichte, a man who, after many adventures, is completely
overwhelmed and thenceforth possessed by a single idea.
No, Schelling possesses directly the wavering passion of
his romantic friends. His kaleidoscopic philosophy,
which changed form with each new essay that he published, was like their whole scheme of life and of art.
Trust your genius; follow your noble heart; change your
doctrine whenever your heart changes, and change your
heart often. Such is the practical creed of the romanticists. The world, you see, is after all the world of the
inner life. Kant cut us off from things in themselves;
Fichte showed us that it is the I, the self, that makes the
world. Let us accept this lesson. The world is essentially what men of genius make it. Let us be men of
genius, and make what we choose. We shall then be as
gods, knowing good and evil.

Herein, as you see, lies at once the great difference between the romantic school and Fichte. Fichte had said:
The world is the world as self-consciousness builds it;
but the essence of self-consciousness is the moral will, the

will to act dutifully, steadfastly, nobly, divinely; and therefore the world is duty solidified to our senses. The romantic spirit says from the very start: The world is indeed the world as self-consciousness builds it; but the true self is the self that men of genius, poets, constructive artists know; hence the real world is such as to satisfy the demands of the man of genius, the artist. Emotion, heart-experience, longings, divinations of the soul, are the best instruments for the philosopher. Dream out your world. It is after all but a dream of the inner life, this vast universe about us. The noblest dreamer will be the man to understand it the best.

The distinguishing features of this group of young men were then, to sum up, so far, these: they proposed in common to create a new literary movement; and whilst they were rather speculative metaphysicians than true poets, they were nevertheless rather romancers than soberly constructive philosophers. They therefore suggest rather than complete. Their lesson is of more importance to us than are their systems. At the start, that is, in the years about 1795, they were under the influence of Fichte, but his ethical idealism soon grew too stern for them. They interpreted the world rather in terms of sentiment and of bold divination than in terms of the moral law. For the rest, external nature interested them, even in their most idealistic moods, more than it had interested Fichte. Of course, the external world is for them too only mind solidified, only a mass of ideas seen from without. But they are dissatisfied with Fichte's moral law as a full account of the essence of this outer mirage of our senses. Art, they hold, is as suggestive as morality for the speculative thinker. Nature is therefore a work of unconscious art, a form which the great Genius of the world gives to his experiences. God is an artist, a poet, who pours out the wealth of his beautiful life in all the world of sense. Of this God, we too are embodiments;

only we are not blind, as his other works are. We are conscious, and therefore it is that we see in sense-form, in nature, our own ideals crystallized. The more inner experiences we ourselves have, the more feelings, longings, ideas we possess, the more means we shall therefore have of interpreting nature. It is in vain, think these men, that you gather and heap up natural facts, if you have no heart. Only a poet can understand nature, for the true laws of nature are through and through analogous to the laws of the heart. If (so the romanticists would say), if we have ever been in love, then and then only we know why the plants grow towards the sunlight, or the free-swinging needles turn to the pole, or why the planets are loyal to the sun. If we are artistically complete in our inner natures, then we comprehend why the crystals love their regular forms. To understand the difference be-tween organic and inorganic matter, you have again to study first your own inner consciousness, and to examine its various stages, as they lead up from disorganized sen-sations to clear and organic reason. For the forms of matter in the outer world are symbolic, are precisely ana-logous, stage for stage, to these processes of the inner life. In brief, to study nature is to sympathize with nature, to trace the likenesses between the inner life and the mag-nets, the crystals, the solar systems, the living creatures, of the physical world. It is the part of genius to feel such sympathies with things; it is the part of philosophy to record your sympathies. Artists are often unconscious philosophers, but great philosophers, from this romantic point of view, are never more than consummate artists. Feeling is an indispensable guide to reason. We should never know God did we not share his nature in our emo-tions. He is only the many-sided and infinite genius. We appreciate him because we young romanticists are geniuses ourselves.

III.

Such philosophy as this was, of course, capable of innumerable forms. Let us illustrate more in detail from the work of particular men: Best do they comprehend truth, declares in substance the young Friedrich Schlegel, best do they comprehend truth who have experienced the most moods. The truly philosophical attitude towards life and reality is therefore one of a sort of courageous fickleness. Schlegel himself called it the romantic irony, and endeavored to found a system upon it. This is his rather grotesque attempt to revive the Socratic method and doctrine. Socrates had founded his whole life as a conversational teacher, who never preached but always asked questions, upon a sort of ironical confession that he was not wise. " This," he used to affirm, " is my only wisdom, to know that I am an utterly ignorant man." Well, somewhat so, but still with a difference, thinks Schlegel, the romantic genius confesses that marvelous as is his present divination of the truth of things, it is, after all, a quick divination, so to speak, which will away again erelong, and will give place to some other theory, equally creditable to its clever possessor, equally true, but also equally fickle and therefore false. " The deepest truth known to me is that erelong my present truth will change : " such, thinks Schlegel, is true wisdom. For the world, as you see, is the world for the self, for the inner life, for the heart. And the heart is so strong and lively a thing that it will change frequently. " The world exists for me ; and to-morrow I propose to make a new world : " such is Schlegel's early interpretation of the essence of Fichte's view. But alas, Fichte's ethical idealism, with the moral law left out, is too grotesque in its mutilation to become a coherent doctrine. Friedrich Schlegel gave up this fickleness in later years, went over to the Catholic church, and devoted himself otherwise to

Oriental studies, wherein he well earned a high and honorable rank. His stupendous poetical genius somehow never came to flower, much less to fruit, and remained therefore a secret close locked in his bosom. He assures us that he possessed it, and no doubt he knew, for in those days, as you are aware, the inner life knew everything.

Novalis, our second illustration, is a more interesting character. His was a profound and noble nature, but fate forbade him to reach maturity. To his beautiful and baffling fragments the sensitive reader returns ever and anon afresh, perplexed, disappointed, and yet always delighted. Novalis never lived to finish anything. His philosophical fragments are after all, however, the best brief compend you could find of the essence of the romantic philosophy, in all its spiritual depth and in all its waywardness. For Friedrich Schlegel, in his metaphysical capacity, as you have just seen, I cannot feel any serious respect. He was wayward and he was *not* deep. But Novalis every one who knows him truly must thoroughly love. His childlike straightforwardness, his amiable plasticity, not to say innocent fickleness of character, his real strength of ideals withal, his sensitiveness to truth, even his very incapacity (so characteristic of his school) to do more than turn chance jewels of truth over and over and hold them up to the light — all these things fascinate us. He is not exactly a great thinker, but of his kind he is so charming. Novalis, or Friedrich von Hardenberg, was born in 1772, the second child of a large and very affectionate family. His childhood was sickly, and until he was nine years old, while he was the object of the kindest care, his mind seemed in no wise extraordinary. Then suddenly, after an acute affection, his health bettered, and he appeared to wake, " as if from sleep," as his biographer says. He was now a quickwitted, studious and imaginative boy, a great inventor and narrator of fantastic fairy tales, tender-hearted, genial, a lover of mystery. From 1790 to 1793 he attended several universities, was then nearly attracted into a soldier's life by the excitement of the revolutionary period, but was erelong led into the hardly less exciting hopes and struggles of the new literary and philosophical movement, through an acquaintance with Friedrich Schlegel and with Fichte himself, who was then at the height of his earlier professional successes. In Arnstadt, in Thuringia, where Novalis went to learn a more practical profession, in government service, he met and loved a very young girl, Sophie von Kühn. Her eyes suggested to him the famous *blaue Blume*, which in his romance, "Heinrich v. Ofterdingen," he afterwards made the symbol of the romantic ideal itself, the mysterious wonder of magic that his hero sees in dream and thenceforth seeks. Readers of Heine's book on the Romantic School will remember this Blue Flower. Sophie was not yet fourteen when Friedrich v. Hardenberg was betrothed to her. They were never married ; and three years later she died, after a long illness, constantly watched to the end by her devoted lover, to whom by this time the worship of his love had become a religion. Her death was the turning-point of his brief career. His mourning for her took a form worthy of a romantic philosopher. He dated a new sacred era from the day of her death, and kept a diary in accordance with his thus established chronology. The diary, which is unfortunately somewhat brief, is devoted to meditations intended to prepare him to meet her in the life beyond. And as for this meeting, he decides to bring it about in a way which shall express and conform his ardent faith in Fichtean principles. Fichte, namely, has said that our will is the master of the universe. Well, to be sure, suicide, in the ordinary sense, is not the philosopher's way to the other world ; but may not one by sheer force of will so purify himself as to become spirit-

ually fit to live in the higher life, and thereupon, not indeed by any mere fading away, but by one supreme *Entschluss*, one resolution, made for and by his deeper self,
simply transfer himself, in a single glorious moment, to
the realm of free spirits? Friedrich persuades himself
that this is possible, and decides to give himself just one
year to prepare his soul for the final act of faith. He
will not go to her in weakness, nor through the door of
illness or of violence. In the full glow of health, in the
ecstasy of a pure love, he will make himself ready, and
then he will pass over in one instant to Sophie's side.
You may be reminded here of the lover in a song which
Schubert's music has rendered so familiar and tear-com-
pelling. I mean the little romanza called "Rosamunde;"
save, indeed, that *das Ende vom Lied*, in case of Novalis,
is somewhat different. During this time of mourning he
planned his wonderful Hymns to the Night, very brief
and mystical rhapsodies in Ossianic prose, interspersed
with verse. His diary, however, soon complains that it is
a little hard to be quite healthy and still to remain wholly
unworldly. One has so many temptations to forgetful-
ness of lofty ideals. One is, after all, but twenty-six;
one loves discussion, friends, philosophy; one plainly has
even a good appetite; and alas! *this* world is so fair,
this age in which one lives is so inspiring! Nay, one is
not yet quite worthy of the world of free spirits, nor of
Sophie. So the days go by; and when the year of the
preparation for the great *Entschluss* is done, not Novalis,
but Sophie has passed — this time not merely into the
world of spirits, but even into the realm of the pure Platonic Ideas themselves. Novalis still worships her glorified essence, but as for his noble Fichtean self, it continues
to surround itself with the sense-facts of the terrestrial
order, and now perceives its duty made manifest to its
eyes in the person of one Julie Charpentier; for to her
Novalis is by this time betrothed after the fashion of the
visible world.

I assure you that I do not repeat this very well-known and even rather famous story here either in any spirit of scoffing, or for the sake of a digression. I can far better suggest the inner sense and the essence of this whole romantic idealism, in all its beauty and its waywardness, by such a tale as this of the love of Novalis than by a much longer homily. Here, you see, is the romantic interpretation of Fichte's doctrine. You see the spirituality, the tenderness, the perfectly honest sentiment of it all; and you also see the essential fickleness, the inevitable arbitrariness, of an idealism that has not yet found any truly objective standards. In a less gentle soul than Novalis this arbitrariness would become cynical. Such noble sentiments have, you see, their even ghastly dangers. Is it feeling that guides you in your interpretation of the world? Are your ideas simply plastic? Do you make your world solely through your own mind? Alas! as Hegel afterwards said, feeling is the mere soil of the forest of life; and from the same soil the noblest tree or the hatefulest weed may spring. Suppose the resolution of Novalis had been by chance not only less fickle, but also less noble; might not his subjective idealism have justified equally well a fierce rebellion against all that humanity justly holds dearest, instead of a mere indifference to what common sense calls obvious? In the later history of the romantic movement the fickleness of wayward idealism did indeed work itself out to the extreme of its painful dialectics, and if you want to know the results, Amadeus Hoffmann's tales of horror, or our own Edgar Poe's gloom, will tell you enough of the story to let you see one of its endings. The Nihilism and the Pessimism of more recent days will give you another outcome of that arbitrary idealism which knows no law. And the lightning of Heine's scorn will show you yet further glimpses of the same lurid world in a fashion that will leave you undecided whether to laugh or to weep.

And yet, all this must not discourage true idealism, and does not discourage it.   What I mean is just what I have already repeatedly pointed out: That as arbitrariness in our interpretation of things is the curse of immature idealism, mature idealism will certainly find out how to return to an order as fixed and as supreme as was Spinoza's substance.

IV.

Schelling, finally, the prince of the romanticists, is an interesting example of a growth of spirit whereby a great thinker was indeed led from Fichte back to Spinoza. Only to the end, while Schelling became the firmest of believers in a supreme and substantial order of things, which impresses itself upon our reason from above, and which we are all forced to obey and to accept, his method remains wayward, imaginative, and, with all his genius, immature.   His Spinozism is such as Spinoza could never have pretended to comprehend ; his idealism early became such as to excite first the suspicion, and finally the violent condemnation of Fichte ; and his whole work is such as only a great genius could have begun, and only a romanticist could have left in the chaos wherein, after a very long life, he finally left it.

Even our brief glance at Schelling's character must take into account the remarkable woman whose counsel and affection made a great part of his most productive years possible.   I doubt whether Schelling, even as philosopher, can be well understood apart from Caroline. She herself was the idol of the whole romantic circle. Her maiden name was Michaelis ; she was twelve years the senior of Schelling.   When Schelling first met her, himself then early in his twenties, she was already married a second time, and to Augustus Schlegel.   Her daughter by her first marriage, Auguste Böhmer, died in 1800, aged seventeen.   As Schlegel, during the closing years of the century, lived in Berlin, and Caroline in Jena, their marriage, although friendly, was not precisely the first interest of either member of the wedded pair. The romantic school, with philosophical consistency, believed in applying their principle of waywardness to marriage also, and approved of elective affinities; and accordingly, absolutely without an unkind word, the marriage of the Schlegels was ultimately dissolved by means of a decree of the obliging Duke at Weimar, and Schelling married Caroline in 1803, after several years of friendship and correspondence. Schelling and Caroline remained on the best terms with Augustus Schlegel until Caroline's death in 1809.

Caroline's letters to Schelling, between 1799 and 1803, are certainly much more than interesting. The wonderful charm of this *herrliche Frau* is once for all an irresistible sensation as you read her intimate self-confessions. She is a marvelous compound of the pathetic, the roguish, the wise, the gay, the deeply sad, and the singularly thoughtful. She has seen, felt, suffered, struggled; and she has conquered. She loves power intensely, is a very good hater, and yet, she has also a childlike and playful gentleness that fairly disarms you. When she is deep in trouble, a light or perhaps a bitter laugh is never far away, wherewith she wins again her composure. She is, in her romantic fashion, as high-minded as she is absolutely fearless, — a sort of Penthesilea, only vastly more tender, and with the heart of a bereaved mother, as well as with the temper of a trained warrior. To her husband Schlegel, in Berlin, she writes meanwhile as straightforwardly and lengthily as you please; only to him she has more to say about literary matters. Philosophy she thought of often, and with just the easy swift insight into subtleties which must have enlightened the young Schelling more than once. Only system-making she regarded with indifference. Hence it was, in part, for her admiration that Schelling must have thought out his subtle, but unsystematic fragments of philosophic creation. They frequently discussed such matters together. Once in conversation, as she writes in 1801 to her husband Schlegel, she and Schelling fell to inventing an appropriate motto in verse for Fichte (the "Sun-clear," as she calls him, after the title of one of his essays, the "Sun clear Exposition of the Essence of Recent Philosophy"), whose solemn and devout appeals to his readers to be honorable men for once, and agree with him, were then growing rather wearisome. They hit upon Hamlet's —

> "Doubt that the stars are fire,
> Doubt that the planets move."

That had an idealistic sound, and seemed to begin a fitting motto for Fichte. They took these lines, of course, in the current German translation, and then Caroline's wit wrought out this as the whole motto : —

> "Zweifle an der Sonne Klarheit,
> Zweifle an der Sterne Licht,
> Leser, nur an meiner Wahrheit
> Und an deiner Dummheit nicht."

I venture, with hesitation, to imitate Caroline in English, but at a long distance, thus : —

> "Doubt that the stars are fire,
> Doubt *all* the things of sense,
> But, reader, doubt not I am wise,
> And thy poor wits are dense."

But Caroline had not only the power to criticise Fichte in this fashion ; she knew also how to write an excellent contrast between Fichte's genius and Schelling's, as follows, in a letter to her young friend himself, who did not marry her until two years later : " It is growing more and more needful now that you produce something eternal, without making so much ado about it. Surely, my dearest friend, you are n't asking *my* opinion about Fichte's power, although you seem to come near it. I have always felt that, with all his incomparable skill in thinking, he has his limits; only, as I have thought, the reason is that he fails of the divine instinct that you possess; and if you have broken through his charmed circle, then I feel as if it was not so much because you are a philosopher, but because you have poetry in you, while he has none. I suppose I use the word 'philosopher' wrongly. If I do, laugh at me. But it is poetical inspiration that has led you to production, as it is simply sharpness of seeing that has led him to consciousness. He has the bright light, but you have the glowing fire; his gift can illuminate, only yours can produce. There, have n't I put that right neatly? As if one should see an immeasurable landscape through a keyhole."

You will now indeed be anxious to learn something of how Schelling had broken through Fichte's charmed circle. Well, his most technical thought will be mentioned next time, when I compare him with Hegel, in whose company he worked for a brief, but important period. For this most significant deed of Schelling's can only be understood in his relations with Hegel. Of Schelling, the poetical friend of Caroline, and the brilliant young creator of the so-called *Naturphilosophie*, I have yet to say a word to-day. The most fruitful problem of Fichte's system was, of course, the problem of the relation of my conscious self to my deeper self, of my private thought to the universal and divine thought, whereof I am the transient expression. Now, it early occurred to Schelling that Fichte had not made all that he could of this relation between the humanly conscious and the divine Ego. My external world, says Fichte, is the product of my own unconscious act; and this act, unconscious to me, is ultimately an expression of God's eternal activity itself. Well, then, is not the true idealism this? The outer world of sense has no existence except as a manifestation of the spirit. And there is but one spirit, after all; but this spirit extends far beyond my little self. He is the

spirit of nature. You cannot comprehend him if you
look only within. In you he is indeed the same that he
is yonder in nature, only in nature his will is writ large,
in dead and in living forces, in gravitation, in magnetism,
in electricity, in vitality. Study these things, not as if
they were ever utterly dead things in themselves, but as
being other expressions of precisely the same life that is
writ fine in your consciousness. Thus, by reversing, as
it were, the Fichtean telescope, you see the human subject indeed as the central being of the human world, only
in himself he now appears less imposing. Turning, however, the right end of the glass towards nature, you see
therein the life of humanity typified, symbolized, crystallized, as it were; for spirit comes to itself in man only
because it has first expressed itself in nature, and is now
striving in us to become conscious of its own work. Thus
viewed, man is indeed simply an evolution from nature;
and Schelling indeed holds that a theory of the evolution
of consciousness is needed as a complement to Fichte's
theory. "In autumn, 1798, I entered upon my lectures
at Jena," says Schelling himself, in one of his autobio-
graphical statements, "full of the thought that the way
from nature to spirit must be as possible as the reverse
way, upon which Fichte had entered." Here, then, is
Schelling's epoch-making idea, and you will see hereafter
that it is the idea which modern philosophic thought will
henceforth be seeking to define. To complete the undertaking of idealism, you need a theory of the facts of
nature, so interpreted as to be in harmony with the view
that only ideas are the realities, and yet so adapted to
experience as to free your idealism from the arbitrariness
of the inner life of mere finite selves. Can we, then,
prove that the very spirit whose life our own consciousness expresses is already present outside and beyond us,
weaving the web of the external world, giving it substance, and yet preserving its ideality and its harmony

with our inner life? If we can, then, our doctrine will
become what is technically called objective idealism.
The outer world is, then, God's thought shown to our
eyes; the inner world is God's thought become conscious
of itself. This doctrine was the centre of Schelling's
Naturphilosophie. Unfortunately he was no man to
prove such a theory. He could only suggest, develop
imaginatively, and in later essays treat with a marvelous,
but fragmentary technical skill. As poet, he indeed
broke through Fichte's charmed circle; but as poet, he
never stated the essence of his *Naturphilosophie* more
clearly or more boldly than he did in a poetic fragment
written under the eyes of Caroline, and meant largely for
her approval. Of this production he himself never published more than a brief portion; in later years it has
been printed from his papers. I refer to his whimsically
so-called *Epikurisch Glaubensbekenntniss Heinz Wider-
porstens,* "Epicurean Confession of Faith of Hans Bris-
tleback."

In this thoroughly wayward sketch in verse, Schelling
assumes a grotesque name and character, in order to give
himself greater freedom to express the heart of his
Naturphilosophie in the boldest and most pantheistic
terms. The meter is borrowed from the well-known revival, in Goethe's "Faust," of the old *Knittelvers,* or
free rhyme of early German poetry. Schelling's hero,
in whose character he speaks, is supposed to be trying to
play the irreligious materialist, whom the priests have
been driving to despair, and who at last rebels. Nature
is his religion, he says. He loves good cheer and fair
faces, and he hates superstition. Is n't this world of the
senses after all the genuine thing? Heinz grows fairly
rollicking in his materialistic and epicurean speeches.
Suddenly, without warning, he assumes another tone,
From beneath the mask of the epicurean, the voice of the
romantic mystic sounds. *Why,* then, is this world of

the senses the world for the truly wise man? Because it
is but the embodiment of one eternal and divine spirit.
Then follows a Schellingian sketch of a process of evolution which, proceeding through the animals, culminates
in us. The world of nature is thus full of the struggle
of the great spirit to win his own higher life. The end
and crown of this whole process is man. In him, blind
nature gets a voice; in him the spirit comes to himself.
And all the universe is one glorious life, in whose contemplation the mystic soul rejoices.

Let me give you, as a close, my own hasty rendering of
some of Schelling's curious lines, with a certain effort to
preserve the unequal metre and even the very unequal
worth of the original. The *Knittelvers*, at its noblest, is
only a sort of glorified doggerel, and is never easy to manage in translation; but I must suggest to you a little of
the romantic intoxication of this sort of pantheism, so
characteristic of one great tendency in German thought.

After his introductory denunciation of priestcraft, asceticism, and superstition, the gay Heinz is made to run on
thus, speaking of course in character : —

> " Therefore religion I forsake,
> All superstitious ties I break,
> No church will I visit to hear them preach,
> I have done with all that the parsons teach.
> And yet there is one faith that masters my will,
> Glows in my verse, and inspires me still,
> Daily my heart with delight doth thrill,
> Eternally showing
> New form ; till I knowing,
> This faith so clear,
> This light so near,
> This poem undying,
> Must witness its truth beyond denying ;
> So that I can nothing hold nor conceive
> Save what it counsels me to believe ;
> Nor aught as certain or right maintain,
> Save what it reveals to my eyes so plain.

.   .   .   .

Thus, then, in my heart am I freed from fear,
Sound in body and soul stand here,
And may, instead of posture and prayer,
Instead of losing my way in the air,
Here on the earth, in her blue eyes see
The deepest depths that exist for me.
Nay, and why should I in the world suffer dread,
I, who know the world from the foot to the head ?
'T is a tame creature, is it not ?
When has it ever its bonds forgot ?
Yields to the yoke of all-ruling law,
Crouches at my feet in awe.

.   .   .   .   .   .

Within it a giant spirit doth dream,
But his soul is a frozen lava stream ;[1]
From his narrow house he cannot away,
Nor his iron chains escape for a day.
Yet often he flutters his wings in his sleep,
Mightily stirs in his dungeon-keep,
Travails in dead and in living things
To know his will and to free his wings.[2]

.   .   .   .   .   .

His power, that fills the veins with ore,
And renews in the spring the buds once more,
Labors unceasing in darkness and night,
In all nature's nooks and crannies for light,
Fears no pang in its fierce desire
To live and to conquer and win its way higher.
Organs and members it fashions anew,
Lengthens or shortens, makes many or few,
And wrestles and writhes in its search till it find
The form that is worthiest of its mind.
Struggling thus on life intent,
Against a cruel environment,
It triumphs at last, in one narrow space,
And comes to itself in a dwarfish race,
That, fair of form, of stature erect,
Stands on earth as the giant's elect,

[1] " Steckt zwar ein Riesengeist darinnen,
      Ist aber versteinert mit seinen Sinnen."
[2] " In todten und lebendigen Dingen
      Thut nach Bewusstseyn mächtig ringen."

Is called in our speech the son of man,
Outcome and crown of the spirit's plan.
From iron slumber, from dreaming set free,
Now marvels the spirit who he may be.
Looks on himself with wondering gaze,
Measures his limbs in dim amaze,
Longs in terror once more to be hid
In nature's slumber, of sentience rid.
But nay, his freedom is won for aye,
No more in nature's peace may he lie ;
In the vast dark world that is all his own,
He wanders his life's narrow path alone.
Yes, he even fears, in his visions dim,
That the giant himself may be wroth with him,
And like Saturn of old, in godlike scorn,
Devour his children scarcely born ;
Know not that he himself is the Sprite
That longingly toiled in the world's dark night ;
Peoples the void with the ghosts of his fear,
Yet could he say, the Giant's peer : —
I am the God who nature's bosom fills,
I am the life that in her heart's blood thrills.[1]
From the first quiver of her mystic power,
Until of life there came that primal hour,
When force new form and body power assumed,
And flowers the beauty showed that lay entombed, —
Yes, now, wherever light, as dawn begins,
A new created world from chaos wins, —
And in the thousand eyes that, from the sky,
Show night and day the heavenly mystery, —
Onwards, to where, in thought's eternal truth
Nature's deep self rewords itself in truth, —
There stirs one might, one pulse-beat all sufficing,
All power retaining, aye, — and sacrificing."

[1] " Ich bin der Gott der sie im Busen trägt,
Der Geist der sich in allem bewegt."

LECTURE VII.

HEGEL.

CONCERNING Hegel, who forms our special topic in this lecture, it is extraordinarily difficult to get or to give any general impressions that will not be seriously misleading. I undertake my task, therefore, with a very strong impression of its importance and its difficulty. The outcome of what we have thus far discussed in these lectures is briefly this: Modern thought began with an endeavor to find a true and rational doctrine about the real outer universe, and to state this doctrine in clear and even mathematical form. The rediscovery of the importance of the inner life led, however, during the eighteenth century, to a skeptical scrutiny of the powers of the human reason itself, and the magnificent systems of earlier thinkers appeared, when examined in the light of such scrutiny, dogmatic and uncertain. Thought endeavored, nevertheless, to re-win its great assurances in a new form. Truth, said Idealism, is essentially an affair of the inner life. The world of truth is the world as it would appear to a complete and fully self-conscious self. The outer universe is only a show world. Its reality is only practical. It is essentially a mirage of the inner life. The real universe is the universe of the spirit. Our deepest relation is not to the natural order at all, but to the one true self, namely, God's own life.

Such, as we found, was the position reached alike by Fichte and the romanticists. But in their further thought they diverged. For Fichte, the centre of the universe, as his idealism conceives it, is the moral law. The infinite self longs for rational and active self-possession. Hence it differentiates itself into numerous forms, as the vine grows out into its own branches. These branchings of the one great vine of the spirit form our finite and essentially incomplete selves.

But for the romanticists, as we found, the centre of the world is not so much the moral law as the interest which every spirit has in a certain divine wealth of emotion and of experience. The world is the world of ideas; things exist because spirits experience them; and spirits experience because, as parts of the divinely complete life, it is their interest to be as manifold and wealthy in their self-realization as possible.

I.

Before we now pass directly to Hegel it is necessary to say yet a word of the more technical speculations of Schelling, of whom, in his character as romanticist, we heard something in the last lecture. Schelling's development, as you already know, was very rapid; his writings were early voluminous. He was a man of mark and a professor at Jena by the time he had reached his twenty-third year. His systematic views during his youthful period seemed to his readers to alter with a dangerously magical ease and swiftness of transformation. He himself meanwhile denied, during the years up to 1809, that there was so far any significant change from the essential doctrines of his early works. He had added, he said, to what he at first taught. More truth had come to him; not a contradiction of former insight. But readers found it suspicious that each new book of Schelling's seemed to supersede all his previous efforts. In 1797, he published his "Ideas towards a Philosophy of Nature." During the next three years appeared his "System of Transcendental Idealism" and his "First Sketch of a System of the Philosophy of Nature." These two latter works were

to be a first statement, so their author declared, of the
two great and seemingly opposed aspects of philosophy.
The outer world was to be shown as after all the manifestation of spirit; the inner world of the self was to be
exhibited as inevitably expressing itself in relation to an
outer, a natural order. The fundamental thought of the
whole doctrine was in substance this: Fichte had declared
that it is the self-assertion of the absolute self, the free
choice of the true Ego, that is the source of all truth.
When I as knower recognize a truth, that is because I as
doer have first made this truth. This view Schelling also
accepts. But now, as one sees, a conscious self is at once
the doer of its present act, and the contemplator of the
results of its past acts. As I look out on the world of
nature, I see crystallized before me the expression of what
my true and absolute self has already been doing. The
same activity that this present consciousness exemplifies
for me has been there from eternity, and nature is the
concrete embodiment to the onlooker of the results of his
own eternal deeds. Nature then is not merely, as Fichte
had said, my duty made manifest to my senses; it is also
my timelessly past spiritual life, — not of course my finite
or individual and private past life, but the life of my
deeper self, of the one and absolute divine spirit. This
autobiography of spirit, manifest to our eyes, is then the
natural order. On the other hand, the inner life as such
is capable of a philosophical treatment; for this is, as it
were, not the record of the spirit's past, but the fullness
of the spirit's conscious actuality. We have thus a twofold philosophy to be wrought out, and Schelling in 1799
and 1800 publishes his two sketches as though in topic,
if not in execution, they completely covered the ground.
But in 1801 appeared a new treatise, called by Schelling
simply " Exposition of my System of Philosophy," and
here the doctrine seems to take a new form, which readers
could only with great difficulty reconcile with what had

gone before. As during the winter of 1800–1801 Schelling expounded this system in lectures, before publishing
the treatise, hearers asserted, as Schelling himself says,
that he had wholly changed his doctrine. On the contrary, says Schelling, in his preface to the new book, this
is the system that I have held all along, and have merely
been keeping to myself so far, because it was too deep a
thing to expound before the time came. The system in
question was called by its author the *Identitäts-System*.
Deeper than both nature and spirit is now something that
Schelling calls by various mysterious names, the "Absolute," the "Identity," the "Indifference of Subject and
Object," the "Unity of Nature and Spirit." It is a curious metaphysical product, this new principle. It resembles Spinoza's Substance; it pretends to be loftier than
Fichte's Divine Self. It is something even dimmer and
vaguer than the Giant Spirit of Nature, of whom Schelling's verses told us in the last lecture. Hegel, a few
years later, rudely called this Schellingian "Identity,"
this "Absolute," in whose indescribable nature all truth
was to be somehow hidden, "the infinite night in which
all cows are black." Its nature was the kind of thing
you think of when you think of nothing in particular.
Yet this nature of the absolute was to be the deepest of
all truth, deeper than the self, deeper than outer nature,
deeper than anything ever before known in philosophy.

I am not minded to trouble you here with a fuller account of Schelling's *Identitäts-System*, whose exposition,
as it chances, is really very deep and suggestive, with
all its vagueness. The thought that there must after all
be some sort of synthesis possible of Kant and Spinoza, was indeed an important thought. And historically
the *Identitäts-System* has a very significant relation to
Hegel's thinking. For Schelling wrote this new treatise
under the direct influence of his intercourse with Hegel,
who had then appeared at Jena, where Schelling was

teaching. What Hegel maintained, and early impressed upon Schelling, was that an end must be put, if possible, to the romantic vagueness of all this dreaming about the relations of the individual and the absolute self, and about the conceptions of the finite and the infinite in general. What philosophy needed was a more exact analysis and proof of the assertion that the individual consciousness and the outer order, the finite self and the infinite self, the world of the moment and the world of the universal, are linked in close spiritual ties. Philosophy must become a system, or else remain naught. This thought Schelling found present in Hegel's mind, and so Schelling for the moment forced his poetical speculations to assume a Spinozistic garb. Largely ineffective, however, Schelling's best efforts remained thenceforth. We shall do well, therefore, to turn at once to the more successful systematizer of the idealistic scheme, namely, Hegel.

II.

With the idealists of the romantic school Hegel had, indeed, many things in common, but he differed from them profoundly in temperament. They had reached their absolute self by various mystical or otherwise too facile methods, which we need not further expound. Hegel hated easy roads in philosophy, and abhorred mysticism. He therefore, at first, in his private studies, had clung closely to Kant's original mode of dealing with the problems of the new philosophy until he had found his own fashion of reflection. To understand what this fashion was we must turn to the man himself.

Yet, as I now come to speak of Hegel's temperament, I must at once point out that of all first-class thinkers he is, indeed, personally, one of the least imposing in character and life.[1] Kant was a man whose intellectual might

[1] The expert reader will easily detect the influence of Haym and of Dr. Hutchinson Stirling's estimates of Hegel's personality in what

and heroic moral elevation stood in a contrast to the weakness of his bodily presence, which, after all, had something of the sublime about it. Spinoza's lonely, almost princely, haughtiness of intellect joins with his religious mysticism to give his form grace, and his very isolation nobility. But Hegel is in no wise either graceful or heroic in bearing. His dignity is solely the dignity of his work. Apart from his achievement, and his temperament as making it possible, there is extremely little of mark in the man. The wonder of him lies in his professional, not in his human aspect. He was a keen-witted Suabian, a born scholar, a successful teacher, self-possessed, decidedly crafty, merciless to his enemies, quarrelsome on occasion after the rather crude fashion of the German scholar, sedate and methodical in the rest of his official life; a rather sharp disciplinarian when he had to deal with young people or with subordinates; a trifle servile when he had to deal with official or with social superiors. From his biographer, Rosenkranz, we learn of him in many private capacities; he interests us in hardly any of them. He was no patriot, like Fichte; no romantic dreamer, like Novalis; no poetic seer of splendid metaphysical visions, like Schelling. His career is absolutely devoid of romance. We even have one or two of his love-letters. They are awkward and dreary beyond measure. His inner life either had no crises, or concealed them obstinately. In his dealings with his friends, as, for instance, with Schelling, he was wily and masterful, using men for his advantage so long as he needed them, and turning upon them without scruple when they could no longer serve his ends. His life, in its official character, was indeed blameless. He was a faithful servant of his

follows. The reader who desires a more eulogistic account will find such, and from a high authority too, in Professor Edward Caird's discussion of Hegel in the volume on that thinker in Blackwood's *Philosophical Classics.*

various successive masters, and unquestionably he reaped
his worldly reward.   His students flattered him, and
therefore he treated them well; but towards opponents
he showed scant courtesy.   To the end he remains a self-
seeking, determined, laborious, critical, unaffectionate
man, faithful to his office and to his household, loyal to
his employers, cruel to his foes.   In controversy he spared
not persons any more than doctrines.   His style in his published books is not without its deep ingenuity and its marvelous accuracy, but otherwise is notoriously one of the
most barbarous, technical, and obscure in the whole history of philosophy.   If his lectures are more easy-flowing
and genial, they are in the end, and as a whole, hardly
more comprehensible.   He does little to attract his reader,
and everything to make the road long and painful to the
student.   All this is not awkwardness; it is deliberate
choice.   He is proud of his barbarism.   And yet — here
is the miracle — this unattractive and unheroic person
is one of the most noteworthy of all the chosen instruments through which, in our times, the spirit has spoken.
It is not ours to comprehend this wind that bloweth
where it listeth.   We have only to hear the sound thereof.

Georg Wilhelm Friedrich Hegel was born in August,
1770, at Stuttgart.   His family was of a representative
Suabian type; his own early surroundings were favorable
to an industrious, but highly pedantic sort of learning.
At the gymnasium in Stuttgart, which he attended from
his seventh year, he was an extraordinarily, but, on the
whole, a very healthily studious boy.   From his fifteenth
until well on in his seventeenth year, we find him keeping
a diary, from which Rosenkranz has published large fragments.   It is in strong contrast to the sentimental diaries
that the characteristic youth of genius, in those days,
might be expected to keep.   In fact there was no promise
of genius, so far, in the young Hegel.   His diary runs on
much after this fashion: "Tuesday, June 28 (1785), I

observed to-day what different impressions the same thing can make on different people. . . . I was eating cherries with excellent appetite, and having a very good time, . . . when somebody else, older than I, to be sure, looked on with indifference, and said that in youth one thinks that one cannot possibly pass a cherry-woman without having one's mouth water for the cherries (as we Suabians say), whereas, in more advanced years one can let a whole spring pass without feeling an equal longing for such things. Whereupon I thought out the following principle, a rather painful one for me, but still a very profound one, namely, that in youth . . . one can't eat as much as one wants, while in age one does n't want to eat as much as one can."

Such was the philosopher Hegel, at fifteen years of age. His diary never records a genuine event. Nothing seems to have happened to this young devourer of cherries and learning, except such marvels as that one day at church he learned the date of the Augsburg Confession; or that, during a walk, one of his teachers told him how every good thing has its bad side; and again, during another walk, tried to explain to him why July and August are hotter than June. Of such matters the diary is full, — never does one learn of an inner experience of any significance. Aspirations are banished. The boy is pedantic enough, not to say out and out a prig; but this at any rate appears as the distinctive feature of his temperament: he is thoroughly objective. He wants to know life as it is in itself, not as it is for him; he desires the true principles of things, not his private and sentimental interpretation of them. Meanwhile, he is at once well instructed in religious faith, and given so far to the then popular and rather shallow rationalism which loved to make very easy work of the mysterious of every kind and grade. He devotes some space to the explanation of ghost stories. He even records, meanwhile, occasional

bits of dry Suabian humor, such as later, in a much
improved form, found place in his academic lectures, and
were so characteristic of his style, not to say of his system.
The boyish form of this interest in the grotesque may be
thus exemplified: January 3, 1787. — Total eclipse of
the moon; instruments prepared at the gymnasium, where
some gathered to see, but the sky was too cloudy.   So
the rector "told us the following: As a boy he himself
had once gone out with other boys, at night, on the pre-
tence of star-gazing.   In reality they had only wandered
about.   The police found them, and were going to take
them into custody; but the gymnasium boys said,
'We're out star-gazing.'   'Nay,' responded the police,
'but you boys ought to go to bed at night, and do your
star-gazing in the day-time!'"   I note this trifle because,
after all, it means more than one would think.   Here and
at other places in the young Hegel's record appear
glimpses of a certain deep delight in the paradoxical, a
delight which, at times merely dry and humorous, at
times keenly intellectual, would mean little in another
temperament, but which is, after all, the determining tendency of Hegel's mind.

In fact, if one has eyes to see it, the Hegelian temperament, although not at all the Hegelian depth, is, even as
early as this, almost completely indicated.   Of the later
philosophical genius, as I have said, there is so far no
promise; but the general attitude which this genius was
to render so significant is already taken by the boy Hegel.
The traits present are, for the first an enormous intellectual acquisitiveness, which finds every sort of learning,
but above all every sort of literary and humane learning,
extremely interesting.   The pedantry which oppresses the
German gymnasiast of that day is relieved, meanwhile, by
this dry and sarcastic Suabian humor, which notes the
oddities and stupidities of human nature with a keen
appreciation.   The humor involves a love of the gro-

tesque, of the paradoxical, of the eternally self-contradictory in human life. The mature Hegel was to discover
the deeper meaning of such paradoxes; for the time being
he simply notes them. For the rest, there is one trait
already manifest which is also of no small significance in
Hegel's life-work. This is a certain observant sensitiveness to all manner of conscious processes in other people,
joined with a singularly cool and impersonal aptitude for
criticising these processes. Here, indeed, is a feature
about Hegel which later, in his mature wisdom, assumed a
very prominent place, and which always makes him, even
apart from his style, very hard for some people to comprehend. We are used in literature to the man who sym-
pathizes personally with the passions of his fellows, and
who thus knows their hearts because of the warmth of his
own heart. We know also something of the tragically
cynical type of man, who, like Swift, not because he is
insensitive, but because he is embittered, sees, or chooses
to describe in passion, only its follies. We have all about
us, moreover, the simply unfeeling, to whom passion is an
impenetrable mystery, because they are naturally blind to
its depth and value. But Hegel's type is one of the rarest, the one, namely, whose representative man will, so to
speak, tell you in a few preternaturally accurate, though
perhaps highly technical words, all that ever you did, who
will seem to sound your heart very much as a skillful
specialist in nervous diseases would sound the mysterious
and secret depths of a morbid patient's consciousness; but
who, all the while, is apparently himself as free from deep
personal experiences of an emotional type as the physician
is free from his patient's morbid and nervous web-spinning. Hegel has this quasi-professional type of sensitiveness about his whole bearing towards life. Nobody
keener or more delicately alive and watchful than he to
comprehend, but also nobody more merciless to dissect,
the wisest and the tenderest passions of the heart. And

yet, it is not all mercilessness in his case. When he has
analyzed, he does not condemn after the cynic's fashion.
After the dissection comes reconstruction. He singles
out what he takes to be the truly humane in passion, he
describes the artistic or the religious interests of man, he
pictures the more admirable forms of self-consciousness;
and now, indeed, his speech may assume at moments a
religious, even a mystical tone. He praises, he depicts
approvingly, he admires the absolute worth of these
things. You feel that at last you have found his heart
also in a glow. But no; this, too, is an illusion. A word
erelong undeceives you as to his personal attitude. He
is only engaged in his trade as shrewd professor; he is
only telling you the true and objective value of things;
he is not making any serious expression of his own piety
or wealth of concern. He is still the critic. His admiration was the approval of the onlooker. In his private
person he remains what he was before, untouched by the
glow of heart of the very seraphs themselves.

In the year 1788, Hegel entered the university of his
province at Tübingen. Here he studied until 1793, being
somewhat interrupted in his academic work by ill health.
His principal study was theology. A certificate given him
at the conclusion of his course declared that he was a man
of some gifts and industry, but that he had paid no serious attention to philosophy. His reading, however, had
been very varied. In addition to theology, he had shown
a great fondness for the Greek tragedians. His most intimate student friends of note had been the young poet
Hölderlin and Schelling himself. Nobody had yet de-
tected any element of greatness in Hegel. The friendship with Schelling was now continued in the form of a
correspondence, which lasted while Hegel, as an obscure
family tutor, passed the years from 1793 to 1796 in Switzerland, and then, in a similar capacity, worked in Frank-
fort-on-the-Main until the end of 1800, when, through

Schelling's assistance, he found an opportunity to enter upon an academic career at the University of Jena. During all these years Hegel matured slowly, and printed nothing. The letters to Schelling are throughout written in a flattering and receptive tone. Philosophy becomes more prominent in Hegel's thought and correspondence as time goes on. To Schelling he appeals as to the elect leader of the newest evolution in thought. From the Kantian philosophy, he says, a great, new creative movement is to grow, and the central idea of this new movement will be the doctrine of the absolute and infinite self, whose constructive processes shall explain the fundamental laws of the world. This notion Hegel expresses already in 1795, when he is but twenty-five and Schelling is but twenty years old. But as to the development of the new system in his own mind he gives little or no hint until 1800, just before joining Schelling at Jena. Then, as he confesses to his friend, "the ideal of my youth has had to take a reflective form, and has become a system; and I now am asking how I can return to life and set about influencing men." He had actually, by this time, written an outline of his future doctrine, which was already in all its essentials fully defined. On his first appearance at Jena, however, he was content to appear as a co-worker and even as in part an expositor of Schelling, and probably he purposely exaggerated the agreement between his friend and himself so long as he found Schelling's reputation and assistance a valuable introduction to the learned world, in which the youthful romanticist was already a great figure, while Hegel himself was so far unknown. In 1801, Hegel began his lectures as *Privat-Docent* at the university. In 1803, Schelling left the university, and Hegel, now dependent upon himself, erelong made no secret of the fact that he had his own relatively independent philosophy, and that he could find as yet nothing definite and final about his friend's writings.

His own first great book, the "Phänomenologie des Geistes," finished at about the time of the battle of Jena, and published early in 1807, completed his separation from Schelling, whose romantic vagueness he unmercifully ridiculed, without naming Schelling himself, in the long preface with which the book opened. In a letter to Schelling accompanying a copy of the "Phänomenologie," Hegel indeed explained that his ridicule must be understood as directed against the misuse which the former's followers were making of the romantic method in philosophy; but the language of the preface was unmistakable. Schelling replied curtly, and the correspondence ended. After the period of confusion which followed the battle of Jena, Hegel, who had been temporarily forced to abandon the scholastic life, found a place as gymnasium director at Nürnberg, where he married in 1811. In 1816, he was called to a professorship of philosophy at Heidelberg. He had already published his "Logic." In 1818, he was called to Berlin, and here rapidly rose to the highest academic success. He had a great following, came into especial court favor, reached an almost despotic position in the world of German philosophic thought, and died of cholera, at the very height of his fame, in November, 1831.

If we now undertake in a few words to characterize Hegel's doctrine, we must first of all cut loose almost entirely from that traditional description of his system which has been repeated in the text-books until almost everybody has forgotten what it means, and has therefore come to accept it as true. We must furthermore limit our attention to Hegel's theory of the nature of self-consciousness, laying aside all detailed study of the rest of his elaborate system. And finally we must be rude to our thinker, as he was to every one else; we must take what we regard as his "secret" (to borrow Dr. Stirling's word) out of the peculiar language in which Hegel chose to express it, and out of the systematic tomb where he would have insisted upon burying it. So treated, Hegel's doctrine will appear as an analysis of the fundamental paradox of our consciousness.

In terms of this paradox he will try to define, first the relation of the finite and the infinite self, then the relation between mind and reality.

III.

The world of our daily life, Kant had said, has good order and connection in it, not because the absolute order of external things in themselves is known to us, but (as I have reworded Kant) because we are sane, because our understanding, then, has its own coherence, and must see its experience in the light of this coherence. Idealism has already drawn the obvious conclusion from all this. If this be so, if it is our understanding that actually creates the order of nature for us, then the problem, " How shall I comprehend my world ? " becomes no more or less than the problem, " How shall I understand myself ? " We have already suggested into what romantic extravagances the effort to know exhaustively the inner life had by this time led. Some profound, but still vague relation was felt to exist between my own self and an infinite self. To this vague relation, which Fichte conceived in purely ethical terms, and which the romanticists tried to grasp in numerous arbitrary and fantastic ways, philosophy was accustomed to appeal. My real self is deeper than my conscious self, and this real self is boundless, far spreading, romantic, divine. Only poets and other geniuses can dream of it justly. But nobody can tell squarely and simply, *mit dürren Worten*, just what he means by it. Now Hegel, as a maliciously cool-headed and sternly unromantic Suabian, did indeed himself believe in the infinite self, but he regarded all this vagueness of the romanticists with contempt, and even with a certain rude mirth. He appreciated all its enthusiasm in his own external way, of course ; he could even talk after that dreamy fashion himself, and once, not to the credit of his wisdom, perhaps not quite to the credit of his honesty, he did so, in an early essay, published, as we must note, while he was still Schelling's academic nursling at Jena. But he despised vagueness, and when the time came he said so. Yet still for him the great question of philosophy lay just where the romanticists had found it, yes, just where Kant himself had left it. My conscious and present self is n't the whole of me. I am constantly appealing to my own past, to my own future self, and to my deeper self, also, as it now is. Whatever I affirm, or doubt, or deny, I am always searching my own mind for proof, for support, for guidance. Such searching constitutes in one sense all my active mental life. All philosophy then turns, as Kant had shown, upon understanding who and what I am, and who my deeper self is. Hegel recognizes this ; but he will not dream about it. He undertakes an analysis, therefore, which we must here re-word in our own fashion, and for the most part with our own illustrations.[1]

Examine yourself at any instant: " I," you say, " know just now this that is now present to me, this feeling, this sound, this thought. Of past and future, of remote things, of other people, I can conjecture this or that, but just now and here I know whatever *is* here and now for me." Yes, indeed, but *what* is here and now for me? See, *even as I try to tell, the here and now have flown.* I know this note of music that sounds, this wave that breaks on the beach. No, not so, even as I try to tell what I now know, the note has sounded and ceased, the wave is broken and another wave curves onward to its fall. I cannot say, " I know." I must always say, " I just

[1] What immediately follows is of course suggested by the opening of the argument in the *Phänomenologie*.

knew." But what was it I just knew? Is it already past and gone? Then how can I now be knowing it at all? One sees this endless paradox of consciousness, this eternal flight of myself from myself. After all, do I really ever know any one abiding or even momentarily finished and clearly present thing? No, indeed. I am eternally changing my mind. All that I know, then, is not any present moment, but the moment that is just past, and the change from that moment to this. My momentary self, then, has knowledge in so far as it knows, recognizes, accepts, another self, the self of the moment just past. And again, my momentary self is known to the self of the next succeeding moment, and so on in eternal and fatal flight. All this is an old paradox. The poets make a great deal of it. You can illustrate endlessly its various forms and shadings. That I don't know my present mind, but can only review my past mind is the reason, for instance, why I never precisely know that I am happy at the very instant when I am happy. After a merry evening I can think it all over, and say, " Yes, I *have been* happy. It all *was* good." Only then, mark you, the happiness is over. But still, you may say, I know that the memory of my past happiness is itself a happy thing. No, not even this do I now directly know. If I reflect on my memory of past joy, I see once more, but in a second reflective memory, that my previous memory of joy was itself joyous. But, as you see, I get each new joy as my own in knowledge only when it has fled in being. It is my memory, that but a moment since or a while since I was joyful, that constitutes my knowledge of my joy. This is a somewhat sad paradox. I *feel* my best joys just when I *know* them least, namely, in my least reflective moments. To know that I enjoy is to reflect, and to reflect is to remember a joy past. But surely, then, one may say, when I suffer I can know that I am miserable. Yes, but once more only reflectively.

Each pang is past when I come to know that it was just now mine. "That is over," I say, "what next?" And it is this horror of the "what next?" this looking for my sorrow elsewhere than in the present, namely, in the dreaded and on-coming fatal future, that constitutes the deepest pang of loneliness, of defeat, of shame, or of bereavement. My illustrations are still my own, not Hegel's.[1]

The result of all this possibly too elaborate web-spinning of ours is not far to seek. We wanted to know who any one of us at any moment is; and the answer to the question is: Each one of us is what some other moment of his life reflectively finds him to be. It is a mysterious and puzzling fact, but it is true. No one of us knows what he now is; he can only know what he *was*. Each one of us, however, is *now* only what hereafter he *shall* find himself to be. This is the deepest paradox of the inner life. We get self-possession, self-apprehension, self-knowledge, only through endlessly fleeing from ourselves, and then turning back to look at what we were.[2] But this paradox relates not merely to moments. It relates to all life. Youth does not know its own deep mind. Mature life or old age reflectively discovers a part of what youth meant, and sorrows now that the meaning is known only when the game is ended. All feeling, all character, all thought, all life, exists for us only in so far as it can be reflected upon, viewed from without, seen at

---

[1] Hegel's illustrations are more commonly from more highly reflective stages of consciousness. Yet the key to the "movement" of the whole "Logic" lies in just this fashion of viewing the facts of life and thought.

[2] Cf. *Logik*, vol. i. (*Werke*, vol. iii.), pp. 99, 114, 152, 283, and 285, for a series of expressions, in highly abstract form, of the nature of this process as manifested in case of various logical constructions and categories. The commonest technical name for the process is *Negation der Negation* (l. c. p. 99), explained further on page 114. On page 152 the verb *zurückkehren* is employed to name the same act; so p. 288.

a distance, acknowledged by another than itself, reworded in terms of fresh experience. Stand still where you are, stand alone, isolate your life, and forthwith you are nothing. Enter into relations, exist for the reflective thought of yourself, or of other people, criticise yourself and be criticised, observe yourself and be observed, exist, and at the same time look upon yourself and be looked upon from without, and then indeed you are somebody, — a self with a consistency and a vitality, a being with a genuine life.[1]

In short, then, take me moment by moment, or take me in the whole of my life, and this comes out as the paradox of my existence, namely, I know myself only in so far as I am known or may be known by another than my present or momentary self. Leave me alone to the self-consciousness of this moment, and I shrivel up into a mere atom, an unknowable feeling, a nothing. My existence is in a sort of conscious publicity of my inner life.[2]

Let me draw at once an analogy between this fact of the inner life and the well-known fact of social life to which I just made reference. This analogy evidently struck Hegel with a great deal of force, as he often refers to it. We are all aware, if we have ever tried it, how empty and ghostly is a life lived for a long while in absolute solitude. Free me from my fellows, let me alone to work out the salvation of my own glorious self, and surely (so I may fancy) I shall now for the first time show who I am. No, not so; on the contrary I merely show in such a case who I am not. I am no longer friend, brother, companion, co-worker, servant, citizen, father, son ; I exist for nobody ; and erelong, perhaps to my surprise, generally to my horror, I discover that I *am* nobody. The one thing means the other. In the dungeon of my

---

[1] The *Kampf des Anerkennens* of the *Phänomenologie.*

[2] Brief general descriptions of the process and paradox of self-consciousness as such are : *Phänomenologie,* p. 125 ; *Logik, Werke,* vol. iii. p. 66, and vol. v. p. 13 ; *Encyklopädie, Werke,* vol. vi. pp. 47, 91.

isolated self-consciousness I rot away unheeded and terror-stricken.   Idiocy is before me, and my true self is far be-hind, in those bright and bitter days when I worked and suffered with my fellows.   My freedom from others is my doom, the most insufferable form of bondage.   Could I speak to a living soul!   If any one knew of me, looked at me, thought of me, yes, hated me even, how blessed would be the deliverance!   Now note the analogy here between the inner life in each of us and the social life that each of us leads.   Within myself the rule holds that I live consciously only in so far as I am known and re-flected upon by my subsequent life.   Beyond what is called my private self, however, a similar rule holds.   I exist in a vital and humane sense only in relation to my friends, my social business, my family, my fellow-workers, my world of other selves.   This is the rule of mental life. We are accustomed to speak of consciousness as if it were wholly an inner affair, which each one has at each mo-ment solely in and by himself.   But, after all, what con-sciousness do we then refer to?   What is love but the consciousness that somebody is there who either loves me (and then I rejoice) or does not (and then I am gloomy or jealous)?   What is self-respect but a conscious appeal to others to respect my right or my worth?   And if you talk of one's secret heart, what is it but just that inner brooding in one's own conscious life which so much the more illustrates, as we say, the very impossibility of know-ing myself except by looking back on my past self.   See, then, it makes no difference how you look at me, you find the same thing.   *All consciousness is an appeal to other consciousness.*[1]   That is the essence of it.   The inner life is, as Hegel would love to express it, *ebensosehr* an outer life.   Spirituality is just intercourse, communion of spir-its.   This is the essential publicity of consciousness, whereby all the secrets of our hearts are known.[2]

[1] *Phänomenologie*, p. 135.
[2] The word "publicity" is a very fair representative of *Allgemein-*

Here, then, Hegel has come upon the track of a process in consciousness whereby my private self and that deeper self of the romanticists may be somewhat more definitely connected. Let us state this process a little abstractedly. A conscious being is to think, or to feel, or to do something. Very well, then, he must surely think or do this, one would say, in some one moment. So be it; but as a conscious being he is also to know that he thinks or does this. To this end, however, he must exist in more than one moment. He must first act, and then live to know that he has acted. The self that acts is one, the self that knows of the act is another. Here, then, there are at least two moments, already two selves. We see at once how the same process could be indefinitely repeated. In order to know myself at all, I must thus live out an indefinitely numerous series of acts and moments. I must become many selves and live in their union and coherence. But still more. Suppose that what our self-conscious being has to do is to prove a proposition in geometry. As he proves, he appeals to somebody, his other self, so to speak, to observe that his proof is sound. Or again, suppose that what he does is to love, to hate, to beseech, to pity, to appeal for pity, to feel proud, to despise, to exhort, to feel charitable, to long for sympathy, to converse, to do, in short, any of the social acts that make up, when taken all together, the whole of our innermost self-consciousness. All these acts, we see, involve at least the appeal to many selves, to society, to other spirits. We have no life alone. There is no merely inner self. There is the world of selves. We live in our coherence with other people, in our relationships. To sum it all up : From first to last the law of conscious existence is this paradox-

heit as applied to self-consciousness by Hegel in the highly important § 436 of the *Encyklopädie, Werke,* vol. vii. 2, p. 283. Here already appears the nature of the true Universal of Hegel's system. Organic interrelationship of individuals is the condition even of their relatively independent selfhood.

ical but real self-differentiation, whereby I, the so-called
inner self, am through and through one of many selves,
so that my inner self is already an outer, a revealed, an
expressed self.   The only mind then is the world of many
related minds.   It is of the essence of consciousness to
find its inner reality by losing itself in outer, but spiritual
relationships.   Who am I then at this moment?   I am
just this knot of relationships to other moments and to
other people.   Do I converse busily and with absorption?
Then I am but just now this centre of the total consciousness of all those who are absorbed in this conversation.
And so always it is of the essence of spirit to differentiate itself into many spirits, and to live in their relationships, to be one by virtue solely of their coherence.

The foregoing illustrations of Hegel's paradox, some of
which in these latter paragraphs have been his own, have
not begun to suggest how manifold are, according to him,
its manifestations.   So paradoxical and so true does it
seem to him, however, that he looks for further analogies
of the same process in other regions of our conscious life.
What we have found is that if I am to be I, "as I think
I be," I must be more than merely I.   I become myself
by forsaking my isolation and by entering into community.   My self-possession is always and everywhere self-
surrender to my relationships.   But now is not this paradox of the spirit applicable still further in life ?   Does n't
a similar law hold of all that we do in yet a deeper sense?
If you want to win any end, not merely the end of knowing yourself, but say the end of becoming holy, is n't it
true that, curiously enough, you in vain strive to become
holy if you merely strive for holiness?   Just pure holiness, what would it be ?   To have never a worldly thought,
to be peaceful, calm, untroubled, absolutely pure in spirit,
without one blot or blemish, — that would indeed be noble,
would it ?   But consider, if one were thus quite unworldly
just because one had never an unworldly thought, what

would that be but simple impassivity, innocence, pure
emptiness? An innocent little cherub, that, just born
into a pure light, had never even heard that there was a
world at all, he would indeed in this sense be unworldly.
But is such holiness the triumphant holiness of those that
really excel in strength? Of course if I had never even
heard of the world, I should not be a lover of the world.
But that would be because of my ignorance. And all
sorts of things can be alike ignorant, — cherubs, young
tigers, infant Napoleons, or Judases. Yes, the very
demons of the pit might have begun by being ignorant of
the universe. If so, they would have been so far holy.
But, after all, is such holiness worth much as holiness? It
is indeed worth a good deal as innocence, just to be
looked at. A young tiger or a baby Napoleon fast asleep,
or a new created demon that had not yet grown beyond
the cherub stage — we should all like to look at such
pretty creatures. But such holiness is no ideal for us
moral agents. Here we are with the world in our hands,
beset already with temptation and with all the pangs of
our finitude. For us holiness means, not the abolition
of worldliness, not innocence, not turning away from the
world, but the victory that overcometh the world, the
struggle, the courage, the vigor, the endurance, the hot
fight with sin, the facing of the demon, the power to have
him there in us and to hold him by the throat, the living
and ghastly presence of the enemy, and the triumphant
wrestling with him and keeping him forever a panting,
furious, immortal thrall and bondman. That is all the
holiness we can hope for. Yes, this is the only true holiness. Such triumph alone does the supreme spirit know,
who is tempted in all points like as we are, yet without
sin. Holiness, you see, exists by virtue of its opposite.
Holiness is a consciousness of sin with a consciousness of
the victory over sin. Only the tempted are holy, and
they only when they win against temptation.

All this I set down here, not merely because I believe it, although indeed I do, but because Hegel's cool diagnosis of life loves to mark just such symptoms as this. "Die Tugend," says he in one passage of his "Logic," "die Tugend ist der höchste, vollendete Kampf." [1] Holiness, then, is the very height of the struggle with evil. It is a paradox, all this. And it is the same paradox of consciousness over again. You want the consciousness of virtue; you win it, not by innocence, but through its own very opposite, namely, through meeting the enemy, enduring and overcoming. Consciousness here once more, as before, differentiates itself into various, into contrasted, forms and lives in their relationships, their conflicts, their contradictions, and in the triumph over these. As the warrior rejoices in the foeman worthy of his steel, and rejoices in him just because he wants to overcome and to slay him; as courage exists by the triumph over terror, and as there is no courage in a world where there is nothing terrible; as strength consists in the mastery of obstacles; as even love is proved only through suffering, grows deep only when sorrow was with it, becomes often the tenderer because it is wounded by misunderstanding; so, in short, everywhere in conscious life, consciousness is a union, an organization, of conflicting aims, purposes, thoughts, stirrings. And just this, according to Hegel, is the very perfection of consciousness. There is nothing simple in it, nothing *unmittelbar*, nothing there till you win it, nothing consciously known or possessed till you prove it by conflict with its opposite, till you develop its inner contradictions and triumph over them. This is the fatal law of life. This is the pulse of the spiritual world.

For see, once more: our illustrations have run from highest to lowest in life. Everywhere, from the most

[1] *Werke*, vol. iv., p. 63. The spirit of the foregoing exposition of the essence of holiness is found expressed in many places, especially in the *Religionsphilosophie*.

trivial games, where the players are always risking loss
in order to enjoy triumph, from the lowest crudities of
savage existence, where the warriors prove their heroism
by lacerating their own flesh, up to the highest conflicts
and triumphs of the spirit, the law holds good. Spirituality lives by self-differentiation into mutually opposing
forces, and by victory in and over these oppositions.
This law it is that Hegel singles out and makes the basis
of his system. This is the logic of passion which he so
skillfully diagnoses, and so untiringly and even mercilessly
applies to all life. He gives his law various very technical names. He calls it the law of the universal *Negativität* of self-conscious life ; and *Negativität* means simply
this principle of self-differentiation, by which, in order
to possess any form of life, virtue, or courage, or wisdom,
or self-consciousness, you play, as it were, the game of
consciousness, set over against yourself your opponent, —
the wicked impulse that your goodness holds by the
throat, the cowardice that your courage conquers, the
problem that your wisdom solves, — and then live by
winning your game against this opponent. Having found
this law, Hegel undertakes, by a sort of exhaustive induction, to apply it to the explanation of every conscious relation, and to construct, in terms of this principle of the
self-differentiation of spirit, the whole mass of our rational
relations to one another, to the world, and to God. His
principle is, in another form, this : that the deeper self
which the romanticists sought is to be found and defined
only by spiritual struggle, toil, conflict ; by setting over
against our private selves the world of our tasks, of our
relationships, and by developing, defining, and mastering
these tasks and relationships until we shall find, through
the very stress and vastness and necessity and spirituality
of the conflict, that we are in God's own infinite world of
spiritual warfare and of absolute restless self-consciousness. The more of a self I am, the more contradictions

there are in my nature and the completer my conquest over these contradictions. The absolute self with which I am seeking to raise my soul, and which erelong I find to be a genuine self, yes, the only self, exists by the very might of its control over all these contradictions, whose infinite variety furnishes the very heart and content of its life.

Hegel, as we see, makes his Absolute, the Lord, most decidedly a man of war. Consciousness is paradoxical, restless, struggling. Weak souls get weary of the fight, and give up trying to get wisdom, skill, virtue, because all these are won only in presence of the enemy. But the absolute self is simply the absolutely strong spirit who bears the contradictions of life, and wins the eternal victory.

Yet one may say, if this is Hegel's principle, it amounts simply to showing us how conflict and active mastery continually enlarge our finite selves. Does it enable us to prove that anywhere in the world there is this absolute self which embraces and wins *all* the conflicts? Hegel tells us how the individual self is related to the deeper self, how the inner life finds itself through its own realization in the contradictions of the outer life. But does he anywhere show that God exists?

To show this is precisely his object. I am not here judging how well he succeeds. The deepest presupposition, he thinks, of all this paradoxical conscious life of ours is the existence of the absolute self, which exists, to be sure, not apart from the world, but in this whole organized human warfare of ours. Only Hegel is not at all content to state this presupposition mystically. He desires to use his secret, — his formula for the very essence of consciousness, his fundamental law of rationality, to unlock problem after problem until he reaches the idea of the absolute self. Of the systematic fashion in which he attacked this task in his "Logic," in his "Encyclopædia," and in his various courses of lectures, I can give no very satisfying notion. To my mind, however, he did his work

best of all in his deepest and most difficult book, the " Phenomenology of Spirit." Here he seeks to show how, in
case you start just with yourself alone, and ask who you
are and what you know, you are led on, step by step,
through a process of active self-enlargement that cannot
stop short of the recognition of the Absolute Spirit himself
as the very heart and soul of your own life. This process
consists everywhere in a repetition of the fundamental
paradox of consciousness : In order to realize what I am I
must, as I find, become more than I am or than I know
myself to be. I must enlarge myself, conceive myself as
in external relationships, go beyond my private self, presuppose the social life, enter into conflict, and, winning
the conflict, come nearer to realizing my unity with my
deeper self. But the real understanding of this process
only comes, according to Hegel, when you observe that
in trying thus to enlarge yourself for the very purpose
of self-comprehension you repeat ideally the evolution of
human civilization in your own person. This process of
self-enlargement is the process which is writ large in the
history of mankind. The " Phenomenology " is thus a sort
of freely told philosophy of history. It begins with the
Spirit on a crude and sensual stage ; it follows his paradoxes, his social enlargement, his perplexities, his rebel-
lions, his skepticism, all his wanderings, until he learns,
through toils and anguish and courage, such as represent
the whole travail of humanity, that he is, after all, in his
very essence the absolute and divine spirit himself, who is
present already on the savage stage in the very brutalities
of master and slave ; who comes to a higher life in the
family ; who seeks freedom again and again in romantic
sentimentality or in stoical independence ; who learns,
however, always afresh that in such freedom there is no
truth ; who returns, therefore, willingly to the bondage of
good citizenship and of social morality ; and who, finally,
in the religious consciousness, comes to an appreciation of

the lesson that he has learned through this whole self-enlarging process of civilization, — the lesson, namely, that all consciousness is a manifestation of the one law of spiritual life, and so, finally, of the one Eternal Spirit. The Absolute of Hegel's "Phenomenology" is no absolute on parade, so to speak, — no God that hides himself behind clouds and darkness, nor yet a Supreme Being who keeps himself carefully clean and untroubled in the recesses of an inaccessible infinity. No, Hegel's Absolute is, I repeat, a man of war. The dust and the blood of ages of humanity's spiritual life are upon him; he comes before us pierced and wounded, but triumphant, — the God who has conquered contradictions, and who is simply the total spiritual consciousness that expresses, embraces, unifies, and enjoys the whole wealth of our human loyalty, endurance, and passion.

IV.

But still you may ask, Does all this yet give us the conditions of a genuine philosophical system? Does it explain outer nature and physical causation? does it explain perception and knowledge? does it tell us the true nature of things? In brief, as you see, all this doctrine of Hegel's seems essentially ethical, practical, an exposition of spirituality, — not a theoretical account of nature. Well, Hegel believes himself to be in possession of devices whereby he can make his essentially practical categories of a deep theoretical significance. Consider, namely, those problems of the external world, of space and time, of cause and effect, of law and phenomena, of substance and show, of nature and of man, which previous philosophy has been treating. How do these problems arise, and what is their universal character? Aren't they always problems about some paradoxical opposition that seems to exist in the nature of reality, and that baffles the human understanding just because both the opposed terms, — say, for instance, knowing subject and known object ; or true reality and seeming reality ; or things in themselves and phenomena ; or finite and infinite, — just because, I say, both these opposed terms in each pair seem to be separate, sundered, mutually irreducible, inaccessible each to other, while yet *both* the opposed things nevertheless continually force themselves upon us, and demand of us an explanation. Philosophy is a nest of such problems. They vex men endlessly ; they gave Kant his troublesome pairs of contradictory assertions about space and time ; they gave Fichte the puzzle about self and not-self ; they gave Hume the problem about facts and laws, about experience that could never find necessity, and necessity that continually pretended to inflict itself upon experience. A logical system of such problems and of their solutions would be a complete theoretical philosophy, an account of the absolute, such as Schelling had dreamed of. Well, in our formula of the universal *Negativität* of the spiritual life, have n't we found precisely the formula that would both state and solve such puzzles as these ? Spirit it is that makes the world. That, you remember, is, since Kant, presupposition of this whole age. The spirit, then, because of its *Negativität*, will everywhere differentiate itself, and therefore, throughout all its universe, from the atoms to the archangels, will create seeming oppositions, will burden itself with a wealth of magnificent paradoxes ; and will do this equally and obstinately in the world of theory, as well as in the world of practice. If, therefore, we have the key to the process whereby the spirit wins unity in the midst of its own oppositions, then the puzzle of Hume and the problems of Kant, the conflicts of empirical research and of *a priori* speculation, — yes, all the puzzles that the history of philosophy shows us, can be stated and solved ; for they will all be cases of the same fundamental paradox of self-consciousness. The talisman of the logic of passion will cause to open the doors of the richest treasure-houses of theoretical research. It is with this notion in mind that Hegel, influenced by Schelling's example, even as Schelling had been by his own, sets out to expound, not merely the history of the human or even of the absolute spirit, but the nature and the solution of every philosophical problem concerning the absolute as the history of philosophy has presented such problems to us, whether in the fundamental questions of logic, or in the inquiries of the philosophy of nature. I need not say that this stupendous undertaking was but indifferently executed.

It is just this undertaking, however, that gives the Hegelian system its peculiarly technical and abstruse formulation.

The system itself is set forth in three divisions: the "Logic," the "Philosophy of Nature," and the "Philosophy of Spirit." The "logic" is an exposition, in the most orderly and technical form, of the fundamental thoughts, or "categories," which are to be found exemplified in all the facts of this our world of the self. As for these categories themselves, the history of philosophy furnishes them to Hegel. They are such fundamental ideas as those of Being and Something; of Many and One; of Quality, and Quantity, and Relation; of Essence and Phenomenon; of Form and Matter; of Inner and Outer; of Law and Substance; of Subject and Object; of Thought and the Absolute. You can't get on in philosophy without using such conceptions. They are the coinage of the spiritual realm. If you try to set forth truth you must employ them; if you want to understand truth, you must comprehend them. And now comprehension of these categories is n't to be got by merely defining them in abstract fashion, as Euclid defines a circle, or Spinoza his substance. Definition, simple, positive, hard and fast as it is, never tells the whole truth about a conception ; for every fundamental conception is really to be comprehended only by viewing it in the true and yet paradoxical relation to its own opposite, that, as a product of self-consciousness, this conception must have. We have already seen how virtue and vice, present consciousness and past consciousness, individual consciousness and social consciousness, inner life and outer life, are indefinable, incomprehensible, save by virtue of an insight into just that wondrous union of conflicting tendencies whereby each of the opposed conceptions gets its meaning for us. It is the flow, the change, the conflict of thought that the philosopher has to follow. In vain, for instance, do you try to define substance after Spinoza's fashion as a *merely* eternal, fixed, congealed, and immobile truth. The substance of *this* world, of this universe of the self, must be a truth that lives in the very stream and struggle of finite and seeming existence. The true substance of the world is n't hidden, but revealed by the passionate change and ebb and flow of the phenomena ; for the true substance is the self, the subject ; and he preserves himself by living, for he is the living God. As such, philosophy has to show him. Therefore you can't abstractly define his nature, apart from finite things and relations. You must concretely realize, even in your notion of substance, the organic unity in endless differentiation of which his universe is the embodiment. Even so it is with other categories. You comprehend them by virtue of their paradoxes. The " Logic " undertakes to be an exhaustive analysis of such paradoxes of the fundamental conceptions.

The method of the " Logic," then, is what Hegel calls the dialectical method. It is the method of what we have called the logic of passion, applied to the most theoretical and seemingly least passionate of human conceptions. Take any notion you please. Hegel at once sees in that notion the traces of the self-conscious strife whereof it is the offspring, or, if you like, the crystallized embodiment. Is it quantity that you are talking about? Then you at once observe that there are two ways of looking at quantity. One, to which we get used in elementary arithmetic, regards quantity as what we call "discrete," that is, as made up of separate units. The other way, to which we get used in geometry and physics, regards quantity as continuous. The one fashion counts by units, the other measures by standards. Now in the ordinary view, this difference in the methods of viewing quantity is thought to correspond to an existent difference in the sorts of quantity that the world contains. There are discrete quantities and there are continuous quantities. But, for Hegel, the notion of quantity, as it truly exists, is a notion that is the product of self-consciousness, and not a mere datum of sense. As such a product of self-conscious-ness, true quantity proves to be, so he holds, at once *both* continuous and discrete, just as virtue proved to be *der höchste Kampf*, and so to involve *both* good and evil. Quantity is a mathematical thing, a seemingly cold and lifeless category, while virtue is obviously a creature of holy passion. But none the less is the paradox of self-consciousness present in the idea of quantity, just as in practical life. Discrete quantity consists of the separate and unjointed units. Continuous quantity resists and even defies description in terms of disjunct ultimate units, as, for instance, a line refuses to be made up of points. Yet, as Hegel thinks himself able to show, each of these sorts of quantity is such that when you try to think out its nature, it *afflicts* itself, so to speak, with the characteristics of the other, takes them on,[1] as Hegel loves

---

[1] A suggestion of Hegel's technical use of *an ihm* or *an ihr*. Cf. *Logik, Werke*, vol. iii. p. 221 : " In gewöhnlichen Vorstellungen von continuirlicher und discreter Grösse wird es übersehen, dass jede dieser Grössen beide Momente, sowohl die Continuität als die Discre-tion, *an ihr* hat."

to say, in all such cases, just as the good will takes on to itself the evil impulse, in order that it may live by overcoming evil. How Hegel tries to show this in case of quantity I have indeed no time to expound.

By means of this dialectical method Hegel seeks, moreover, not only to show each logical category as in itself an organism of opposed and yet mutually complementary elements, but also to show all these fundamental notions as forming one system, wherein the most apparently diverse and disparate ideas are actually interrelated as parts of the one highest and inclusive category, the divine *Idee*, or total thought of the world, whose full realization is the absolute self in its spiritual wholeness. The absolute *Idee* is the notion of the complete self, regarded just as a logical category. As true self, it appears to us later, in the philosophy of spirit. In the " Logic " it is only this *thought of the total nature of things as being in the Hegelian sense self-determined.* This thought contains all the subordinate categories as organic parts of the total, and as parts whose organic relation is precisely such as this dialectical, this paradoxical nature of self-consciousness demands. What the citizens are to the state, such are the individual categories of thought to the absolute logical *Idee*. In themselves they are endlessly conflicting, and they are yet complementary to one another. In their totality they form but one highest category, the category of the organic unity of all thoughts in one. The *Idee* is also called by Hegel an *objectiver Begriff*,[1] the real law of laws, the thought of the organic relation of all things and thoughts in one universal order.

One may thus obviously define the " Logic " as an effort to set forth all fundamental human thoughts as forming an organic system. This character of the " Logic " the most superficial reader at once sees. What is missed by the superficial reader of the " Logic " is an insight into what,

[1] *Logik, Werke*, vol. v. p. 230.

according to Hegel's notion, constitutes organic unity, into
what is the linkage that ties together the members of *his*
kind of organism.   This linkage, as we now sufficiently
know, is the one that the nature of self-consciousness alone
explains.   It is therefore through and through a linkage
of opposing and complementary members by reason of
their very oppositions.   This is the source of the perplexing analysis of contradictions whereof the " Logic " is full.
The success or failure of the " Logic " therefore depends
upon its author's right to read the processes of the higher
practical spirituality into the products of purely theoretical thinking.   Here is the *crux* of the system.

One fundamental consideration remains to be mentioned
as characterizing the "Logic."   Old-fashioned logic called
itself formal.   It discussed categories and methods of
thinking, but it did not undertake to construct concrete
truths.   Its forms of thought were never real things for
it.   But Hegel's categories are, of course, more than this.
The laws of thought are n't mere abstractions; they are
the soul of things.   In the " Logic" one is constructing
the very essence of the world-self.

Now, Hegel further expressed this aspect of the matter
by his remarkable doctrine about the relation between
Begriffe, or universal notions, and the individual facts
that fall under these notions.   There is an old controversy as to whether individual things, or the classes that
correspond to general conceptions, are the deepest realities in the world.   Science, as Aristotle said, is always of
the general.   When we think, we always think of classes,
of categories, in brief, of universals.   But, on the other
hand, the facts of the world always appear to our senses
to be individual.   Man, as a mere abstraction, does n't
exist; individual men do.   Here is one of the most perplexing of the paradoxes of common sense: The business
of science, namely, is with truth, and truth is always universal, is known to us as the notion of things, the law of

things, the essence of the world. And, on the other hand, science is to be true of facts, and yet the facts, at all events as sense views them, are n't universal, but are just the individual facts. This opposition between the form of science, which is universality, and the matter of science, which is individual fact, gave much trouble already to Aristotle,[1] into whose system it introduced a fundamental contradiction. Hegel was well aware of this contradiction between the Aristotelian ideal of universal knowledge, and the actual theory of the relation of universals and individuals, as Aristotle developed it in his logical treatises.[2] But this ancient paradox, which had given ground for one of the most famous of the controversies of the philosophy of the Middle Ages, was precisely the kind of paradox that Hegel's method was peculiarly apt to characterize and deal with. In attempting his own solution of the problem he was therefore fully conscious of its difficulty, and of the relative novelty of his own theory. " The universal in its true and inclusive sense is a thought," he once says,[3] " that it has cost thousands of years to bring to human consciousness, and that received its full recognition only through the aid of Christianity. The Greeks knew neither God nor man in their true universality." The philosophical formulation of this thought is of course, according to Hegel, later than its concrete realization ; yes, this philosophical formulation of the "inclusive" nature of the universal is to be one of Hegel's own peculiar contributions to philosophical theory.

[1] See Zeller's *Philosophie der Griechen*, part II. section 2, pp. 304–313 (3d edition), for a technical exposition of the resulting difficulties.

[2] Compare the two accounts of Aristotle's method of work in Hegel's own lectures on the History of Philosophy, *Werke*, vol. xiv. pp. 279, 282. See, also, the characterization of Aristotle's Logic, *id.*, p. 368.

[3] In a lecture, as reported by one of his students, *Werke*, vol. vi. p. 321.

The true universal, namely, or as Hegel calls it, the *Be-griff*, whose highest expression is to be the absolute *Idee*, is the organic union of the universal truth and the individual facts, an union determined by the principle that every truth is a truth constructed by the thought of the world-self, and that as such it will exemplify just that multiplicity of individual facts in the all-embracing and so universal unity of self-consciousness, which we have now so fully exemplified. The true universal of the whole world is, then, the divine *Idee*, or " all-enfolding " nature of things, the true genus *within* which all individual facts fall. This universal is no abstraction at all, but a perfectly *concrete* whole, since the facts are, one and all, not mere examples of it, but are embraced in it, are brought forth by it as its moments, and exist only in relation to one another and to it. It is the vine; they, the individuals, are the branches. It is in nature the self. They are the individual thoughts, aspects, finite expressions, embodiments of the self. "*All reality*," says Hegel, in one striking passage, " *is the Idee.* . . . The individual being is some aspect (*Seite*) of the *Idee*. As such it therefore needs other realities [beside it], which seem as if they also existed all by themselves; yet only *in them together and in their relationship is the universal realized. The individual by itself does not embody its universal.*" [1]

Thus the paradox of the relation of universal and individual is to be solved in a manner peculiarly characteristic of the whole system. The true law is to be the organic total of the facts that fall under it. The true general class, the actual object of science, is not an abstract something *exemplified* by the individuals, nor yet an essence that is to be found *in each individual.* There is no such thing for Hegel as a merely individual object of thought existent all alone for itself. The total world of the interrelated individuals is all that exists. The uni-

---

[1] *Werke,* vol. vi. p. 385.

versal is therefore realized in this totality of individual
life. For the nature of the universal is the nature of the
self, and the self is a world of organically interrelated
selves, moments of the infinite organism, phases of its
infinity.[1]

One could not mention a formula more characteristic
of the Hegelian doctrine than this account of what Hegel
calls the " concrete universal," which constructs, brings
forth, in the endless play and toil of rationality, its own
" differences," the individuals of the world of experience.
It is this which for him explains how in the church or in
the state we, the individuals, find ourselves " members
one of another." It is this that shows us the whole world
as an organism. Wherever this sort of universality is *not*
found, as is the case in the world of uncomprehended
sense-facts, where, for instance, only *men* as individuals
seem to exist, and *man* appears to us as a dead abstraction, we are *not* dealing with the world of truth. The
first sign that we are dealing with the truth itself is our
success in discovering an organic connection amongst
things. For organism is selfhood or personality viewed
in its outward manifestation. There is, then, for Hegel a
lower form of thinking that reaches only a *Verstandes-
Allgemeinheit.* Such thinking finds itself in the presence
of individual facts, and regards the universal either as a
bare abstraction, or else as present only in each individual
as its inner and separate nature. For such thinking the
only *concrete* truth is the world of individual things as
such. But the deeper insight into the world is revealed

[1] Hegel's first published exemplification of this doctrine was in
the before-mentioned theory of the *Allgemeinheit des Bewusstseins,* as
expounded in the *Phänomenologie.* In the *Logik* the doctrine receives
a most intricate and elaborate exposition. It is in later writings made
the basis for Hegel's doctrine of the state and of the religious consciousness, although it was almost certainly reached, in the first place,
through an examination of just these instances. For further citations
see Appendix C.

to us through a reflection upon the nature of self-consciousness, wherein the universal, or self, is the organic total of the facts of consciousness, which exist not save as related to one another, and to this universal. The true Universal of Hegel's theory is, then, what our own Shelley so well described when he told us in the "Prometheus" of the

> "One undivided Soul of many a soul
> Whose nature is its own divine control,
> Where all things flow to all, as rivers to the sea." [1]

Of the philosophy of nature (Hegel's most unfinished and weakest undertaking), and of the philosophy of spirit (whereof the foregoing has already contained a suggestion), it is not our office here to treat. These matters belong in their fullness to technical expositions, upon whose province I have now doubtless too much trespassed.

And herewith I must close this account. It will, perhaps, be already obvious to you all that there is a great deal in this Hegelian analysis of self-consciousness that seems to me of permanent and obvious value. As to the finality of the philosophical doctrine as a whole, that is another matter not here to be discussed. Still, I may, perhaps, do well, in closing, to suggest this one thought: People usually call Hegel a cold-hearted system-maker, who reduced all our emotions to purely abstract logical terms, and conceived his absolute solely as an incarnation of dead thought. I, on the contrary, call him one who knew marvelously well, with all his coldness, the secret of human passion, and who, therefore, described, as few others have done, the paradoxes, the problems, and the glories of the spiritual life. His great philosophical and systematic error lay, not in introducing logic into passion,

---

[1] The Hegelian theory of universals is well sketched in Principal Caird's *Philosophy of Religion*, pp. 229–232. See, also, p. 241, where Principal Caird illustrates the true universal by the example of a family with many members.

but in conceiving the logic of passion as the only logic; so that you in vain endeavor to get satisfaction from Hegel's treatment of outer nature, of science, of mathematics, or of any coldly theoretical topic. About all these things he is immensely suggestive, but never final. His system, as system, has crumbled, but his vital comprehension of our life remains forever.

LECTURE VIII.

SCHOPENHAUER.

I NEED hardly remark in the presence of this audience that the name of Schopenhauer is better known to most general readers, in our day, than is that of any other modern Continental metaphysician, except Kant. The reputed heretic has in this field the reward of his dangerous reputation, and I scarcely know whether to fear or to rejoice, as I now approach the treatment of so noteworthy and significant a man, at the position in which Schopenhauer's fame puts his expositor. In one respect, of course, my task is rendered easier by all this popular repute of my hero. Of his doctrine most of us have heard a good deal, and many of us may have followed to a considerable extent his reasoning; at all events we have become acquainted, at least by hearsay, with the fact that his outcome was something called Pessimism. And thus, in dealing with him, I am not voyaging with you in seas unknown to all but the technical students of philosophy, as was last time the case, when I told you of Hegel. On the other hand, the kind of reputation that his writings have very naturally won is decidedly against me when I undertake to treat him with genuinely philosophical fairness. It is so much easier to be edifying than to face with courage certain serious and decidedly tragic realities! Let me be frank with you, then, at the outset about my difficulty. It is, plainly stated, simply this: You have heard that Schopenhauer is a pessimist. You, meanwhile, are surely for the most part no pessimists. Therefore, as we approach Schopenhauer, you want me, in your secret hearts,

if not in your expressed wishes, to refute Schopenhauer.
Now refutation is, as I have already tried to maintain, a
thing of only very moderate service in the study of philosophy. We may refute a great thinker's accidental mis-
judgments; we can seldom refute his deeper insights.
And as I must forthwith assure you, and shall very soon
show you, Schopenhauer's pessimism is actually expres-
sive of a very deep insight into life. This insight is indeed not a final one. We must transcend it. But surely
you would justly discover me in a very unphilosophical, and
in fact very unworthily self-contradictory, attitude if now,
after all these successive efforts to show you a continuity
and a common body of truth in the modern philosophers,
I should suddenly, at this point of my discourse, assume
the airs of a champion of the faith against the infidels,
and should fall to hewing and hacking at Schopenhauer
with genuinely crusading zeal. In fact it is not my calling to do anything of the sort. I always admire the cru-
saders, but my admiration is due rather to their enthusiasm than to their philosophical many-sidedness; rather to
the vitality of their faith than to the universality of their
comprehension. I fear that if I should try to join myself unto them they would not accept me without reserve.
I cannot therefore treat Schopenhauer as a crusader would
treat him. He is to me a philosopher of considerable
dignity, whom we could ill spare from the roll of modern
thinkers; whom I do not by any means follow as disciple,
but to whom I owe, in common with other philosophical
students, a great deal, for his skillful analysis and for his
fearlessly clear assertion of his own significant temperament.

I.

But as to pessimism itself, Schopenhauer's famous doctrine, as to this terrible view that life is through and
through tragic and evil, what is my attitude towards that?
I must, you will probably say, either accept it, and then

must avow it in manly fashion, or I must reject it. And
if I reject it, then I am bound to refute it. My answer
to the question is not far to seek. As an actual fact I
do accept, and avow with perfect freedom, what to many
gentle minds seems, as I am aware, a pessimistic view of
life; namely, precisely the view that at the last time we
found Hegel maintaining and expanding into his marvelously ingenious and technical doctrine of what he called
Negativität as the very essence of the passionate spiritual existence. The spiritual life is n't a gentle or an
easy thing. It is indeed through and through and forever
paradoxical, earnest, enduring, toilsome ; yes, if you like,
painfully tragic. Whoever hopes to find it anything else,
either now or in some far-off heaven, hopes unquestionably
in vain. If that is pessimism, — and in one sense, namely,
in the sense in which many tender but thoughtless souls
have used the phrase, it is pessimism, being opposed to
the gentle and optimistic hopes of such, — then I am now,
and always shall be, in that very sense no optimist, but a
maintainer of the sterner view that life is forever tragic.
In so far as Schopenhauer has sought to make this plain,
I follow him unhesitatingly, and honor him for his mercilessness. Why I do so I shall try to make plain before
this lecture is done. In so far, however, as Schopenhauer
held that the tragedy of life disheartens every spirit that
has once come to know the truth, I as plainly and absolutely reject so much of his outcome. The world is, on the
whole, very nearly as tragic as Schopenhauer represents
it to be. Only spirituality consists in being heroic enough
to accept the tragedy of existence, and to glory in the
strength wherewith it is given to the true lords of life to
conquer this tragedy, and to make their world after all
divine. The way to meet Schopenhauer's pessimism is,
not to refute its assertions, but to grapple practically with
its truths. And if you do so, you will find as the real
heart and significance of Schopenhauer's own gloomy

thought, a vital, yes, even a religious assurance, which
will make you thank God, that, as we tried to suggest by
a phrase quoted in an earlier lecture, the very ice and
cold, the very frost and snow, of philosophy praise and
magnify him forever. In short, my attitude towards pessimism is one that, some years ago, in an article written
for a Harvard College journal, I tried to express in words
suggested by the then current accusation that too many
Harvard students of ability were accustomed to pose as
pessimists. If I quote now my former words, it is only
because the right bearing towards such matters seems to
me so simple that when I try to express it, I am troubled
with a poverty of phrases, and have to fall back on oft
repeated formulæ, for which perhaps some defiant inter-
jection, hurled into the face of our common enemy, namely,
the inner spiritual sluggishness wherewith a man is so
easily beset, would be the best embodiment. But, at all
events, these were my poor words: —

"One hears nowadays, very often, of youthful pessimism, prevalent, for instance, among certain clever college
students. When I hear of these things, I do not always
regret them. On the contrary, I think that the best man
is the one who can see the truth of pessimism, can absorb and transcend that truth, and can be nevertheless an
optimist, not by virtue of his failure to recognize the evil
of life, but by virtue of his readiness to take part in the
struggle against this evil. Therefore, I am often glad
when I hear of this spread of pessimistic ideas among
studious but undeveloped youth. For, I say to myself, if
these men are brave men, their sense of the evil that hin-
ders our human life will some day arouse them to fight this
evil in dead earnest, while if they are not brave men, optimism can be of no service to cowards. But in any case I
like to suggest to such brave and pessimistic youth where
the solution of their problem must lie. It surely cannot
lie in any romantic dream of a pure and innocent world,

far off somewhere, in the future, in heaven or in the isles of the blessed. These things are not for us. We are born for the world of manly business, and if we are worthy of our destiny, we may possibly have some good part in the wars of the Lord. For nothing better have we any right to hope, and for an honest man that is enough."

If these words which I have quoted seem to you rather unfeeling in their hardness, I beseech you to wait until I am done, not merely with to-day's exposition of Schopenhauer, but with my whole course, before you judge them. As for living up to this obvious, but tremendously difficult kind of courage, of course you will not need to hear me say that a student of philosophy finds that quite as hard a task as do any of his neighbors. I am only stating the doctrine. A coward is not an admirable person, but it is only too easy to be one.

Thus, then, forsaking for the moment my position as chronicler, I try to tell you, in this wholly unoriginal fashion, what, to be sure, has always been the creed of brave men ever since our remote ancestors, or their cousins, struggled with the climate of the glacial period. And having thus freed my mind and defined my attitude towards pessimism, I can venture to assume once more the position of the historical student, and to set forth something of Schopenhauer's contribution to the great philosophic task of modern humanity.

II.

The general character and worth of this contribution I must first describe, and in doing so I shall follow in the main the view of a recent German writer on the history of philosophy, namely, Professor Windelband, to whose well-known book, " Die Geschichte der neueren Philosophie," these lectures have owed throughout not a little. Modern idealism, as it developed since Kant, was from the first an effort to discover the rationality of our world through an

analysis of the nature of consciousness. Such analysis
was the problem that Kant bequeathed to his successors.
For Kant showed that we know the world only in terms
of consciousness and its laws, so that the understanding
is the creator of the show nature that stands before our
senses. Fichte tried to solve this Kantian problem by
proving that it is the moral law which is the very heart
and essence of our consciousness, so that our seemingly
outer world is there as a means whereby we can do our
work and win our deeper self. The romanticists, however, felt that consciousness was no more exhaustively
expressed by the moral will than by any other humane interest of the self. Thus, there entered into philosophy a
reign of caprice, to which even Hegel did not put an end.
Once understand the nature of this caprice, and you will
see the place which Schopenhauer's system is to hold in
the development of doctrine.

Were it not, says all idealism, were it not that I am
just such a conscious being as I am, my world would be
a wholly different one from the world that I see. To
know the real nature of my world I must therefore understand my own deeper self. Is there anything fixed,
stable, necessary, about my nature? If so, then I am
necessarily forced to exist in just this sort of world. But
if I am essentially of no one fixed and necessary nature,
then at any moment my whole world might alter. The
ordinary realism of common sense does n't fear this,
does n't feel the necessity of an ultimate appeal to anything stable or fixed about me as the real source of truth,
because ordinary realism holds that the truth is there
beyond me, as something knowable to all people of good
intelligence, in the hard and fast matter of the world of
sense. There is the moon yonder. For ordinary realism,
the moon is as permanent as nature makes it, and stays
there whether any one knows it or not. Hence, in order
to ask whether there is anything stable about the world,

ordinary realism has to put no questions to the inner life. But the very essence of idealism it is to say, *My* moon, the moon that I see and talk about, the moon of my own world of outer show and of empirical knowledge, is just one of my ideas. *You* see the *same* moon only in so far as in *your* world, in your inner life, there is a fact truly corresponding to what I call the moon in my inner life. Therefore, if you and I are to continue to see the same moon, that must be because both of us have some common and necessary deeper nature, a true and abiding oneness of spirit, that forces us to agree in this respect as to our inner life. Hence, not the abiding matter of the moon, as something that should stay there when you and I had both departed, but some common law that holds for your spirit as for mine, is the basis for the seeming permanence and common outer reality of the moon for us. The moon has the same sort of objective existence that, for instance, at this moment, my lecture has. The lecture exists as thought in me, and as experience in you. But because of a certain community of our thoughts, we all of us have the same lecture more or less present to us. We all of us, moreover, regard the lecture as an outer reality, and we therefore seem to be as much in presence of an objective fact as if the lecture were made of real atoms, instead of ideas. Or again, for the idealistic view, the existence of the events in matter, or of any other external events, resembles the existence at any instant of the price of a stock in the stock-market, or the credit of a great firm in the commercial world. A consensus of the thoughts of the buyer and sellers exists at any moment, which, however well founded, or again however arbitrary and changing this consensus may be, is expressed for the instant as if it were a hard and fast material thing in a genuinely outer world. In fact, prices and credits are ideas, and exist in the show-world of market values and of commercial securities, being but the projections of the various ideas of people as these at any moment agree to express themselves. Even so, then, just as this lecture is at this instant a fact because our minds agree in making it so, and just as the price of the stock, or the credit of the great firm, is an often irresistible fact, to which the individual dealer must yield in so far as his own financial might is n't equal to altering it, even so the moon yonder is likewise for us all an outer fact, because we are forced to agree in regarding it as outer. But our agreement itself is a fact of the deeper life of our common selfhood.

Such common ideas being, then, the idealist's true world, his problem it is to determine whether there is any deeper and impersonally human necessity which guarantees that our ideas *shall* thus in any wise agree. This necessity must be sought, if at all, in our own hidden nature. Constructive idealists have always sought it in that common band of rationality which, as they conceive, so links us all together that we are organically related parts or moments of one deeper self. This self, which shall express itself in you, in me, in everybody, is to link your experience to mine in such fashion that we shall see related outer worlds. Because this self in you constructs a show-space in three dimensions, and does a similar thing for me, therefore we alike look out into the depths of space, where the same stars seem to glitter for us all. Unity, fixity, assurance, we get, if we get such prizes at all, only by virtue of that rational and spiritual unity that is beneath our lives. Can the philosopher find the true heart and essence of this our common selfhood? If he can, then idealism becomes a system. We are, then, all in one world of truth. The outer world is indeed show, but no illusion; and our life has an organic fixity, a lawful completeness about it, such as every philosophy longs for.

But now, unfortunately, when idealists set about deducing this unity and consistency of the spiritual world from some deep inner principle, their reflection always leaves us

in one great respect dissatisfied. We very certainly,
namely, can never deduce from the idea of our common
spirituality the idea of any particular sense thing, such as
the moon. Or, to repeat one of my former illustrations,
idealists can't tell us *why* we are spiritually or rationally
bound all alike to perceive a starry world, wherein there
shall be a belt of telescopic asteroids between the orbits of
Mars and Jupiter. Such facts idealists get, like their
neighbors, from daily experience or from science. Idealists may say in general, as Fichte said, that the moral law
needs a world of outer experience as the material for its
embodiment. They cannot show why just *this* material
is needed. There remains, then, an element of brute fact,
a residuum, if you choose, of spiritual caprice, in their
world of the all-embracing self. Perhaps we have, as
they say, the one deeper self in common, perhaps this
deeper self has rational grounds for building in us all
alike just this world of sense, of moons, of asteroids, or
comets, of jelly-fish, and of all the rest, only there is still,
from our finite point of view, a vast element of at least
apparent caprice about the entire universe of the spirit as
thus built. And all idealists have to recognize this fact
of the seeming capriciousness of the external order. The
universal reason builds the world, says idealism; but then
does not the universal reason seem to build many irrational facts into its world? You see then the difficulty.
Our common spiritual nature is to guarantee the truth of
our common experience. Unless this nature has some
hard and fast necessity in it, of which we can form an
adequate conception, there is no satisfaction in our philosophy. But when we try to develop this idea of the universal necessity of the world of our common selfhood, we
come once more against an element of the most stubborn
caprice. Idealism seems to be an insight as suggestive
and inspiring as it is limited. The nature of this divine
self has something seemingly irrational about it. Our

attempted account of the world in terms of the universal reason therefore remains so far a mere programme, a postulate, almost a dogma. And yet dogmas were just what our philosophy had all along been trying to reduce and to rationalize.

In view of this common perplexity of all the idealistic systems, there were certain to arise, upon the historical basis of the Kantian theory, philosophies that not only accepted the perplexity, but that magnified it, that referred it to the very nature of the quasi-mental reality behind the world of sense, and that declared: " Deeper than reason, in this world of the ideal existence, is the caprice which once for all expresses itself in the wealth of nature's facts." Of such systems Schopenhauer's philosophy is the classic representative. Not that Schopenhauer was in this general tendency alone. Windelband very properly classes under the same head Schelling's later theologico-philosophical speculations (not studied in these lectures) along with two or three other doctrines. Windelband calls them all by the common name *Irrationalismus*. A doctrine of this sort, upon a Kantian basis, must run somewhat as follows: The world as we see it exists only in our ideas. We all have a common outer show-world because we all possess a common deeper nature, wherein we are one. You are essentially the same ultimate being that I am. Otherwise we should not have in common this outer projected world of seeming sea waves, star clusters, and city streets. For, as ideas, those things have no outer basis. As common to us all, they must have a deep inner basis. Yet this their basis can't be anything ultimately and universally rational. For in so far as we actually have reason in common, we think necessary, clearly coherent, exactly interrelated groups of ideas, such, for instance, as the multiplication table. But about the star clusters and the sea waves there is no such ultimate rational unity and coherency.

Natural laws only bind such things together, in the fashion that Kant so prettily explained, in case the phenomena to be bound together are once for all there. Why, given sea waves and star clusters and city streets, we should be bound to think them as in *some* sort of interconnection, Kant has told us. Only no such laws of nature can explain why there should be the phenomena there that are thus to conform to law. This is capricious. This is due to our common but irrational nature. The world of the true idealism is n't so much the world of the rational and divine self, as it is the world of the deep unreason that lies at the very basis of all of our natures, of all our common selfhood. Why should there be any world at all for us? Is n't it just because we are all actually minded to see one? And is n't this being minded to see a world as ultimately and brutally unreasonable a fact as you could name? Let us find for this fact, then, a name not so exalted as Fichte's high-sounding speech would love. Let us call this ultimate nature of ours, which forces us all alike to see a world of phenomena in the show forms of space and time, simply our own deep common Will. Let us drop the divine name for it. Will, merely as such, is n't precisely a rational thing; it's capricious. It wills because it does will; and if it wills in us all to be of such nature as to see just these stars and houses, then see them we must, and there is the end of it.

Thus stated, you have an irrationalism on an idealistic basis, a doctrine that may be summed up in three propositions; —

1. The world has existence only as we see it.

2. What facts we are to see can only be learned from experience, and cannot be found *a priori* through any absurd transcendental deductions of the so-called essence of any absolute spirit.

3. The deepest ground, however, for all these seen facts, and for the community of our various visible worlds,

is the common and single World-Will, which, expressed in all of us equally, forces us to see alike, but does so simply because this is the particular caprice that it happens to have, so that it embodies itself for us and in us as just this show-world, rather than any other, because such is its fashion of willing.

The obvious value of such a theory is that it is at once idealistic in its analysis of the presuppositions of life, just to the direct and irresistible reality of the facts of experience, and disposed, after all, to go deeper than experience in its search for the ultimate truth of the world. Final it certainly is not in this form. But it has an obvious advantage over the sort of caprice that, as we saw, was characteristic of the philosophy of the romantic school. Their caprice was the fickleness of private and individual choice. For them you can change, as it were, at any moment of time, your show-world. For them the man of genius makes whatever world he chooses. But for this theory of Schopenhauer's there is but one caprice, and that is the caprice of the World-Will itself, which once for all has hit upon this particular world of facts in time and in space. For us, in our individual capacity, there is no further caprice. We are in presence of this world now, because we ourselves are embodiments of the world-will. We cannot help the fact any longer. Experience is experience; fact is fact; the show is going on for us all alike; the world-will has chosen; but it has not chosen at any point in time. Hence in the world, as it is in time, there is no further caprice, only fact. Time itself is indeed not any ultimate reality. Time belongs to the show-world, and is there like any other fact or form of things, because the world-will fancies such a form for the things of sense. But just for this very reason, we, as individuals, are just where we are, and the realities of sense and of science, although susceptible of so deep and mysterious an interpretation as this, are as inevitable and as objective for us

as ever the most naive and unreflectively superficial realism made them. As against such realism our doctrine
possesses depth, philosophical keenness of analysis, idealistic insight. As against the romantic idealism, our doctrine has the advantage of objectivity and fixity. Just
because our common temporal existence is part of the
caprice of the World-Will, this temporal existence itself
has for us individuals reality and fixity.

So much for the theoretical side of our author's doctrine. On the practical side, in respect, namely, of his
pessimism, we shall find Schopenhauer in a very interesting historical relation to Hegel. In fact, as we shall
learn, our author's pessimism is but another aspect of the
same insight into the paradoxical logic of passion which
we have discovered at the heart of Hegel's doctrine. It
is true that Schopenhauer's World-Will, this blind power
that, according to him, embodies itself in our universe,
appears in his account, at first, as something that might
be said to possess passion without logic. Yet this first
view of the World-Will soon turns out to be inadequate.
The very caprice of the terrible principle is seen, as we go
on, to involve a sort of secondary rationality, a logic, fatal
and gloomy, as well as deeply paradoxical, but still none
the less truly rational for all that. Schopenhauer's world
is, in fact, tragic in much the same sense as Hegel's.
Only, for Schopenhauer the tragedy is hopeless, blind,
undivine ; while for Hegel it is the divine tragedy of the
much-tried Logos, whose joy is above all the sorrows of
his world. Were this difference between these two thinkers merely one of personal and speculative opinion, it
might have little significance. But since it involves, as
we shall find, one of the most truly vital problems of our
modern life, one which meets us at every step in our literature and in our ethical controversies, we shall find it well
worth our while to study the contrast more closely. First,
then, here, let us see something of the man Schopenhauer,
and afterwards we may estimate the doctrine.

III.

Arthur Schopenhauer, born in 1788, was probably descended, on the father's side, from a Dutch family. He was the son of a wealthy merchant of Danzig. His mother, the once noted Johanna Schopenhauer, brilliant novelist, and in her later years ambitious hostess in the literary circles at Weimar, had married, as she very frankly tells us, not from love, but for position. On both sides, Schopenhauer's ancestry was somewhat burdened, as we should say, in respect of nerves, although this fact is decidedly more marked on the father's side. The philosopher's paternal grandmother was declared insane during the latter years of her life; and of his uncles, on the same side, one was idiotic, and one was given to excesses of the neurotic type. Schopenhauer's father, a busy and uncommonly intelligent man, many-sided and successful, still suffered, towards the last, from the family trouble. He showed at fifty-eight years of age occasional but acute symptoms of an excited form of derangement, lost, meanwhile, his memory for well-known persons, and very soon died under mysterious circumstances that strongly indicated an insane suicide. Johanna herself was indeed personally quite free from noteworthy nervous defect, unless heartlessness be reckoned as such. The philosopher himself, as is well known, lived in excellent general health until past seventy, dying in 1860, of a cause having no apparent relation to nervous difficulties. Still, especially in youth, he was vexed by his hereditary burden enough to enable us without question to associate his pessimism in some measure with his temperament. Several neurasthenic symptoms are reported, showing themselves in sporadic but decided forms, — night-terrors, of a known pathological type; causeless depressions; a persistent dread of possible misfortunes; a complaining and frequently unbearable ill humor, with attendant crises of violent temper. A troublesome and slowly growing deafness, similar to one manifest in his father, is referred to the same cause. Against these stood always a very fine general constitution and a rather over-anxiously guarded fashion of life. The question suggested by all these facts, — the well-known question whether Schopenhauer's pessimism was mainly due to mere morbidness of temperament, was in short mere *Stimmungspessimismus*, — is not so easy to decide as some of his critics fancy. In fact, the man was unquestionably incapable of a permanently cheerful view of life, — was a born outcast, doomed to hide and to be lonely. Unquestionably, moreover, he was given to pettiness in the minor relations of life, was vain, uncompanionable, and bitter. But then, many clever men have had all these burdens to bear, without being able to see the tragedy of life as wisely and deeply as Schopenhauer saw it. He would have said of his own unhappy temper very much what he once said of the crimes of Napoleon's career, namely, that there are conditions which make manifest the latent evil of human selfishness, the dangers of the restless will that is in us all alike, better than do other conditions, but which do not therefore create their latent evil. It will not do in any case to state the case against Schopenhauer's pessimism in such shallow fashion as to make it appear that, whilst all pessimism is mere pettiness, all optimism is *prima facie* noble-mindedness. Optimists also can be selfish and even intolerable. In fine, then, I am disposed to say, as a matter of mere historical judgment, that Schopenhauer's nervous burdens unquestionably opened his eyes to the particular aspect of life which he found so tragic, but that meanwhile the fact of such burdens is of positively no service to us in forming our estimate of the ultimate significance of our philosopher's insight, — an insight which, for my part, I find as deep as it was partial.

The Italian psychologist, Lombroso, in his well-known

work on the relations of genius and insanity, makes use of course of Schopenhauer in his catalogue of pathological geniuses. The only value which such observations have, in the present chaotic condition of our knowledge upon the subject, is to remind us that we cannot dispose of a man's intellectual rank, or of his doctrine, by merely observing that he was weighted with morbid tendencies of mind. Genius has often, although by no means always, a background of a pathological sort; while, on the other hand, the nervously burdened, whether geniuses or not, actually do a great part of the world's work and of the world's thinking, and may be all the wiser by reason of the depth of their nervous experiences. Specially interesting, however, in Schopenhauer's case, is the relation of contrast between the peevishness of his private temper and the self-controlled calm and clearness of his literary style. To such a man intellectual work is a blessed relief from the storms of trivial but violent emotion. His reflective thought stands off, as it were, on one side, and surveys with a melancholy freedom his daily life of care and of bondage. His thinking rejoices in the wondrous craft whereby it has outwitted passion. His reflection, therefore, throughout, is a negative self-criticism, a sort of *reductio ad absurdum* of the tempestuous natural man. It does not embody the peevishness of this natural man, but rather scorns the vanity of his unwisdom. As Schopenhauer himself says: "Since all grief, because it is a mortification, a call to resignation, has in it the possibility of rendering one holy, therefore it is that great sorrow, deep pangs, arouse in us a certain reverence for the sufferer; but the sufferer becomes wholly venerable only when, seeing his whole life as one chain of sorrow, he yet does not dwell on the enchainment of circumstances that brought grief to just his life; . . . for then he would still be longing for life, only under other conditions. But he is truly venerable only when his look is turned from the petty to the universal; when he becomes, as it were, a genius in respect of ethical insight; when he sees a thousand cases in one, so that life seen as one whole . . . moves him to resignation. . . . A very noble character," continues Schopenhauer, " we always conceive with a certain tinge of melancholy in it, — a melancholy that is anything but a continual peevishness in view of the daily vexations of life (for such peevishness is an ignoble trait, and arouses suspicions of maliciousness), but rather a melancholy that comes from an insight into the vanity of all joys, and the sorrowfulness of all living, not alone of one's own fortune." Thus, as we see, Schopenhauer's philosophy is not founded upon any summing up of the malicious judgments of his natural peevishness, but is an expression of a calm and relatively external survey and confession of his temperament in its whole-ness. This it is that is expressed in the lucidity of his style, and that gives permanent value to his insight. The strong opposition between will and contemplation is one of the chief features of his doctrine.

As for this style in itself, it suggested Jean Paul's famous characterization of the first edition of Schopenhauer's " Welt als Wille und Vorstellung": "A book of philosophical genius, bold, many-sided, full of skill and depth, — but of a depth often hopeless and bottomless, akin to that melancholy lake in Norway, in whose deep waters, beneath the steep rock-walls, one never sees the sun, but only the stars reflected; and no bird and no wave ever flies over its surface." Just this calm of Schopenhauer's intellect is the characteristic thing about his writing; and no one who knows the highly intellectual and reflective type of the nervously burdened genius will fail to comprehend the meaning of the contrast between the man's peevishness, which tortured him, and his thinking, wherein he found rest. More cheerful spirits may think and will in the same moment, may reflect with vigorous vitality and work with keen reflection. But for men of Schopenhauer's type there is a profound contrast between their contemplative and their passionate life, precisely the same contrast that the ascetic mystics, with whom, once more, like Spinoza, Schopenhauer as philosopher had many things in common, have always loved to dwell upon and to exaggerate. Do you give yourself over to passion? Then, as they will have it, you may be clever, well informed, ingenious; in short, as all the ascetic mystics would say, you may be as wily as you are worldly; but through it all you will be essentially ignorant, thoughtless, irrational. Do you attain the true enlightenment, even for a moment? Then you stand aside from passion; its whirlwind goes by, and you remain undisturbed; your thought, to use an old comparison that was a favorite of Schopenhauer's, pierces through passion as the sunlight through the wind. You see it all, but it moves you not.

Such mysticism is essentially pessimistic; we find it so even in Spinoza, or in the "Imitation of Christ;" only, in the "Imitation," contemplation has the glory of God to turn to above and beyond the storm of sense and of vanity. A formula for Schopenhauer is that his pessimism is simply the doctrine of the "Imitation" with the glory of God omitted; but as the glory of God in the latter book is described in purely abstract, mystical, and essentially unreal terms, one may see at once that the road from the mediæval mystic to Schopenhauer's outcome is not so long as some people imagine. "I saw in my dream," says Bunyan, at the end of his "Pilgrim's Progress," when the angels carry off poor Ignorance to the pit, — "I saw in my dream that there was a way to the bottomless pit from the very gate of Heaven, as well as from the City of Destruction." Now, Schopenhauer's mission it was to explore this highly interesting way with considerable speculative skill. The mystic who forsakes the world because of its vanity finds his comfort in a dream of something called the divine perfection, — something pure, abstract, extra-mundane. He comes on "that which is," and catches, like Tennyson in the famous night vision on the lawn, in the "In Memoriam," "the deep pulsation of the world." Only by and by morning comes. Your mystic must awake; his vision must vanish, "stricken through with doubt." Tennyson seems to have endured the waking better than others. But, generally speaking, the pessimist of Schopenhauer's type is simply the mystic of the type of the "Imitation," at the moment when he has awakened from the false glory of this religious intoxication.

The events of our hero's life may be briefly disposed of. His father took or sent him on long travels during his early youth, made him well acquainted with both French and English, and insisted that he should in due time learn the mercantile business, and train himself to be a busy, intelligent, and many - sided man of the world. Scholarship and the university formed no part in the father's plans. The boy spent also considerable time on his father's country estate, loved nature, but was always a lonely child. As youth waxed, moodiness tormented him; he already showed also the metaphysical turn. His father's death, in 1805, left him free to follow his own plans. He forsook the hated counting-house, where he had already set about his work, and began to study for the university; making rapid progress in Latin, quarrelling with his elders, and writing rhetorically gloomy letters to his mother, who had now entered on her Weimar career. The son's native pessimism was still far, of course, from the later philosophical formulation, but he already perceived that one great evil about the world is its endless change, which dooms all ideal interests and moods to alteration and defeat. "Everything," he writes to his mother, "is washed away in time's stream. The minutes, the numberless atoms of pettiness into which

every deed is dissolved, are the worms that gnaw at
everything great and noble, to destroy it." His mother
found this sort of thing rather tedious, and especially inconsistent with her son's social success as an occasional
inmate of her house at Weimar. There already a most
brilliant company often gathered, Goethe at the head. A
youth of twenty or thereabouts could not add grace to
such a scene so long as he could talk of nothing but time
and worms. She wrote him plainly, being a woman as
clear-headed as she was charming: " When you get older,
dear Arthur, and see things more clearly, perhaps we
shall agree better. Till then let us see that our thousand
little quarrels shall not hunt love out of our hearts. To
that end we must keep well apart. You have your lodg-
ings; as for my house, whenever you come you are a
guest, well received, of course, only you must n't interfere.
I can't bear objections. Days when I receive, you may
take supper with me, if you'll only be so good as to re-
frain from your painful disputations, which make me
angry, too, and from all your lamentations over the stupid
world and the sorrows of mankind; for all that always
gives me a bad night and horrid dreams, and I do so like
a sound sleep."

In 1809, Schopenhauer began his university studies at
Göttingen, devoted himself to Kant and Plato, and rapidly acquired the type of erudition which he kept to the
end, an erudition vast rather than technical, the learning
of one who saw swiftly rather than studied exhaustively,
remembered rather than systematized, enjoyed manifold
labors rather than professional completeness. He was
always a marvelous reader, of wide literary sympathies,
especially fond of the satirists, the mystics, and the keen
observers of all ages. For the processes of the exact
sciences he had a poor comprehension; for natural phenomena of a suggestive sort his eye was always very wide
open; he longed to catch the restless World-Will in the

very act of its struggle and sorrow. He loved books
of travel, energetic stories, strongly written historical
sketches, tragic as well as satirical dramas, and books of
well-described natural history. In nature itself, he was
very fond of observing flowers, while, after his fashion,
he loved animals passionately. They show the will naked,
in all its naive cruelty, guilt, and innocence.

Edifying literature of all but the purely mystical type,
most systematic schemes of constructive thought, all
merely sentimental poetry, and above all such moralizing
poetry as Schiller's "Don Carlos," he in general bitterly
despised. These things seemed to him to hover above
life. He wanted to contemplate the longing of life in
itself. His critical and historical judgments are deep and
yet wayward. He is once more on the lookout for types,
not for connections ; he had, for so learned a man, a poor
eye for detecting unscholarly and fantastic theories, and
frequently accepts such when they relate to topics beyond
his immediate control. His literary sense was after all
his best safeguard in scholarship. Here his fine contemplative intellect guided him. He could not make a bad
blunder as to a purely linguistic question ; but where his
taste and instinct for the immediate inner life of things
and of people were unable to guide him, he wandered too
often in the dark. On all matters of learning his judgment remains, therefore, largely that of the sensitive man
of the world. His sense of humor was of the keenest.
The will is once for all as comic in its irrationalities as it
is deep in its unrest. A distinguishing feature of his style
is due to this wide reading, namely, his skill in metaphor
and in other forms of comparison. In this respect he
rivals those wonderful masters of comparison, the Hindoo
metaphysicians, whom he knew through translations, and
admired much. One further trait may yet be mentioned
as pervading his study and his whole view of life. He
was an intense admirer of the English temperament, just

as he was an intense hater of many English institutions.
Not, of course, the English Philistine, but the English
man of the world, attracted him, by that clear-headedness
and that freedom from systematic delusions which are so
characteristic of the stock. To sum all up in a word, the
maxim of his whole life as a learner was, See and record
the vital struggles and longings of the will wherever they
appear.

Such scholarship as this was ill-fitted to prepare Schopenhauer for an academic life. In 1813, he printed his
dissertation for the doctor's degree, on the "Fourfold
Root of the Principle of Sufficient Reason." It is his
most technical book, with least of his genius in it. In
1818 was published the first edition of his "Welt als
Wille und Vorstellung." In 1820, he entered on his work
as *Privat-Docent* at the university of Berlin, and immediately made a sufficiently complete academic failure to
discourage him from any serious effort to continue. Embittered by the indifference with which both his books
and his attempts as a teacher were received, he gradually
acquired that intense hatred of all professors of philosophy, and of the whole post-Kantian speculative movement
in Germany, which he expressed more than once in a
furious form, and which wholly misled him as to his own
historical relations. After 1831, he retired to Frankfort-
on-the-Main, and lived upon his little fortune until the
close of his life. How he came slowly to be publicly
known, in spite of the indifference with which academic
circles treated him; how in old age there gathered round
him a little circle of well-received flatterers; how young
Russians used to come and stare at the wise man; how he
loved the attentions of all such people, and better still the
more intelligent understanding of two or three faithful
disciples, but best of all his dinner and his dog; how he
died at last suddenly, when he was quite alone, — are not
all these things written in the books of modern literary

gossip? I need not dwell upon them further; nor need I repeat how Schopenhauer had only to die to acquire general fame, until now his name is everywhere a symbol for all that is most dark and deep and sad and dangerous about the philosophy of our time. Of the pettier incidents of his life, of his quarrels, of his one or two outbursts of temper which led to public scandals, of his other eccentricities numberless, I have no time to speak further.

IV.

Schopenhauer's principal work, "Die Welt als Wille und Vorstellung," is in form the most artistic philosophical treatise in existence, if one excepts the best of Plato's "Dialogues." In its first edition it was divided into four books; a later edition added in a second volume comments upon all four. Of these books, the first summarizes the Kantian basis of Schopenhauer's own doctrine. The world is, first of all, for each and for all of us, just our *Vorstellung*, our Idea. It is there because and while we see it; it consists in its detail of facts of experience. These, however, are, for our consciousness, always interpreted facts, seen in the sense forms of space and of time, and within these forms, perceived through and by virtue of our universal form of comprehension, namely, the principle of causation. When I experience anything, I inevitably seek for a cause in space and in time for this experience. When I find such a cause, I localize the experience as an event manifesting some change in something there in space and in time; but these forms of space and of time, as well as this principle of causation, are all alike simply formal ideas in me. Kant's great service lay, in fact, in his proving the subjectivity, the purely mental nature, of such forms. The space and time worlds, with all that they contain, exist accordingly for the knowing subject. No subject without an object, and no object without a subject. I know in so far as there is a world to know; and the world yonder exists in so far as I know it. In vain, moreover, would one seek for any thing in itself really outside of me as the cause of my experiences. For cause is just an idea of mine, useful and valid for the events of the show world, but wholly inapplicable to anything else.. Within experience the law of causation is absolute, because such is my fashion of thinking experience and of perceiving the localized things of sense. But beyond experience what validity, what application, can one give to the principle of causation? None. There is no cause to be sought beyond my own true nature for my own experiences.

But what *is* this my nature? The second book answers the question. My nature, you must observe, is something very wealthy. It does not indeed *cause* my experiences, in any proper sense; for cause means only an event that in time or in space brings another event to pass; and there is nothing that, in time or in space, brings to pass my own deepest, timeless, and spaceless nature. As phenomenon in time, my body may move or die, as other events determine; but my deepest nature is so superior to space and time that, as we have just shown, space and time are in fact *in me*, in so far as they are my forms of seeing and of knowing. Therefore my true nature neither causes, nor is caused; but, as one now sees, it in truth *is*, comprises, embodies itself in, all my world of phenomena. Hence you see how wealthy my true nature must be in its implications. Yes, in a deeper sense, you also, in so far as you truly exist, must have the same deepest nature that I have. Only in space and in time do we seem to be separate beings. Space and time form, as Schopenhauer says, the dividing principle of things. In an illusory way they seem to distinguish us all from one another; but abstract space and time, with all their manifold and illusory distinctions of places and moments, and the real world collapses into one immanent nature of things.

Since my own deepest nature is beneath and behind the time form of the apparent world, it follows that, in an essential and deep sense, I am one with all that ever has been or that ever will be, either millions of ages ago or millions of ages to come. And as for space, there is no star so remote but that the same essential nature of things which is manifest in that star is also manifest in my own body. Space and time are, as the Hindoos declared, the veil of Maya or Illusion, wherewith the hidden unity of things is covered, so that, through such illusion, the world appears manifold, although it is but one.

To answer, therefore, the question, What is the nature of things? I have only to find what, apart from my senses and my thought, is my own deepest essence. And of this I have a direct, an indescribable, but an unquestionable awareness. My whole inner life is, namely, essentially my will. I long, I desire, I move, I act, I feel, I strive, I lament, I assert myself. The common name for all this is my will. By will, of course, Schopenhauer does not merely mean the highest form of my conscious choice, as some people do. He means simply the active nature of me, the wanting, longing, self-asserting part. This, in truth, as even the romantic idealists felt, lies deeper than my intellect, is at the basis of all my seeing and knowing. Why do I see and acknowledge the world in space and in time? Why do I believe in matter, or recognize the existence of my fellow-men, or exercise my reason? Is not all this just my actual fashion of behavor? In vain, however, do I seek, as the idealists of Fichte's type often pretended to seek, for an ultimate reason why I should have this fashion of behavior. That is a mere fact. Deeper than reason is the inexplicable caprice of the inner life. We want to exist; we long to know; we make our world because we are just striving to come into being. Our whole life is as ultimate and inexplicable an activity as are our particular fashions of loving and of hating. *So* I am; this is the nature of me, — to strive, to long, to will; and I cannot rest in this striving. My life is a longing to be somewhere else in life than here, where I am.

Here, then, is the solution of our mystery in so far as it can have a solution. The world is the Will. In time and space I see only the behavior of phenomena. I never get at things in themselves, but I, in my timeless and spaceless inner nature, in the very heart, in the very germ, of my being, am not a mere outward succession of phenomena. I am a Will, — a will which is not there for the sake of something else, but which exists solely because it desires to exist. Here is the true thing in itself. The whole world, owing to the utter illusoriness of time and space, has collapsed into one single and ultimate nature of things. This nature, immediately experienced in the inner life, is the Will. This Will, then, is that which is so wealthy that the whole show world is needed to express its caprice. Look, then, on the whole world in its infinite complication of living creatures and of material processes. These, indeed, are remote enough from your body. Seen in space and time, you are a mere fragment in the endless world of phenomena, a mere drop in the ocean, a link in an endless chain. But look at the whole world otherwise. In its inmost life and truth it must be one, for space and time are the mere forms in which the one interest of the observer is pleased to express itself. Look upon all things, then, and it can be said of you as, once more, the Hindoos loved to say, "The life of all these things, — *That art Thou.*"

Schopenhauer himself was fond of quoting this well-known phrase of the Hindoo philosophy as expressing the kernel of his own doctrine. New about his philosophy was, he felt, the synthesis that he had made of Kant's thought and the Hindoo insight; but with this insight itself he essentially agreed. "The inmost life of things is one, and *that life art thou.*" This sentence expresses to his mind the substance of the true thought about the world. Let us, then, quote a paragraph or two from one of the Hindoo philosophic classics called the "Upanishads," much read and loved by Schopenhauer, to illustrate his view. In the passage in question a teacher is represented as in conversation with his pupil, who is also his son. " 'Bring me,' says the father, 'a fruit of yonder tree.' 'Here it is, O Venerable One.' 'Cut it open.' 'It is done.' 'What seest thou therein?' 'I see, O Venerable One, very little seeds.' 'Cut one of them open.' 'It is done, Venerable One.' 'What seest thou therein?' 'Nothing, Venerable One.' Then spake he: 'That fine thing which thou seest not, my well beloved, from that fine thing (that life) is, in truth, this mighty tree grown. Believe me, my well beloved, *what* this fine (substance) is, of whose essence is all the world, that is the Reality, that is the Soul, — *That art Thou*, O Çvetaketu.' "

" 'This bit of salt, lay it in the (vessel of) water, and come again to-morrow to me.' This did he. Then spake (the teacher): 'Bring me that salt which yesterday even thou didst lay in the water.' He sought it and found it not, for it was melted. 'Taste the water here. How tastes it?' 'Salt.' 'Taste it there. How tastes it?' 'Salt.' 'Leave the vessel and sit at my feet.' So did he, and said, '(The salt) is still there.' Then spake the teacher: 'Verily, so seest thou the truly Existent not in bodies, yet is it truly therein. What this fine substance is of whose essence is all the world, that is the Reality, that is the Soul, — *That art Thou*, O Çvetaketu.' "

" 'Just as, O my well beloved, a man whom they have led away out of the land of the Gandharis with eyes blindfolded, and have loosed him in the wilderness, — just as he wanders eastwards or westwards, southwards or northwards, because he has been led hither blindfolded and loosed blindfolded, but after some one has taken off the blind from his eyes, and has said, "Yonder lies the land of the Gandharis; yonder go," he, asking the way in village after village, instructed and understanding, comes home at last to the Gandharis, — even so, too, is the man who here in the world has found a teacher; for he knows "to this (world) I belong only until I am delivered; then shall I come to my home." What this fine (substance) is, of whose essence is all the world, that is the Reality, that is the Soul, — *That art Thou*, O Çvetaketu.'"

Here, one sees, is the Hindoo way of getting at the substance. It is also Schopenhauer's way. Look for the substance within, in your own nature. You will not see it without. It is the life of your own life, the soul of your own soul. When you find it, you will come home from the confusing world of sense-things to the heart and essence of the world, to the reality. *That art Thou.*

Since for Schopenhauer this soul of your soul is the capricious inner will, there is no reason to speak of it as God or as Spirit; for these words imply rationality and conscious intelligence. And intelligence, whose presence in the world is merely one of the caprices of this will itself, finds itself always in sharp contrast to the will, which it can contemplate, but which it can never explain. However, of contemplation there are various stages, determined in us phenomenal individuals by the various sizes and powers of our purely phenomenal brains. Why any intelligence exists at all, and why it is phenomenally associated with a brain, nobody can explain. The will thus likes to express itself. That is the whole story. However, once given the expression, this intelligence reaches its highest perfection in that power to contemplate the whole world of the will with a certain supreme and lofty calm, which, combined with an accurate insight into the truth of the will, is characteristic of the temperament of the productive artist. Art is, namely, the embodiment of

the essence of the will as the contemplative intelligence
sees it. And to art Schopenhauer devotes his third book.
The will has certain ultimate fashions of expressing itself,
certain stages of self-objectification, as Schopenhauer calls
them.   These, in so far as contemplation can seize them,
are the ultimate types, the Platonic ideas, of things, all
endlessly exemplified in space and time by individual objects, but, as types, eternal, time-transcending, immortal.
They are the ultimate embodiments of passion, the eternal
forms of longing that exist in our world.   Art grasps
these types and exhibits them.   Architecture, for instance, portrays the blind nature-forces, or longings, of
weight and resistance.   Art is, then, the universal appreciation of the essence of the will from the point of view
of a contemplative onlooker.   Art is, therefore, disinter-
ested, embodying passion, but itself not the victim of passion.   Of all the arts, according to Schopenhauer, Music
most universally and many-sidedly portrays the very essence of the will, the very soul of passion, the very heart
of this capricious, world-making, and incomprehensible
inner nature of ours.   Hence music is in some respects
Schopenhauer's favorite art.   Music shows us just what
the will is, — eternally moving, striving, changing, flying,
struggling, wandering, returning to itself, and then beginning afresh, — all with no deeper purpose than just life
in all its endlessness, motion, onward-flying, conflict, fullness of power, even though that shall mean fullness of
sorrow and anguish.   Music never rests, never is content;
repeats its conflicts and wanderings over and over; leads
them up, indeed, to mighty climaxes, but is great and
strong never by virtue of abstract ideas, but only by the
might of the will that it embodies.   Listen to these cries
and strivings, to this infinite wealth of flowing passion,
to this infinite restlessness, and then reflect, — *That art
Thou;* just that unreposing vigor, longing, majesty, and —
caprice.

Of all Schopenhauer's theories, except his pessimism itself, this theory of art has become the most widely known and influential. As he stated it, it was, indeed, evidently the notion, not of the systematic student of any art, but of the observant amateur of genius and sensibility. It lacks the professional tone altogether. Its illustrations are chosen whimsically from all sorts of directions. The opposition between will and contemplation reaches for the first time its height at this point in the system. On one side, the world of passion, throbbing, sorrowing, longing, hoping, toiling, above all, forever fleeing from the moment, whatever it be; on the other side, the majesty of artistic contemplation, looking in sacred calm upon all this world, seeing all things, but itself unmoved. Plainly, in this contemplative intellect the will has capriciously created for itself a dangerous enemy, who will discover its deep irrationality.

This enemy is none other than that Wagnerian Brünhilde, who is destined to see, through and through, the vanity of the world of the will, and who, not indeed without the connivance of the high gods of the will themselves, is minded to destroy the whole vain show in one final act of resignation. There arise from time to time in the world, thinks Schopenhauer, holy men, full of sympathy and pity for all their kind, full of a sense of the unity of all life, and of the vanity of this our common and endless paradox of the finite world. These men are called, in the speech of all the religions, saints. Whatever their land or creed, their thought is the same. Not the particular griefs of life, not the pangs of cold and hunger and of disease, not the horrors of the baseness that runs riot in humanity, — not these things do they weigh in the balance with any sort of precision or particularity, although these things, too, they see and pity. No, the source of all these griefs, the will itself, its paradox, its contradictory longing to be forever longing, its irrational striving to be for-

ever as one that suffers lack, — this they condemn, com‹
passionate, and — resign. They do not strive or cry.
They simply forsake the will. Life, they say, *must* be
evil, for life is desire, and desire is essentially tragic, since
it flees endlessly and restlessly from all that it has; makes
perfection impossible by always despising whatever it happens to possess, and by longing for more; lives in an eternal wilderness of its own creation; is tossed fitfully in
the waves of its own dark ocean of passion; knows no
peace; finds in itself no outcome, — nothing that can
finish the longing and the strife.

And this hopelessly struggling desire, — so the saints
teach to each one of us in our blindness, — *That art Thou.*
The saints pity us all. Their very existence is compassion. They absent them from felicity awhile, that they
may teach us the way of peace. And this way is what?
Suicide? No, indeed. Schopenhauer quite consistently
condemns suicide. The suicide desires bliss, and flees only
from circumstance. He wills life. He hates only this
life which he happens to have. No, this is not what the
saints teach. One and all they counsel, as the path of
perfection, the hard and steep road of Resignation. That
alone leads to blessedness, to escape from the world.
Deny the will to live. Forsake the power that builds the
world. Deny the flesh. While you live be pitiful, merciful, kindly, dispassionate, resisting no evil, turning away
from all good fortune, thinking of all things as of vanity
and illusion. The whole world, after all, is an evil dream.
Deny the will that dreams, and the vision is ended. As
for the result, " we confess freely," says Schopenhauer,
in the famous concluding words of the fourth book of
his first volume, " what remains, after the entire annul-
ling of the will, is, for all those who are yet full of the
will, indeed nothing. But, on the other hand, for those
in whom the will has turned again, and has denied itself,
this our own so very real world, with all her suns and
Milky Ways, is — Nothing."

V.

The estimate of the doctrine which we now have before us will be greatly aided if we bear in mind the nature of its historic genesis. The problem bequeathed by Kant to his successors was, as we have seen throughout both this and the preceding discussion, the problem of the relation of the empirical self of each moment to the total or universal self. This problem exists alike for Hegel and for Schopenhauer. Hegel undertakes to solve it by examining the process of self-consciousness. This process, developed according to his peculiar and paradoxical logic, which we have ventured to call the Logic of Passion, shows him that in the last analysis there is and can be but one self, the absolute spirit, the triumphant solver of paradoxes. Sure of his process, Hegel despises every such mystical and immediate seizing of the Universal as had been characteristic of the romanticists. With just these romanticists, however, Schopenhauer has in common the immediate intuition whereby he seizes, not so much the universal self as, in his opinion, the universal and irrational essence or nature that is at the heart of each finite self, and of all things, namely, the Will. Yet when he describes this will, after his intuition has come to grasp it, he finds in it just the paradox that Hegel had logically developed. For Hegel, self-consciousness is, as even Fichte already had taught, essentially the longing to be more of a self than you are. Just so, for Schopenhauer, if you exist you will, and if you will you are striving to escape from your present nature. It is of the essence of will to be always desiring a change. If the Will makes a world, the Will as such will be sure, then, thinks Schopenhauer, to be endlessly dissatisfied with its world. For, once more, when you will, the very essence of such will is discontentment with what is yours now. I no longer make that an object of desire which I already possess. I will what I have not yet, but hope to get, as a poor man wills wealth, but a rich man more wealth. I will the future, the distant, the unpossessed, the victory that I have not yet won, the defeat of the enemy who still faces me in arms, the cessation of the tedium or of the pain that besets me. Do I attain my desire, my will ceases, or, which is the same thing, turns elsewhere for food. Curiously enough, this, which is precisely the thought that led Hegel to the conception of the absolutely active and triumphant spirit, appears to Schopenhauer the proof of the totally evil nature of things. Striving might be bearable were there a highest good, to which, by willing, I could attain, and if, when I once attained that good, I could rest. But if will makes the world and is the whole life and essence of it, then there is nothing in the world deeper than the longing, the unrest, which is the very heart of all willing. Does n't this unrest seem tragic ? Is there to be no end of longing in the world ? If not, how can mere striving, mere willing, come to seem bearable ? Here is the question which leads Schopenhauer to his pessimism. Precisely the same problem made Hegel, with all his appreciation of the tragedy of life, an optimist. Hegel's Absolute, namely, is dissatisfied everywhere *in* his finite world, but is triumphantly content *with* the whole of it, just because his wealth is complete.

An historical lecture like the present one has not to decide between the metaphysical claims and rights of the Schopenhauerian immediate intuition of the Universal and the Hegelian logic. As theories of the absolute, these two doctrines represent conflicting philosophical interests whose discussion would belong elsewhere. Our present concern is the more directly human one. Of the two attitudes towards the great spiritual interests of man which these systems embody, which is the deeper ? To be sure, even this question cannot be answered without making a confession of philosophical faith, but that I must here do in merely dogmatic form.

For my part, I deeply respect both doctrines. Both are essentially modern views of life, modern in their universality of expression, in their keen diagnosis of human nature, in their merciless criticism of our consciousness, in their thorough familiarity with the waywardness of the inner life. The century of nerves and of spiritual sorrows has philosophized with characteristic ingenuity in the persons of these thinkers, — the one the inexorable and fairly Mephistophelian critic of the paradoxes of passion, the other the nervous invalid of brilliant insight. We are here speaking only of this one side of their doctrines, namely, their diagnosis of the heart and of the issues of life. How much of the truth there is in both, every knowing man ought to see. Capricious is the will of man, thinks Schopenhauer, and therefore endlessly paradoxical and irrational. Paradoxical is the very consciousness, and therefore the very reason, of man, finds Hegel; and therefore, where there is this paradox, there is not unreason, but the manifestation of a part of the true spiritual life, — a life which could not be spiritual were it not full of conflict. Hegel thus absorbs, as it were, the pessimism of Schopenhauer; while Schopenhauer illustrates the paradox of Hegel.

But if both doctrines stand as significant expressions of the modern spirit, a glance at our more recent literature — at the despairing resignation of Tolstoi, with its flavor of mysticism, and at the triumphant joy in the paradoxes of passion which Browning kept to the end — will show us how far our romancers and poets still are from having made an end of the inquiry as to which doctrine is the right one. My own notion about the matter, such as it is, would indeed need for its full development the context of just such a philosophical argument as I have declined to introduce at the present stage of this course. As constructive idealist, regarding the absolute as indeed a spirit, I am in sympathy with Hegel's sense of the triumphant rationality that reigns above all the conflicts of the spiritual world. But as to Schopenhauer's own account of life, I find indeed that his pessimism is usually wholly misunderstood and unappreciated, as well by those who pretend to accept as well by those who condemn it. What people fail to comprehend concerning these deep and partial insights which are so characteristic of great philosophers is that the proper way to treat them is neither to scorn nor to bow down, but to experience, and then to get our freedom in presence of all such insights even by the very wealth of our experience. We are often so slavish in our relations with doctrines of this kind! Are they expressed in traditional, in essentially clerical language, as in the "Imitation" or in some other devotional book, then the form deceives us often into accepting mystical resignation as if it were the whole of spirituality, instead of bearing, as it does bear, much the same relation to the better life that sculptured marble bears to breathing flesh. But if it is a Schopenhauer, a notorious heretic, who uses much the same speech, then we can find no refuge save in hating him and his gloom. In fact, pessimism, in its deeper sense, is merely an ideal and abstract expression of one very deep and sacred element of the total religious consciousness of humanity. In fact, finite life is tragic, very nearly as much so as Schopenhauer represented, and tragic for the very reason that Schopenhauer and all the counselors of resignation are never weary of expressing, in so far, namely, as it is at once deep and restless. This is its paradox, that it is always unfinished, that it never attains, that it throbs as the heart does, and ends one pulsation only to begin another. This is what Hegel saw. This is what all the great poets depict, from Homer's wanderings of the much tossed and tried Odysseus down to "In Memoriam" of Tennyson, or the "Dramatic Lyrics" of Browning. Not only is this so, but it must be so. The only refuge from

spiritual restlessness is spiritual sluggishness; and that, as
everybody is aware, is as tedious a thing as it is insipid.
For the individual the lesson of this tragedy is always
hard; and he learns it first in a religious form in the
mood of pure resignation. "I cannot be happy; I must
resign happiness." This is what all the Imitations and the
Schopenhauers are forever and very justly teaching to the
individual. Schopenhauer's special reason for this view
is, however, the deep and philosophical one that at the
heart of the world there seems to be an element of capricious conflict. That fact was what drove him to reject
the World Spirit of the constructive idealists, and to speak
only of a World-Will. But is this the whole story? No;
if we ever get our spiritual freedom, we shall, I think,
not neglecting this caprice which Schopenhauer found
at the heart of things, still see that the world is divine
and spiritual, not so much in spite of this capriciousness,
as just because of it. Caprice is n't all of reason; but
reason needs facts and passions to conquer and to rationalize, in order to become triumphantly rational. The
spirit exists by accepting and by triumphing over the
tragedy of the world. Restlessness, longing, grief, —
these are evils, fatal evils, and they are everywhere in the
world; but the spirit must be strong enough to endure
them. In this strength is the solution. And, after all,
it is just endurance that is the essence of spirituality.
Resignation, then, is indeed part of the truth, — resignation, that is, of any hope of a final and private happiness.
We resign in order to be ready to endure. But courage
is the rest of the truth, — a hearty defiance of the whole
hateful pang and agony of the will, a binding of the
strong man by being stronger than he, a making of life
once for all our divine game, where the passions are the
mere chessmen that we move in carrying out our plan,
and where the plan is a spiritual victory over Satan. Let
us thank Schopenhauer, then, for at least this, that in his

pessimism he gives us an universal expression for the whole negative side of life. If you will let me speak of private experience, I myself have often found it deeply comforting, in the most bitter moments, to have discounted, so to speak, all the petty tragedies of experience, all my own weakness and caprice and foolishness and ill fortune, by one such absolute formula for evil as Schopenhauer's doctrine gives me. It is the fate of life to be restless, capricious, and therefore tragic. Happiness comes, indeed, but by all sorts of accidents; and it flies as it comes. One thing only that is greater than this fate endures in us if we are wise of heart; and this one thing endures forever in the heart of the great World-Spirit of whose wisdom ours is but a fragmentary reflection. This one thing, as I hold, is the eternal resolution that if the world *will* be tragic, it *shall* still, in Satan's despite, be spiritual. And this resolution is, I think, the very essence of the Spirit's own eternal joy.

LECTURE IX.

IDEALISM, in several of its most significant phases, has been described in the lectures on the movement from Kant to Hegel. In this lecture I have to discuss another phase of what I have several times called the return to the outer order. In looking back for a moment at certain of the suggestions of the last lecture, I shall not ask you to dwell any more upon Schopenhauer's pessimism. Of that topic we have had doubtless enough for the present. Coming as we do to a more cheerful chapter of modern philosophy, we want only to remind ourselves, at the out-set, of another element in Schopenhauer's thought, and one which will be of importance for the work that we now have in hand.

Schopenhauer, as you may remember, while he was in his own way an idealist on a Kantian basis, was not, on the whole, what one would call, somewhat technically, a constructive idealist. That is, while he was very positive in saying that the world which we see and feel is just the world of our ideas, and nothing else, he did not follow out the plan of Fichte or of the romanticists by trying to show constructively what sort of a world we are all rationally bound to see. On the contrary, as Schopenhauer holds, the world that we see is at once the world of the self, of the inner life, and is also the world of that capricious will which is the very heart of the inner life. You cannot deduce *a priori* anything about the sorts of reality which this world must express and contain. You cannot say, with Fichte, that it must be the world of the moral

law, *das versinnlichte Material unserer Pflicht.* You
cannot say, with Schelling, that it must be the world
which expresses in symbolic form the life of a rational
and gigantic World-Spirit. You must take the world as
you find it. You may be sure indeed of its unity, yet
this assurance rests only upon your power to prove that
all diversity is due to our sense-forms of time and space,
and is therefore illusory. But the longing and struggling
will cannot be described apart from experience. The
philosopher must become a naturalist. He must look
upon the world as the spectator looks on during a tragedy
which he knows beforehand to be full of action and of
suffering, but which he must watch before he can know
the plot.

It is this thought of Schopenhauer's that brings him
very near to the position of most students of modern science. Schopenhauer marks then, in the history of
thought, the transition from the romantic idealism to the
modern realism, the return to the natural order. He is
indeed an idealist of a Kantian type. He is philosopher
in his sense of the unity of things, in his assurance that
all phenomenal plurality is a mere illusion, in his reitera-
tion of the Hindoo *That art Thou,* and in his Kantian
idealism itself. But as to the individual facts of the
world, he is proud to be a naturalist, who studies men
and beasts and art and flowers, merely to find out what
the Will is doing.

I.

What I now want you to feel is that all this was in so
far a natural and a healthy turn for the idealistic philosophy to take. Philosophy had begun, in modern times,
with the external order and with dogmatic assertions
about it. Growing doubtful and self-critical, it had next
fallen to scrutinizing the inner life. Becoming bold and
clear as to both its powers and its limitations it had later
said, with Kant: "Things in themselves, indeed, are n't

for me; but as for the order and unity of phenomenal nature, that is mine, and is even of my own creating." Waxing, however, afresh, still bolder, thought had next asserted: " Not only the order of nature, but the very content of nature is spiritual, and is even the creation of the very spirit whom my life embodies in finite form." " I therefore," it continued, " have a right to seize hold upon and to master the very deepest mysteries of this whole spiritual creation. There shall be no limits to my ventures, and no things in themselves shall stand between me and the rational construction of reality at which I aim." But here, indeed, the idealist had been doomed to fresh disappointment. That the world is the world of the absolute spirit he could make indeed plausible, — how plausible we ourselves have hardly had time in our brief survey to see. That, deeper than your conscious nature or than mine, there is a truth at the heart of the inner life of which we as finite spirits are embodiments, all this the idealist could try to explain by showing how the community of our sense-worlds, our own human power to act in practical and rational concert, and all the other presuppositions of our spiritual existence, lead us to postulate that the whole environment of our inner life is spiritual, that there is but one self, and that this self is God. But, after all, even granting the force of these considerations, one difficulty remained which the idealists could not conquer. Whatever your formula for the postulated spiritual world, whether it were Fichte's moral law or the various wayward theories of the romanticists, an element of stubborn caprice remained. From the constructions of your ideal philosophy to the empirical facts of outer nature remained a long and hopelessly tangled way. The world might be thus rational, but it was evident that the absolute spirit must be thinking of many things that you, in your finite weakness, could not well presume to construct *a priori*.

In view of all this, thought, as we now see, must be content to take one more step, not, as many superficial students of modern thought have supposed, the step of repenting once for all of the whole undertaking of the idealistic period, but rather the step of returning, enriched by the experience and the depth of insight which this period had produced, to the cautious scrutiny and rational interpretation of the external order itself. The first charge of idealism upon the fortress of the spiritual mys-- teries of the world was indeed in one sense a failure. Constructive idealism meant, as the romanticists showed, no small danger of arbitrary speculative guesses, of way-wardness, and of dreaming. If Hegel sought to put an end to all this capriciousness by his marvelously skillful construction of the essence of the absolute spirit in terms of a formula derived from the study of the inner life, still, as we saw, this formula also was quite inadequate to the expression of the facts of outer nature. Hegel made a skillful diagnosis of the logic of passion. He pointed out how spirituality means conflict. He tried to show how this conflict proceeds from lower to higher stages, and how, in its evolution, all the forms of spirituality which human civilization in its growth exemplifies are necessa-rily produced. In this way Hegel built up, after his own fashion, an inadequate but profoundly suggestive philoso-phy of history, as well as a sort of rational construction of the whole content of human, social, and political life. In other words, Hegel tried to show how, on a Kantian basis, the world of human passion can be explained, and how we can escape from what we called the prison of the inner life, and prove ourselves to be in the world of the infinite spirit. Every step of Hegel's investigation was indeed open to some question, but in his own proper field he discovered what might be said to offer very high hopes to the rational idealist. But not even Hegel could really get into the charmed circle of the empirical sciences, and construct the facts of nature upon the postulates of idealism. He attempted this after a certain limited fashion, as Schelling had attempted it; but he failed. Both his pretensions in this regard and the nature of his failure have indeed been distorted and misrepresented by unjust opponents; but in any case there remains the fact that, as I just said, the first onslaught of idealism upon the central mysteries of reality failed; and it became necessary to consider what next to do.

How simple, then, under these circumstances, for idealists, or for men who had been trained in the idealistic school, but who saw this incompleteness of constructive idealism, — how simple for them now to say: "That the world is spiritual, that the inner life is in fact at the heart of it, seems, after Kant, clear. But equally clear it is that, at the depth of this nature which the inner life thus reveals to us, there are spiritual mysteries which for us, in our present ignorance, are so far unfathomable. Doubtless these mysteries are n't unfathomable in themselves; doubtless the one spirit whose life embodies itself in all our inner natures knows what he means, and has some sort of interpretation for even the apparently most capricious of his truths. But as for us, in our conscious nature, we only know that we, just now, are forced to see this sense-world and to work in it. Let us then turn for the solution of our mysteries back again to the long and painful road of experience. Why we are bound by our inner nature to see this world of sense-facts we can surely never say, until we shall have first learned empirically what sense-facts we are bound to see. This, however, only science can teach us."

We return to the natural order, as you see, in company with such thinkers, but by no means as if, in returning, we left our idealism behind us. We return, but, once more, not to *that* outer order which we left for the paths of speculation in the seventeenth century. The empirical sciences, which, in their own way and largely apart from any but indirect speculative influences, have been developing ever since the seventeenth century, which have been extending their field, elaborating their theories, tilling their vast and fruitful fields, will indeed no doubt at first misinterpret our return. Their servants, full of the learning and the successes of two centuries of inductive research, will scornfully say: " See these idealists ! They long tried to call the world their dream, and to construct it *a priori*. But they grew hungry in their wilderness, feeding the swine of strange masters, and longing for the very husks of speculative guess-work and delusion. Now they come back like prodigals, hoping that experience, our master, will have facts enough and to spare for them. In truth, had they remained at home, their reflective cleverness might have been of much use to science. But they took the portion of intelligence that belonged to them, and went away; and here they come now, in all the rags of their poor systems." So, perhaps, the scoffers will insist. But this sort of scorn will not impose upon us. We know that we were not prodigals, but rather spies, sent to spy out the land of promise, and what we bring back with us are great clusters of grapes as specimens of the wealth of a land of milk and honey beyond the Jordan of mystery. That land is still unconquered. We return to the friendly camp in the wilderness of this world, and we ask its followers to arise and go with us, that we may yet enter into that land, and possess it.

But, figures aside, our undertaking as we return to the study of the natural order is simply this: the mystery of the world is for us through and through an ideal, a spiritual mystery. This great order is once for all divine. And thus much our idealism has taught us, namely, (1) by showing us that, *except* for the world of ideas, except for the phenomena that appear as outer to beings with minds, or that have their place in the inner life of such beings, there is *no* reality at all ; (2) by showing us, as Kant has shown, that there can be no rational order in nature unless the thought of some rational being introduces such order, and (3) by leading us to postulate, as all the post-Kantian constructive idealists have postulated, that beneath the nature of our conscious self, which finds itself forced to recognize this or that as outer, there must lie a complete, an infinite Self, which somehow, whether by a divine caprice or by a divine rationality, or by both combined, is actually and of its own nature not outwardly forced, but inwardly minded, to express itself in this whole vast world of ours.   If, with all this at heart, we return to the outer order, it is because we desire our idealism to remain no longer barren, abstract, afraid of experience, capricious, wayward, sentimental, or fantastic. We want our idealism to do a manly work.   We want it to enter upon its true task, not of dreaming of a possible perfection, but of transforming, of enlivening, of spiritualizing, the concrete life of humanity.   Idealism on one side, dreaming its splendid dreams ; science on the other side, condemned to an irrational and Philistine enmity to the spiritual, — what spectacle could be more unworthy of humanity !   In fact, nobody has ever really desired such a situation.   In its most fantastic moments idealism, unless it were perchance the romantic irony of some young Friedrich Schlegel, has been sincerely anxious to embody experience, and to get at the truth of life.   Science, on the other hand, in the person and work of any earnest and sensible investigator, however narrow his specialty, however unspiritual seemed his facts, has been through and through spiritual in its inmost conception of reality. Divorced from speculation, as it has usually chosen to be, during the latter half of the eighteenth century and the first decades of the nineteenth century, it still has never lost sight of its task, namely, to elaborate the facts of experience in such wise as to find and to make apparent in them the laws, the essential truths, the ideas of things. When in Laplace's "Celestial Mechanics," and in Lagrange's completion of the system of the whole mechanical science of his day, a vast multitude of the most confusing natural phenomena were reduced to expressions of a very few ultimate and rigid thoughts, what was this but an embodiment of the search for rationality in nature? And all modern science up to the moment of which we are now speaking has been one vast and toilsome poem of rationality, fragmentary indeed, but even in its fragments how beautiful!

The business of speculation is then already outlined. What science seeks is essentially what we are seeking, — to catch the rhythm and the very pulse-beat of the reason that is and must be, amidst all the caprice of nature, yes, even because of this wealth of caprice in nature, at the very heart of the world. We return to the world of science, then, to enrich its postulates by our idealistic interpretation, and to enrich our own too abstract fashion of conceiving the rationality of things through the wealth of nature's facts.

Thus, as you see, I am now trying, still, of course, in my attitude as mere chronicler, to express the spirit in which, in the early decades of this century, many men of considerable speculative training set about their work in various departments of empirical research. They were idealists at heart; they became scientific specialists by profession. Of course, such is the narrowness of human nature, that only with great difficulty could such persons keep at once the purity of their idealistic faith and the exactness of their powers of empirical observation, equally well in sight as they toiled. Some of them, especially in Germany, remained for a long time the prey of various forms of systematic delusion, and warped their observations in order to illustrate their voluminous speculations. Still more of them, however, in turning their attention to exact scholarship, or to physical science, sought as much as possible to lay aside whatever speculative concern they had ever possessed. But still, after all, say what one will, one cannot fairly examine the thinking of this our century without seeing that during its whole course empirical research and the truly philosophical spirit have been bound in a close marriage tie compared to which all previous unions of speculation and of experience have been but the most passing moods of mutual admiration.

The most noteworthy offspring and illustration of this marriage tie has been the vast industry that has gathered about what we now call the idea of evolution, as a law, or rather, a group of laws, of nature.

II.

The philosophy of evolution was, in fact, to be my special topic to-day, and doubtless I have spent too long a time in approaching this topic itself. But so much I have gained if I have now prepared the way for a brief preliminary statement of the nature of the process whereby this philosophy arose in modern thinking. The way was this: Idealism having proved as unable to construct the visible world upon any *a priori* rational scheme, as it was successful in laying the foundation for the spiritual philosophy of the future, the problem that the earlier idealists had left to their successors was now: *To comprehend the world of experience in terms of the fundamental idealistic postulates.* In a search for the solution of this problem, thought was led to the rational study of human history. Surely if the great Spirit is anywhere to be manifest to us, then it should be in the growth of humanity. To see this growth as a spiritual process became, therefore, an object of serious concern. Of course here, as everywhere else in science, some of the first efforts were bold and crude enough, but they were suggestive. They led in time to that vast undertaking known as modern historical research, a sort of study that, strange as it may seem to say so, is not yet a century old. For, as we shall see, what used to be called historical research was something that in former centuries embodied a spirit very different from what we now know as the historical spirit. But the interest thus aroused spread to other branches of science. Natural history, which formerly had been, notwithstanding its name, a merely descriptive science, began to be pursued upon a deeper plan; it became truly historical, examined into the genesis of organic forms, and, in the field of geological study, set about the study of the succession of organic forms upon the earth's surface. The field thus entered upon proved unexpectedly fruitful. The century became the typical century of the historical theory of creation. In previous periods of modern thought, thinkers had deliberately neglected the history of things. Nature, not as it grows, but as it eternally is, was that which constituted the outer order known to the seventeenth century. Events had little concern to a doctrine like Spinoza's. Newton's conception of physical science was founded, indeed, upon the observation of the actual events of nature; but these events were to be explained, if possible, by eternal laws like gravitation, and history was to be absorbed in mechanism. When the eighteenth century turned its eyes towards the inner life, it still studied an ideally permanent thing called human nature, which savage life illustrated in its primitive innocence, civilized life in its artificial disguises, but which nothing in heaven or earth, except the will of its creator, could essentially change. But for our nineteenth century it is just the change, the flow, the growth of things, that is the most interesting feature of the universe. Old-fashioned science used to go about classifying things. There were live things and dead things; of live things there were classes, orders, families, genera, species, — all permanent facts of nature. As for man, he had one characteristic type of inner life, that was in all ages and stations essentially the same, — in the king and in the peasant, in the master and in the slave, in the man of the city and in the savage. The glory of science lay just in its power to perceive this essence of the eternally human everywhere in man's life. The dignity of human nature, too, lay in just this its permanence. Because of such permanence one could prove all men to be naturally equal, and our own Declaration of Independence is thus founded upon speculative principles that, as they are there stated, have been rendered meaningless by the modern doctrine of evolution. Valuable, indeed, was all this unhistorical analysis of the world and of man, valuable as a preparation for the coming insight; but how unvital, how unspiritual, how crude seems to us now all that eighteenth-century conception of the mathematically permanent, the essentially unprogressive and stagnant human nature, in the empty dignity of its inborn rights, when compared with our modern conception of the growing, struggling, historically continuous humanity, whose rights are nothing until it wins them in the tragic process of civilization, whose dignity is the dignity attained as the prize of untold ages of suffering, whose institutions embody thousands of years of ardor and of hard thinking, whose treasures even of emotion are the bequest of a sacred antiquity of self-conquest! Not inalienable, but hard won and painfully kept are the true rights of man. Not a special creation, but a living organism is our nature; an organism not permanent in its structure, but the outcome of labor; an organism with a long embryonic development, capable of degeneration as well as of growth, and needing therefore our constant care lest it lose all the spirituality and all the rights that it has thus far acquired.

Thus, I say, the historical conception of the world, and above all, of the world of human nature, has appeared in our modern life. I am now to trace more precisely the

growth and the consequences of this doctrine of evolution.
As in the case of the study of Schopenhauer, at the last
time, my task is at once aided and hindered by the popular reputation of my topic.   Many of the things that one
can most easily say about evolution are nowadays almost
too familiar, having been discussed even in the newspa-
pers until we are weary of them.   On the other hand, a
deeper insight into the true problems suggested by evolution is rather the more difficult on account of this familiarity; for the aspect of a deep subject which we most
need to reflect upon is never the one which purely popular discussion is likely to favor.   My difficulty is, therefore, in part like the difficulty of one writing an essay
upon Hamlet's Soliloquy, or on the Beatitudes.   The
words are so familiar that the meaning comes to seem
remote.   Even so here; the word "evolution" occurs on
very many modern title-pages, until one too easily forms
a habit of shutting any new book in which he chances to
encounter a term thus often repeated, but seldom appreciated.

The modern historical spirit assumed a definite form
not far from the time of the battle of Waterloo.   The
two events were, in fact, not at all disconnected.   In Germany, the romantic school proper had by this time fallen
into a decline.   The romantic movement, in a wider sense,
was, however, still flourishing, and, in fact the new historical movement was a direct outgrowth of this romantic
interest in life.   As for the mechanism of the process,
that is very obvious, but as it is not so frequently described to our public as it has been to the German public,
I must dwell for a moment on the main aspects of the intellectual situation in Germany in the first decade of the
century.   Germany itself, as you know, was at this time
a land trodden under the invader's foot, corrupted by the
invader's appeals to the avarice of its minor princes, and
left, in general, in a hopeless political situation, which,

strangely enough, aroused no strong lamentations in the
minds of the nation's own best men. Hegel, for example,
warmly admired for a time Napoleon, whom he saw in
person about the time of the battle of Jena, and whom he
then looked upon wonderingly as upon a sort of *Welt-
geist zu Pferde*, as the philosopher in effect expressed
himself. This political indifference, this free intellectual
curiosity, which marveled at the changes of the age and
felt no patriotic longings, was typical of the mood of all
Germany's intellectual class from Goethe down. Thought
was, after all, free; one had the empire of the air and the
recesses of the heart to one's self, and one let contemporary history go its course as it would. Meanwhile, however, this idealism without concrete and visible ideals was,
as we have seen, not only a capricious but a dangerous
thing. The representative younger poets of the time
reveled, as we know, in emotion and in mystery. The
whole romantic movement might be defined as a consciously wayward and, before it was done, a fairly morbid
reflection upon the heart of man viewed merely as the
heart. You felt, you experienced, you sang, you grew
constantly more sentimental, you gloried in the wealth of
your feelings, you wept in public with your numberless
lyrics, and then you felt and experienced and sang again
with endless ardor and garrulity. If you studied nature,
you loved above all things mere mysteries, divining rods,
magic, the night-side of nature generally. But, of course,
in all this there had to be, after all, something objective
as a foundation. Even feelings and mysteries must look
for facts to support them, and, greatly to our advantage,
the romanticists early turned their attention to certain
records of humanity's past experience which had been,
until very recently, almost wholly neglected by modern
students. Such records were of various classes, but had
in common this, that they all alike stood for ancient, or
else for very remote experiences, the product either of

quite mysterious or of little understood times and peoples. The favorite sources of such records were the
Orient and the Middle Ages. One could not have named
two regions of learned research that were more remote
from the customary thought of the middle of the eighteenth century than mediæval and Oriental civilization ;
one could not name any two branches of study that
appealed more to the distinctively romantic spirit than
did these. The Middle Ages, at any rate as men then
conceived them, were of course the typical period of romance. Then emotion had possessed every possible object
wherein to revel, — mysteries, magic, unknown countries,
crusades, knightly ideals, fairy tales, religious ardor, freedom of artistic forms, adventures, castles, saints, and the
Holy Roman Empire. Now that all these things had per-
ished, what better could romantic poets and readers do
than recall the long-past glories, and revive the buried
emotions. As for the Orient, what wisdom might lie
treasured there was still only faintly to be conjectured.
The prosaic Englishmen indeed, having conquered India,
had fallen to making learned researches into the literature, the thought, and the laws of their new subjects,
mainly with a view to the practical business of government. These researches had begun to become known on
the Continent. Sacred books, some of them philosophical,
had been translated. Meanwhile Mohammedan civilization also, from Persian and Arabic sources, was finding
its way to the renewed attention of European scholars.
No amateur esoteric Buddhist of our own day has felt a
deeper curiosity about what this Oriental wisdom might
mean, or has labored harder to find out, than did numerous
scholarly youth of this romantic period. Poets imitated
Oriental forms ; Hindu pantheism, or Persian Sufism, was
clothed in melodious verse by such voluminous singers as
Rückert ; men like the Schlegels forgot the romantic
irony, to learn Sanskrit ; a Wilhelm von Humboldt ex-

pounded the Bhâgavat-gita. Thus began the scholarship
that has produced the science of modern comparative philology, and our whole knowledge of the true life of the
far East.

Now the thing to note, for our purpose, in all this new
study, is, that its motive was at first mainly romantic, but
that its outcome was very significantly scientific. The
scholars of the two previous centuries had been linguists,
with a great love, in many cases, of the æsthetic aspects
of scholarship, but with little sense for what we now
think to be the truly human element in the study of the
languages and literatures of the world. It was the romantic love of passion, of mystery, and emotion, that now
set the heart's blood of scholarship fairly bounding in the
veins of the new learning. Sanskrit, Arabic, Persian, the
tongues of Europe in the Middle Ages, the old chroni-
clers, the poems of the mediæval Empire, — why, all
such things, if the eighteenth-century scholar had even
deigned to think of them with respect at all, would have
seemed to him but a series of crabbed linguistic puzzles,
not worthy for an instant of comparison with the problems
of classical philology. But the romantic movement
changed all that. The very spirit that in Great Britain
expressed itself in Scott's romances, once wedded to the
minuteness of German scholarship, was destined to transform the whole study of history.

For see, it was history that the romanticists thus found
themselves erelong devotedly studying. Men who had
set out to be merely fantastic dreamers perceived that the
far-off humanity of Asia or of mediæval Europe, had
dreamed better than they themselves could ever hope to
dream. As they studied the records of this humanity,
the dead past became once more alive. It was the present that now seemed, in its swift changes and in its un-
steady ideals, the unessential expression of the spirit of
humanity. Above all, men felt how those far-off times had

possessed, in their more permanent institutions, a treasure which the nineteenth century was daily risking,
if not losing, in the shifting conflicts of the Napoleonic
period.   And thus the institutions of humanity, whose
study has become so characteristic of our whole modern
movement, first came into the foreground of attention.
Laws, customs, religions, began to show a human worth
which students had, up to that time, persistently ignored.

In the keen interest that now quickly grew and con-
creted itself, nothing was too insignificant to deserve observation, if it illustrated the passions or the deeper faiths
of men.   Fairy tales, preserved in the mouths of the country people, ballads, rural superstitions, seemed interesting
to the wisest thinkers.   Even the rude dialects of the
illiterate began to acquire dignity.   The human was not
of necessity the cultivated.   The human was the wide-
spread or the ancient in speech or in behavior.   It was
the deep, the emotional, the thing much loved by many
men, the poetical, the organic, the vital, in civilization.
Scholars looked for it not in modern books, but in the
lore of forgotten ages, or heard it from the mouths of the
very peasantry of their own time.   The brothers Grimm
began to collect their German popular tales.   Poets were
proud to imitate the ballads of the people.

Nor did classical philology itself remain uninfluenced
by the romantic movement.   On the contrary, this movement transformed its very ideals and methods.   It was
no longer to favor mere linguistic skill, nor to cultivate
taste by analyzing the finest models of ancient literary
art.   It was rather to comprehend the inner life of antiquity, to set forth the nature of Greek and Roman
institutions, beliefs, and conduct, to show what relation
that civilization had to our own, to make linguistic study
a handmaid of truly humane scholarship, to treat the
classical history, not as a mere collection of examples for
moral or for literary edification, but as an evolution.   For,

already, as you see, the idea of what we call evolution was dawning on the minds of the scholars of that day. Far off indeed was our modern theory, with all its world-embracing inductions; but the spirit which it was to embody was born of the very dreams of the romantic period. Herein lies the continuity of thought which connects us, in all the so-called realism of our prosaic modern research, with the dreamers who dreamed, with the fantastic poets who failed, in the first decades of our century.

III.

But I have already somewhat anticipated. I said a moment since that the battle of Waterloo was not disconnected with the first bloom of the new historical study. The connection is not far to seek. Before 1815 the helplessness of Germany, bleeding and corrupted, left for the intellectual leaders of the people no resource equal to their dreams and their abstract idealism. The end of the Napoleonic episode brought room on earth for the feet of those who had long been traversing the empire of the air. The romanticists, however, did not on that account forsake contemplation. They only found themselves more disposed to scholarship, and less given to fantasy. I called the return to the natural order, a little while since, a return to the wilderness of this present world. Of course, I might reverse the Scripture metaphor and, appealing now to the book of Revelation, say that, as Satan lay bound in St. Helena, the church of the spirit could return from the wilderness into which it had fled; and that it swiftly did so. The scholarly motives that we have just been analyzing produced hereupon, in quick succession, a long series of epoch-marking historical books. Moreover, there was yet another reason why the political changes of the time were favorable to historical study. When great events are past, and a passionate episode of our lives is completed, we are easily disposed to the writing of chronicles. After one's first love affair, one keeps a diary for a season, or perhaps begins an autobiography, with special reference to the story of one's mightier passions. The doctrine of evolution took its rise in such an effort of humanity to write its own autobiography, after a terrible experience of being in love with what it had believed to be liberty, and of being jilted by what proved to be despotism. Thus all things worked together to the same end. It is surprising to look over the list of these great books, each one of which marks an era in modern investigation, and so many of which belong to the years between 1815 and 1835. The list shows a constant widening and deepening of the historical interest. General literature, Roman law, mediæval traditions and institutions, classical philology, Oriental literature, comparative philology, and at last Christian theology itself, are assailed after the historical fashion, and one research leads to another. The two Humboldts, the Schlegels, the Grimms, Niebuhr, Boeckh, Ranke, were all in the front rank of the students of the day, and a list, if complete, would name works by all of them, and by numerous other scarcely less important scholars. Curious was the fate that drove every scholarly specialty to become more and more historical. A book like Strauss's " Life of Jesus " might be in itself so novel in its methods, so tentative and imperfect in its hypotheses, that its own author would entirely change erelong his opinion about some of his own most noteworthy contentions. Yet the storm of controversy that it aroused would drive friend and foe to historical researches of a new sort ; and the whole of modern Christology, orthodox as well as unorthodox, has been profoundly modified by the indirect effect of Strauss's bold and suggestive investigation.

As for the outcome of all this ferment, it was inevitably the conception of the higher human life as one vast and connected growth from lower to nobler conditions,

with episodes, indeed, of stagnation and degeneracy, and
with vast outlying regions of almost changeless barbaric
or imperfectly civilized mankind, but with a meaning,
after all, about even the saddest of its phenomena, such
as the moralizing historians of former generations had
never understood.   This meaning lay in the physical dependence of man, for his whole civilization and culture,
upon the former generations of men.   After a fashion
people had, of course, always recognized such dependence.
But how deep and how concrete the new history found
the dependence to be!   Our language, our institutions,
our beliefs, our ideals, whatever in short, is mightiest and
dearest in all our world, all this together is a slow and
hard-won growth, nobody's arbitrary invention, no gift
from above, no outcome of a social compact, no immediate expression of reason, but the slowly formed concre-
tion of ages of blind effort, unconscious, but wise in its
unconsciousness, often selfish, but humane even in its selfishness.   The ideals win the battle of life by the secret
connivance, as it were, of numberless seemingly un-ideal
forces.   Climate, hunger, commerce, authority, superstition, war, cruelty, toil, greed, compromise, tradition, con-
servatism, loyalty, sloth, — all these coöperate, through
countless ages, with a hundred other discernible tendencies, to build up civilization.   And civilization itself is,
in consequence, a much deeper thing than appears on the
surface of our consciousness.   Instinct has a larger share
in it than reasoning.   Faith counts for more in it than
insight.   It embodies in concrete form that deeper self
that the idealists loved to talk about.   Your deeper self is
plainly a sort of abstract and epitome of the whole history of humanity.   A new and wiser form of the doctrine of metempsychosis occurs to you.   The humanity
that toiled and bled and worshiped of old has trans-
mitted to you, in your language and institutions, in the
ancient lore that your fathers teach you, in your preju-

THE SPIRIT OF MODERN PHILOSOPHY.

dices, in your faults, in your conscience, in your religion, the very soul of its agony and of its glory. You can read in history your personal instincts written in the language of evolution. You can watch the human spirit in its growth with a deeper sense of the "That art Thou" than you had ever before possessed. The metaphors of your heathen ancestors are crystallized in every word that you utter. The very horrors of their superstitions are the true though humble origin of your loftiest and most sacred devotions. Humanity never really forsakes its past. The days of mankind are bound each to each in mutual piety.

All these ideas have now, to be sure, become, by dint of much repetition, too commonplace. It is well for us to remember that the most cultivated thinkers of the last century scarcely in any measure possessed them. The unity of humanity, as the last century conceived it, was, I repeat, an abstract unity, a dead and permanent thing. All men had erect stature, language, reason, and the power to laugh. As some men stood straighter than others, so some men had more wit, and of such were the enlightened souls of that century. That was to their own minds the whole story of the unity of human life, and as for the growth of institutions, and all the agony of the winning of our life by the men of old, — the eighteenth century, at least until its very last decades, thanked God that it knew too much of wisdom to worry itself about any of the men of old except the wise ones, such as Cicero, or the elegant ones, such as Horace. Superstition you outgrew, the customs of your ancestors you prudently forgot, and of history you remembered only what it would be pleasing to narrate on a social occasion. Hence, as we see, our modern commonplace is after all something of a novelty, even a paradox.

I have dwelt so long upon this transformation of our notion of human history, because people too frequently regard the doctrine of evolution as having for the first time flashed upon the world after the appearance of Darwin's "Origin of Species." Nobody can value more than I do the significance for the general student of the splendid achievement of Darwin; but it was a splendid achievement for humanity at large because the age was ripe for the extension of the historical conception far beyond the boundaries of humanity proper. And, once more, the age was thus ripe because by this time scholarship had brought into existence this very conception of history itself in the modern sense of the word. If you can conceive Darwin's knowledge of natural history, his investigations, and his marvelous induction that led to the principle of natural selection, with all its consequences, if, I say, you can conceive all this transferred to the last century, some properly informed naturalists might, no doubt, have been convinced; but the world at large could have found no place for the doctrine. It would have been to them only one oddity the more in nature, or rather in speculation. They would have called it Darwin's paradox, and would have banished it into the realm of curiosities. It was coming into an historical age that made Darwin's book so great a prize, and the idea of natural selection so deeply suggestive to philosophy.

And now, having spent so much time in laying our foundation, we can swiftly suggest in a few words the climax of the doctrine of evolution which the natural sciences have at last made possible. Germany began the historical movement. It was left for England to complete the ascendency of the new thought. It is matter of popular knowledge that geology, in its modern form, is largely due to the British mind. Lyell's researches substituted for the catastrophes which the earlier geologists conceived relatively uniform natural processes, whereby, as they worked through long ages, the earth's crust had been slowly modified. On the basis of this uniformitarian geology, a doctrine of the transformation of species began to look more reasonable. Such a doctrine, indeed, as a mere speculation, is one of the oldest guesses of infant science, and even the Darwinian notion of natural selection had been first formulated in Greek speculation by Empedocles, before the time of Socrates. But such guesses, however finely a Schelling might write out their substance in poetical form, as we found him doing awhile since, could never mean much for science until modern geology had made probable that the earth's crust itself has a genuine history, wherein there is more of unity than of catastrophic change. But herewith came very quickly the time when natural history as a whole could assume the truly historical shape. Von Baer's embryological researches, and the classifications and embryological studies of Agassiz, showed that wonderful parallelism between the growth of the individual life and the relation of each animal form to its neighbors and predecessors on the earth, which soon came to have so deep a scientific meaning. The appearance of Darwin's " Origin of Species " in 1859, however, brought to a focus all these tendencies of modern research. With the one exception of Newton's " Principia," no single book of empirical science has even been of more importance to philosophy than this work of Darwin's. And you know now wherein the importance lay. The world was longing for an historical view of phenomena. The historical interest was already excited to the keenest pitch. Human civilization was already conceived as an evolution. The earth's crust was already known to embody a history whose gaps, still, even at this present moment, very large, were already, in 1859, sufficiently reduced to make probable the notion that a continuous series of physical process, without violent convulsions, had produced the whole succession of geological strata. The old nebular hypothesis of Kant and La Place suggested that the whole growth of our solar system to its present form had been part of the very process that has ended in our own geological history. Only the boundary line between species and species, only the difficulty of conceiving in scientific terms the growth of animal forms without the interference anywhere of special creations, only this, which was, of course, most felt in case of the distinction between man and the animals, remained as an apparently impassable obstacle in the way of the triumph of the historical movement. Darwin's book removed this last great obstacle. In the working of natural selection he found an agency sufficient to explain, in part, if not in the main, the transformation of species. And there could be no question, after his researches, that natural selection is a *vera causa*, that is, is actually at work in the organic world. Moreover, he showed, in his first and in his later works, that the whole mass of evidence for the transformation of species and the animal origin of man is far greater than the evidence that natural selection itself is the only natural agency at work. In fact, since Darwin, while naturalists differ endlessly as to the degree to which natural selection is responsible for the transformation of species, further investigation has put it farther and farther beyond question that, once granting the postulates of empirical science, the doctrine of the transformation of species, and of the animal origin of man, is simply beyond question. All modern naturalists of note are in this sense followers of Darwin, not that they all hold his views about natural selection, but that they all teach the doctrine of transformation.

But our interest is just now much less in this bit of empirical science as such than in the philosophical views to which it has led men.

IV.

The doctrine of evolution had its rise, as we have now seen, in a twofold interest. This interest was first an historical one, the offspring of the idealistic interest in the meaning of things, the product of an age for which the processes of the world were primarily spiritual processes, or were to be interpreted in the light and by the analogy of such processes. But, on the other side, this interest was a strongly empirical one, the offspring of a dread of the extravagances of the idealistic period, the product of a hard-learned lesson in caution, the embodiment of an unwillingness to mistake fantasy for truth. On the one side, then, the doctrine of evolution is to be sharply distinguished from the naturalism of the seventeenth century. Unlike that naturalism our modern doctrine is primarily disposed, not merely to explain, but to estimate nature. It tries to find growth in the world as well as mechanism, progress as well as law, ideally interesting products as well as absolutely rigid processes. But, on the other hand, the same doctrine has become more and more disposed, as time has gone on, to suppress, or at all events to subordinate its own original idealism ; for it is a doctrine about experience, a theory founded on observation ; and mere experience as such does n't show us ideal forces at work in nature, only facts that we, as observers, are able to interpret, if we like, in terms of ideals. Without interest in the historical aspect of things, without, then, an essentially idealistic concern for what the events of the world *mean*, for what story they seem to embody, we should never have come upon this notion of evolution at all. But without a patient devotion to facts, and a rigid self-control as to our romantic interpretations, we should never have done the work necessary to verify the notion. There remains, then, something conflicting, something inherently self-contradictory in the views nowadays current as to the nature of the process of evolution itself. This inner conflict of modern thought furnishes one of the most characteristic problems of to-day. It is the problem of the so-called Philosophy of Evolution. The empirical generalization that the whole life of our planet is in all probability one continuous process, free from unintelligible or magical breaks and interferences, is one great outcome of modern research, — an outcome inconceivable except on the basis of numerous presuppositions which philosophy must analyze, but for all that an outcome that appeals for proof to the facts of experience, rather than to the romantic intuitions of the age of Schelling. But the interpretation of this generalization, — the inner sense of it, — what of that? Have we hereby banished ideals from the world? have we really restored the faith in the rigid outer order of Spinoza? or have we not rather, for the first time, got a true empirical verification of the presence of the great active Spirit in his world? Is it the continuity, the physical necessity, the unalterably fatal law of the process that our science is beginning to make clear? or is it rather the immanence in nature of ideal powers, of significant tendencies, that from the beginning so moulded the atoms, so predetermined the laws of their mechanism, so endowed them with swift flight and with close affinity, that the outcome of ages of their motion has been spiritual, — is it this that we are now discovering by our experience? Here the thought of our day pauses, hesitant; here the spirit in which the whole labor of the century was begun stands in conflict with the spirit of positive and empirical science that the century has developed as it has proceeded.

But whatever is to be the outcome of this conflict, let me point out to you that at all events those who are nowadays accustomed to speak of a Philosophy of Evolution, ought to have no doubt as to what their expression, *if* it is to mean anything, must mean. A *doctrine* of evolution may be, like Darwin's doctrine of natural selection, a purely empirical theory, a generalization from facts with a use of the postulates of science, and nothing more. How nature came by this seemingly ideal character of her processes, such an empirical doctrine need not try to explain. But a *philosophy* of evolution, if there is ever to be one, must face just that ultimate question, Has the world a meaning? and, as a philosophy of a true *evolution*, must answer that question in the affirmative; for a philosophy, or at all events an affirmative, a positive phi-losophy, is, as we have seen all along, an effort to express, and by criticism to establish, the presuppositions of the age which it reflects upon. Now the presumption of an historical age is that there is a history embodied in the known world, and a philosophy of evolution must be an effort to give voice to this presupposition. If there is anything true in a philosophy of evolution, then there is something *more* than mere physical causation, mere mechanism in the world; for how there can be history in the world, no causal explanation, no appeal to mechanism as such, can ever directly express. In so far as you find mechanism only in the world, you find neither growth nor decay; you find no story at all. The return to the outer order in our century has therefore in its presupposition not been a return to the old outer order of the seventeenth century. It has been a return to a world pervaded, as it were, with the spirit of idealism. If there is not merely a group of sciences having a fictitiously historical interest, but a true evolution, then there are ideal interests expressed in this outer order of nature, spiritual passions (to borrow Schelling's romantic expression) frozen into this lava stream of nature's mechanism. Those who have believed that the spirit of the age of evolution removed ideals, removed teleology from the world, have, then, failed to see that the presupposition of our historical age, ever since Rousseau and the romantic period, has been that history is worth studying for its own sake, and that therefore ideals are responsible for nature's mechanism.

But just herein, you see, lies once more the deepest problem of recent philosophy. The seventeenth century, before doubt and idealism came, used to say: " We know

that there are rigid and necessary laws of nature's mechanism; and as all is necessary, therefore the historical is
insignificant. The world of to-day is the world of eternity." But our age, returning to a seemingly rigid outer
order, returns with idealism in its reflective thought, with
spiritual passion as its deepest presupposition, and insists
that, whatever nature's mechanism, there is still no knowledge so profound as the knowledge of the history of
things. Yet how can this insistence be defended? The
doctrine of evolution, I assert, is in heart and essence the
child of the romantic movement itself. Can the child,
inheriting its mother's depth and longing for wisdom,
defend this inheritance in this vast outer universe of rigid
order and absolute law? That is the true problem of the
philosophy of evolution. I know many who regret the tendency in our day to apply the doctrine of the transformation of species to humanity, who fear the apparently
materialistic results of the discovery that the human mind
has grown. For my part there lies in all this discovery
of our day the deeply important presupposition that the
transition from animal to man is in fact really an evolution, that is, a real history, a process having significance.
If this is in truth the real interpretation of nature, then
the romantic philosophy has not dreamed in vain, and the
outer order of nature will embody once more the life of a
divine Self.

v.

Yet we must not too much anticipate later results.
Presuppositions are not yet the philosophy which is to
establish them; passions are not yet proofs. Let me try,
as I close, to suggest something of those attitudes towards
the problems of our day which are now best known and
most characteristic. Thus I shall be able to conclude our
historical sketch, and to pass to the second and more positive part of our survey of modern problems.

Towards the vast world of science with the endless mul-

titude of its facts, collected as they have been under the
influence of the spirit that I have been describing in the
present lecture, it is possible to take the attitude of declaring that, whatever interest led to their collection, the
facts are now so numerous and complex as to exclude
henceforth and forever any attempts at a philosophy.
The fantastic failures of the idealistic age may be looked
upon as illustrating the weakness of human powers. A
modest sense of the puzzling mystery of things may regard as final in Kant's doctrine only its confession of
ignorance; and may find in the later systems only romances. The business of to-day, one may declare, is with
science, with the world of experience, with the facts.
The world in its wholeness is too much for us. The outcome of philosophy has been the one lesson of the need of
recognizing our limitations.

This result of the return to the outer order is nowadays
natural and familiar enough. In so far as it expresses a
mere private and personal unwillingness on the part of
many people to undertake the philosophical task, I respect
this spirit, and urge no argument against those who happen to be possessed by it. Reflection is not a man's
whole business. Our modern world is indeed vast. There
is a great diversity of gifts amongst us. Many of us are
better men without philosophy. Let such as are so cling
to experience. I will not molest them. These lectures
are not addressed to them.

I object to this way of looking at the modern situation
of human thought only when those who assume it declare
that the history of thought teaches this sort of resignation, or that the problems and results of modern science
demand it of us in any novel or peculiar sense. On the
contrary, if ever there was an age that demanded not resignation, but industry in philosophy, it is our own. The
incomplete results of the previous periods of thought, the
wondrous suggestiveness of Kant, the marvelous analyses

of self-consciousness, and of its relation to truth, whereof
the idealistic age is full, this new problem suggested by
the doctrine of evolution, — are not all these things a
challenge to our time, a challenge such as previous ages
have never heard ?   What our age is challenged to do is,
not to invent some revolutionary novelty in philosophy,
but to organize the outcome of earlier reflection.   Organization — it is the one greatest idea of our time.   Synthesis — it is the one undertaking of our century.   Do you
find a mass of fragmentary little states, spiritually related
by tongue and literature, sundered by bitter fortune, —
then by blood and iron you make them into one empire.
Is your republic endangered by local jealousies and private interests, — then at the cost of years of warfare you
force these factions to know their own brotherhood.   Is
society imperiled by too much individualism, — then your
leaders become filled with the spirit of social organization.
Everywhere the same spirit is abroad.   Shall thought
remain untouched by it?   Shall reflection, frightened by
the diversity of opinions, refuse to attempt their synthesis?
For what is needed, I repeat, is not some new gospel,
preached by an angel from heaven, but a synthesis of the
truth that we now have ready at hand.   Schopenhauer
and Hegel, Spinoza and Kant, mechanism and teleology,
nature and evolution, experience and reason, — these are
all, not mere names for warring tendencies, whose conflict
proves that all things are and must remain a mystery to
us men ; these stand rather for embodiments now of
this, now of that deeper truth.   Their existence is, I repeat, a challenge to us, not to see how much they differ,
but how well they belong together.   No other age ever
had so rich a suggestion of such a synthesis of truth.
Can we afford to neglect our opportunity ?

It is n't despair, then, that the complexity of modern
thought teaches us.   It is rather the wondrous beauty of
the philosophical problem of the age that is shown us by

this very complexity. Nor is the return to the outer order necessarily a forsaking of philosophic theory for experience. No, experience itself is meaningless without presuppositions. Every one has an unconscious philosophy. Every one has beliefs about the world as world, and in its wholeness. One may neglect or even hate a conscious philosophy. Nobody is without the faith that it would need a whole philosophy to make articulate. The question, What is experience? was Kant's own question; and to that question the whole idealistic age was a fragmentary answer. In vain, then, do you say: I, for my part, hold fast by experience, and forsake theory. There is in truth no experience without theory, and philosophy is simply theory brought to consciousness of itself.

VI.

But now, if, still following the history of current tendencies, one passes to a mention of those thinkers who, recognizing the true situation of modern thought, and not abhorring reflection, have undertaken this great synthetic task of philosophy itself, and have done so from the modern point of view, you will at once think, especially in connection with the doctrine of evolution, of the name of Mr. Herbert Spencer. You will ask of me, at this point, some suggestion of the relation of this noteworthy thinker to the movement whose growth I have been following. The barest suggestion, indeed, is all that I can make. Mr. Spencer will be to me here an illustration of one way of meeting the modern situation as it has now been described. Mr. Spencer, as everybody who knows anything of his career is aware, did not wait for the appearance of Darwin's "Origin of Species" before seizing upon the idea of his general "Formula of Evolution." The thought that the processes of nature are historical, that the very mechanism of the physical world is such as is bound to show to the onlooking spectator the spectacle of a rhythmic alternation of growth and decay, and that in this rhythmic alternation all the various histories of the solar system, of the earth's crust, and of the life of the animals and of men, are contained, — this thought came early to the mind of this singularly patient and many-sided student of science and of politics. During the fifties he thought out the main outlines of his future system of synthetic philosophy, published the first edition of his " Psychology," and embodied in periodical essays his notion of " Progress, its Law and Cause," as well as the application of this notion to several important problems of natural history, of social science, and of the history of humanity. Early in the sixties his system began to appear ; but it was not until after 1870 that he won the general recognition which has made him, in this country, in the eyes of so many, the one true prophet of the philosophy of evolution, and that has given him a worthy name and influence throughout the realm of European scientific inquiry. To-day his system is still unfinished. A world of new investigations, which he follows industriously but without noteworthy change of his opinions, has grown up about him, inviting him to eternally new labors, but always only confirming in his mind his own convictions. He undertook long since the task of a Titan. He has pursued this task for full thirty years with the patience of an enthusiast. The skillful devotion of the man is unquestionable. His value as an awakener and organizer of research is vast. What can we say of his place in the history of philosophy ?

Mr. Spencer stands in a singular position, whether you regard him as an Englishman or as a philosopher. Englishman he is, but how unlike Locke or Berkeley, with their classical limitations of outlook and of inquiry, with their doubtful attitude towards researches that lay beyond the circle of their immediate interests, with their unwillingness to apply philosophy to more than a few problems.

Mr. Spencer in his position amongst English thinkers is so far more like Hobbes. The whole range of problems seems to concern him. He attempts fearlessly the most stupendous of tasks. He would unify science. His province is the world of experience in its entirety. He is fond of mentioning in the same sentence or paragraph nebulæ and starfishes, savages and molecules, the laws of motion and the institutions of Europe. Nor is this wide range chosen by him because of mere waywardness, or from the mere love of variety in illustration. He mentions all these things because he seems to himself to have a formula for them. Unlike Hobbes he is, on the other hand, in his fondness for the letter of this formula itself, in his fearlessness about the use of highly abstract phrases, in his endless repetitions and illustrations of a few principal aspects of his fundamental thought. All this, I say, this combination of universality of purpose with abstractness of expression, is an un-English trait in Mr. Spencer. It allies him so far with Hegel, and with the other inventors of world-embracing formulas. An Englishman who writes on philosophy usually loves the Socratic fashion of posing as a plain man of simple undertakings and of obvious ideas. Mr. Spencer speaks rather as one having authority. If you criticise him, he replies that you have failed to comprehend the subtlety and the many-sidedness of his thought. He does not reply as Socrates or as Berkeley would have done, that it is the critic who is too subtle and artificial to grasp the concrete ideas of a plain man. On the contrary, Mr. Spencer, more after the fashion of Hegel, knows that his formula is only for trained minds, like his own, for men who, like himself, have lived long amidst deep contemplations, and who are accustomed to world-compelling synthetic thought. In this synthetic character of his thought, again, that seems to give him a place amongst the characteristic thinkers of this our third period of modern philosophy. As we have

now repeatedly seen, the great business of modern thought
is the discovery of the unity of apparently diverse lines of
investigation, the reconciliation of seemingly hopeless contradictions, the unification of the world which anarchical
passion and analytic reflection have conspired to rend
asunder.   And Mr. Spencer undertakes everywhere to be
a reconciler, an unifier, one who harmonizes through synthesis, and who brings to light oppositions only to enrich
thought by suggesting their organic unity.   Science and
religion, empiricism and rationalism, Locke and Kant,
egoism and altruism, mechanism and evolution, nature
and history, — such are some of the seemingly opposing
forces that he would critically reunite, even in the act of
dwelling upon their warfare.   His world, too, is rent by
great conflicts; but its unity is to be more than its conflicts.   Mr. Spencer's great popular reputation is largely
due to this organizing spirit that everywhere shows itself
in his writings.   That, again, is why young men love him
so intensely.   And their love is so far well suggested by
his imposing dignity of enterprise.   His categories, meanwhile, look so much more empirical and concrete than
Hegel's, or than those of other similar philosophic unifiers.
The redistribution of matter and motion is so much more
scientific-sounding a phrase for the description of the process of nature than is Hegel's notion of the absolute.   The
passage from the indefinite and homogeneous to the definite and heterogeneous, which Mr. Spencer makes the
type of all cosmical evolution, is so much more readily
conceivable than is Hegel's *Negativität*.   But one thus
indeed forgets, as one reads, that over every statement of
Mr. Spencer's about the outer world broods that dim and
shadowy Unknowable of his, whose mystery gives to every
assertion about the unity of its own processes an air of
doubt and of unintelligibility.   In the same breath Mr.
Spencer, in fact, seems to assure you that he knows all and
nothing about this unity of scientific truth.   The real outer

world is according to him this Unknowable itself.   The
Absolute is an impenetrable mystery.   Consciousness cannot transcend its own boundaries.   The limitation of knowledge is thus for Mr. Spencer the tragic defeat of the highest purpose of knowledge.   Human thought will never
reach its real goal, and that, not because human thought is
merely unfinished, but because genuine knowledge of outer
truth is in its very essence inconceivable, contradictory,
hopeless.   Yet all the while Mr. Spencer has that universal formula, namely, his law of evolution.   And this formula shall be true, and true about objective nature, about a
real world, about something that does transcend consciousness.   Idealistic constructions of the absolute shall be
impossible, just because the absolute is unknowable.
But unification of science, an empirical construction of an
universally valid and objective law, shall be possible,
although the outer truth is essentially unknowable.

This well-known paradox of Mr. Spencer's is extremely
characteristic of the halting attitude of much contemporary thought.   As for the Unknowable itself, we shall
have something to say of it hereafter, in the second part
of our course.   For the present one may note, as an
historical fact, that both doubters and mystery-mongers
(of whom our time is full) often take an almost equal
delight in Mr. Spencer's theory of the Unknowable: the
one class because they perceive that he, too, doubts, the
other class because they find in Mr. Spencer's vague
speech, as to this matter, words that arouse their most
religiously unutterable longings and croonings.   Kant's
things in themselves were, indeed, somewhat similar to
this Unknowable; yet they were at least sharply distinguished from the knowable phenomena.   All that Kant
ever pretended, even provisionally or partially, to " unify "
was the world of the inner life.   But in Mr. Spencer's
doctrine it is our knowledge of the outer world which is
to be " unified; " and yet this outer, as such, cannot truly

be known save as to the bare fact of its existence. The
union of knowable and unknowable in Mr. Spencer's system is thus a painfully corrupt one.   " Reconciled " they
are in the system much as science and religion are reconciled at the outset of the " First Principles."   In case of
most of Mr. Spencer's " reconciliations," the opposing
interests are, in fact, first more or less developed, and then
deliberately ignored.   The reconciled terms and interests
enter into the reconciling formula, much as the dead in
Job's lamentation enter Sheol, and find peace: " The
small and the great are there, and the servant is free
from his master."   " The prisoners rest together, they
hear not the voice of the oppressor."   " The wicked cease
from troubling and the weary are at rest."   So, I say, are
the great interests of humanity, the great problems of
philosophy, the concerns of science, and the passions of
religion, at rest in the dim recesses of the Spencerian
fórmulas.

One of the most noteworthy and valuable features of
Mr. Spencer's thought, meanwhile, in its influence upon
our age, is seen in the curious fact of the actual fruitfulness for modern discussion of some of his very vaguest
formulas.   Mr. Spencer lives in a time when no accent of
the Holy Ghost fails to reach the ear of some breathless
listener.   So hungry is this our modern world for truth
that the least hint suggests to it a feast of insight.   And
that is why Mr. Spencer's comprehensive syntheses have
been so significant for many minds, and, despite their
vagueness, will have a part in the outcome of human philosophy.   The whole doctrine of Mr. Spencer remains, to
my mind, a vast programme of a philosophy of evolution.
The author's idea, namely, to give a general account of
the nature of the historical process as such, is a great
idea.   I do not find in his actual formula anything at all
successful or satisfying.   The processes of differentiation
and of integration, which he tries to describe and unite in

this formula, are ill universalized through his famous definition of evolution. Not all historical processes are described by even these abstract terms. Still less are all
the processes that his formula includes historical in their
nature. But still the thought of the whole, which is the
thought that the world of natural mechanism must be
shown to be also, in another aspect of its nature, historical, is a deep and thoroughly modern thought, and that
is the thought which I believe to be the outcome of the
whole work of the century.

VII.

Outside of the circle of the special teachings of Mr.
Spencer we find, meanwhile, a group of doctrines which
make a more or less serious effort at being philosophical,
and which retain of idealism only a few fragmentary elements. But these doctrines are withal so significant of
our age and of its problems, that I should do ill, even in
this fragmentary sketch, if I wholly failed to characterize
them. I allude to the doctrines best known by the very
general epithet, Monistic. In them the idealistic tradition still lives, but in an unconscious fashion. The coy
doctrine of the world as spirit, pursued too hotly by
former lovers, has been metamorphosed, and now survives
in a sort of Daphne-like slumber, under such names as
the Mind-Stuff theory, or the doctrine of the Double
Aspect. Readers of modern discussion are not unfamiliar with such statements as that the doctrine of evolution has taught us the "Oneness of all Existence;" this
oneness meaning that the world is somehow made of one
stuff, and that this stuff is at once essentially physical
and essentially mental in its qualities. Schopenhauer,
whose real system was at heart a much more subtle and
profound doctrine than much of this modern monism,
used phrases that already suggest its formulas. The will,
he used to say, is just nature's physical causation " seen

from within;" while the laws of nature are the will "seen from without." Using this phrase, and avoiding Schopenhauer's own systematic context for the phrase, many recent thinkers have sought to reconcile science and philosophy after much the following fashion: —

Nature, they say, shows us material processes, subject to fixed law. Matter is known to be real, for experience tells us so. The idealistic views of post-Kantian thought are mere romances. Kant's own subjectivism was unscientific. The real world first appears as the physical world, full of matter in motion. But now what is this matter in motion? Experience makes clear that in certain very highly complex organisms, and, in particular, in the nerve-centres of these organisms, certain masses of matter exhibit mental characteristics, so that here molecular motion is accompanied by consciousness. The more highly organized the nerve-centres in question, the higher the consciousness; the simpler the organism, the simpler the consciousness, until, low in the scale, we come to what seem to be unconscious organisms, and lower still, to what seems to be inanimate matter. The doctrine of evolution teaches us that the transition from lower to higher has been, so far as the material processes are concerned, a continuous process. The more complex has evolved from the simpler. The organisms that possess consciousness are the offspring of an ancestry which in earlier stages of evolution would have seemed to possess none. Moreover, each conscious individual, in his growth from the egg, passes from the condition of a little mass of protoplasm to the condition of a knowing and thinking being. As matter organizes, mind gives evidence of its presence. As the brain disintegrates in old age or in disease, mind alters or disappears. What now is the meaning, the outcome, of all these facts? Is it not this? As the material elements of the brain existed before the brain, and came together to form it, so the elements of the mind existed

apart from and before the conscious mind itself, and by
their synthesis have produced it. And what, once more,
can this mean? Does it not signify that the elements of
the mind and the elements of the brain are *not* two sorts
of substance, but one; that the consciousness is, as it
were, only the inner aspect of that which, seen from without, appears as the brain; and that each atom of the
brain is only the representative, in the world of physics, of
that which, otherwise viewed, is in its essence an element
of the mind? The world that the doctrine of evolution
shows us is, in fact, a world of one continuous process.
At one end of this process we find what seems to be dead
matter. At the other end we find, say in our own inner
life, what seems to be pure mind. How can one process
show such different things? Yet the continuity of the
process, its persistence through all the ages of the evolution of our planet, the absence of proof of external interference, all these indicate that there must have been one
real stuff present throughout, despite the variety of its
manifestations. The various manifestations must then be
only in seeming and not in ultimate foundation various.
The so-called dead matter was always in essence mental.
The consciousness known to us in our inner life has that
physical aspect which the observer calls our brain. The
same substance it is, then, that " seen from within " appears as mind, and that " seen from without " is called
matter.

A well-known passage of M. Taine's book on " The Intellect " uses, to state this doctrine, the figure of a text
and interlinear translation, which, in the book of nature,
appear in some places side by side, as the two series: the
mental and the physical phenomena of the world. In
some regions the text only appears to the observer (as
each one of us, and he only, knows his own inner life);
while elsewhere, as in our observation of " dead " matter,
only the translation appears to us, not the text. The in-

ference is that, mutilated as our copy of the text may be, both text and translation are meant in the original of our book to be parallel, correspondent, and, in deepest sense, one. This, then, is the theory of Monism, as the doctrine of evolution has suggested it to many recent thinkers.

In further development the expressions of the doctrine differ widely. The lamented Clifford, in one of the most brilliant of his essays, that on "Mind-Stuff," gave to modern monism one of its most suggestive formulations. Independently, Dr. Morton Prince, of Boston, in a book on "The Nature of Mind and Human Automatism," reached, a number of years since, the same thought. So stated, monism declares that the real stuff of the world is *not* an unknown somewhat, an *x*, that when viewed as we view our own states appears as mind, and that when viewed from without appears as matter. On the contrary, this real stuff of things is, for Clifford and for Dr. Prince, nothing but mind itself, known to us directly and in its true essence when we know our own feelings, known to us indirectly and obscurely when it is formed of the feelings that are *not* ours, and that, affecting our feelings from without, are represented therein by our ideas of material things beyond us. The world is thus in reality mind, but not of necessity conscious mind, rather only a vast congeries of elementary feelings, out of which, when they come into close relations to one another, as they do in our organisms, complex mental life, and finally consciousness, can be and is made. The process of evolution is the process of the organization of this mind-stuff. The laws of nature's mechanism are the laws of the relations of mind-stuff atoms ; and there is but this one stuff in all things.

Other lovers of this modern monism are not always so simple in their formulations. To many the truth of the doctrine lies in the thought that matter and mind are simply diverse aspects of one ultimate substantial stuff. But what this is, conscious or unconscious, feeling or not-feeling, we are not to know. The true stuff is an x with two faces, a substance more like Spinoza's, whose two attributes, material and physical, we comprehend by experience, but whose essence is only made articulate for us in terms of these its attributes.

Such is a suggestion of this, one of the best-known tendencies of recent speculation. You see its tentative and empirical character; you see its close relation to the doctrine of evolution; you see also how far it is from meeting the critical requirements that, since Kant, are necessarily made of a philosophy. This naive acceptance of the possibility that out of a mass of feelings you can build up a self, this faith that feelings can somehow "come together" or "organize themselves," when we know of no such thing in experience as a loose feeling out of organization at all, or apart from the unity of a self, this belief in the "oneness" of things on the basis of an uncriticised experience, — all these things make modern empirical monism rather a suggestion than a philosophy. In some ways, as you will later see, I prize it highly and make use of its insight. I cannot rest content with it.

VIII.

Herewith ends my sketch of the rise of the doctrine of evolution. Of the positive significance of the doctrine for philosophy, a later discussion must say something. And herewith, as sometimes before in my lectures, I lay aside the attitude of the mere chronicler; only this time I lay it aside finally and altogether. We have traveled a long road in company; we have now, at last, reached the problems of the present day. Heretofore I have tried to tell a story, — in my own words indeed, generally with my own illustrations, often in so untechnical a fashion as to run the risk of leaving my author sadly misunderstood; but always with a desire to let the history in some fashion unfold its own inner meaning, display its own continuity, and furnish its own criticism of the errors and partial insights which we have encountered. You have seen throughout, I suppose, where my sympathies have been lying; at the outset I confessed to you the nature of my own philosophical creed; and on several occasions, especially in recent lectures, I have freely supplemented history by personal expressions of opinion. But from this time forth I am no longer to be a chronicler who frequently criticises, but a student who risks his own positive creed for whatever it may prove to be worth. The substance of this creed I shall in the concluding lectures suggest, with special reference to the point that we have now reached in our study. I shall try to make my doctrine the legitimate outcome of the reflective process that I have been describing to you. I am, as you now know, an idealist. I find Kant's analysis of our knowledge in its essence the true one. Kant erred chiefly in what he omitted to analyze, and in his assumption of those useless things in themselves. As far as his deeper study of the inner life of the intellect went, he was on his own ground, and he knew it wonderfully well, for all his burden of technical subtleties and for all his pedantic schematism. He held that space and time are mental. To my mind this is unquestionable. He held that all judgment is essentially only an appeal to my own deeper Self, and that all knowledge depends on my unity with my deeper Self. This seems to me the profoundest truth of philosophy. What Kant did not make clear was what this, my deeper Self, is. It certainly is n't my empirically conscious self. It certainly is n't the person called by my individual name. I find in the later idealists many suggestions as to what this deeper Self is. I am very fond, as you have seen, of Hegel's tragic but highly vital formula for the paradox of consciousness, the struggle of self-knowledge and self-mastery, as the very life of this passionate deeper Self. I do not, however, think that Hegel has told the whole truth about the Self. I find great interest in saying, with

Schopenhauer, that to know the Self we must first watch it as it plays the world-game, not as if the facts of the world were ever really external to thought, but because the deeper Self, although one, needs an infinity of sense-facts to express its will, and writes its ideas in a vast hieroglyph, whose characters we call experience. Hence it is that I love to study science. And when I study science I do so naively, submissively, straightforwardly, just as if the atoms and the suns and the milky-ways, the brains and the nerve-cells and the reflex mechanisms, were all things in themselves. They are n't things in themselves; they are mere manifestations of the Self. But I must for this very reason accept them as they come. Nor do I try, as the romanticists did, to find obvious symbolic interpretations for hastily recorded facts of sense before cautious science has scrutinized these facts thoroughly. I have confidence enough in the depth of meaning that the Self has to embody in the world, not to try to guess this meaning of its hieroglyph before a good deal thereof has been empirically examined. I do not grow restive in listening to the story of evolution, merely because I am well aware that the whole temporal view of things is largely illusory, and that the true Self, far from being subject to time, creates time. I rather delight in this craft whereby the Self thus hides its true nature in energetic nebulous masses and in flying meteors, pretends to be absent from the inorganic world, pretends to have descended from relatives of the anthropoid apes, pretends, in short, to be bounded in all sorts of nutshells; yes, plays hide and seek amongst the æons of forgotten time, when this planet was not, and demurely insists that without phosphorus it could not possibly have learned how to think. The Self has its comedies as well as its tragedies; and these comedies are as far from being mere farces as the tragedies are from being the mere horror-plays at which Schopenhauer's saints turned pale, until they grew ineffectively holy, and finally vanished. No, the comedies are as deep as the tragedies. The Self is as truly present in evolution as he is in sin and in ignorance. These are the World-Spirit's garments that we see him by. Only we must see patiently, watching every fold and listening to every rustle of the garment; for behind this garment stirs the infinite life, and to each one of us philosophy says, *That art Thou.* It is only after a patient scientific scrutiny has revealed, as is the case with the doctrine of evolution, a vast unity in a long series of phenomena; a growth like this which links civilized to savage man; and savage man to an animal ancestry; and the animal ancestry to unicellular organisms; and these to the inorganic matter of a primitive earth-crust; and this crust to an antecedent fluid earth-ball, glowing, and parting with its bulky satellite, the moon; and this glowing ball to a primitive nebula; and perhaps this nebula to a previous manifold streaming of multitudinously clashing meteors, — it is only then, I say, when such a book as this splendid history of life lies open before us, only partly deciphered, but still suggestively grasped in its magnificent outlines, daily more clearly read by science, that we have a right to ask: Who, then, is this Self, and what manner of life is this he writes in this book, itself merely a waif from the lost tales of endless time, just as the endless time also is merely an illusory form wherein the Self is pleased to embody and manifest this truth? Its illusory form is not wholly an illusion. For the Self is all that is, and his world is the chosen outcome of his eternal reality. Beyond all these illusions must lie a meaning deeper than we have ever yet comprehended, higher than our thought will soon reach. What fragment, then, of the meaning does the story of evolution convey? To give that question a precise definition and to risk a sharp answer, to make this answer less mystical and more concrete than the one now suggested, and to develop before you something of its proof, will be my business in the remaining lectures.

PART II.

SUGGESTIONS OF DOCTRINE.

LECTURE X.

WE begin herewith the task of thinking for ourselves
concerning the problems of philosophy. We shall have
learned little from the preceding historical discussions, if
they have not strongly suggested to us that the world of
truth must be something very unlike the naive notions
of its nature that our primitive consciousness gives us.
Empirical science is full of romantic surprises; but philosophy has shown itself to be far more so. Copernicus
transformed the universe for the natural man; but Kant's
"Copernican discovery" suggested a far more wondrous
transformation. Our own work we have defined in advance as an effort to bring into synthesis the thoughts
that the history of modern philosophy has suggested to
us. Following, then, in the paths of Kant and of his
successors, we shall not expect to get glimpses of less
marvelous things than they beheld. What we desire is
that these insights of ours should be reasonable, and
should be adjusted to the facts of life and of nature.

I.

It is the world of the outer order in which our historical studies have left us. The idealistic interpretation of
this world that I suggested as I closed the last lecture
will not at first sight appear to you more than a mystical
romance. Let it pass, for the moment, as such. I shall
not here begin with it; I shall begin with the assumption
of realistic science, with the hypothesis of our own age,

namely, that there is a real world, which our senses more or less truly perceive, which a well-guarded experience can fruitfully investigate, and which our natural science has been learning in some measure to comprehend. This assumption is one presupposition of our age. We shall study it as critically as we can. If it needs a peculiarly cautious scrutiny, if it lacks in any sense foundation, or if it must be transformed before it can be accepted, we shall hope to discover the fact in the course of our analysis.

That, once granting the foregoing presupposition, the reflection of a metaphysician should have any rights as against the stupendous acquisitions of the sciences of experience, would seem at first glance absurd enough, were it not that the highest flights of science are precisely the ones that, to reflective persons, are always most suggestive of the need of a philosophy. At the close of the remarkable address of the president of the British Association at Cardiff (delivered in August, 1891), I find noteworthy words, concluding a presentation of the recent marvels of the progress of astronomy : —

"Astronomy, the oldest of the sciences," says Dr. Huggins, "has more than renewed her youth. At no time in the past has she been so bright with unbounded aspirations and hopes. Never were her temples so numerous, nor the crowd of her votaries so great. . . . Happy is the lot of those who are still on the eastern side of life's meridian. . . . Since the time of Newton our knowledge of the phenomena of nature has wonderfully increased, but man asks, perhaps more earnestly now than in his days, What is the ultimate reality behind the reality of the perceptions ? Are they only the pebbles of the beach with which we have been playing ? Does not the ocean of ultimate reality and truth lie beyond ? "

Let these words of Dr. Huggins be the text of what is immediately to follow. The more one becomes absorbed

in the study of the wonders of nature, the nearer must
lie the thought, that these things are not what they seem ;
that space and time, and matter and motion, and life and
our human consciousness, are but the show, the finite embodiment, the temporal manifestation, of a deeper truth.
If this world of experience is indeed real, its reality must
be far profounder than our experience. May not an analysis of the conditions of experience suggest to us wherein
lies this profounder actuality, behind the show, and yet
incorporated in it ?

This world of scientific realism is first of all a world
in space and in time. Space and time are themselves, as
Kant has shown us, such puzzling conditions of natural
law and of human knowledge, that we should run the
risk of complicating hopelessly our inquiry if we here
already dwelt afresh upon their paradoxes. Let us post-
pone such a consideration until later ; let us look rather
at the contents of the space world, as experience shows
them to us. In space we find the universe of the stars
and the nebulæ, as the world wherein occur all the
changes that fall within our ken. These changes, as
physical science knows them, are, to use the well-known
phrase, "redistributions" of matter and of energy. So
far as we know, neither matter nor energy is ever altered
in quantity. It is their distribution, the form of the
physical world, which changes. As for the general extent and character of these changes, the astronomer tells
us (to quote once more from Dr. Huggins's address)
something of the following nature : —

"The heavens are richly but very irregularly inwrought
with stars ; the brighter stars cluster into well-known
groups upon a background formed of an enlacement of
streams and convoluted windings and interwined spirals
of fainter stars, which becomes richer and more intricate
in the irregularly rifted zone of the Milky Way.

"We who form part of the emblazonry can see only

the design distorted and confused; here crowded, there scattered, at another place superposed. The groupings due to our position are mixed up with those which are real.

"Can we suppose that each luminous point has no relation to the others near it than the accidental neighborship of grains of sand upon the shore, or particles of the wind-blown dust of the desert? Surely every star, from Sirius and Vega down to each grain of the light dust of the Milky Way, has its present place in the heavenly pattern from the slow evolving of its past. We see a system of systems, for the broad features of clusters and streams and spiral windings which mark the general design are reproduced in every part. The whole is in motion, each point shifting its position by miles every second, though from the august magnitude of their distances from us and from each other, it is only by the accumulated movements of years or of generations that some small changes of relative position reveal themselves."

A "system of systems," then, with the "broad features" "reproduced in every part," is before us. Its very outlines suggest a general process of physical evolution. This impression is after a fashion confirmed by two well-known considerations, one of which is relatively older in science, while the other is at the moment in process of highly novel development through spectroscopic research. The first consideration relates to the fact that the energy of this vast material system is now distributed in a manner that, from the nature of the case, is, so to speak, peculiarly unstable, and that appears to involve enormous future changes of distribution; while if we look backwards we see that there must have been involved in the past a long and continuous process of a particular type leading towards the present state. The hot stars, in cold space far from one another, are just now continually dissipating their heat by radiation. If one inquires into the

most probable source of all this heat-energy, now so waste-
fully poured out, one finds but one highly plausible hypothesis, which has been suggested after a very considerable
study of the phenomena of our own sun. Contraction,
under the influence of gravity, most probably furnishes
the source of this heat in case of each of the great stellar
masses. Contraction, read backwards, and interpreted in
the light of the well-known and now pretty widely confirmed nebular hypothesis, indicates that each star must
once have been far larger than it now is, and that the
energy now radiated as heat must once have been stored
up as the energy of position of widely diffused matter,
whose particles gravitated towards one another, and whose
state is probably indicated to us by such vast masses as
certain of the nebulæ show us. Condensation, the conversion of the energy of position into heat, radiation of
heat, the continued contraction of stellar masses : such is
the process that we now probably see indicated before us.

The recent spectroscopic study of the stars furnishes a
second and subordinate sort of evidence, which adds still
further plausibility to the idea of this unity of process
throughout the heavens. The stars seem, we are told, to
fall into classes, whose physical condition strongly suggests, although it cannot yet prove, just such varieties of
age, just such different stages in the process of condensation and of cooling, as we might expect to discover in a
universe of a stellar evolution of the sort that the nebular
hypothesis demands. The confirmation from this source,
incomplete though it is, is highly significant.

Granting these hypotheses about the world-system around
us, — hypotheses rendered daily more probable in the light
of that general unity of material structure and of physical
law which the spectroscope so wonderfully reveals, — then
the process that is going on has a character that renders
it very highly problematic. The energy of this system is
being transformed, as we have seen ; but the average

transformations appear to conform to a type which suggests that the bright world of the hot stars, as it now is, must be destined to only a finite period of existence. These transformations, namely, are taking place in one direction. The energy of the stellar world seems to be " running down," that is, to be passing from " available " to " unavailable " forms. The total quantity of energy in the world remains constant; but its serviceableness for continuing the world-process that we now observe and admire must be growing momentarily less. We cannot with serious probability discover any compensating process of sufficient magnitude and universality to enable us to see how the stellar evolution could go on forever, in any one part of space, however large, without an entire change in the character of the events involved. A rhythm of growth and decay, a passing of energy from " higher " to " lower " forms, and then back again from " lower " to " higher " forms, in case that were the law of the process before us, would suggest an ultimately stable " moving equilibrium " in the universe, whose " broad features," " reproduced in every part," would be those of an endless life of ripening and decaying solar and stellar systems. But unfortunately, the greater part of the energy involved in this world of the hot stars and the cold space no sooner reaches the form of heat energy, shown in the glowing stellar surfaces themselves, than it is radiated off into space; and there is nothing rhythmical, so far as we can see, about the results of the process of radiation. The fashion of this world changes; and no restoring process adequately compensates for the change. The stellar universe continually casts this bread of its energy on to the waters of infinite space. When shall it be found again? To speak of the facts more particularly, each star tends to cool off, since it is radiating enormous quantities of heat. What can supply the loss, and keep the star hot? The answer is, that the contraction of each stellar mass, by reason of gravitation, continually converts energy of position into heat-energy. But in no single case could this contraction go on indefinitely. The stars that we know must one and all grow old and die. What could restore life to the cooling universe? Collisions of stellar masses? These in any one case would bring to pass enormous diffusions of matter, would form fresh nebulæ, would begin the vast processes of single systems once more; but would do so only by drawing afresh on the store of the higher forms of energy (that is, upon the energy of position and the energy of relative stellar motions). The energy thus won, and made available, would be radiated off in the end; would be lost in the depths of space; and the process would continue only at a loss.

This law of the "degradation" of energy, of the tendency everywhere for higher forms of energy, such as those of the energy of position and the energy of the motion of masses of matter, to pass, when transformed, into the lower form of energy, namely, heat, and then to be radiated off into space, is a well-known tendency, present in all sorts of physical processes. Only at a certain loss can heat-energy be transformed back into higher forms of energy, even by the best of known devices. Heat water, here at the earth's surface, and you can make steam, and get the steam to raise bodies to higher levels, and so get some of your heat-energy stored up once more in forms that will be later "available" for useful service. But you can do so only at a loss. In order to transform some of the heat-energy at your disposal into a higher and more useful form, you have to waste a good deal of heat, by letting it heat up the bodies in the neighborhood of the water that you use, and by so letting it ultimately diffuse itself through space by radiation. Lost heat you can't restore. Energy you employ, then, only by giving part of it away as waste heat, and using the remainder to do your work. That seems to be the way of our universe. Its energies continually diffuse themselves through infinite space in "degraded" form as ether vibrations. The stars waste vastly more than they can give to their planets. And even what they give to their planets is continually being lost, as our own earth shows us, through radiation.

If, then, this stellar universe possesses at present any *finite* quantity of "kinetic" or of "potential" energy in available undiffused forms, that is, if the process before us is confined to any finite portion of space, then the energy seems to be so tending to lose itself in diffused form, that in some finite time the whole process must "run down." The evolution must cease.

So, at least, it would seem. The problem as suggested to us in the other direction is obvious. If this evolution must sometime cease, how, carrying it backwards, can we conceive it as having been without a beginning? A rhythmical process, in which there is a regular alternation of certain conditions, can easily be conceived as having always existed. Look back, namely, as far as you will, and you will find this process present at any moment of time, in some stage of its endlessly repeated rhythm. But a physical process that shall have gone on through endless time, and yet always in the same direction, an endless wasting of energy by the continual conversion of higher into lower forms, — how hard to conceive of such a process as having already gone on forever! The only plausible hypothesis that makes such a conception possible seems at first sight to be the one discussed by Professor W. K. Clifford, in his brilliant lecture on "The First and Last Catastrophe."[1] In order to follow Clifford's thought, let us fix our attention for a moment on the case of the earth. If, says Clifford, we follow back the probable condition of the earth itself, we find that, according to certain computations, this planet must have solidified a lim-

[1] See his *Lectures and Essays*, vol. i. pp. 191–227 ; in particular, the passages, pp. 220, 221.

ited number of millions of years since. "Before that, it was cooling as a liquid." And before this again, further computations would show that, at a certain time, the earth had passed from the gaseous to the liquid state. And then, continues Clifford : —

"If we went further back still we should probably find the earth falling together out of a great ring of matter surrounding the sun, and distributed over its orbit. The same thing is true of every body of matter; if we trace its history back, we come to a certain time at which a catastrophe took place; and if we were to trace back the history of all the bodies in the universe in that way, we should continually see them separating up into smaller parts. What they have actually done is to fall together and get solid. If we could reverse the process we should see them separating and getting fluid; and, as a limit to that, at an indefinite distance in past time, we should find that all these bodies would be resolved into molecules, and all these would be flying away from each other. There would be no limit to that process, and we could trace it as far back as ever we liked to trace it. So that on the assumption — a very large assumption — that the present constitution of the laws of geometry and mechanics has held good during the whole of past time, we should be led to the conclusion that, at an inconceivably long time ago, the universe did consist of ultimate molecules, all separate from one another and approaching one another. Then they would meet together and form a great number of small, hot bodies. Then you would have the process of cooling going on in these bodies, exactly as we find it going on now. But you will observe that we have no evidence of such a catastrophe as implies a beginning of the laws of nature."

Clifford, as you will see from his words, does not regard this hypothesis as more than a very provisional one. All that we are seeking for the moment, however, is a plausible way of regarding the world that now is as continuously linked with what was, and with what will be, by a world process that extends indefinitely both towards the past and towards the future. Towards the future, as we have seen, it is very hard to conceive the present process as indefinitely extended without coming to what Clifford himself (page 224 of the same lecture) describes thus : —

" If we were to travel forward, . . . and consider things as falling together, we should come finally to a great central mass, all in one piece, which would send out waves of heat through a perfectly empty ether, and gradually cool itself down. As this mass got cool it would be deprived of all life and motion ; it would be just an enormous frozen block in the middle of the ether."

In the past, again, extending the present process backwards, we come, as Clifford has shown us, to a condition of greater and greater diffusion of matter, to a state where more and more energy took the form of energy of position, and where there was less and less of the present condition of stellar systems with highly heated solar surfaces. In both cases our effort to conceive the world-process as *one* process is founded, as Clifford points out, on the " large assumption " that the " present constitution of the laws of geometry and mechanics has held good during the whole of past time," or in other words that the world is what it now seems to be to our more exact scientific consciousness. The question now is whether the conception that we thus get is an essentially coherent one.

At the present stage of our inquiry it would be mere Philistinism to dwell, as many are disposed to do, upon the disheartening notion of the past and future state of our universe which these considerations and hypotheses so far suggest. Our criticism of the presuppositions of modern inquiry will have, in due time and place, to study the moral and religious aspect of the real world. But just now we dare not call in question hypotheses as to nature, merely because they do not meet the longings of our hearts. Our criticism must go deeper.

Turning back at once, however, to the theoretical aspect of the matter, we find that this conception of the real world is, as we have already observed, at all events a very highly problematic one. We may well doubt the ultimate coherence of these our empirical notions of the physical world when thus driven, as it were, to their limits, when pressed into service to define a possible world-process that shall include the known phenomena, and that shall still be continuous and boundless in time. Yet not in vain will have been our efforts so far if we take into account a consideration that just now becomes highly important for us.

There is, namely, no more useful experiment in philosophy than just such an effort as the one now before us, to universalize our conceptions of things, to try what becomes of them when we *do* pass to the limit, and suppose them true for all the world and for all time. Such an experiment often is for philosophy what a crucial test in a laboratory is for physics. It decides for us, namely, what sort of conception we are dealing with; and that is why these speculations are worth our while. A conception that could consistently be thus universalized, that could be used to define an absolute or a self-completed world-process, that thus could have an essentially boundless application, might be a conception of an objective and well-founded type, true of the real world apart from our merely human point of view. But a conception that you can't universalize, that seems to contradict itself, or that gives rise to highly suspicious incongruities, so soon as you press it to the limit, so soon as you suppose it to apply *semper et ubique*, is thereby shown to be in all probability a conception of an essentially human character or else of no world-wide objectivity. It may have truth about it, but this truth will in part be due to our own limited point of view, to our particular station in the universe. This notion will be, so to speak, a *mortal* conception of things, not a conception of a really eternal truth. For example : the notion of the earth as supported by an elephant that stood on a tortoise was such an essentially transient and merely human conception, just because it was derived from the analogy of a very special and limited experience of ours, and was obviously incapable of true universalization. Seeking to pass to the limit, you found yourself in a world whose law was that all things needed support from beneath, while you could never find a real supporter *in* the world, whether for the earth or for anything else. For any supporter in your world-series would be such only in so far as he was first conceived to be supported. And so as no unsupported supporter could be found in a series thus defined, while an unsupported supporter would be essentially needed somewhere to give all above him a real foundation, the defined series would be worthless for the purpose of explaining the earth's apparent stability. Very different, however, is the conception (a purely ideal one, to be sure) of the stability of a gravitative system in otherwise absolutely empty space, — a system that should consist, say, of a sun and a planet, both moving with perfect freedom about their common centre of gravity, both uninfluenced by disturbances from without, and both rigid and homogeneous spherical bodies. Such a system, although it does not exist in our physical world, can be conceived as existing. Such a system, moreover, under the law of gravity, would give us an endless rhythmic change of position on the part of its members, the small planet revolving in an established orbit about its large sun, or rather both moving about their common centre. The motion in question would be a stable one. There would be no difficulty in predicting the position, velocity, and acceleration of the planet at any time, from its position and motion at any other. The possible positions of the planet in its orbit would form a closed curve. One complete cycle of the system would exhaustively exemplify all, and would not be in need of a support or explanation from any source outside the system. The motion in an universe so consti- tuted would be, as defined, essentially endless. In this empty space no physical condition could have produced or begun it; and nothing could end it. The conception of such an universe is essentially self-completed, and so as an universe possible. Such an universe, then, although it is not real, might be real. The universe where the stabil- ity of things was only to be explained by such a notion as that of the earth supported by elephant and tortoise, *can't* be real; for either elephant and tortoise, as con- ceived, would not be real supporters at all, or else *if* they were, then, like the conceived earth itself, they would need support ere they could become supporters, whilst in the world as so conceived they could find no ultimate support whatever.

I exemplify this rather abstruse-seeming distinction between essentially coherent and essentially incoherent notions of the universe in its wholeness, not for the sake of involving my argument in unnecessary subtlety, but for the sake of preparing the way for what seems to me a not unimportant step forwards in our discussion.

II.

No one doubts the validity of the foregoing inductions of physical science when judged by their own presupposi- tions, and taken within their chosen limits. But they are confessedly inductions about the world as it seems. As they are originally made, they therefore do not profess to give us a theory about the ultimately real world. It is our own reflective interest that has now suggested to us the mere experiment of seeing whether the conceptions that these inductions involve are capable of being universalized, of being pressed to the limit, and whether they remain coherent when this is hypothetically done. The purpose of the experiment is to see whether the world as it seems to outer experience can really be viewed as a fair specimen of the world as it really is.

Supposing this process of the aggregation of matter and the radiation of energy into space to be a specimen of the ultimately real process of nature, can we, with Clifford, regard this as a process that, uncertainties apart, can without incoherence be conceived as boundless in time? As an example of a hypothetical process that *can* be so conceived, we have just had the case of the ideal system of rigid sun and planet, alone in space and changeless in inner physical structure. Their rhythm would be a perfect one. Their motion would occur in closed cycles. Beginning or end of their process would be physically unintelligible. An universe that contained them and them only would be logically as well as physically complete. No evolution would occur there; and none would be needed or conceivable. Is our seeming world that is now one of a "running-down" energy, constant in quantity, but such that it is tending to "degradation" in form, a world that we can coherently conceive as eternal?

Difficulties at once occur to us. Let us put them as simply as possible. A process called aggregation shall have been endlessly going on. What stage has it now reached? The answer is, one of very imperfect aggregation. The masses of matter now coherent in the world before us are, despite their imposing size, after all comparatively small. Their number is, meanwhile, comparatively speaking, very great. Many millions of suns, — no sun in sight that we are forced to regard as after all so very much larger than our own sun. Some stars may be several hundreds or thousands of times the mass of our own sun. None, however, are big enough to show us across the interstellar spaces any disk. What we see are mere points of light. Where instead of points we see large nebulæ, of considerable apparent area, we get evidence of the presence of diffused gas and perhaps, also, of meteor - swarms, not of highly aggregated and still extremely vast masses of matter. As to the significance of this fact, there is indeed nothing exact, as yet, about our present consideration. So far it merely arouses our suspicion. If aggregation has been going on endlessly, there ought to be, one would think, at least a few prodigious centres of aggregation, as big, say, in angular size, when seen even across these prodigious spaces, as the larger nebulæ appear to us, and still as coherent at least as is the mass of Sirius. The small average size of the suns is precisely what one might expect to see if at some finite time in the past aggregation had begun hereabouts in space, the nebular gaseous matter, or the meteoric swarms, having at the beginning of that time filled pretty evenly our part of space. But this is not what our hypothesis, carried to the limit, pretends to suggest. Universal aggregation, going on wherever there was matter, — this is what shall have filled the endless past. And still, — this incomplete result!

I repeat, I do not at all exaggerate the force of so inexactly formulated a consideration. Clifford's way of stating his hypothetical case of a look into the past might already seem to have forestalled our objection. But I give it this form by way of introducing later a more serious reflection.

Meanwhile, a second doubt comes to mind, and this time with regard to the energy of our world. It shall have tended always towards the final state of indefinite degradation and dispersion. And yet there is so much of it still "available!" These stars are so hot, this store of energy, wasted for an infinite time, shall have left us after all still so far from the frozen termination of all

evolution! Is not this incompleteness another cause of
suspicion? Can our conceptions thus be fully universalized without a curious inconsistency? Ought not a process that from all eternity has taken but one direction to
have been completed long ago?

But I hasten to correct these inexact considerations by
opposing to them Clifford's very simple way of stating
the case for the inner coherence of our present conceptions of natural law. What "the bodies of the universe"
"have actually done," he says, "is to fall together and
get solid. If we could reverse the process we should see
them separating, . . . and as a limit . . . at an indefinite
distance in past time we should find that all these bodies
would be resolved into molecules, and" [if we read the
process backwards] "all these would be flying away from
each other. There would be no limit to that process, and
we could trace it as far back as ever we liked to trace it."
In this way, thinks Clifford, we should get a definable
endless process for the physical universe. That we ourselves happen to live and to be sentient just at the moment when the infinite process has reached *this* stage, is,
after all, not more marvelous than that we live at all.
Infinite past and future time being once assumed, we ourselves must of course come somewhere in the process, and
we come just where we actually find ourselves, the process being in a peculiarly critical and transitional stage.

But it is not our own existence that is just here the
problem. It is the real world which thus conceived has,
when viewed in time, a very singular character. There is
a stage in its endless life, when, for a finite period, which
we may call E (meaning thereby the portion of time during
which what we call processes of evolution are possible),
there is a considerable, but still not an extreme aggregation of its matter, and yet a considerable, though not an
extreme retention of energy of position on the part of its
constituent masses. During this time suns and systems

form, stars are hot, and planetary life may, as on our earth,
be possible. Before this period lies an endless time P, a
past when aggregation was small, but when there were
nebulæ, meteor swarms, yes, if you go far enough back,
separated molecules. These had much energy of position,
or of motion, or of both. They had not yet, on the average, converted much of it into heat. There were in those
times no processes of evolution possible. Then beyond
and after the time E there is to lie an endless future F,
wherein once more the matter is aggregated but cold, the
energy is dispersed through space in the ether, and what
we call evolution is over. The result is an absolute division of infinite time into the three parts : —

<————————————— P | E | F————————————>

and this division shall be not merely our private and finite
interpretation of the thing, but the truth of nature. The
world of high temperatures, of large and rapidly condens-
ing masses, of planets and suns, of all the complex natural processes, electrical, magnetic, chemical, connected
with the life of solar systems, — this world is an exception in the wastes of infinite time. P contains nothing
of the sort. F contains nothing of the sort. Only the
select region E, of the temporal process, gives birth to
such things.

Now a natural process that is essentially confined to one
part of infinite time, and that finds no place elsewhere,
is the real anomaly with which we have so far to deal.
We wanted to conceive nature as one process. We have
really conceived it as a drama in three acts, essentially
separate in physical character from one another, despite
the continuity of motions that joins them. This anomaly
needs, at all events, further scrutiny. This is an odd
world that we have got ourselves into. How odd, we shall
in some measure comprehend only after I have taxed your
patience with yet one more subtlety, to which I now invite
your brief, but very careful attention.

III.

Whatever other difficulties this conceived world may or may not contain, it is sure that its boundlessness in time, and the fashion of its presence in boundless space, are of a sort very different from those which we before ascribed to the conceived simple gravitative system consisting of two bodies. In the latter world, namely, there was always going on a certain cyclical process of one fixed type. The sun and its conceived planet were somehow there in space. Looking back as far as we liked, we should always find the pair occupying some one of the determinate relative positions that they pass through during their endlessly repeated cycles. Looking backwards or forwards, therefore, we should not be driven by any special physical problems of this conceived world to puzzle ourselves about the sense in which there is any real infinity of space and time at all. It is true, as everybody has heard, that there are obvious and serious difficulties in the way of conceiving how space and time are to be really infinite actualities, — how, off yonder, there can actually exist parts of space infinitely remote from us, or how, looking backwards, we can say that there ever did occur events an infinitely long time ago. But now, as we see, the world of our closed cycle of planet revolving about sun suggests by no marked physical peculiarity of its processes any question about this reality of infinite space and infinite time as such. We have called its existence boundless in time. We mean by that only that its supposed existence would seem to be as endless as is time, — not less so, not more so. If there is any trouble about conceiving of infinite time, that is the fault of time, not of this simple mechanical rhythm of planet swinging about sun. Whatever endless time means, that the rhythm of this conceived simple system is adequate to fill. Even so, too, in case of space. We have supposed our sun and planet to be alone in boundless space. Just what an actually boundless space is, it is hard to define. One soon comes to suspect, when one tries a definition, that one is dealing with a self-contradictory notion. But be that as it may, the conceived sun and planet, there together in space, require space to exist in, but have by hypothesis no physical relations to infinite space, do not trouble themselves, as it were, about whether space is infinite or no. If a really infinite space can exist, then the sun and planet can be in it; but for their physical relations they require only the finite bit of space within their own masses and within the planet's orbit. The existence of such a system, then, is to be called essentially boundless in time just because its physical properties drive us to *no* assumptions about what boundless time is and means, but are processes that, as being rhythmical and self-completed, arouse no question as to how or when they could have begun, and are therefore boundless in whatever sense time itself proves to be boundless. This same existence is again intelligible as a conceived fact in boundless space, because, whatever boundless space means, this process, as being a definite and limited one, could find its place in such a space.

But now (and here is the important point), the world of the "running-down" energy, and of the endlessly consolidating matter, differs from this simple world of the sun and planet, in that its existence has, as conceived, an essentially physical relation to an actually infinite space and time, so that its processes cannot be conceived as boundless in time, merely because they suggest to us, like the sun and planet, no possible beginning; but can only be conceived as boundless by first meeting and overcoming all the difficulties as to an actually infinite space and time. Infinite space and time as such become, in such a theory, matters, not of dim possibility, but rather parts of a physical hypothesis. They render this physical hypothesis,

therefore, peculiarly hard to conceive with congruity.
This is no place for dwelling in full upon what these difficulties about infinite space and time really are. I am not
here setting forth at length a philosophy, but only suggesting one. What I have to point out, however, may be
indicated by returning to a former analogy. I have said
that this world, where all the processes take the one direction towards the consolidation of matter, is very unlike the
simple and rhythmical world of the conceived sun and
planet. What I now have to point out is that this our
world of the endlessly consolidating matter, if taken as
an absolutely real world, would much resemble in one
feature that other conceived world where the elephant
rested on the tortoise. The trouble with *that* world was
that support was assumed to be needed, and yet none was
ever defined. The trouble with *this* world is that the
store of available energy at any moment, lacking both
permanency in itself and any tendency to get, through
rhythmic processes, a periodic restoration of its previous
quantity, sends us backwards endlessly in time for a
definition of the very physical process and constitution
to which its present quantity shall have been due. Now
some sort of endless regress in time is in one sense forced
upon us by every physical process. The simple rhythm
of the sun and planet also sent us back endlessly into
time; not in order that we should find out what sort
of process it was (for that we learned from any one cycle), but only in order that we should see how such a
process as that could *not* be conceived to have a physical
beginning. But this process of the endlessly consolidating
world, as Clifford defines it, sends us back into time much
as the earth, elephant and tortoise series would send us off
into space. Would it be any answer to an objector to
say, in case of the elephant and tortoise series : — Oh, the
tortoise, too, is supported by another creature, say a giant;
and he by a tree; that by something else; and so on *ad*

infinitum? No, for thus no support would to all infinity ever begin to be explained. Even so, although a perfectly rhythmical and complete physical process can easily, without incongruity, be regarded as unbounded when we look backwards, — a boundless regress where, on the other hand, all the character of the process *changes* as we go backwards, and changes, wholly without rhythm or any sort of reversal of type, in one general direction, does and must involve incongruity.

What incongruity may now be finally and succinctly pointed out. Any moment of time, however remote, must actually have been passed through in order that our consolidating world should have reached its present state. To any such past moment, would correspond some actual physical state of our supposed world. Far back in time its state would have been one of greater and greater disintegration. Passing to the limit we can say that our hypothesis would suppose, (1) that at an infinite past time the particles of matter now together in the stars must have been infinitely distant from one another ; and (2) that, since every state, even the present one, presupposes and demands *all* the previous states of this unrhythmical process as physically necessary antecedents, the present state of the universe could not be unless that antecedent state of the mutually infinite remoteness of its parts actually did precede.

The idea of infinite remoteness, as being an actual physical fact, is, however, notoriously hard to conceive. It is one thing to say that our space is such that, however far you go out into its depths, you could always go further. To mention that character of space is merely to state a fact of our space conception, — a fact that nobody has any trouble to conceive. It is quite another thing to try to conceive a state of the world in which there are actually two particles of matter that shall be an infinite number of leagues apart. The conception of the boundlessness of space is, in the first case, a mere expression of our actual failure to conceive of a boundary. This failure is a fact of immediate observation for our consciousness. But if I say, in the second case: There are, in a certain state of the world, two particles of matter, p and q, and the distance between these two particles is an infinite distance, I contradict myself. For the line pq which joins these particles must by hypothesis end in one direction at p and in the other direction at q, — in other words must be finite.

And yet our present hypothesis as to the real world demands of us the assertion that such a contradictory state of things must have been real in order that the present state of the world should have come to pass.

Clifford himself, in stating the hypothesis, avoids our present incongruity by saying only that, in case of the endlessly consolidating world, the behavior of things is such that if we go back as far as ever we like, we shall find the particles of matter further and further apart. But unfortunately such a statement does not exhaust the difficulty in case this seeming process has always been an absolutely real one. Fixing our attention once more on two particles, p and q, we see that, by the hypothesis, at a time (t_1) they were a certain distance apart (d_1), and that an earlier time (t_2) they were yet further apart (say a distance d_2), and so on indefinitely. But now in order that they should reach the distance apart that we have called d_1, they must *before* have been *actually* at the distance from another that we have called d_2. Passing to the limit, then, we have to say that in order to reach the less distances they must universally have been *first* at the greater distances, so that unless one presupposes the greater as real, and so at the limit, the infinite distance as actually precedent, the finite distances cannot have been reached. It is n't merely the case, then, that we are dealing with an hypothesis of a process that, however far *we* choose to follow it, proves to be for our consciousness, and from our point of view, unlimited. The trouble is that unless we *first* conceive the unlimited distances as real, the limited distances can never be reached. Therefore, if the process is what it seems to be, namely, an absolutely real one, the unlimited distances must have been real. Our infinite in this case is n't the indefinite beyond that *we* do not attain, however far back we go. It is the impossible that yet must have been actually and absolutely attained *before* any of the states of the world that we experience could have been reached. Only by passing through this impossible infinite distance from one another, can the particles p and q have reached the conceivable finite distances from one another.

The parallel between this supposed real world and that of the elephant and tortoise is now fairly plain. The true supporter of the elephant-tortoise earth must, *if* he exists at all, be infinitely remote and yet real. Without him elephant and tortoise, by hypothesis, could not support anything, being themselves unsupported. Even so, the true antecedent of our present physical world must, on Clifford's hypothesis, be a state in which the space relations of the smallest particles of matter were relations of infinite remoteness from one another. Dropping out the consideration of the infinite time, we can then say in absolute terms that, on this hypothesis, there was formerly a real state of the world in which its ultimate particles were at infinite distances from one another. Is this not as if we said of the elephant and tortoise: There *is*, at an infinite distance, that which supports the whole series and them?

I repeat, upon the more technical aspect of the difficulties regarding infinite space and time, I have not here further to dwell. What we have found is simply this: —

1. There are *possible* physical processes that you *can* conceive as universalized, as essentially boundless in time,

as existent in boundless space, without any effort to define what the positive nature of a really infinite time and space are. Such processes are the ones known as " cyclical." In case of these processes, the definition of one cycle involves the description of all. A " cyclical " physical process, conceived as isolated in space, could not change its character through any physical cause. However long, therefore, you followed it forwards or backwards, you would find only the same thing repeated. In this conception there is nothing difficult. Such a process you would call essentially endless; meaning thereby that whatever endless time really means, and whatever its ultimate nature turns out to be, the processes in question would be adequate to that endlessness. Of such processes our supposed sun and planet example is an illustration. There is no incongruity involved in universalizing such processes.

2. But there are, on the other hand, possible physical processes that you *cannot* thus universalize, without presupposing infinite space and time as being themselves, in all their infinity, elements in the definition of certain states of the physical process in question. Of such physical processes the world of the elephant and tortoise series, and the world of Clifford's hypothesis, are possible examples, so soon as you suppose them to be not seeming but genuinely real worlds. Common sense will at once say that as we have no notion of infinite space and time as actual physical wholes, we can have no right thus to universalize such processes, in case we meet with special examples of them in our experience. Philosophy goes deeper, and declares that thus to universalize such physical process involves us in incongruity, involves the presupposition of a real past state of the world whose very definition is self-contradictory.

The result, so far, is that the world of the endlessly consolidating matter can't be the ultimately real world, but must be only a seeming world whose anomalous character is due to our private and human point of view. Seen as we see it, the empirical truth about matter and energy must be only the show of a deeper truth. This apparent law of the endless consolidation of the universe must be only a fragmentary aspect. These stars and "intertwined spirals" and "convoluted windings" of stars, these hypothetical molecules that have been forever falling nearer and nearer together, this process that has been forever taking one direction without reaching as yet its goal, — all these things must belong to the show of reality. The substance, the soul of it all, must lie behind. The real world process cannot thus be essentially a paradox, essentially incomplete, fundamentally absurd. It must have at least as much unity and self-consistency as a "cyclical" physical process. When we see it as we do, in this ragged and unintelligible shape, that must be because, in our experience, we are but playing with the "pebbles on the beach." The "ocean of ultimate reality and truth" must lie beyond.

In all the foregoing I have not wished to create difficulties ; I have merely found them where they exist. Nor have I wished to make light of the world of our modern realism. On the contrary, as I repeat, those who study this world most devotedly are often the first to acknowledge not only its mystery, but its probable fragmentariness, its suggestion of a hidden truth beyond. "Unknowable," some investigators call this real world on account of such paradoxes. It is, however, precisely the men who thus call reality unknowable, who seem to me to make light of the serious business of science. What one learns from such puzzles is not that our scientific experience is untrue, but that it isn't the revealer of the whole truth, — not that matter and energy and their laws are illusions, but that they are partial revelations only of what, seen from a higher point of view, would have to get the unity

and completeness that our human point of view so far
lacks. These puzzles, then, do not turn us away from the
world of science ; they rather encourage us to philosophize as to the meaning of the presuppositions that lie beneath science. If you find a significant limitation in
your knowledge, philosophy bids you scrutinize the bases
of your knowledge to see what in the human point of view
it is that is the source of this limitation.

Clifford, whose way of stating the hypothesis of the law
of endless consolidation we have been criticising, was himself one of the first to insist, although for other reasons,
upon the probable inadequacy of this hypothesis. Himself one of the most admirable minds of recent British
thought, he was restlessly at work, during his brief career,
at the task of criticising the fundamental postulates of
science. That the laws of physics and even of geometry
are probably not ultimate truths about the nature of
things, he used to argue with all the clearness of the ma-
thematician and all the reflective skill of the born speculator. Our space and time, with their paradoxical infinities, he used to regard as very suspicious appearances. In
criticising him I have therefore, after all, only borrowed
certain of his own methods of thinking. He was his own
keenest critic. He dwelt on the borderland of philosophy.
It is a source of deep regret that he never lived to enter
into that land with the powers which he had been training
so skillfully. He would there have proved himself a
great conqueror.

IV.

The considerations of the foregoing discussion must
have been wearisome enough in their abstractness. I
hasten to suggest their more concrete bearings.

The problem of the outer order, as we conceive it in
these modern days, is the problem of the true relation of
nature and evolution. The question of the previous discussion has been only a highly abstract formulation of

this problem. The seeming world, as we find it in space and time, is one whose matter and energy are permanent in quantity, while their distribution is endlessly changing. The changes of distribution going on about us on this planet have been, for what we call a long time, favorable to evolution. These same changes will, however, so far as we can see, lead to the ultimate extinction of evolution on our planet. The question arises, Does the same relation between the nature of the physical world and the evolution, the progress, of the significant features of its various parts, hold true universally? The heavens, too, in their wholeness, suggest to us, from one point of view, a vast process of cosmical evolution. Examined more carefully, however, their physical phenomena seem to show that this evolution is but a transient stage of the endless world-process. The further question arises hereupon: Can we form a conception of the world-process in its true and entire nature, and so make out how it is actually related to what we call evolution? To this question we have found thus far only such an answer as suggests that the true world, whose mere show is embodied in these physical events now before our eyes, is at all events very inadequately represented by them. For the solution of our problem, if it is to find any, we must search deeper.

In what direction we have to search, our argument itself very readily suggests. It is plain that in what we said about the incongruity of such physical conceptions as involve the existence of an actually infinite space and time, and of actually infinite distances between bodies, we have touched close upon those considerations concerning the objectivity of space and time themselves which we have now learned to associate with the name of Kant. What if the foregoing paradoxes of the world of the "running down" energy, and of the endlessly consolidating matter, were due to the fact that we have been trying to give an hypothetical account of an absolute world-process in terms of human forms of conception and of experience? What if the truly complete world-process does not occur in time at all, but can only be conceived "under the form of eternity," as Spinoza would have said? "Such existence," said Spinoza, speaking of eternal truths, "cannot be explained by means of continuance or time." What if both the permanent laws and energy of nature on the one hand, and what we know as the process of evolution on the other, were but the temporal sign of something whose significance is to be otherwise conceived? Doubtful phrases these, one may say; yet, after all, what more doubtful than the ultimate truth of a physical world in which occur such paradoxical processes as we have been examining?

On the other hand, what more obvious than that *if* one conceives man as the product of a physical evolution of the type that we have heretofore been discussing, if one says that a planet-crust, at a particular stage of its history, brought forth man, while the heat of a slowly dying sun sustained his life, as it had done the lives of his countless animal ancestors before him, — if one holds all this to be true, then one must indeed look with equal wonder upon the power of such a creature to conceive at all of the real universe, or of the eternal, and upon the *naïveté* that trusts, without analysis and criticism, his notions of space and of time, his natural perceptions of the outer world, as if they were sure to be well-founded. The marvel of marvels, that this being, evolved from inorganic nature, from the stuff and the energy of a cooling solar system, — this mortal bit of mechanism — should after all *know*, should look forwards and backwards to eternity, and learn so much of the nature that gave him birth, — such a marvel surely calls for a deeper scrutiny. The world where such things appear is surely not what it seems; and the lesson is that, in the critical study of just this *knowing* power of ours, in the scrutiny of our most fundamental ideas, is to be found, if anywhere, the key to these mysteries. We have been so far inquiring into this or that truth. Now, more than ever, we see the need of assailing the problem, What is truth itself? What are our powers to know? And what validity have our ideas of the world and of its endless life?

And thus we are prepared, by the paradoxes of the outer order, to return for awhile, in order to seek a solution of them, to the recesses of the inner life, there to examine our conceptions of the world once more with a truly philosophical reflectiveness.

Does our result so far seem nothing but a sense of the mystery of things? Then remember at least that, as all modern thought has been teaching us from the start, the outer world is n't merely foreign to us. What we call the dark external universe yonder is, after all, *our* universe, even when we only go so far as to doubt or to wonder about it. Whatever the success or the failure of this or that idealistic theory, the permanent lesson of modern idealism has been that the inner and the outer worlds *must* have organic relations. If one of them is the world of the thinker, the other is the object of his thought. Ignorant as he may be of numberless facts in it, it has to echo somehow, even from its remotest heavens, the magic words that utter his deepest beliefs about it. Philosophy promises help, just because, when it speaks of the world whose mystery man's mind longs to penetrate, it also speaks of the mind itself whose nature it is to acknowledge, yes, and in acknowledging, just so far to penetrate the mystery. For, as we shall hereafter see, I cannot recognize a rational problem even as a problem, unless I already know a good deal about the object whose nature gives me this problem. What I definitely recognize as unknown must have such a knowable nature as enables me to make sure that it is unknown. An object of my conscious and rational ignorance is still an object, determined as such for me by my thought, and so in one aspect known to me, even in order that in some other aspect it may be unknown. Ignorance, if only it be definite ignorance, is sure to be partial knowledge. In so far as our study has made us aware of the mysteries that are in the world, it has already taught us much about the world. We don't know the precise value of the ratio of the circumference of a circle to its diameter. That is a good example of a rational mystery. For it is a definite, a highly scientific mystery. But see, we don't know this ratio just because we *do* know enough about the nature of a circle to be sure that this ratio is absolutely unstateable in any finite form. Well, even so, if philosophy shows us in any definite way how mysterious the world is, that will only be because philosophy will tell us enough about the true nature of the world to make clear to us where the mystery lies. Vague mysteries are the amusement of fools. Precise and rational mysteries are, in one sense, the goal of science. In defining our relation to nature, then, in making clear the issues of science, philosophy will aid us, not to solve all mysteries, as a dream might pretend to do, but to know where the deepest problems of the world lie, and thereby to show us something of the very essence of the reality which we have a right to find obscure.

It is in this spirit that I shall in the next lecture undertake to give you, in brief, my reasons for holding that an idealistic interpretation of the physical world, and in particular the theory of one absolute Self as the truth embodied in both nature and mind, is a doctrine that, without any presumptuous effort to transcend our human powers, may be explained and established.

LECTURE XI.

SUCH brief essays as I am to embody in these untechnical discussions must needs fail somewhere. I shall be glad, at all events, if they do not fail in frank statement of opinion. I do not want to weary you with bare assurances; I do not want to leave you with nothing to remember but my own word that in case I had time, I *would* expound my meaning and my reason for it; but I do want, above all things, in so far as I see any glimpse of truth, to risk in your presence a plain confession of it. If I must come short of the purpose of these lectures, let it be in technical exactness, since once for all that belongs elsewhere; but let me not fail of showing you that I have convictions, such as they are, whether I can make you agree with them or not. I do not know how you have found it, but for my part, as I have read the writings of some of the modern authors whose intelligence and caution I most value, I am frequently tormented with their tenderness of conscience about risking a statement of their personal beliefs. They have been driven to take this attitude, no doubt, through the warning which is given them by the traditional dogmatism of certain theologians. Longing to escape from the over-assurance and intolerance of such, the writers to whom I now refer lay more stress upon liberality, caution, patience, and learning, than even upon courage. I hope that I do not undervalue liberality or caution, and I am sure that I long for vastly more learning and patience than I shall ever possess; but, after all, it is what a man by chance believes, not what he does *not* believe, that enables him to be of service to his fellows as a thinker; and whatever fragment of knowledge one may possess will surely remain undiscovered unless he sometime ventures assertion of his temperament for whatever it may happen to be worth.

The business of the present lecture is to tell you in what sense and for what reasons I am an idealist. In the next following lectures, returning to the study of the outer order, I shall try to explain how, in consequence, I venture to conceive our human relationships to that physical world from which we have sprung and of which we are a part. In my concluding lecture I shall set forth what practical consequences I conceive to flow from my philosophy concerning that which constitutes the vocation of man. You will not require me to say that, as to all these three matters, I must needs be not only very fragmentary and unpersuasive, but also highly unoriginal. Other investigators may deal with novelties. It is the fate of the philosophical student to be cut off, by his very task, from all but a very relative and imperfect sort of originality. He is simply making articulate the life which he is privileged to enjoy. He invents nothing; he only confesses. Prophets create ideals; he critically expounds them. Poets, whose relation to passion is more direct and momentary, and therefore less universal, less abstract, less critical, less systematic, have for this very reason far more of the inventive about them. The student of philosophy is privileged to survey, to contemplate life from without, to reword. Others create; he observes. Consequently, were a philosophy original, it would be *ipso facto* untrue. The doctrines of philosophy are borrowed from passion. If, for instance, idealism is true at all, that is because all of you are already idealists. The philosopher only tells you so. He does not make you so. The fashion of my exposition in the following lectures may

have this or that of my own about it. The matter is as
old as it is true ; or, if it is not old, then that is because
it is not true.

But in still another sense is this discussion unoriginal.
The time is long past when really intelligent thinkers
sought to do anything outside of intimate relations to the
history of thought.   It still happens, indeed, that even in
our day some lonesome student will occasionally publish
a philosophical book that he regards as entirely revolutionary, as digging far beneath all that thought has ever
yet accomplished, and as beginning quite afresh the labors
of human reflection.   Such men, when they appear nowadays, as once in a while they do appear, are anachro-
nisms ; and you will always find them either ignorant of
the history of the very subject that they propose to revo-
lutionize or incapable of reading this history intelligently.
What they give you is always an old doctrine, more or
less disguised in a poorly novel terminology, and much
worse thought out than it has already been thought out,
time after time, in the history of speculation.   It is one
of the defects of the current liberalism in matters of opinion that it does encourage, only too often, this sort of
thinking ; and the sole corrective of the error is a certain
amount of philosophical study of an historical sort before
one begins to print one's speculations.

Now, as you know, I have been fearing such unhistorical fashions of procedure so much that I have been devoting myself wholly, during the first part of these lectures,
to telling a story, and adding occasional criticisms. It follows that I have no doctrine to teach save the one that
this history has taught me.   Personal conviction, then,
offered for whatever it is worth, — a reflective confession
of my own temperament — but all this reflection guided
throughout by the light which the history of thought gives
me about what is really human and worth confessing
in this temperament of mine, — such must be the busi-

ness of these concluding lectures. For how it is that a man can thus be at once merely the critic of his own deeper nature, and still merely the mouthpiece for the telling of the lesson that he has learned from the history of thought, you will now after all these discussions surely be able to see. The philosophical student confesses his own ideals; for what others has he to confess? He learns, however, from history what amongst his ideals have any permanent human value; for the history of thought is the school in which alone one *can* learn to humanize one's reflective processes, and to distinguish the accidental from the essential in one's temperament.

I.

I am very sorry that I cannot state my idealism in a simple and unproblematic form; but the nature of the doctrine forbids. I must first of all puzzle you with a paradox, by saying that my idealism has nothing in it which contradicts the principal propositions of what is nowadays called scientific Agnosticism, in so far, namely, as this agnosticism relates to that world of facts of experience which man sees and feels and which science studies. Of such agnosticism we learned something in our last lecture. But I must go on to say that the fault of our modern so-called scientific agnosticism is only that it has failed to see how the world in space and time, the world of causes and effects, the world of matter and of finite mind, whereof we know so little and long to know so much, is a very subordinate part of reality. It will be my effort to explain how we do know something very deep and vital about what reality is in its innermost essence. My explanation will indeed be very poor and fragmentary, but the outcome of it will be the very highly paradoxical assertion that while the whole finite world is full of dark problems for us, there is absolutely nothing, not even the immediate facts of our sense at this moment,

so clear, so certain, as the existence and the unity of that
infinite conscious Self of whom we have now heard so
much.   About the finite world, as I shall assert, we know
in general only what experience teaches us and science
records.   There is nothing in the universe absolutely sure
except the Infinite.   That will be the curious sort of
agnosticism that I shall try in a measure to expound.
Of the infinite we know that it is one and conscious.   Of
the finite things, that is, of the particular fashions of behavior in terms of which the infinite Consciousness gives
himself form and plays the world-game, we know only
what we experience.   Yet doubtless it will at once seem
to you that in *one* important respect my announced doctrine is in obvious conflict with a wise agnosticism.   For
is it not confessedly anthromorphic in its character ?
And is not anthropomorphism precisely the defect that
modern thinkers have especially taught us to avoid ?

Anthropomorphism was the savage view, which led
primitive man to interpret extraordinary natural events
as expressions of the will of beings like himself.   However he came by his fancy, whether by first believing in
the survival of the ghosts of his ancestors, and then conceiving them as the agents who produced lightning, and
who moved the sun, or by a simple and irreducible instinct
of his childish soul, leading him to see himself in nature,
and to regard it all as animate ; in any case he made the
bad induction, created the gods in his own image, and
then constituted them as the causes of all natural events.
His ignorant self-multiplication we must avoid.   Shall
our limited inner experience be the only test of what
sorts of causation may exist in the world?   What we
know is that events happen to us, and happen in a certain
fixed order.   We do not know the ultimate causes of these
events.   If we lived on some other planet, doubtless
causes of a very novel sort would become manifest to us,
and our whole view of nature would change.   It is self-

contradictory, it is absurd, to make our knowledge the measure of all that is! The real world that causes our experience is a great x, wholly unknown to us except in a few select phenomena, which happen to fall within our ken. How wild to guess about the mysteries of the infinite!

But now *this* agnosticism, too, as I assure you, I ardently and frankly agree with, so far as it concerns itself with precisely *that* world in which it pretends to move, and to which it undertakes to apply itself. I have no desire to refute it. Touching all the world in space and time beyond experience, in the scientific sense of the term experience, I repeat that I know nothing positive. I know, for instance, nothing about the stratification of Saturn, or the height of the mountains on the other side of the moon. For the same reason, also, I know nothing of any anthropomorphic dæmons or gods here or there in nature, acting as causes of noteworthy events. Of these I know nothing, because science has at present no need for such hypotheses. There may be such beings; there doubtless are in nature many curious phenomena; but what curiosities further experience might show us, we must wait for experience to point out ere we shall know. I repeat, in its own world, agnosticism is in all these respects in the right. For reasons that you will later see, I object indeed to the unhappy word *unknowable*. In the world of experience, as in the world of abstracter problems, there are infinitely numerous things unknown to us. But there is no rational question that could not somehow be answered by a sufficiently wise person. There are things relatively unknowable for us, not things absolutely so. There are numberless experiences that I shall never have, in my individual capacity; and there are numberless problems that I shall never solve. But the only absolute insoluble mysteries, as I shall hereafter point out to you, would be the questions that it is essentially absurd to ask.

Still, not to quarrel over words, what many agnostics mean by unknowable is simply the stubbornly unknown, and, in that sense, I fully agree and indeed insist that human knowledge is an island in the vast ocean of mystery, and that numberless questions, which it deeply concerns humanity to answer, will never be answered so long as we are in our present limited state, bound to one planet, and left for our experience to our senses, our emotions, and our moral activities.

But, if I thus accept this agnostic view of the world of experience, what chance is left, you will say, for anything like an absolute system of philosophy? In what sense can I pretend to talk of idealism, as giving any final view of the whole nature of things? In what sense, above all, can I pretend to be a theist, and to speak of the absolute Self as the very essence and life of the whole world? For is this not mere anthropomorphism? Is n't it making our private human experience the measure of all reality? Is n't it making hypotheses in terms of our experience, about things beyond our experience? Is n't it making our petty notions of causation a basis for judging of the nature of the unknown first cause? Is n't it another case of what the savage did when he saw his gods in the thunder-clouds, because he conceived that causes just like his own angry moods must be here at work? Surely, at best, this is sentiment, faith, mystical dreaming. It can't be philosophy.

I answer, just to change our whole view of the deeper reality of things, just to turn away our attention from any illusive search for first causes in the world of experience, just to get rid of fanciful faith about the gods in outer nature, and just to complete the spiritual task of agnosticism by sending us elsewhere than to phenomena for the true and inner nature of things, — for just this end was the whole agony of modern philosophy endured by those who have wrestled with its problems. Is any one agnos-

tic about the finite world? Then I more. I know nothing of any first cause in the world of appearances yonder. I see no gods in the thunder clouds, no Keplerian
angels carrying the planets in conic sections around the
sun; I imagine no world-maker far back in the ages,
beginning the course of evolution. Following Laplace, I
need, once more, no such hypothesis. I await the ver-
dict of science about all facts and events in physical
nature. And yet that is just *why* I am an idealist. It
is my agnosticism about the causes of my experience that
makes me search elsewhere than amongst causes for the
meaning of experience. The outer world which the
agnostic sees and despairs of knowing is not the region
where I look for light. The living God, whom idealism
knows, is not the first cause in any physical sense, at all.
No possible experience could find him as a thing amongst
things or show any outer facts that would prove his existence. He is n't anywhere in space or in time. He makes
from without no worlds. He is no hypothesis of empirical science. But he is all the more real for that, and his
existence is all the surer. For causes are, after all, very
petty and subordinate truths in the world, and facts,
phenomena, as such, could never demonstrate any important spiritual truth. The absolute Self simply does n't
cause the world. The very idea of causation belongs
to things of finite experience, and is only a mythological
term when applied to the real truth of things. Not because I interpret the causes of my experience in terms of
my limited ideas of causation is the universe of God a
live thing to me, but for a far deeper reason; for a reason which deprives this world of agnosticism of all substantiality and converts it once for all into mere show. I
am ignorant of this world just because it is a show-world.

And this deeper reason of the idealist I may as well
first suggest in a form which may perhaps seem just now
even more mysterious than the problem which I solve by

means of it. My reason for believing that there is one absolute World-Self, who embraces and is all reality, whose
consciousness includes and infinitely transcends our own,
in whose unity all the laws of nature and all the mysteries
of experience must have their solution and their very
being, — is simply that the profoundest agnosticism which
you can possibly state in any coherent fashion, the deepest
doubt which you can any way formulate about the world or
the things that are therein, already presupposes, implies,
demands, asserts, the existence of such a World-Self.
The agnostic, I say, already asserts this existence —
unconsciously, of course, as a rule, but none the less inevitably. For, as we shall find, there is no escape from the
infinite Self except by self-contradiction. Ignorant as I
am about first causes, I am at least clear, therefore, about
the Self. If you deny him, you already in denying affirm
him. You reckon ill when you leave him out. Him when
you fly, he is the wings. He is the doubter and the
doubt. You in vain flee from his presence. The wings
of the morning will not aid you. Nor do I mean all this
now as any longer a sort of mysticism. This truth is, I
assure you, simply a product of dry logic. When I try
to tell you about it in detail, I shall weary you by my
wholly unmystical analysis of commonplaces. Here is,
in fact, as we shall soon find, the very presupposition of
presuppositions. You cannot stir, nay, you cannot even
stand still in thought without it. Nor is it an unfamiliar
idea. On the contrary, philosophy finds trouble in bringing it to your consciousness merely *because* it is so familiar. When they told us in childhood that we could not
see God just *because* he was everywhere, just because his
omnipresence gave us no chance to discern him and to fix
our eyes upon him, they told us a deep truth in allegori-
cal fashion. The infinite Self, as we shall learn, is actually asserted by you in every proposition you utter, is
there at the heart, so to speak, of the very multiplication

table. The Self is so little a thing merely guessed at as
the unknowable source of experience, that already, *in* the
very least of daily experiences you unconsciously know
him as something present. This, as we shall find, is the
deepest tragedy of our finitude, that continually he comes
to his own, and his own receive him not, that he becomes
flesh in every least incident of our lives; whilst we, gazing
with wonder upon his world, search here and there for
first causes, look for miracles, and beg him to show us the
Father, since that alone will suffice us. No wonder that
thus we have to remain agnostics. "Hast thou been so
long time with me, and yet hast thou not *known* me?"
Such is the eternal answer of the Logos to every doubting
question. Seek him not as an outer hypothesis to explain
experience. Seek him not anywhere yonder in the clouds.
He is no "thing in itself." But for all that, experience
contains him. He is the reality, the soul of it. "Did not
our heart burn within us while he talked with us by the
way?" And, as we shall see, he does not talk merely tc
our hearts. He reveals himself to our coolest scrutiny.

II.

But enough of speculative boasting. Coming to closer
quarters with my topic, I must remind you that idealism
has two aspects. It is, for the first, a kind of analysis of
the world, an analysis which so far has no absolute character about it, but which undertakes, in a fashion that
might be acceptable to any skeptic, to examine what you
mean by all the things, whatever they are, that you believe in or experience. This idealistic analysis consists
merely in a pointing out, by various devices, that the
world of your knowledge, whatever it contains, is through
and through such stuff as ideas are made of, that you
never in your life believed in anything definable *but* ideas,
that, as Berkeley put it, "this whole choir of heaven and
furniture of earth" is nothing for any of us but a system

of ideas which govern our belief and our conduct. Such idealism has numerous statements, interpretations, embodiments : forms part of the most various systems and experiences, is consistent with Berkeley's theism, with Fichte's ethical absolutism, with Professor Huxley's agnostic empiricism, with Clifford's mind-stuff theory, with countless other theories that have used such idealism as a part of their scheme. In this aspect idealism is already a little puzzling to our natural consciousness, but it becomes quickly familiar, in fact almost commonplace, and seems after all to alter our practical faith or to solve our deeper problems very little.

The other aspect of idealism is the one which gives us our notion of the absolute Self. To it the first is only preparatory. This second aspect is the one which from Kant, until the present time, has formed the deeper problem of thought. Whenever the world has become more conscious of its significance, the work of human philosophy will be, not nearly ended (Heaven forbid an end!), but for the first time fairly begun. For then, in critically estimating our passions, we shall have some truer sense of whose passions they are.

I begin with the first and the less significant aspect of idealism. Our world, I say, whatever it may contain, is such stuff as ideas are made of. This preparatory sort of idealism is the one that, as I just suggested, Berkeley made prominent, and, after a fashion familiar. I must state it in my own way, although one in vain seeks to attain novelty in illustrating so frequently described a view.

Here, then, is our so real world of the senses, full of light and warmth and sound. If anything could be solid and external, surely, one at first will say, it is this world. Hard facts, not mere ideas, meet us on every hand. Ideas any one can mould as he wishes. Not so facts. In idea socialists can dream out Utopias, disappointed lovers can imagine themselves successful, beggars can ride horses, wanderers can enjoy the fireside at home. In the realm of facts, society organizes itself as it must, rejected lovers stand for the time defeated, beggars are alone with their wishes, oceans roll drearily between home and the wanderer. Yet this world of fact is, after all, not entirely stubborn, not merely hard. The strenuous will can mould facts. We can form our world, in part, according to our ideas. Statesmen influence the social order, lovers woo afresh, wanderers find the way home. But thus to alter the world we must work, and just because the laborer is worthy of his hire, it is well that the real world should thus have such fixity of things as enables us to anticipate what facts will prove lasting, and to see of the travail of our souls when it is once done. This, then, is the presupposition of life, that we work in a real world, where house-walls do not melt away as in dreams, but stand firm against the winds of many winters, and can be felt as real. We do not wish to find facts wholly plastic; we want them to be stubborn, if only the stubbornness be not altogether unmerciful. Our will makes constantly a sort of agreement with the world, whereby, if the world will continually show some respect to the will, the will shall consent to be strenuous in its industry. Interfere with the reality of my world, and you therefore take the very life and heart out of my will.

The reality of the world, however, when thus defined in terms of its stubbornness, its firmness as against the will that has not conformed to its laws, its kindly rigidity in preserving for us the fruits of our labors, — such reality, I say, is still something wholly unanalyzed. In what does this stubbornness consist? Surely, many different sorts of reality, as it would seem, may be stubborn. Matter is stubborn when it stands in hard walls against us, or rises in vast mountain ranges before the path-finding explorer. But minds can be stubborn also. The

lonely wanderer, who watches by the seashore the waves
that roll between him and his home, talks of cruel facts,
material barriers that, just because they *are* material, and
not ideal, shall be the irresistible foes of his longing
heart. "In wish," he says, "I am with my dear ones,
but alas, wishes cannot cross oceans! Oceans are material facts, in the cold outer world. Would that the world
of the heart were all!" But alas! to the rejected lover
the world of the heart *is* all, and that is just his woe.
Were the barrier between him and his beloved only made
of those stubborn material facts, only of walls or of
oceans, how lightly might his will erelong transcend them
all! Matter stubborn! Outer nature cruelly the foe of
ideas! Nay, it is just an idea that now opposes him, —
just an idea, and that, too, in the mind of the maiden he
loves. But in vain does he calls this stubborn bit of disdain a merely ideal fact. No flint was ever more definite
in preserving its identity and its edge than this disdain
may be. Place me for a moment, then, in an external world
that shall consist wholly of ideas, — the ideas, namely,
of other people about me, a world of maidens who shall
scorn me, of old friends who shall have learned to hate
me, of angels who shall condemn me, of God who shall
judge me. In what piercing north winds, amidst what
fields of ice, in the labyrinths of what tangled forests, in
the depths of what thick-walled dungeons, on the edges
of what tremendous precipices, should I be more genuinely in the presence of stubborn and unyielding facts
than in that conceived world of ideas! So, as one sees,
I by no means deprive my world of stubborn reality,
if I merely call it a world of ideas. On the contrary, as
every teacher knows, the ideas of the people are often the
most difficult of facts to influence. We were wrong, then,
when we said that whilst matter was stubborn, ideas could
be moulded at pleasure. Ideas are often the most impla-
cable of facts. Even my own ideas, the facts of my own

inner life, may cruelly decline to be plastic to my wish.
The wicked will that refuses to be destroyed, — what rock
has often more consistency for our senses than this will
has for our inner consciousness! The king, in his soliloquy in "Hamlet," — in what an unyielding world of
hard facts does he not move! and yet they are now only
inner facts. The fault is past; he is alone with his conscience.

> " What rests ?
> Try what repentance can. What cán it not ?
> Yet what can it, when one cannot repent ?
> O wretched state ! O bosom black as death !
> O limëd soul, that, struggling to be free,
> Art more engaged ! "

No, here are barriers worse than any material chains.
The world of ideas has its own horrible dungeons and
chasms. Let those who have refuted Bishop Berkeley's
idealism by the wonder why he did not walk over every
precipice or into every fire if these things existed only in
his idea, let such, I say, first try some of the fires and the
precipices of the inner life, ere they decide that dangers
cease to be dangers as soon as they are called ideal, or
even subjectively ideal in me.

Many sorts of reality, then, may be existent at the
heart of any world of facts. But this bright and beautiful sense-world of ours, — what, amongst these many possible sorts of reality, does that embody ? Are the stars and
the oceans, the walls and the pictures, real as the maiden's
heart is real, — embodying the ideas of somebody, but
none the less stubbornly real for that ? Or can we make
something else of their reality ? For, of course, that the
stars and the oceans, the walls and the pictures have *some*
sort of stubborn reality, just as the minds of our fellows
have, our analysis so far does not for an instant think of
denying. Our present question is, what sort of reality ?
Consider, then, in detail, certain aspects of the reality

that seems to be exemplified in our sense-world. The sublimity of the sky, the life and majesty of the ocean, the interest of a picture, — to what sort of real facts do these belong? Evidently here we shall have no question. So far as the sense-world is beautiful, is majestic, is sublime, this beauty and dignity exist only for the appreciative observer. If they exist beyond him, they exist only for some other mind, or as the thought and embodied purpose of some universal soul of nature. A man who sees the same world, but who has no eye for the fairness of it, will find all the visible facts, but will catch nothing of their value. At once, then, the sublimity and beauty of the world are thus truths that one who pretends to insight ought to see, and they are truths which have no meaning except for such a beholder's mind, or except as embodying the thought of the mind of the world. So here, at least, is so much of the outer world that is ideal, just as the coin or the jewel or the bank-note or the bond has its value not alone in its physical presence, but in the idea that it symbolizes to a beholder's mind, or to the relatively universal thought of the commercial world. But let us look a little deeper. Surely, if the objects yonder are unideal and outer, odors and tastes and temperatures do not exist in these objects in just the way in which they exist in us. Part of the being of these properties, at least, if not all of it, is ideal and exists for us, or at best is once more the embodiment of the thought or purpose of some world-mind. About tastes you cannot dispute, because they are not only ideal but personal. For the benumbed tongue and palate of diseased bodily conditions, all things are tasteless. As for temperatures, a well known experiment will show how the same water may seem cold to one hand and warm to the other. But even so, colors and sounds are at least in part ideal. Their causes may have some other sort of reality; but colors themselves are not in the things, since they change with the light that falls on the things, vanish in the dark (whilst the things remained unchanged), and differ for different eyes. And as for sounds, both the pitch and the quality of tones depend for us upon certain interesting peculiarities of our hearing organs, and exist in nature only as voiceless sound-waves trembling through the air. All such sense qualities, then, are ideal. The world yonder may — yes, must — have attributes that give reasons why these qualities are thus felt by us; for so we assume. The world yonder may even be a mind that thus expresses its will to us. But these qualities need not, nay, cannot resemble the ideas that are produced in us, unless, indeed, that is because these qualities have place as ideas in some world-mind. Sound-waves in the air are not like our musical sensations; nor is the symphony as we hear it and feel it any physical property of the strings and the wind instruments; nor are the ether-vibrations that the sun sends us like our ideas when we see the sun; nor yet is the flashing of moonlight on the water as we watch the waves a direct expression of the actual truths of fluid motion as the water embodies them.

Unless, then, the real physical world yonder is itself the embodiment of some world - spirit's ideas, which he conveys to us, unless it is real only as the maiden's heart is real, namely, as itself a conscious thought, then we have so far but one result: that real world (to repeat one of the commonplaces of modern popular science) is in itself, apart from somebody's eyes and tongue and ears and touch, neither colored nor tasteful, neither cool nor warm, neither light nor dark, neither musical nor silent. All these qualities belong to our ideas, being indeed none the less genuine facts for that, but being in so far ideal facts. We must see colors when we look, we must hear music when there is playing in our presence; but this *must* is a must that consists in a certain irresistible presence of an idea in us under certain conditions. *That* this idea must

come is, indeed, a truth as unalterable, once more, as the
king's settled remorse in Hamlet.   But like this remorse,
again, it exists as an ideal truth, objective, but through
and through objective *for* somebody, and not *apart from*
anybody.   What this truth implies we have yet to see.
So far it is only an ideal truth for the beholder, with just
the bare possibility that behind it all there is the thought
of a world-spirit.   And, in fact, *so* far we must all go together if we reflect.

But now, at this point, the Berkeleyan idealist goes one
step further.   The real outside world that is still left un-
explained and unanalyzed after its beauty, its warmth, its
odors, its tastes, its colors, and its tones, have been rele-
gated to the realm of ideal truths, what do you now *mean*
by calling it real?   No doubt it *is* known as somehow real,
but *what* is this reality *known as* being?   If you know
that this world is still there and outer, as by hypothesis
you know, you are bound to say *what* this outer character
implies for your thought.   And here you have trouble.
Is the outer world, as it exists outside of your ideas, or of
anybody's ideas, something having shape, filling space,
possessing solidity, full of moving things?   That would
in the first place seem evident.   The sound is n't outside
of me, but the sound-waves, you say, are.   The colors are
ideal facts ; but the ether-waves don't need a mind to
know them.   Warmth is ideal, but the physical fact called
heat, this playing to and fro of molecules, is real, and is
there apart from any mind.   But once more, *is* this so
evident?   What do I *mean* by the shape of anything, or
by the size of anything?   Don't I mean just the idea of
shape or of size that I am obliged to get under certain
circumstances ?   What is the meaning of any property
that I give to the real outer world?   How can I express
that property except in case I think it in terms of my
ideas?   As for the sound-waves and the ether-waves, what
are they but things ideally conceived to explain the facts

of nature ? The conceptions have doubtless their truth, but it is an ideal truth. What I mean by saying that the things yonder have shape and size and trembling molecules, and that there is air with sound-waves, and ether with light-waves in it, — what I *mean* by all this is that experience forces upon me, directly or indirectly, a vast system of ideas, which may indeed be founded in truth beyond me, which in fact *must* be founded in such truth if my experience has any sense, but which, like my ideas of color and of warmth, are simply expressions of how the world's order must appear to me, and to anybody constituted like me. Above all, is this plain about space. The real things, I say, outside of me, fill space, and move about in it. But what do I mean by space? Only a vast system of ideas which experience and my own mind force upon me. Doubtless these ideas have a validity. They have *this* validity, that I, at all events, when I look upon the world, am bound to see it in space, as much bound as the king in Hamlet was, when he looked within, to see himself as guilty and unrepentant. But just as his guilt was an idea, — a crushing, an irresistible, an overwhelming idea, — but still just an idea, so, too, the space in which I place my world is one great formal idea of mine. That is just why I can describe it to other people. "It has three dimensions," I say, "length, breadth, depth." I describe each. I form, I convey, I construct, an idea of it through them. I know space, as an idea, very well. I can compute all sorts of unseen truths about the relations of its parts. I am sure that you, too, share this idea. But, then, for all of us alike it is just an idea ; and when we put our world into space, and call it real there, we simply think one idea into another idea, not voluntarily, to be sure, but inevitably, and yet without leaving the realm of ideas.

Thus, all the reality that *we* attribute to our world, in so far as *we* know and can tell what we mean thereby, becomes ideal. There is, in fact, a certain system of ideas, forced upon us by experience, which we have to use as the guide of our conduct. This system of ideas we can't change by our wish; it is for us as overwhelming a fact as guilt, or as the bearing of our fellows towards us, but we know it only *as* such a system of ideas. And we call it the world of matter. John Stuart Mill very well expressed the puzzle of the whole thing, as we have now reached the statement of this puzzle, when he called matter a mass of " permanent possibilities of experience " for each of us. Mill's definition has its faults, but it is a very fair beginning. You know matter as something that either now gives you this idea or experience, or that would give you some other idea or experience under other circumstances. A fire, while it burns, is for you a permanent possibility of either getting the idea of an agreeable warmth, or of getting the idea of a bad burn, and you treat it accordingly. A precipice amongst mountains is a permanent possibility of your experiencing a fall, or of your getting a feeling of the exciting or of the sublime in mountain scenery. You have no experience just now of the tropics or of the poles, but both tropical and polar climates exist in your world as permanent possibilities of experience. When you call the sun 92,000,000 miles away, you mean that between you and the sun (that is, between your present experience and the possible experience of the sun's surface) there would inevitably lie the actually inaccessible, but still numerically conceivable series of experiences of distance expressed by the number of miles in question. In short, your whole attitude towards the real world may be summed up by saying: " I have experiences now which I seem bound to have, experiences of color, sound, and all the rest of my present ideas; and I am also bound by experience to believe that in case I did certain things (for instance, touched the wall, traveled to the tropics, visited Europe, studied physics), I then should get, in a determinate order, dependent wholly upon *what* I had done, certain other experiences (for instance, experiences of the wall's solidity, or of a tropical climate, or of the scenes of an European tour, or of the facts of physics)." And this acceptance of actual experience, this belief in possible experience, constitutes all that you mean by your faith in the outer world.

But, you say, Is not, then, all this faith of ours after all well founded ? Is n't there really something yonder that corresponds in fact to this series of experiences in us? Yes, indeed, there no doubt is. But what if this, which so shall correspond without us to the ideas within us, what if this hard and fast reality should itself be a system of ideas, outside of our minds but not outside of every mind? As the maiden's disdain is outside the rejected lover's mind, unchangeable so far for him, but not on that account the less ideal, not the less a fact in a mind, as, to take afresh a former fashion of illustration, the price of a security or the objective existence of this lecture is an ideal fact, but real and external for the individual person, — even so why might not this world beyond us, this "permanent possibility of experience," be in essence itself a system of ideal experiences of some standard thought of which ours is only the copy ? Nay, must it not be such a system in case it has any reality at all ? For, after all, is n't this precisely what our analysis brings us to ? Nothing whatever can I say about my world yonder that I do not express in terms of mind. *What* things are, extended, moving, colored, tuneful, majestic, beautiful, holy, *what* they are in any aspect of their nature, mathematical, logical, physical, sensuously pleasing, spiritually valuable, all this must mean for me only something that I have to express in the fashion of ideas. The more I am to know my world, the more of a mind I must have for the purpose. The closer I come to the truth about the things,

the more ideas I get. Is n't it plain, then, that *if* my
world yonder is anything knowable at all, it must be in
and for itself essentially a mental world? Are my ideas
to *resemble* in any way the world? Is the truth of my
thought to consist in its *agreement* with reality? And
am I thus capable, as common sense supposes, of *conforming* my ideas to things? Then reflect. What can, after
all, so well agree with an idea as another idea? To what
can things that go on in my mind conform unless it be to
another mind? If the more my mind grows in mental
clearness, the nearer it gets to the nature of reality, then
surely the reality that my mind thus **resembles** must be in
itself mental.

After all, then, would it deprive the world here about
me of reality, nay, would it not rather save and assure
the reality and the knowableness of my world of experience, if I said that this world, as it exists outside of my
mind, and of any other human minds, exists in and for a
standard, an universal mind, whose system of ideas simply constitutes the world? Even if I fail to prove that
there is such a mind, do I not at least thus make plausible that, as I said, our world of common sense has no fact
in it which we cannot interpret in terms of ideas, so that
this world is throughout such stuff as ideas are made of?
To say this, as you see, in no wise deprives our world of
its due share of reality. If the standard mind knows
now that its ideal fire has the quality of burning those
who touch it, and if I in my finitude am bound to conform in my experiences to the thoughts of this standard
mind, then in case I touch that fire I shall surely get the
idea of a burn. The standard mind will be at least as
hard and fast and real in its ideal consistency as is the
maiden in her disdain for the rejected lover; and I, in
presence of the ideal stars and the oceans, will see the genuine realities of fate as certainly as the lover hears his
fate in the voice that expresses her will.

I need not now proceed further with an analysis that will be more or less familiar to many of you, especially after our foregoing historical lectures. What I have desired thus far is merely to give each of you, as it were, the sensation of being an idealist in this first and purely analytical sense of the word idealism. The sum and substance of it all is, you see, this: you know your world in fact as a system of ideas about things, such that from moment to moment you find this system forced upon you by experience. Even matter you know just as a mass of coherent ideas that you cannot help having. Space and time, as you think them, are surely ideas of yours. Now, what more natural than to say that *if* this be so, the real world beyond you must in itself be a system of somebody's ideas? If it is, then you can comprehend what its existence means. If it isn't, then since all you can know of it is ideal, the real world must be utterly unknowable, a bare *x*. Minds I can understand, because I myself am a mind. An existence that has no mental attribute is wholly opaque to me. So far, however, from such a world of ideas, existent beyond me in another mind, seeming to coherent thought essentially *un*real, ideas and minds and their ways, are, on the contrary, the hardest and stubbornest facts that we can name. *If* the external world is in itself mental, then, be this reality a standard and universal thought, or a mass of little atomic minds constituting the various particles of matter, in any case one can comprehend what it is, and will have at the same time to submit to its stubborn authority as the lover accepts the reality of the maiden's moods. If the world *isn't* such an ideal thing, then indeed all our science, which is through and through concerned with our mental interpretations of things, can neither have objective validity, nor make satisfactory progress towards truth. For as science is concerned with ideas, the world beyond all ideas is a bare *x*.

III.

But with this bare x, you will say, this analytical idealism after all leaves me, as with something that, spite of all
my analyses and interpretations, may after all be there
beyond me as the real world, which my ideas are vainly
striving to reach, but which eternally flees before me. So
far, you will say, what idealism teaches is that the real
world can only be interpreted by treating it as if it were
somebody's thought. So regarded, the idealism of Berkeley and of other such thinkers is very suggestive; yet it
does n't tell us what the true world is, but only that *so
much* of the true world as we ever get into our comprehension has to be conceived in ideal terms. Perhaps,
however, whilst neither beauty, nor majesty, nor odor, nor
warmth, nor tone, nor color, nor form, nor motion, nor
space, nor time (all these being but ideas of ours), can be
said to belong to the extra-mental world, — perhaps, after
all, there does exist there yonder an extra-mental world,
which has nothing to do, except by accident, with *any*
mind, and which is through and through just extra-mental,
something unknowable, inscrutable, the basis of experience, the source of ideas, but itself never experienced as
it is in itself, never adequately represented by any idea
in us. Perhaps it is there. Yes, you will say, *must* it
not be there? Must not one accept our limitations once
for all, and say, "What reality is, we can never hope to
make clear to ourselves. That which has been made clear
becomes an idea in us. But always there is the beyond,
the mystery, the inscrutable, the real, the x. To be sure,
perhaps we can't even know so much as that this x after
all does exist. But then we feel bound to regard it as
existent; or even if we doubt or deny it, may it not be
there all the same?" In such doubt and darkness, then,
this first form of idealism closes. If that were all there
were to say, I should indeed have led you a long road in

vain. Analyzing what the known world is for you, in case there is haply any world known to you at all, — this surely is n't proving that there is any real world, or that the real world can be known. Are we not just where we started ?

No; there lies now just ahead of us the goal of a synthetic idealistic conception, which will not be content with this mere analysis of the colors and forms of things, and with the mere discovery that all these are for us nothing but ideas. In this second aspect, idealism grows bolder, and fears not the profoundest doubt that may have entered your mind as to whether there is any world at all, or as to whether it is in any fashion knowable. State in full the deepest problem, the hardest question about the world that your thought ever conceived. In this new form idealism offers you a suggestion that indeed will not wholly answer nor do away with every such problem, but that certainly will set the meaning of it in a new light. What this new light is, I must in conclusion seek to illustrate.

Note the point we have reached. *Either*, as you see, your real world yonder is through and through a world of ideas, an outer mind that you are more or less comprehending through your experience, *or else*, in so far as it is real and outer it is unknowable, an inscrutable *x*, an absolute mystery. The dilemma is perfect. There is no third alternative. Either a mind yonder, or else the unknowable; that is your choice. Philosophy loves such dilemmas, wherein all the mightiest interests of the spirit, all the deepest longings of human passion, are at stake, waiting as for the fall of a die. Philosophy loves such situations, I say, and loves, too, to keep its scrutiny as cool in the midst of them as if it were watching a game of chess, instead of the great world-game. Well, try the darker choice that the dilemma gives you. The world yonder shall be an *x*, an unknowable something, outer, problematic, foreign, opaque. And you, — you shall look upon it and believe in it. Yes, you shall for argument's sake first put on an air of resigned confidence, and say, "I do not only fancy it to be an extra-mental and unknowable something there, an impenetrable x, but I know it to be such. I can't help it. I did n't make it unknowable. I regret the fact. But there it is. I have to admit its existence. But I know that I shall never solve the problem of its nature." Ah, its nature is a *problem*, then. But what do you mean by this "*problem*"? Problems are, after a fashion, rather familiar things, — that is, in the world of ideas. There are problems soluble and problems insoluble in that world of ideas. It is a soluble problem if one asks what whole number is the square root of 64. The answer is 8. It is an insoluble problem if one asks me to find what whole number is the square root of 65. There is, namely, no such whole number. If one asks me to name the length of a straight line that shall be equal to the circumference of a circle of a known radius, that again, in the world of ideas, is an insoluble problem, because, as can be proved, the circumference of a circle is a length that cannot possibly be exactly expressed in terms of any statable number when the radius is of a stated length. So in the world of ideas, problems are definite questions which can be asked in knowable terms. Fair questions of this sort either may be fairly answered in our present state of knowledge, or else they could be answered if we knew a little or a good deal more, or finally they could not possibly be answered. But in the latter case, if they could not possibly be answered, they always must resemble the problem how to square the circle. They then always turn out, namely, to be absurdly stated questions, and it is their absurdity that makes these problems absolutely insoluble. Any fair question could be answered by one who knew enough. No fair question has an unknowable answer. But now, *if* your unknowable world out there is a thing of wholly, of absolutely problematic and inscrutable nature, is it so because you don't *yet* know enough about it, or because in its very nature and essence it is an absurd thing, an *x* that *would* answer a question, which actually it is nonsense to ask? Surely one must choose the former alternative. The real world may be unknown; it can't be essentially unknowable.

This subtlety is wearisome enough, I know, just here, but I shall not dwell long upon it. Plainly *if* the unknowable world out there is through and through in its nature a really inscrutable problem, this must mean that in nature it resembles such problems as, What is the whole number that is the square root of 65? Or, What two adjacent hills are there that have no valley between them? For in the world of thought such are the *only* insoluble problems. All others either may now be solved, or would be solved if we knew more than we now do. But, once more, *if* this unknowable is only just the real world as now unknown to us, but capable some time of becoming known, then remember that, as we have just seen, only a mind can ever become an object known to a mind. If I know you as external to me, it is only because you are minds. If I can come to know *any* truth, it is only in so far as this truth is essentially mental, is an idea, is a thought, that I can ever come to know it. Hence, if that so-called unknowable, that unknown outer world there, ever could, by any device, come within our ken, then it is already an ideal world. For just that is what our whole idealistic analysis has been proving. Only ideas are knowable. And nothing absolutely unknowable can exist. For the absolutely unknowable, the *x* pure and simple, the Kantian thing in itself, simply cannot be admitted. The notion of it is nonsense. The assertion of it is a contradiction. Round-squares, and sugar salt-lumps, and Snarks, and Boojums, and Jabberwocks, and Abracadabras; such, I insist, are the only unknowables there are.

The unknown, that which our human and finite selfhood has n't grasped, exists spread out before us in a boundless world of truth ; but the unknowable is essentially, confessedly, *ipso facto* a fiction.

The nerve of our whole argument in the foregoing is now pretty fairly exposed.   We have seen that the outer truth must be, if anything, a " possibility of experience." But we may now see that a *bare* " possibility " as such, is, like the unknowable, something meaningless.   That which, whenever I come to know it, turns out to be through and through an idea, an experience, must be in itself, before I know it, either somebody's idea, somebody's experience, or it must be nothing.   What is a " possibility " of experience that is outside of me, and that is still nothing *for* any one one else than myself?   Is n't it a bare *x*, a nonsense phrase ?   Is n't it like an unseen color, an untasted taste, an unfelt feeling ?   In proving that the world is one of " possible " experience, we have proved that in so far as it is real it is one of actual experience.

Once more, then, to sum up here, *if*, however vast the world of the unknown, only the essentially knowable can exist, and *if* everything knowable is an idea, a mental somewhat, the content of some mind, then once for all we are the world of ideas.   Your deepest doubt proves this. Only the nonsense of that inscrutable *x*, of that Abracadabra, of that Snark, the Unknowable of whose essence you make your real world, prevents you from seeing this.

To return, however, to our dilemma.   *Either* idealism, we said, *or* the unknowable.   What we have now said is that the absolutely unknowable is essentially an absurdity, a non-existent.   For any fair and statable problem admits of an answer.   *If* the world exists yonder, its essence is then already capable of being known by some mind.   If capable of being known by a mind, this essence is then already essentially ideal and mental.   A mind that knew the real world would, for instance, find it a something possessing qualities. But qualities are ideal existences, just as much as are the particular qualities called odors or tones or colors. A mind knowing the real world would again find in it relations, such as equality and inequality, attraction and repulsion, likeness and unlikeness. But such relations have no meaning except as objects of a mind. In brief, then, the world as known would be found to be a world that had all the while been ideal and mental, even before it became known to the particular mind that we are to conceive as coming into connection with it. Thus, then, we are driven to the second alternative. The real world must be a mind, or else a group of minds.

IV.

But with this result we come in presence of a final problem. All this, you say, depends upon my assurance that there is after all a real and therefore an essentially knowable and rational world yonder. Such a world would have to be in essence a mind, or a world of minds. But after all, how does one ever escape from the prison of the inner life? Am I not in all this merely wandering amidst the realm of my own ideas? *My* world, of course, is n't and can't be a mere *x*, an essentially unknowable thing, just because it *is my* world, and I have an idea of it. But then does not this mean that *my* world is, after all, forever just *my* world, so that I never get to any truth beyond myself? Is n't this result very disheartening? My world is thus a world of ideas, but alas! how do I then ever reach those ideas of the minds beyond me?

The answer is a simple, but in one sense a very problematic one. You, in one sense, namely, never *do* or can get beyond your own ideas, nor ought you to wish to do so, because in truth all those other minds that constitute your outer and real world are in essence one with your own self. This whole world of ideas is essentially *one* world, and so it is essentially the world of one self and *That art Thou.*

The truth and meaning of this deepest proposition of all idealism is now not at all remote from us. The considerations, however, upon which it depends are of the dryest possible sort, as commonplace as they are deep.

Whatever objects you may think about, whether they are objects directly known to you, or objects infinitely far removed, objects in the distant stars, or objects remote in time, or objects near and present, — such objects, then, as a number with fifty places of digits in it, or the mountains on the other side of the moon, or the day of your death, or the character of Cromwell, or the law of gravitation, or a name that you are just now trying to think of and have forgotten, or the meaning of some mood or feeling or idea now in your mind, — all such objects, I insist, stand in a certain constant and curious relation to your mind whenever you are thinking about them, — a relation that we often miss because it is so familiar. What is this relation? Such an object, while you think about it, need n't be, as popular thought often supposes it to be, the *cause* of your thoughts concerning it. Thus, when you think about Cromwell's character, Cromwell's character is n't just now *causing* any ideas in you, — is n't, so to speak, doing anything to you. Cromwell is dead, and after life's fitful fever his character is a very inactive thing. Not as the *cause*, but as the *object* of your thought is Cromwell present to you. Even so, if you choose now to think of the moment of your death, that moment is somewhere off there in the future, and you can make it your object, but it is n't now an active cause of your ideas. The moment of your death has no present physical existence at all, and just now causes nothing. So, too, with the mountains on the other side of the moon. When you make them the object of your thought, they remain indifferent to you. They do not affect you. You never saw them. But all the same you can think about them.

Yet this thinking *about* things is, after all, a very curi-

ous relation in which to stand to things. In order to
think *about* a thing, it is *not* enough that I should have
an idea in me that merely resembles that thing. This
last is a very important observation. I repeat, it is *not*
enough that I should merely have an idea in me that resembles the thing whereof I think. I have, for instance,
in me the idea of a pain. Another man has a pain just like
mine. Say we both have toothache; or have both burned
our finger-tips in the same way. Now my idea of pain is
just like the pain in him, but I am not on that account
necessarily thinking about *his* pain, merely because what
I am thinking about, namely my own pain, resembles his
pain. No; to think about an object you must not merely
have an idea that resembles the object, but you must *mean*
to have your idea resemble that object. Stated in other
form, to think of an object you must consciously aim at
that object, you must pick out that object, you must already in some measure possess that object enough, namely,
to identify it as what you mean. But how can you *mean*,
how can you *aim at*, how can you *possess*, how can you
pick out, how can you *identify* what is not already present in essence to your own hidden self? Here is surely a
deep question. When you aim at yonder object, be it the
mountains in the moon or the day of your death, you
really say, " I, as my real self, as my larger self, as my
complete consciousness, already in deepest truth possess
that object, have it, own it, identify it. And that, and
that alone, makes it possible for me in my transient, my individual, my momentary personality, to mean yonder object, to inquire about it, to be partly aware of it and partly
ignorant of it." You can't mean what is utterly foreign
to you. You mean an object, you assert about it, you talk
about it, yes, you doubt or wonder about it, you admit
your private and individual ignorance about it, only in so
far as your larger self, your deeper personality, your total of normal consciousness already *has* that object. Your

momentary and private wonder, ignorance, inquiry, or assertion, about the object, implies, asserts, presupposes, that your total self is in full and immediate possession of the object. This, in fact, is the very nature of that curious relation of a thought to an object which we are now considering. The self that is doubting or asserting, or that is even feeling its private ignorance about an object, and that still, even in consequence of all this, is *meaning*, is *aiming at* such object, is in essence identical with the self for which this object exists in its complete and consciously known truth.

So paradoxical seems this final assertion of idealism that I cannot hope in one moment to make it very plain to you. It is a difficult topic, about which I have elsewhere printed a very lengthy research,[1] wherewith I cannot here trouble you. But what I intend by thus saying that the self which thinks about an object, which really, even in the midst of the blindest ignorance and doubt concerning its object still means the object, — that this self is identical with the deeper self which possesses and truly knows the object, — what I intend hereby I can best illustrate by simple cases taken from your own experience. You are in doubt, say, about a name that you have forgotten, or about a thought that you just had, but that has now escaped you. As you hunt for the name or the lost idea, you are all the while sure that you mean just one particular name or idea and no other. But you don't yet know what name or idea this is. You try, and reject name after name. You query, "Was this what I was thinking of, or this?" But after searching you erelong find the name or the idea, and now at once you *recognize* it. "Oh, that," you say, "was what I meant all along, only — I didn't know what I meant." Did not know? Yes, in one sense you knew all the while, — that is, your deeper self,

[1] See *The Religious Aspect of Philosophy* (Boston, 1885), ch. xi., " The Possibility of Error," pp. 384–435.

your true consciousness knew. It was your momentary self that did not know. But when you found the long-sought name, recalled the lost idea, you recognized it at once, because it was all the while your own, because you, the true and larger self, who owned the name or the idea and were aware of what it was, now were seen to include the smaller and momentary self that sought the name or tried to recall the thought. Your deeper consciousness of the lost idea was all the while there. In fact, did you not presuppose this when you sought the lost idea? How can I mean a name, or an idea, unless I in truth am the self who knows the name, who possesses the idea? In hunting for the name or the lost idea, I am hunting for my own thought. Well, just so I know nothing about the far-off stars in detail, but in so far as I mean the far-off stars at all, as I speak of them, I am identical with that remote and deep thought of my own that already knows the stars. When I study the stars, I am trying to find out what I really mean by them. To be sure, only experience can tell me, but that is because only experience can bring me into relation with my larger self. The escape from the prison of the inner self is simply the fact that the inner self is through and through an appeal to a larger self. The self that inquires, either inquires without meaning, or if it has a meaning, this meaning exists in and for the larger self that knows.

Here is a suggestion of what I mean by Synthetic Idealism. No truth, I repeat, is more familiar. That I am always meaning to inquire into objects beyond me, what clearer fact could be mentioned? That only in case it is already I who, in deeper truth, in my real and hidden thought, *know* the lost object yonder, the object whose nature I seek to comprehend, that only in this case I can truly *mean* the thing yonder, — this, as we must assert, is involved in the very idea of *meaning*. That is the logical analysis of it. You can mean what your deeper self

knows ; you cannot mean what your deeper self does n't
know.   To be sure, the complete illustration of this most
critical insight of idealism belongs elsewhere.   Few see
the familiar.   Nothing is more common than for people
to think that they mean objects that have nothing to do
with themselves.   Kant it was, who, despite his things in
themselves, first showed us that nobody really means an
object, really knows it, or doubts it, or aims at it, unless he
does so by aiming at a truth that is present to his own
larger self.   Except for the unity of my true self, taught
Kant, I have no objects.   And so it makes no difference
whether I know a thing or am in doubt about it.   So
long as I really *mean* it, that is enough.   The self that
means the object is identical with the larger self that
possesses the object, just as when you seek the lost idea
you are already in essence with the self that possesses the
lost idea.

In this way I suggest to you the proof which a rigid
analysis of the logic of our most commonplace thought
would give for the doctrine that in the world there is but
one Self, and that it is *his* world which we all alike are
truly meaning, whether we talk of one another or of
Cromwell's character or of the fixed stars or of the far-
off æons of the future.   The relation of my thought to
its object has, I insist, this curious character, that *unless*
the thought and its object are parts of one larger thought,
I can't even be *meaning* that object yonder, can't even
be in error about it, can't even doubt its existence.   You,
for instance, are part of one larger self with me, or else
I can't even be meaning to address you as outer beings.
You are part of one larger self along with the most mysterious or most remote fact of nature, along with the
moon, and all the hosts of heaven, along with all truth
and all beauty.   Else could you not even intend to speak
of such objects beyond you.   For whatever you speak of
you will find that your world is meant by you as just

your world. Talk of the unknowable, and it forthwith becomes your unknowable, your problem, whose solution, unless the problem be a mere nonsense question, your larger self must own and be aware of. The deepest problem of life is, "What is this deeper self?" And the only answer is, *It is the self that knows in unity all truth.* This, I insist, is no hypothesis. It is actually the presupposition of your deepest doubt. And that is why I say: Everything finite is more or less obscure, dark, doubtful. Only the Infinite Self, the problem-solver, the complete thinker, the one who knows what we mean even when we are most confused and ignorant, the one who includes us, who has the world present to himself in unity, before whom all past and future truth, all distant and dark truth is clear in one eternal moment, to whom far and forgot is near, who thinks the whole of nature, and in whom are all things, the Logos, the world-possessor, — only his existence, I say, is perfectly sure.

V.

Yet I must not state the outcome thus confidently without a little more analysis and exemplification. Let me put the whole matter in a slightly different way. When a man believes that he knows any truth about a fact beyond his present and momentary thought, what is the position, with reference to that fact, which he gives himself? We must first answer, He believes that one who really knew his, the thinker's, thought, and compared it with the fact yonder, would perceive the agreement between the two. Is this *all*, however, that the believer holds to be true of of his own thought? No, not so, for he holds not only that his thought, as it is, agrees with *some* fact outside his present self (as my thought, for instance, of my toothache may agree with the fact yonder called my neighbor's toothache), but also that his thought agrees with the fact with which it *meant* to agree. To *mean* to agree, however, with a specific fact beyond my present self, involves such a relation to that fact that if I could somehow come directly into the presence of the fact itself, could somehow absorb it into my present consciousness, I should become immediately aware of it as the fact that I all along had meant. Our previous examples have been intended to bring clearly before us this curious and in fact unique character of the relation called *meaning* an object of our thought. To return, then, to our supposed believer: he believes that he *knows* some fact beyond his present consciousness. This involves, as we have now seen, the assertion that he believes himself to stand in such an actual relation to the fact yonder that were it in, instead of out of his present consciousness, he would recognize it both as the object *meant* by his present thought, and also as in agreement therewith; and it is all this which, as he believes, an immediate observer of his own thought and of the object — that is, an observer who should include our believer's present self, and the fact yonder, and who should reflect on their relations — would find as the real relation. Observe, however, that only by *reflection* would this higher observer find out that real relation. Nothing but Reflective Self-consciousness could discover it. To believe that you know anything beyond your present and momentary self, is, therefore, to believe that you do stand in such a relation to truth as only a larger and reflectively observant self, that included you and your object, could render intelligible. Or once more, so to believe is essentially to appeal confidently to a possible larger self for approval. But now to say, I know a truth, and yet to say, This larger self to whom I appeal is appealed to only as to a possible self, that need n't be real, — all this involves just the absurdity against which our whole idealistic analysis has been directed in case of all the sorts of fact and truth in the world. To believe, is to say, I stand in a *real* relation to truth, a relation which transcends wholly my present momentary self; and this real relation is of such a curious nature that only a larger inclusive self which consciously reflected upon my meaning and consciously possessed the object that I mean, could know or grasp the reality of the relation. If, however, this *relation* is a real one, it must, like the colors, the sounds, and all the other things of which we spoke before be real *for* somebody. Bare possibilities are nothing. Really possible things are already in some sense real. If, then, my relation to the truth, this complex relation of meaning an object and conforming to it, when the object, although at this moment meant by me, is not now present to my momentary thought, — if this relation is genuine, and yet is such as only a possible larger self could render intelligible, then my possible larger self must be real in order that my momentary self should in fact possess the truth in question. Or, in briefest form, The relation of conforming one's thought to an outer object meant by this thought is a relation which only a Reflective Larger Self could grasp or find real. If the relation is real, the larger self is real, too.

So much, then, for the case when one *believes* that one has grasped a truth beyond the moment. But now for the case when one is actually in *error* about some object of his momentary and finite thought. Error is the actual failure to agree, not with any fact taken at random, but with just the fact that one had meant to agree with. Under what circumstances, then, is error possible? Only in case one's real thought, by virtue of its meaning, does transcend his own momentary and in so far ignorant self. As the true believer, meaning the truth that he believes, must be in real relation thereto, even so the blunderer, really meaning, as he does, the fact yonder, in order that he should be able even to blunder about it, must be, in so far, in the same real relation to truth as the true believer. His error lies in missing that conformity with the meant object at which he aimed. None the less, however, did he really mean and really aim; and, therefore, is he in error, because his real and larger self finds him to be so. True thinking and false thinking alike involve, then, the same fundamental conditions, in so far as both are carried on in moments; and in so far as, in both cases, the false moment and the true are such by virtue of being organic parts of a larger, critical, reflective, and so conscious self.

To sum up so far: Of no object do I speak either falsely or truly, unless I mean that object. Never do I mean an object, unless I stand in such relation thereto that were the object in this conscious moment, and immediately present to me, I should myself recognize it as completing and fulfilling my present and momentary meaning. The relation of meaning an object is thus one that only conscious Reflection can define, or observe, or constitute. No merely *foreign* observer, no external test, could decide upon what is meant at any moment. Therefore, when what is meant is outside of the moment which means, only a Self inclusive of the moment and its object could complete, and so confirm or refute, the opinion that the moment contains. Really to mean an object, then, whether in case of true opinion or in case of false opinion, involves the real possibility of such a reflective test of one's meaning from the point of view of a larger self. But to say, My relation to the object is such that a reflective larger self, and *only* such a reflective and inclusive self, could see that I meant the object, is to assert a fact, a relation, an existent truth in the world, that either is a truth for nobody, or is a truth for an actual reflective self, inclusive of the moment, and critical of its meaning. Our whole idealistic analysis, however, from the beginning of this discussion, has been to the effect that facts must be facts for somebody, and can't be facts for nobody, and that *bare* possibilities are really impossible. Hence

whoever believes, whether truly or falsely, about objects
beyond the moment of his belief, is an organic part of a
reflective and conscious larger self that has those objects
immediately present to itself, and has them in organic
relation with the erring or truthful momentary self that
believes.

Belief, true and false, having been examined, the case
of doubt follows at once. To doubt about objects beyond
my momentary self is to admit the "possibility of error"
as to such objects. Error would involve my inclusion in
a larger self that has directly present to it the object
meant by me as I doubt. Truth would involve the same
inclusion. The inclusion itself, then, is, so far, no object
of rational doubt. To doubt the inclusion would be
merely to doubt whether I meant anything at all beyond
the moment, and not to doubt as to my particular knowledge about the *nature* of some object beyond, when once
the object had been supposed to be meant. Doubt presupposes then, whenever it is a definite doubt, the real
possibility, and so, in the last analysis, the reality of the
normal self-consciousness that possesses the object concerning which one doubts.

But if, passing to the extreme of skepticism, and stating
one's most despairing and most uncompromising doubt,
one so far confines himself to the prison of the inner
life as to doubt whether one ever does mean any object
beyond the moment at all, there comes the final consideration that in doubting one's power to transcend the moment, one has already transcended the moment, just as we
found in following Hegel's analysis.[1] To say, It is impossible to mean any object beyond this moment of my
thought, and the moment is for itself " the measure of all
things," is at all events to give a meaning to the words
this moment. And *this moment* means something only in
opposition to *other* moments. Yes, even in saying *this*

[1] See, in the lecture on Hegel, pp. 204–207.

moment, I have already left this moment, and am meaning and speaking of a past moment. Moreover, to deny that one can mean an object " beyond the moment " is already to give a meaning to the phrase *beyond the moment,* and then to deny that anything is meant to fall within the scope of this meaning. In every case, then, one must transcend by one's meaning the moment to which one is confined by one's finitude.

Flee where we will, then, the net of the larger Self ensnares us. We are lost and imprisoned in the thickets of its tangled labyrinth. The moments are not at all in themselves, for as moments they have no meaning ; they exist only in relation to the beyond. The larger Self alone is, and they are by reason of it, organic parts of it. They perish, but it remains ; they have truth or error only in its overshadowing presence.

And now, as to the unity of this Self. Can there be many such organic selves, mutually separate unities of moments and of the objects that these moments mean ? Nay, were there *many* such, would not their manifoldness be a truth ? Their relations, would not these be real? Their distinct places in the world-order, would not these things be objects of possible true or false thoughts ? If so, must not there be once more the inclusive real Self for whom these truths were true, these separate selves interrelated, and their variety absorbed in the organism of its rational meaning ?

There is, then, at last, but one Self, organically, reflectively, consciously inclusive of all the selves, and so of all truth. I have called this self, Logos, problem-solver, all-knower. Consider, then, last of all, his relation to problems. In the previous lecture we doubted many things ; we questioned the whole seeming world of the outer order ; we wondered as to space and time, as to nature and evolution, as to the beginning and the end of things. Now he who wonders is like him who doubts. Has his wonder any rationality about it ? Does he *mean* anything by his doubt ? Then the truth that he means, and about which he wonders, has its real constitution. As wonderer, he in the moment possesses not this solving truth; he appeals to the self who can solve. That self must possess the solution just as surely as the problem has a meaning. The real nature of space and time, the real beginning of things, where matter was at any point of time in the past, what is to become of the world's energy : these are matters of truth, and truth is necessarily present to the Self as in one all-comprehending self-completed moment, beyond which is naught, within which is the world.

The world, then, is such stuff as ideas are made of. Thought possesses all things. But the world is n't unreal. It extends infinitely beyond our private consciousness, because it is the world of an universal mind. What facts it is to contain only experience can inform us. There is no magic that can anticipate the work of science. Absolutely the *only* thing sure from the first about this world, however, is that it is intelligent, rational, orderly, essentially comprehensible, so that all its problems are somewhere solved, all its darkest mysteries are known to the supreme Self. This Self infinitely and reflectively transcends our consciousness, and therefore, since it includes us, it is at the very least a person, and more definitely conscious than we are ; for what it possesses is self-reflecting knowledge, and what is knowledge aware of itself, but consciousness ? Beyond the seeming wreck and chaos of our finite problems, its eternal insight dwells, therefore, in absolute and supreme majesty. Yet it is not far from every one of us. There is no least or most transient thought that flits through a child's mind, or that troubles with the faintest line of care a maiden's face, and that still does not contain and embody something of this divine Logos.

LECTURE XII.

PHYSICAL LAW AND FREEDOM: — THE WORLD OF
DESCRIPTION AND THE WORLD OF APPRECIATION.

WE return from the general notion of the world as the
universe of the Logos, to the business of trying to interpret the facts of experience. "Ye men of Galilee, why
stand ye gazing up into heaven?" We must go into all
the world and preach the gospel of this rationality and
unity of the truth, until the most unspiritual and misbelieving of phenomena shall have been converted. Our
business is not that of gazing, but of interpreting. And
it is hard indeed so to interpret idealism that it shall seem
to the ordinary mind anything but an idle comment upon
the general connectedness of things.

The business of the present lecture is with the idealistic
interpretation of the outer order. In what precise sense
is this world in space and in time still real for us? Is
the true world one of rigid necessity, or is it a world of
free and spiritual ideals? What place in it have the scientific notions of causality, and of such physical truths as
energy and matter? In what sense has the doctrine of
evolution a place in this universe of the Logos? Is this
world a moral order? And is it a world where a man's
mind is still dependent upon his nervous mechanism, as
empirical science assures us? And what ultimate connection does idealism recognize between finite mind and the
truth that physical science calls matter?

These questions, technically called the problems of a
philosophical cosmology, are before us. The study of
them is hard and dry. The exposition must of necessity

be in some places extremely intricate, in others far too
dogmatic and aphoristic. The outcome may be unexpected, and even light-giving. The fashion wherein we
shall attack the undertaking will be in some respects different from the traditional one ; but we shall still at every
step be guided by the lessons of our historical lectures.

I.

Despite our idealism, and in fact even because of our
idealism, the world of experience is to appear to us, in
what follows, as at least the outward aspect of a genuinely
real world. We have asked, *What sort of a world is it ?*
The answer has been, It is a world of outer and ideal
truth, a world of mind. The doctrine of the idealist is
not one that involves or encourages any doubt that there
is truth beyond his own private and finite selfhood. A
popular and trivial objection to idealism, often repeated
by critics who comprehend it not, accuses each finite idealistic thinker of believing more in this his finite self than
in anybody or anything else. But, on the contrary, as
we have seen, it is only the idealist who has a reasonable
account to give of his faith in outer truth, and of his own
relation thereto. This outer truth is for him the content
of the transcendent personality of the Logos, of whom our
experience is a fragmentary suggestion. As I have
pointed out elsewhere, in the book to which I have already
referred, it is just the popular, the common-sense notion
of external reality, for which the outer world is a bare
postulate, a mere practical assumption.[1] Only idealism,

[1] *Religious Aspect of Philosophy*, pp. 304–305. — " If the history
of popular speculation on these topics could be written, how much of
cowardice and shuffling would be found in the behavior of the natural mind before the question : ' How dost thou know an external
world ? ' Instead of simply and plainly answering, ' I mean by the
external world in the first place something that I accept or demand,
that I posit, postulate, actually construct on the basis of sense-data,'
the natural man gives us all kinds of vague compromise answers. . . .

with its theory of the world of the Logos as the one objective reality, implied by every doubt and half-conscious belief of every finite fragment of this true self, finds a warrant for the postulates of common-sense, converts the mere faith in the outer world into an insight, possesses an objective truth in coming thus to an awareness of our relation to our own deepest nature, and interprets our own deepest nature by showing that it is *not* our finite self-hood merely as such, but is through and through objective.[1]

II.

This being premised as to the idealist's attitude towards the objective truth, our next undertaking must be, to define more exactly the characteristics that objective truth, as such, possesses. For such a definition will of necessity throw light on the nature of the world in which we find ourselves. This task is a very hard one, and can be accomplished only by advancing from one tentative definition to another.

We must begin, therefore, with a provisional definition of the genuine outer reality as distinguished from any seeming outer world. What character, we ask, is the essential character of an objective truth as such? What do we *mean* by the outer order? The natural and provi-

The ultimate motive with the every-day man is the will to have an external world. . . . We construct but do not receive the external reality." I quote this passage here because some of my critics have taken it, strangely enough, as the expression of my own idealism. On the contrary, it is expressly stated in the book in question as the substance of the popular and every-day point of view, to which only a genuine idealism ever gives any sound and objective basis.

[1] It is of this objective truth that on p. 332 of the *Religious Aspect* I ventured to speak as of something "not our postulate." Of this *absolute* aspect of the outer truth, later chapters of that work sought to give proof. Yet, in common with other objective idealists, I have occasionally had the fortune to be spoken of as one who does not pretend to *know* any truth beyond the finite self, but only to postulate such truth.

sionally acceptable answer is, that from our human point
of view, the outer order, in so far at least as it is the
object of science, is simply so much of the truth of the
self as is revealed, through our experience, and to our
finite consciousness, in aspects that are universal and
abiding, and not merely private, fleeting, and momentary.
The contrast between the inner and the outer is generally
recognized, in fact, as the contrast between the transient
and the permanent in our outer experience. What persists in experience, must, we say, correspond to some real
truth beyond our private selves. In this sense we call a
dream unreal, because all the dream-people and the
dream-objects vanish when we awake. On the other
hand, we call the matter of physical nature real, because
its quantity appears to be unchangeable, in so far as our
experience enables us to measure this quantity. For a
similar reason it is that Professor Tait has frequently
argued that from the physical point of view the two certain realities of the outer order are matter and energy
(the latter being distinguished very decidedly from what
is technically called force). For these two, says Professor Tait, are permanent throughout the whole range of
scientific experience. But at all events, whether any
given theory as to what the permanent elements in experience may be proves correct or no, it seems very fair
indeed to say, at the outset, that the objective, the outer
reality is for us mortals that which is experienced as
enduring.

Yet permanence, as such, is not the only character of
the reality that we call outer. There is another character,
closely associated with permanence, that is of still deeper
meaning. We are accustomed, namely, to distinguish the
inner from the outer by saying that their contrast is that
between what only some *one* finite consciousness, or only
a certain limited number of such consciousnesses experience, in their relative and fleeting life of limitations,

and that which *all* must experience, in so far as they share in a common rationality. As I now am, I feel pain or pleasure. That is, in itself considered, just *my* pain or pleasure, in so far as I am this finite and changing bit of a self, bound here to these moments of time. That pleasure or pain, then, for the first, exists only in me and in nobody else. The world of the true and absolute Self contains that fact, but contains it here only. The true Self has the pleasure or pain, but only in so far forth as he is limited to me. *You* know nothing directly concerning it. You are another bit of a self, like me ; you have your feelings, I mine. It is true that in order even to be thus bounded in time and experience, we must have a real and organic communion of life in and through the one Spirit. It is he who feels and works in us. No fragment of our life but is his. But our feelings, the facts of our inner life as such, are his only in so far as he is conceived under the form and the limitations of our various finite selves and moments of life.

On the other hand, I now can think of numbers, and when I think that three and two together make five, I think by virtue indeed of feelings that are mine and not yours, but with reference to a truth that I mean, and that in the finite and individual sense of the words is neither yours nor mine, but that is truth for all of us. So space and time, if indeed they are more than mere seemings of our human point of view, are such universal and consequently ever present truths. To say that space and time are objectively real is to say, then, that these things, revealed though they are through your feelings and through mine (and so far merely facts of the inner life), are yet truth for all of us, like the numbers, and not only for all of us men, but for every intelligent bit of a self in all the universe, be he archangel or dweller in Mars. To doubt the reality of space is to doubt just this opinion.[1]

[1] An objector may say that, if this account of the nature of outer

There is, then, for us, this provisional contrast between the inner order and the outer. Whether this contrast expresses the last word of philosophy, we have yet to see. So far it is n't a contrast that enables us to separate the two orders, but it is one that does enable us to distinguish them. This contrast is that between the permanent and universal elements of experience on the one hand, and the private and fleeting elements of experience on the other. Our finite life has its inner aspect in so far as it is just individual, the truth of our moments as such, the breaking of just our waves of consciousness on the beach. But our finite consciousness relates to outer and physical truth in so far as it *means* something that may be present for any and all intelligent moments and individuals. When one questions, as we did in an earlier lecture,

truth be even provisionally accepted, the laws of number would be objectively true in no other sense than the laws of physics. But (so the objector will ask) *are* numbers real in the same sense in which matter is real? I answer, It is a familiar proposition of what is called modern positivism in philosophy that the laws of arithmetic, of geometry, and of mathematics generally, are merely physical truths of a peculiar simplicity and abstractness. This proposition of positivism I fully accept. Numbers, in so far as they are abstractions, are indeed unreal, because our experience is always of a number of physical facts. But the *laws* of arithmetic are laws of the physical world, and are true because they are so. To be sure, the physical world is not what many who call themselves positivists take it to be. It is the world of the truth, in so far forth as this truth is public property for all finite intelligences; it is the world of the truth that lasts, and that can be shared, that is n't the private property of momentary consciousness, like our feelings, but that, although revealed to each of us through his feelings, has a communicable, an universal aspect. In this sense, the principle that three and two make five, or such a principle as the binomial theorem, is as genuinely physical a law as is the law of gravitation; save that the last-mentioned law deals with a far more complex and concrete reality, and may have, for that very reason, a far more limited scope. In what sense the arithmetical laws are *a priori* and absolutely universal, we shall see later.

whether the world of the interwoven spirals and streams
of stars, the world of the consolidating matter and of the
" running down " energy, is what it seems to be, one's
question means this : Is this world that we men have been
thinking out as we interpreted our human feelings, a
world of truth that would necessarily be present to other
than human intelligences in the same form as those in
which it is present to us? If the archangels can count,
if the inhabitants of Mars can add, they will all agree
with us that three and two make five. But we know not
as yet whether they would or would not, in case they came
to think of the same truth that we think of when we look
at the stars, agree with us as to the forms and laws of
this truth. Therefore, and in no other sense, do we
doubt whether the world of the stars is what it seems,
and whether we are after all playing with the " pebbles
on the beach."

III.

What we want, then, next in order, is a fuller statement of what is implied in this provisional criterion of
objectivity. Each of us is thinking in more or less fragmentary ways and moments. We want some means of
distinguishing the essentially private in our thoughts from
the permanent, the public, and the universal.

Our effort to define such a criterion must begin in an
extremely naive and simple fashion. If I am dealing
with my neighbor, and he says that he has experiences
which stand for outer truth, and which are n't merely his
private feelings, my first disposition is to demand that he
shall put me where I can get these experiences, too, or
something that we shall both recognize as similar experiences. If he sees a rainbow, and regards it as standing
for a real and outer truth, as being essentially an objective idea, and I doubt that he sees the rainbow, I ask
to be shown it. If, looking towards the quarter of the
heavens to which he points, I see that to which I readily

apply the same name, I am quickly convinced, from the point of view of untutored common sense, that we are both seeing the same rainbow. A very close and critical observation would, however, erelong prove to us both, as he and I moved about, that his rainbow and mine do not occupy precisely the same apparent place, with reference to our experiences of other objects. If we become aware of this fact, we may first begin to differ as to whose rainbow is the real one, and later, with proper instruction, we shall come to see that just because an essential character of the visible rainbow, namely, its seeming place in the world of the things upon whose reality we are already agreed, is a matter of the point of view, the rainbow itself must have a decidedly different sort of physical objectivity from that possessed by other objects, say, for instance, trees and mountains.

So far, then, the test of objectivity is the apparent similarity of our human experiences when two or more of us are in given circumstances. This similarity, however, is critically examined by comparing, as far as possible, the accounts that we can give to one another of the *relations* amongst the objects of our experience. In other words, the test of objectivity is, so far, permanence and community of ideas, and the test of the permanence and community of ideas is the sameness of the *description* that we can give to one another of the relations amongst the various parts of our private experience.

Here at once appears an important distinction in our private experiences themselves. As they come to us, they are very complex, and they interest us from moment to moment in ways that embody just our private mood. But *one* interest we take in them which brings to pass for us just that distinction upon which the whole of natural science depends. This is the interest in describing them. The distinction that it introduces is one between what is *describable*, and what is only *appreciable*. As my expe-

rience comes to me at any moment, I may, namely, be
said to *appreciate* it in some fashion. That is, it feels
to me so or so. I like it or I hate it. Or again, where
pleasure and pain are n't marked, still there is an essentially indescribable value that my experience has for me
when regarded just as my own feeling. Tastes have one
sort of worth for me, colors another. An electric shock
from a Leyden jar is appreciated as a peculiar and atrocious interruption of all other trains of feeling, such that
its painful value is surely, but inexpressibly, different
from that of all other experiences. Such elementary and
personal interests in the passing moment, such essentially
dumb *appreciations*, have in them few elements or none
whereby we can test whether or no we have them in
common with our neighbors. Real sympathy, real sharing of even the most elementary appreciations there may
be ; and of the significance of such, in case they exist, we
shall hear something later on. For the moment we are
disposed to call our elementary appreciations indescribable, and to regard them as the most characteristic instances of private and individual experience, which reveal
merely *wie es uns zu Muthe ist*, not what can be called
objective.

On the other hand, there are certain elements of our
experience which we regard as describable. How my own
hat feels when I pick it up, taking it from amongst a large
number of hats in a dimly lighted cloak-room, is something
that I can only appreciate. I know my hat by the *feel*
of it when I pick it up. *How* I know it I can't tell you.
On the other hand, that I find my hat hung a peg higher
than I myself left it, that it is hung on the right or the
left side of the room, that just as I took it the clock struck
ten, these are experiences that I pretend to be able to
describe. I can tell you, so I say, just what I mean by
them. I hold them to be experiences that anybody might
have, whether he felt about my hat as I do, or did not.

Now the character that makes an experience describable, involves two facts concerning its nature. The first fact is that an experience, just in so far forth as it is describable, is reproducible at pleasure by the person who can describe it. For him, indeed, the act of description is always a voluntary and more or less complete or abbreviated reproduction of the experience described. As he thus reproduces for the purpose of description, he has a sense of his own power over the reproduction. The feeling was confined to the moment; the description already involves a communication from moment to moment within a man's own life. Here, already, is a partial interpretation of the permanence which we before recognized as a character of outer truth. The describable, as such, has for us one sort of permanence. The second fact is that, in the unity of consciousness, the relations amongst feelings which permit us to describe the content of any moment must themselves fall under certain general types, or, as we more technically say, under either Forms or Categories of experience. By forms of experience we mean the characteristics which we express by saying that our experience involved ideas of space or of time; that is, that our feelings were those of extensive size or of shape, or of duration. By categories of experience we mean at present the characteristics which enable us to say, that what we experienced consisted of one or of many feelings, of like or of different feelings, or again, of feelings that differed from one another, or resembled one another, in quantity or in quality. There are many other such categories used in the work of physical science. Here is no place to enumerate or to explain them. Our meaning at present is that the formless and uncategorized experience, in so far as it is such, appears, from our present and provisional point of view, a merely private appreciation, which does not reveal outer truth, while the well formed and sharply categorized experience is in so far regarded as capable of description, and therefore as apt to reveal outer truth. I can't tell you much about the curious minor feelings of vague depression that once followed, in my own case, an attack of influenza. If ycu have passed through a similar experience, you may appreciate my feelings. But I can never be quite sure that you do. On the contrary, I can tell you, if I like, a good deal about any experience that I can define in terms of known geometrical figures, of numbers, of duration, of size, or of some law of the recurrence of experiences. " Ten strokes of the clock," " two feet to the right," " a regular recurrence of wind and rain, following, on several occasions, a rapidly falling barometer," — all these are phrases of description, — not indeed of unlimited or of complete description ; for all these phrases suggest elementary experiences of sound, of sight, and of other indescribable feelings, that are in so far mere appreciations. But they are phrases of description in so far as they express definite relations in space and in time, and relations that fall under such typical categories as quantity, number, recurrence, likeness, regularity, and other such notions, — these relations of experience being so far under our control that we can reproduce at will typical instances which exemplify them. All such phrases pretend to tell something about a conceived outer reality. Of such is the kingdom of natural science.

To recapitulate : (1) An experience is indescribable if I lose it beyond clear recall as soon as it is gone. In order to be describable it must contain aspects that I can reconstruct out of their elements at pleasure, so long as my intelligent memory lasts. I can describe only what I can keep and permanently think out. (2) In the next place, this my power to think out and reconstruct my experience must, in every case of description, depend upon my discovery of the forms and the categories that the experience exemplifies. (3) Only that which is re-

vealed through our experience in describable form, however, has, so far in our discussion, approved itself as
objective, as public property, as universal. It may indeed
be that we shall need to modify soon this provisional and
tentative account ; and that some of the objective truths
are indescribable. But so far we have not found instances of the sort. Thus far describable facts and objective facts mean pretty much the same thing for us who
live under ordinary human limitations. The business of
natural science is the " description of the world of experience." And the real is so far the describable.

With such a provisional definition of the real in mind,
let us glance back at the world of the mere appreciations,
to bring out the contrast now defined. The noblest and
the most stupid appreciations, it would seem, *may*, and
in many cases do alike exemplify this formless and uncategorized character of the merely private and so far illusory
experience. On the other hand, the most artistically
worthless fact in what we call nature, the physical thing
that we appreciate least and regard as of least worth, will
exemplify, in so far as it is an outer fact, this definable,
this universal character, this conformity to rules of description, this presence in space and in time, this submission to categories, which together make natural science
possible. The reasons in both cases appear so far to be
ones already pointed out. What is describable is as such
public property. A man who knows it once for what it
is, and who keeps his wits, can think out its characters,
can mentally reproduce the relationships of its elements,
can tell his neighbor about it, and can feel tolerably sure
that if any intelligent being got into the right place in
the world-order, he too would experience something of
much the same description, however colored his inner feelings might be. On the other hand, what *is n't* so defined
by space and time and number and quantity, and the
other types of intelligent experience, as to have the rela-

tions of its parts describable is, first of all, when once it is past, like the " tender grace of a day that is dead." It comes not back. While it is present it is like " the tears, idle tears," whereof " I know not what they mean." It is like —

> " That sense, which at the winds of spring
> In rarest visitation, or the voice
> Of one beloved, heard in youth alone,
> Fills the faint eyes with falling tears which dim
> The radiant looks of unbewailing flowers,
> And leaves this peopled earth a solitude
> When it returns no more."

The merely appreciable, then, as such, is, in our human world, notoriously fleeting. So with all the lovely things in Schiller's lines : —

> "*Warum bin ich vergänglich, O Zeus ?* So fragte die Schönheit.
> *Macht dich doch*, sagte der Gott, *nur das Vergängliche schön !*
> Und die Liebe, die Jugend, der Thau und die Blumen vernahmen 's ;
> Alle gingen sie weg, weinend von Jupiter's Thron."

The atoms, as describable, seem thus far to be realities, and they survive. The noble emotions of youth and of lovers die. *If*, however, this provisional definition of the real is to be in any way supplemented, and if the appreciations too are to become of eternal significance, as the poets desire, then the appreciations, it would seem, must not be the appreciations of *merely* temporal and transient beings, but of some being that himself does not live in moments, as we mortals on earth do, but that appreciates in eternity, or that shares in such an eternal appreciation. " Only that which never has been," in our world of time, as Schiller tells us, " that alone grows never old." He is speaking of course of appreciable realities, not of physical ones. Or, again, the enduring appreciation may be conceived as belonging to an immortal soul, that survives the loveliness of all passing moments : —

> " Sweet spring, full of sweet days and roses,
> A box where sweets compacted lie,

My music shows ye have your closes,
And all must die.

" Only a sweet and virtuous soul
Like seasoned timber never gives ;
But though the whole world turn to coal
Then chiefly lives."

Or finally, a community of such free spirits might share together the lasting appreciation. But such eternal appreciation is confessedly, for us mortals, far too much an ideal. Whether we do in any measure partake of such an appreciative consciousness remains to be seen, and forms one of the deepest problems of constructive philosophy. For the moment, we have suggested to us, in this distinction between the outer reality which is describable, and the inner appreciation which is unreal, one tragedy of our finitude, namely, that our descriptive consciousness, coldly and dispassionately devoting itself to the typical, to the relatively universal structure of our experience, seems to seize upon what is for that very reason real, abiding, yes, like the numbers and the atoms, everlasting in time, while, on the other hand, that which makes the moment often so dear to us, its appreciable aspect, its value, is indescribable, and so essentially private and fleeting. This it is that makes science often so cold to us, and facts so lifeless, while the glowing world of appreciation appears to be, after all, so fantastic and vain ; —

" Grau, theurer Freund, ist alle Theorie,
Und grün des Lebens goldener Baum.'

So far, however, we have come seeking for the consequences of our provisional definition of the essential nature of the outer order. We see now, plainer than at first, that the outer order as viewed by us men must be one of well-knit and universal law, structure, order, that it must be in definite forms, subject to categories, inde-

pendent of momentary caprices. All this, as we begin to
see, it must be in order to be describable. And describable it must appear to us in order that the content of one
intelligent moment of conscious life should be, under the
conditions of our finite human existence, communicable to
another. In short, the outer and natural order is beginning to show itself in its complete character as a " World
of Description," that, as such, is bound to appear in our
experience as a world of permanence and of necessity.
Forms and categories are necessary to description, and
these mean order and fixity of type.

On the other hand there may already appear, on the
horizon of our discussion, the notion of another sort of
conceivable reality, different from our natural order, but
as possible in the logical sense as ours, namely, the reality of what we may call a World of Appreciation. For
consider, were our human intercourse of another sort,
were all the moments of all our human lives directly
appreciable by us together and at our pleasure, — *then*
the world of our accessible truth would have quite another
aspect from that of the world of description. Conceive,
namely, for the sake of argument, and as an ideal, of
beings who were so aware of their common relations to
the true Self that their life together was one of an intimate spiritual communion, so that the experience of each
was an open book for all of them. In other words, conceive of beings who were mutually perfect mind-readers
one of another. Their highest spiritual world would be
for them what, in our finite bondage, our physical world
of the outer order is not for us, a world of " one undivided
soul of many a soul." The truth of it would be universal,
without having to be first abstractly described. Or, to
remind ourselves of what we learned in studying Hegel's
characteristic theory of universals, the community of
truth, in the world of such spirits, would be rather of the
Hegelian type of universality, than of the ordinary type

of the more abstract universality. Forms and categories
there would doubtless be in the experience of such beings,
but the necessity for such forms would be of another
kind. The experience of each individual would there be
directly and organically related to the experience of all.
It would n't be necessary to put it into abstract shape
before communicating it. Nor would the appreciative
moment, once passed, be for each individual beyond recall,
leaving this peopled earth a solitude when it returned no
more. For each spirit in that free world would read at
pleasure his own past mind and experience as well as his
neighbor's, would not abstractly and discursively reconstruct, but would directly acknowledge the world of his
whole inner and of his whole outer order, by virtue of
the one organic and complete form of intercourse which
would there exist. In such a world of spiritual intercourse, all the thoughts of one man would become directly
the object of his neighbor's thought. In such a case we
should stand in the presence of an order in which the distinction of outer and inner would be no ultimate one. All
would be appreciable, spiritual, significant. But, as such
appreciative mind-reading is under ordinary human conditions denied us, what *we* mean by having common
objects, a common truth, and the same nature of things
present to us all, is expressible only by saying that in so
far as we can describe the contents of our moments of
experience, and communicate these descriptions through
imitative gestures, or through conventional speech, — so
far and no further does our experience appear to us to
represent the permanent, the outer, the objective. And
hence, however the objective world may appear to freer
spirits, or however it ultimately appears to the Self in his
wholeness, to us it must appear, for the first, as a world of
formed and well-categorized experience, that is, as a world
of orderly universality. For only orderly universality is
describable.

IV.

I must beg you to glance back once more over the course of this necessarily intricate argument. We have been trying to define what is meant by the true and objective, as distinct from the private and merely subjective elements of our human experience. We have provisionally defined the physically real, for us men, as *that which we experience and can describe*. We have defined the business of natural science, therefore, as the description of the content of experience. We have formed a provisional notion of nature, as being " the World of Description." As only that which has Form, Categories, Universality, about it is describable, we have asserted already that this world of description must be a world of rigid necessity.

On the other hand, however, we have suggested hypothetically what a " World of Appreciation " might be. It would be a world such as the organic Self in his wholeness might have present to him at a glance, or such as the community of conceived spiritual mind-readers might share. It would be a world whose Universals were of the type that Hegel defined. It might be free from the type of necessity that our order of nature possesses. It might be a world altogether inspired by appreciative ideals ; and yet it would be a world of objective truth, for each individual in it, each conscious moment of it, would find the others as outer and yet not foreign facts.

But now we must turn back from the hypothetical suggestion of that world of appreciation, whose reality we have yet by no means verified, and must study a little more closely the world of description, — the world, as we have seen, in which our actual human science moves.

This world of empirical science suggests a well-known philosophical problem to which we must next refer. Science, as everybody knows, assumes that the physical world is one where the law of causation rules, where nature is uniform, and where, in general, what have been called axioms, namely, certain obvious and *a priori* principles, are valid.   Now it is an old problem how empirical science comes by these *a priori* principles.   You remember Hume's doubts about the "original of our idea of necessary connection."   You remember the controversy over the innate ideas.   You remember Kant's "Transcendental Deduction of the Categories."   Now in our day many students of the philosophy of science, following more or less unconsciously in the footsteps of Kant, have been more and more inclined to agree upon an account of the nature of these so-called "axioms" that I myself regard as unquestionably on the right track, although there is still much to be done in developing this view in all its details.[1] According to this view the one postulate of physical science is that the real objects revealed to us in our experience are describable in universal terms, and are so whether these objects are "things" or "events."   In order to be describable, the things and the events must appear, to us men, in space and in time, because these forms of our experience are actually the aspects of our conscious life that we have to use as the basis of every description.   Furthermore, in order to make our description valid for all intelligent human beings, the fashions of our description have to be universal.   We can't describe the unique, *e. g.*, Shelley's "sense that at the winds of spring," etc.   That we have to appreciate.   Therefore it is n't an object of scientific experience.   Moreover, in order to describe, we

---

[1] The present is no place for a bibliography.   I must refer to the now almost classic discussions in the introductory lecture of Kirchhoff's *Vorlesungen über Mathematische Physik*, in the *Lectures and Essays* of Clifford, vol. i. pp. 111–123, and in Mach's *Die Mechanik in ihrer Entwickelung*, etc.   See, for a popular suggestion of some related views, the interesting book on *Fundamental Problems*, by Dr. Paul Carus.   The present use of the word "description" I borrow from Kirchhoff, extending, however, his notion in my own way.

have to reduce the transient to the permanent. Otherwise the description would *not* be independent of the appreciative content of the moment. Hence we have to describe in terms of assumed changeless things (*e. g.*, atoms, elements, media, — in a word, substances). And in so far as the world of experience endlessly changes, we have to refer (1) these changes of experience to changes of space and time relations amongst the assumed substances, and (2) the ways of changing themselves, so far as possible, to universal laws. The axiom of the "permanence of substance" has this very simple meaning, namely, that in so far as I can describe my experience to other men, who stand quite outside of this moment, there must be elements in the thing that is the object of this experience which are quite independent of the particular time when I experienced the object itself. In fact, so far as anybody else, at any other time, could conceivably experience this same thing, it must, *ipso facto*, be changeless. And *unless* anybody else you please could conceivably experience this same thing, either at the same time, or at any other time you please, the object is n't public property, and I am doubtless in so far busied with my private appreciation. The changing elements in my experience of things may, however, themselves be described, in so far as they involve changes of relation amongst the permanent things that have been assumed to exist in space and time. For *types* of change must have permanent descriptions.[1] From this point of view events too, as well as things, may be objects of scientific experience, *i. e.*, may be freed from

---

[1] The discovery of the exact meaning of this truth by Galileo and his contemporaries gave rise later to the Calculus, which is especially devoted to the mathematical description of the permanent types of change (*cf.* Newton's name, Theory of Fluxions), and eventually has brought within the prospective range of exact science the vast world of "sublunary" changes, which ancient thought found almost hopeless, or only sought to appreciate in terms of ideals ; *cf.* Lasswitz, *Die Atomistik,* vol. i. pp. 79–85 and 175–183.

the appreciative privacy of the momentary experience. The axiom of Causation is the axiom of the Describability of Events, in so far as they are real and public and are not merely events as privately appreciated. The axiom of the Uniformity of Nature is the axiom that the event once described, *i. e.*, reduced to an universal type, is described forever. Is that event one of a type that may become a possible object of anybody's experience, — then it has universal and unchangeable characteristics. These constitute its law. Whoever experienced an event of the type, *i. e.*, an event involving the same things in the same time and space relations, would observe in it these same characteristics. For otherwise there is something incommunicable, *i. e.*, merely appreciable about the event.

All these thoughts I have to suggest very dogmatically. Let a few brief illustrations indicate, not their proof, but their meaning.

First then, all the so-called axioms of natural science relate to things and events in so far as they are describable. There is notoriously no axiom as to the caprices of maidens, or as to the wayward human heart generally. The axioms of natural science are about number, space, time, motion, force (in the technical sense of the word), — all describable matters.[1]

In the second place our *most* assured and universal axioms all relate to matters of the completest describability. I know that all beings, if only they can count, must find that three and two make five. Perhaps the angels can't count; but if they can, this axiom is true for them. If I met an angel who declared that his experience had occasionally shown him a three and a two that did *not* make five, I should know at once what sort of an angel he was.

---

[1] Or about matters assumed to be describable. A deeper study than there is here room to undertake would show how limited our actual powers of description are. At the basis of every description, *e. g.*, of space, one finds a fundamental and irreducible appreciation.

But now *why* am I so sure of this? Simply because my description of three and of two is so free from merely appreciative elements, because I know so perfectly their precise structure, and know that it *is* their structure, and is not any part of the appreciative content of the feelings of the moment when I count three and two. My feelings may be of what you will, of notes of music or of chalk-marks. I count; that is enough. The numbers as numbers are producible and reproducible at my pleasure by my counting, and are not matters of my feelings. They are then indeed *in* my experience, but are not *of* the moment.

Of geometrical axioms there is no time to speak at present. Let us pass immediately to more concrete instances. Take the ancient case of the principle that " all men are mortal." This is confessedly no axiom. It is an induction from experience. What is the reason why we are so sure of it? If anybody, *e. g.*, the angel aforesaid, told us that in his experience there were cases of men who had lived a hundred thousand years, and who appeared to him to be essentially immortal, what should we reply? If we thought already pretty highly of the angel in question, we might not respond according to our first impulse, but might reflect a little. If we did thus hesitate, what axiomatic answer to his assertion could we very soon suggest? Very obviously this: That *if* this indeed were so, then the people that he called men *must be in some fashion of a very different description* from the people to whom we are accustomed to limit the name. That answer would express the scientific postulate very precisely. If any man is a real man, and not a creature in a dream, then he must have some sort of public and definite description, capable of being put into universal terms; and this description must be such as to follow him through all his fortunes to the end. The description will be one involving substances, and changes in the relations of these substances, the changes having a definable type. If this definable type of change is such as to involve some day the death of the man, — well then, anybody else who corresponds to this same description must also be doomed to death. That is the whole story of the universal mortality of man. That is all that we know about it, except indeed in so far as our knowledge of the description of the typical process of heredity enables us to say that the offspring of men must be describable as a man, and must therefore be as mortal as his fathers.

To take another illustration : the Paul of Acts xxviii. 2–6 gathered sticks to make a fire, and thereupon the viper came out of the heat, and stung him. The barbarians, looking on, anticipated his death, and made appropriate but rather narrowly appreciative comments. But "he shook off the beast into the fire, and felt no harm." So, "after they had looked a great while and saw no harm come to him, they changed their minds, and said that he was a god." The reasoning, granted the facts of the narrative, was crude, but not extraordinary. Evidently these barbarians used, after their fashion, the principle of the uniformity of nature. And what was this principle in their eyes ? It was the principle of the universality and consequent permanence of descriptions. A man was described, according to their notion, as a being who, amongst other general characters, possessed that of swelling up and dropping down dead when stung by a viper. The description was inexact, but it served for lack of a better. Now Paul did not do this. He felt no harm. Well then, what followed ? Not that one changed one's description of a man, but that one looked for another class with another description, wherein to place Paul. Paul's companions already had in mind a certain sub-class of men, described as apostles, who were, amongst other general characteristics, exempt from injury by the touch of "deadly things." To them, therefore, the classification as "god" was both superfluous and excluded.

The real axiom is then, that both things and events, in so far as they are objective, have universal and permanent descriptions, in whose unity all that is real concerning the events is so bound up that a given grouping of characteristics can be predicted for any object that corresponds to the given description. All prediction of natural events is therefore of necessity hypothetical. The sun will certainly rise to-morrow *if* in this part of the cosmos the same bodies keep moving in the present ways; and this they will do *unless* some describable physical catastrophe (*e. g.*, the blowing into small fragments of the earth from some enormous internal tension) takes place before to-morrow; and this catastrophe, again, will not take place, *unless* describable physical changes are now going on in the earth and in the universe at large that are tending towards such an explosion, and tending in such manner as to lead to it before to-morrow. So one must always state one's predictions. That the same causes lead to the same effects means, when interpreted in exact mechanical terms, that certain definable motions, velocities, and accelerations of certain definite bodies are such, that *when* you describe them mathematically and exactly, you find certain earlier conditions of a system of bodies leading to and involving, as part of the whole description, certain later states. The belief that there is physical causation is then the belief that such mathematically exact descriptions of the things and events of the world are possible, whether we have found them as yet or not. And the genuine foundation of this belief is the observation that only by thus categorizing and formalizing our experience do we find ourselves able to make its content public property, for our later thought, or for our neighbors. I must *reconstruct* my experience, or it is not publicly mine, is not universal, is not impersonal. And to reconstruct it I must lay stress upon so much of it as exemplifies forms and categories.

One returns then, for the sake of characterizing this whole world of description, to the suggestion that the case of the rainbow already brought before us at the outset. My neighbor experiences this or that. He says that this experience was not his alone, but was an experience of universal truth. *Well then*, we say, *tell us what it was*. In so far as he does this, with exactness, and under the conditions of scientific rigidity, he describes. If he describes successfully, he tells us, then, of definite and permanent things, in space and time, that behave in definite and permanent ways. Does he fail of this rigidity of description (as our imperfect science is continually failing, in all but its mathematical departments), what is our conclusion? It is one that first voices itself thus: *Then*, as we say, *you have not yet experienced enough of your object. Go back to it, and study it and its relations to other objects until you have reached mathematical exactness.* Does our observer now reply: — " But I can't reach such exactness, with any amount of study, because the object itself is n't exact, conforms to no laws, behaves in no permanent way, is n't a lasting or a definite object "? — Then our final answer is : Ah, very well, if this be so, your object is n't an object, but your private feeling. This *Gewühl von Erscheinungen* we have heard of before from Kant. It is the very essence of the private and personal experience, uncategorized, incapable therefore of being shared by anybody else, and therefore not objective.

So much then for a sketch of the world of description. So much for the gist of what I take to be the only possible " deduction of the categories " of physical nature. Therefore is this our physical world one of rigid law, of immovable order, of atoms and ether vibrations and well-conserved energy. Therefore, moreover, is it an essentially *human* world, the world not of the fully conscious Self as such, in his eternal completeness, but of beings who never communicate with exactness through any devices but those of abstract description.

V.

It hardly needs a very elaborate proof to show that this world of description as it has now at length been defined for us cannot be the *whole* of the real world. Our provisional assumption has indeed aided us thus far very well. It has defined for us the world of exact natural science, a world of boundless intellectual concern to us men, and surely a part or at all events an aspect of the real world. But our assumption has not pretended to be adequate to the account of *one* sort of outer reality, in which we all believe, and which we continually long to know.

Here in my world of daily experience is my friend. In what sense is he real to me? Very imperfectly I can describe him — a man of such height, so or so conditioned and habited as to this space form, wherein I find all the things of my world. Science teaches me to guess at a closer description of him. If one saw him through and through, as with my poor eyes I see him not, one would ultimately experience as the describable physical facts about him, — a quivering mass of molecules. I need not go further as to the constitution of these molecules. Enough, they would be flying about together, a swarm of trillions upon trillions, — restless with the pent-up energy of their unstable mutual positions, and with the live energy of their swift and ceaseless flight. Multitudes of them would be perpetually leaving, at every breath he draws, the form that I call his. Multitudes of new ones would take the place of what he had lost. Especially complex with intertwined spirals and streams of multitudinous molecules would be each of the many tens of millions of cells of his brain. In this "system of systems," like the astronomer in the boundless heavens, I the observer, were I acute enough to witness all this, would be lost. Thus my friend, however, might be found, as a fact in space and time, public before all men and angels in so far as they too were able to view him. Thus he might be found? Nay, I have as yet found him not at all. I did not *mean* this maze of molecules by my friend. I meant his intelligence, which he more or less transmits to me through his own descriptive gestures and speech, — this and his appreciations themselves, which, as I have all along been saying, are his, and his alone, purely private facts of his inner life, but which, after all, I value most about him. His ideals, which I so admire, his will, which is often so much wiser than mine, his approval, which I prize so highly, — where are all these? Are they for me *facts* in my world? Yes, for I mean to speak of them. I think about them, and either they are real as I think them to be, or else, if I am in error, the true Self, who knows all things, is aware of what place in the true and absolute order the genuine object of my thoughts occupies, and knows what facts really constitute that to me inaccessible object. Facts they are for me; and they are not facts *within* me; nor yet are they describable facts in my space and in my time. The forms of my world contain them nowhere. The categories of my understanding cannot be impressed upon them. And yet they are real. They are in truth amongst the most vitally real objects of my faith, of my thinking, and of my will.

What sort of reality then is this? Is it not a most familiar kind of reality, in which our human social consciousness is absolutely bound up, without constant reference to which we speak hardly a waking word? And yet is it not a reality that as such absolutely transcends our private consciousness, and absolutely defies our powers of physical description?

And still all along, even in trying so resolutely to confine the objective consciousness to the consciousness of whatever is describable, were we not meanwhile recognizing and appealing to this objective other consciousness of our fellows? Yes, we were; for we were speaking of what truth we could describe, and so share with the beings who possess this other consciousness. What we pretended to share, however, with them, was some abstraction or other, which in their experience we hoped that they could *also* realize. Their experience as such we never hoped to share. That was private, inner, incommunicable. What we could describe would be real for them only in case they too could experience what they could then abstractly describe in the same forms as those used by us. What was shared was then never consciousness, but only the imitative abstract and epitome of it, rendered cold and unappreciative, in order that it might the better be transferred, through word and gesture, from our appreciative inner life to their foreign but equally warm and glowing world of feeling. Yet all along they were real for us and for one another. Their monad-like privacy, their windowless isolation of momentary consciousness, — we acknowledged its existence, and we pretended to intrude upon it with our descriptions of our own space and time world, descriptions which we asked them to verify. What could we be meaning by all this?

Our answer, as idealists, is already fully prepared and indicated. The reality that I attribute to my friend, the genuine external existence that (even while we defined the outer order as that which could be experienced and described) we all the while had to attribute to the appreciations of our fellows (which we can never, in our finite capacity, either experience or describe), — all this is unintelligible except in so far as one recognizes that we seemingly isolated and momentary beings do share in the organic life of the one Self. I *mean* my friend's inner life when I am fond of him. And yet my friend's inner life is not one of my finite experiences at all; nor can it ever become so, however much I peer about for his mind in all my own world of space and of time; nor can I describe how it must seem to all beholders, as I describe the things of nature. What do I mean by him, then? Anything definite? Yes, a most definite, although not a physical fact. I mean a fact in the same conscious spiritual realm with me, a fact whose relation to me, as the true object of my thought, only the inclusive Self, in whose thought, for whose reflection, both my friend and I exist, — only he can know, and knowing can constitute.

Neither my friend's inner life, nor the human lives all about me whose experience I try to re-word in abstractly universal terms in my descriptive science, are themselves describable objects. They are, nevertheless, real; and so there is a sense in which, despite my limitations, I know myself as in a world of appreciation, a world whose facts are hard and fast, are beyond my private life, cannot be expressed in terms of my space and time, and yet must be present and united in the organic universality of the one Self. And I presupposed this world at every step, even while I spoke provisionally as if the objective and the describable were one and the same. The communion of spirits, then, is genuine, although we have no consciousness of a spiritual mind-reading of other finite beings. Our relations with the universe are essentially social. The world of description itself but expresses, in so far as it is the truth, one aspect of this fact of our spiritual intercourse. Because we can communicate with each other, therefore we can so far identify our descriptive accounts of our various inner experiences as to know that we have truth in common. But we could not even mean to communicate with each other, did we not presuppose, as an objective fact, such organic spiritual relations as cannot possibly be expressed in any physical terms, but only in terms of the assertion that all the spirits are truly together in one Spirit.

VI.

The facts of the world of appreciation have already forced us to alter in one respect our definition of the nature of this world. At the outset it was for us the world of essentially private appreciations, that is, of what we called feelings. In so far as we regard ourselves as beings bounded in time and space, the appreciative facts do indeed still retain this private and inner nature. But what we have now further found is the truth that the facts of this universe of appreciative feelings are not as isolated as at the outset they seemed to be, or as, in the world of space and of time, they must still seem. My friend yonder is, as fact of space and time, real to me only in so far as his inner life is foreign. But in so far as I truly communicate with him, we are members of the same world of appreciation; and in this sense he is real to me by virtue of our organic unity in the one Self. This organic unity, whereby the monads of the spiritual world cease to be *merely* monads, has already introduced that form of universality into the world of the appreciations which we have just recognized. This world is one whose parts never become public property for one another, in so far as you observe them from without. Their ties are of another sort. They are " windowless " (as Leibnitz said of the Monads that in his doctrine made up the universe of finite beings); but they are windowless only to one another's finite view in the world of space and time relations. From above they are open to the light of the reflective Self, in whom they live and move and have their being. It is with their relations as it is already *within* our own finite lives, in so far as we are individual bits of the Self. For the moments of our lives are all separate in time, — isolated as the various finite selves are, yet in reflection we commune within ourselves, and catch in one moment the *meaning* of a thought that was only half articulate in another ; or correct, or otherwise review and reword the ideas that, left solely to time, would seem to be lost and dead forever. However small a bit of a self I am, I already, then, possess something of the inclusive transcendency of the true Self, for I "look before and after," and join in my one consciousness more of time than the mathematical instant would possess. And as the moments of my finite thought are to me when I reflect upon my own meaning, and upon the relations of many moments of my life, so my neighbors and I are to the larger Self when, discoursing together about the same objects, we find ourselves as it were but moments in his inclusive unity.

The world of appreciation is, then, one of a sort of *reflective* " publicity " and interconnectedness ; and such an interconnection and publicity is, as we have seen, the very presupposition of the existence of any genuine truth in the world of description. If I cannot really communi- cate with my neighbor, and think of meanings that are like his, there is no truth in any of our descriptions. Without the multitude of genuinely interrelated expe- riences, no true similarities, no describable universality of experience ; without the facts of appreciation, no laws of description ; without the cloud of witnesses, no ab- stract and epitome of the common truth to which they can bear witness. Destroy the organic and appreciable unity of the world of appreciative beings, and the de- scribable objects all vanish ; atoms, brains, " suns and milky ways " are naught. On the other hand, if you destroy our describing kind of intercommunication, you can at least conceive of beings, as we did before, whose communications were of a direct and appreciative sort, as those of mother bird and nestlings now often seem to be as we look at them. The world of science, then, *presup- poses the world of spiritual oneness* ; the unity of the Self is through and through His Own, and is in so far appreciative.

Nor are all appreciations dumb. The whole Moral World presupposes a sharing of definite and express appreciations amongst moral beings,[1] a " realization " of the life of one by another. Describable phenomena may aid this mutual realization, but can never assure it ; and only when it is assured does the moral life begin. What Kant called the Practical Reason, the moral nature of man, is through and through appreciative, but it is not on that account merely emotional. It is like the true Self, thoroughly and reflectively rational. The moral law itself is in no physical sense an outer reality. You cannot describe its facts as you can those of gravitation, by looking on and computing ; but none the less is the moral law a truth, — a truth, namely, of the universal appreciation of the world of finite ideals and strivings, all of them inner facts, but, in their totality, an universe of genuine objectivity. The world of appreciation is, then, the deeper reality. Its rival, the world of description, is the result of an essentially human and finite outlook.

Not on that account, however, is the latter unreal. It is simply the way in which the world of appreciation, the world of the true and spiritual Self, *must needs appear when viewed by a finite being whose consciousness experiences in the forms of our space and of our time*, and who is interested in giving to his fellows a dispassionate and universalized account of how he views it. Here is the permanent truth of Kant's doctrine.

But now, ere we pass to a closer study of the relations of these two aspects of reality, shall we not restate the modified view that we have gained of the nature of the world of appreciation ? As we now view it, it is the world whose categories are not those of abstractly formal description, but are not the less true categories. They are the Categories of Self-Consciousness as such. When one

[1] See *The Religious Aspect of Philosophy*, chap vi. : *The Moral Insight*, p. 131 sqq.

is describing an object of physical science, he is so much
concerned with the structure of this object, that it is his
business to forget, as we say, himself, and to live solely
in the process of constructive imitation whereby he seizes
upon what is enduring about this object. When he appreciates, he says, on the contrary: So this thing is for me.
Hence it was that, at the outset, appreciation appeared to
us a sort of private exercise of each self-consciousness. It
was, as we first found it, a sort of speaking with tongues,
whereby each little bit of a self edified himself, but not
the brethren. Now, however, we have learned a more
excellent way. The truly objective and universal appreciation is like the Pauline charity. It is none the less
self-conscious because it seeketh not its own, and rejoiceth
rather in the truth. It stands for the unity of self-consciousness of the one Spirit, whom all finite things and
experiences presuppose. His appreciations are indeed his
own ; for he is alone and none beside him. Yet in them
we all share, for that fact is what binds us together.

Categories the universal appreciation has, and what are
they ? They are the categories of the self-conscious and
of the significant world, the categories of the realm of
inter-related interests, and of the mutual dependence of
each finite consciousness upon others for its own truth
and meaning. In this realm it is, too, that thoughts have
objects beyond them and true relations to these objects.
Here, also, the categories of objective worth and of purpose have validity ; for it is self-consciousness that gives
worth to things, and that reflectively compares the worth
of things seen from one point of view with their worth as
estimated otherwise. The world of appreciations is, then,
the world of ideals. In space and in time you find no
such things as worth and ideals ; there you find only hard
facts. The consciousness of us finite beings who know
and judge the things of space and time is the source of
the transient worth which appears to us here or there in

our world. Only the eternal consciousness, in its time-
transcending completeness, can know the really abiding
and eternally true value of the world.

On the other hand, the specific categories of the world
of description have no application to this world of appreciation, in so far as it is regarded in itself. It is real, but
there is no physical necessity in it, no natural causation
links together its parts; and we know this, at present,
because we have found what is the nature of physical
necessity and of natural causation. In so far as two
finite beings, A and B, separated in space and time, are
to communicate with each other by abstract rewording of
experience, they must find present in the experience
of each of them a world of facts that submit to the categories of science; and of these one is that of physical
necessity. But in so far as A considers what he means by
the inner existence of B, he finds here a fact, to wit, another self-consciousness, recognized by him as real. This
fact, however, is one that he cannot describe. He can
describe the outward seeming of B, but never the inner
appreciations of B as such. It is useless to say, therefore,
that the category of physical causation applies to the true
relations of B and A. A's body, indeed, by virtue of its
changes, causes changes in the body of B. So far physical causation reigns supreme ; but A's body and B's body
are describable phenomena in the world of space and time,
and only describable phenomena have physical relations.
A and B, however, are in their actual and appreciable
relations by virtue of the part they both play in the inner
self-consciousness of the organic and inclusive Self, who,
being what he is, embodies his personality in numerous
finite bits of selfhood, whereof A and B are examples.
In him they are together, in so far as each of them thinks
of the other. Another person of whom I think is, as
such, not the cause, but the appreciable object of my
thoughts. Where real things are in this relation, they

are not in the describable relation called that of cause
and effect. The spiritual world, as such, then, *causes* in
me no thoughts. I think of it thus or thus by virtue of
my place in its organic wholeness. The more of a self I
am, the more and the deeper do I know its truth. And
as a whole the world of the self is caused by nothing, is
what it is by virtue of its own self-knowledge, is constituted by the reflective self-consciousness in and for which
it has its own being. It is, then, through and through, a
world of Freedom ; its own significance is what occasions
it thus to express itself. Nothing causes or explains it
from without. It is its own excuse for being.

As for the proof of all this, I can now only refer you
again to the argument as to the nature of objective truth,
and as to our relation thereto, that I so imperfectly set
forth at the last time. Just this problematic but real
relation of a thought to its object is the one implied in
every least assertion of our lives. It is not true that we
believe in outer objects because we suppose somehow, *a
priori*, that our inner experiences must have adequate
causes, and *then* make hypotheses as to the nature of
these causes. On the contrary, unless I first believed in
outer objects, and in the validity of my thoughts about
them, I should never talk of laws and of causes at all.[1]
The objects of my thought are not the producers of my
thought, but the truths that correspond thereto. A cup
of coffee may, as I say, " set me thinking," that is, may
increase the activity of my nerve-centres ; but what I
think of may, then, be, not the coffee, but the feelings of
my fellow-men, or the nature of things, or the preparation of this lecture. The relation of object to thought
is here, you see, not a physical, but a logically appreciable
one, — one that only my relation to the inclusive Logos
can explain or express. And this case is typical. Rela-

[1] A fuller exposition of these considerations will be found in the
Religious Aspect of Philosophy, pp. 354–360.

tions of causation, however, exist *amongst* certain objects of thought, in a certain aspect of their nature. Is an object, namely, to be regarded by me in so far forth as it is abstractly describable, *then*, and only then, does it stand in causal relations to other objects. As for causes that affect me personally, these do so, once more, only in so far as I, too, am conceived, not in my inner and appreciable nature, but as myself capable of being looked upon and described from without, that is, as myself an object amongst objects, existent in space and time, and public to all men. " The coffee sets me thinking : " this expression refers to the physical fact of the essentially describable relation of a certain alkaloid to the physiological changes that its presence in my blood produces in my nerve centres. Of this describable change in me as phenomenal thing my own inner life, after I drink coffee, is the appreciable aspect.

VII.

Our last word, "aspect," suggests to us at once how near in one way we have now come to the language of the so-called " Monism " of recent times.[1] In fact, unsatisfactory as the " mind-stuff " theory seems to an idealist in the ordinary formulation of this theory, he has only to substitute his own interpretation of the fundamental truth of things for certain of the statements of Clifford and of the other Monists, and the doctrine of the " Double Aspect " becomes at once luminous and inevitable. We shall aid ourselves greatly if we interpret the theory now in our hands by the aid of this monistic formula. In doing so we shall again survey, but from a new outlook, our whole argument.

The true world is, to state our theory afresh, the system of the thoughts of the Logos. His unity, as we have seen, is a reflective, a self-conscious, and so an appreciable, but not, in its deepest truth, a describable unity. We know

[1] See above, Lecture IX., pp. 300–304.

this unity just in so far forth as we ourselves consciously and rationally enter into it and form part of it. There-fore, in so far as we have inner unity of thinking, in so far as we commune with our fellows, and in so far as we rightly see significance in the outer universe, we are in and of the world of appreciation that embodies the thought of the Logos.

On the other hand, once having recognized ourselves as finite beings, *distinct* from our fellows in so far as we are different centres of appreciative consciousness, and *sundered* from them in so far as we are all only bits of the true Self, we become aware of our private world of inner truth as distinguishable from the truth as experienced by other men, and from the universal truth of the all-know-ing world-consciousness. A new question then arises: — *How much* of this private truth of ours is a revelation to us in our finitude of what other finite selves can also know? Then comes the answer: So much as can be *described* to these other finite selves and then, in their ex-perience, appreciatively *verified*, may be regarded as not our private content, but as universal. Herewith began a little while ago our effort to describe the content of our experience. Using the space and time forms, and the cate-gories of theoretical science, we get, as the result of a long-continued common effort of humanity at describing things, the world of science. But again the question returns upon us, In what sense is this world of description real? The only answer is, It is real in so far as it is in very truth an aspect of the world of the Logos, such an aspect, namely, as can be expressed by finite consciousness in terms of the space and time forms, and of the categories of empirical science. Only as such an aspect has the physical world a reality. Consequently all its laws, all its necessity, its causation, its uniformity, belong, not to its inner nature as such, but to the external show of this nature. If we could grasp the whole truth at a glance, as the Logos does, we should see what now is dark to us, namely, why and how the world of appreciation, when viewed under the conditions of our finite experience, has thus to seem a world of matter in motion. As it is, however, we already know that the world of matter in motion is simply an external aspect of the true and appreciable world. That is, in substance, the whole of our philosophical insight into the matter. Therefore it is perfectly true to say that my friend's brain, with its countless molecules, is simply the outward aspect of my friend's inaccessible inner life, in so far as this life is expressed, symbolized, translated, into the language of my personal experience of time and space phenomena. My friend, as he is in himself, is therefore not a new sort of thing, called a soul or mind, existent somewhere yonder in space, in amongst his brain molecules, — a thing imprisoned in his body. No, he is himself the reality that, when I look at his body, I am vainly trying to see and describe. What I see and describe is simply the physical, the phenomenal aspect of his inner and appreciative life. That he does appear at all in my world of phenomena is due to the fact, not further explicable from the human point of view, that he and I, by virtue of our places in the world-order, have spiritual relations, think of each other, and do somehow indirectly commune together. That this relation of his inner life to me is symbolized by the describable facts of his physical organism, is due in general to my nature as a being who can perceive and describe only what appears to me in space and in time. That just this particular set of facts, however, should symbolize to me his inaccessible inner life, is once more, for us human beings, an ultimate datum. The Logos knows, not we, *why* inner feelings, outwardly symbolized in space and time to our perceptions, should appear as nerve-centres made up of countless flying molecules. The twofold aspect itself is, however, a certain truth of our experience. There *is* my friend.

He is for himself conscious, *i. e.*, appreciative. The only aspect of this appreciative life that can become manifest to me actually appears to me as matter in motion. And *this* is describable. Herewith we have however *only* the fact of the double aspect. The inner intelligibility of this fact is regarded by us as something that must be un-derstood by the Logos. It is for us a problem; but is not so for our true Self, who completes the insight that for us is so fragmentary.

Our theory, then, does *not* declare, as do other forms of the double aspect theory, that there is a curious kind of substance in the world, a substance mysterious and essen-tially inscrutable, that has the two aspects, the mental and the physical. For our theory undertakes to know what this substance is. It is the conscious life of the Logos, whereof my friend is a finite instance, and whereby I too am so conceived as to be in appreciable relations to him. Nor yet do we say, as the mind-stuff theory says, that my friend is a mass of mind-stuff atoms, which pro-duce effects upon my mass of mind-stuff atoms. On the contrary, for our theory, my true friend stands in relations to me that are essentially appreciable, not physical at all. He causes no effects in me whatever. His body affects my body; but that is an affair of physics, not of inner life. I am genuinely related to him in so far only as the insight of the Logos reflectively so constitutes our mutual concern for each other that, as a fact, it is what it is. My friend then is no cause in the world of physical phenomena, at all. He is neither matter nor energy. His thoughts move no molecules. His feelings towards me innervate no muscles, set in motion no bodily limbs, release no phy-sical energy. But his organism, as it appears in space and time, is the describable show and symbol of the inner and appreciable reality that is his; and, even so, the physical effects that his organism produces upon mine are merely the describable show of our spiritual and appreciable inter-

relationships. His matter and energy, his nervous tre-
mors and his innervated muscles, his deeds and their physical effects are the phenomenal aspect of his part of the
world-order. His mind does not influence his body. His
body is merely a very imperfect translation of his mind
into the describable language of space. The physical
causation that I attribute to him should be attributed,
therefore, solely to this body. For all physical causation
is only the describable translation of the inner meaning of
things into terms of relations amongst bodies. The relations of the world of appreciation, which is the true world,
to the world of description, which is its show, are therefore themselves in no wise relations of cause and effect.
I as observer, interpreting the true world in terms of our
human forms and the categories of theoretical science, am
bound to see, in the world as thus interpreted, rigid laws
of causation. But the laws thus seen are symbols of
deeper truth, and not the physical effects of this truth.
This deeper truth itself is not causal. It is only such
truth as, in order to be describable, must show the aspect
that the laws of causal connection in our experience interpret in their own imperfect way.

VIII.

Three further and closing considerations occur to us, in
this connection, as giving fuller expression to our form
of the doctrine of the "double aspect." The first of
these is suggested by the problem of the relation of the
inorganic world to our human consciousness. The second
is suggested by the problem of the real nature of physical
evolution. The third has to do with the problem of the
freedom of the will.

The theory of the "double aspect," applied to the facts
of the inorganic world, suggests at once that they, too, in
so far as they are real, must possess their own inner and
appreciable aspect. Upon this suggestion we have no

time to dwell at great length.   In general it is an obvious
corollary of all that we have been saying.

When I think of the stars and of matter, of space and
of the energy that appears forever to be dissipating itself
therein, I think of something real, or else of merely a private experience of mine.   If, now, the common experience
of humanity is our sufficient warrant for assuming some
universal reality as actually embodied in these hot stars
and cold interspaces, of what sort must this reality be?
In and for itself, we now answer, it must be an appreciable reality, the expression of what, in Schopenhauer's
sense of the word, may be called a World-Will; as well
as of what, in Hegel's sense, may be called an Universal
Self-Conscious Thought.   But to say this is not to commit
ourselves to the acceptance of those paradoxes of the seeming outer order which we set forth in our tenth lecture.
These paradoxes were due to the assumption of infinite
space and time as themselves outer and real, and to their
introduction into our account of the physical processes of
the stellar world.   We now have reached a deeper insight.
The " antinomies " of the physical order no longer terrify
us.   They are due to our trying to express the whole
appreciable system of things in our human forms of space
and time.   Here before us is the order of the embodied
Logos.   We try to describe it.   Our science undertakes
the task ; our highest descriptive synthesis encounters incongruities.   What do these mean?   They mean simply
that our descriptive science is, indeed, in one aspect of its
work, playing with " pebbles on the beach."   For the
fashion of this world of space and time is such as to
give us no united and intelligible definition of the world-
process in its wholeness.   Only the self-completed is intelligible ; and our physical world in endless time and
in infinite space, being no world of self-completed, that is,
of " cyclical " processes, is a mere aspect of the true world,
and is also an aspect that must be but fragmentary.

Higher beings than we may have other forms of descriptive science, based upon a consciousness, say, of some other form of space and time, *e. g.*, of a "non-Euclidean" space of three dimensions, or of a space of four or more dimensions, and of a time that includes the truth of ours, and that still makes clear how the world-process somehow returns into itself. Such higher forms of consciousness we can speculatively view as possibilities. They may be adequate to a description of the whole world of phenomena as viewed by such higher beings. We, however, in our limitation, know only that the Self must have unity in himself, — an appreciable wholeness in his conception of the world. We speak of him as infinite; we do not mean that he is vaguely infinite, so that however much of his thought one might consider there would always be more to consider. On the contrary, he knows himself as one, and so as eternally complete, — as a finished whole. Otherwise he would be no self. Therefore our vague infinities of space and time, never finished, never explorable as wholes, are very poor embodiments of his truth. His infinity, however it is constituted, must mean self-completion. We may expect, therefore, so soon as *we* approach the limits of our science about the phenomenal things in space and time, to get warnings that our descriptive knowledge is an inadequate translation of the truth. Such a warning we got in the study of the outer order a little while since. The world of the stars, then, and of the "running down" energy is not really what it seems. It is a "well-founded phenomenon," but not a final truth.

On the other hand, we have, indeed, a perfect right thus to say that the world of the stars is, like the brains of our friends, the well-founded show in space and time of an appreciative consciousness, and that the unity of the laws of physical nature is the outer aspect of some deep spiritual unity of will and plan in the world. We have a right to interpret this unity, in hypothetical forms, as well

as we are able. Only we must not say that this will and
plan are in any physical sense the causes of our show-
world. On the contrary, all physical causation is itself
part of the show, in so far as the show is describable.
They are perfectly right, therefore, who deny designs as
factors in natural processes. The true World-Will, being
no phenomenon in space and time, is no form of physical
energy, and moves no matter. The laws of matter more
or less completely portray, but do not, physically speaking, result from the Logos. No creative fiat produced the
world at any moment in past time. To say that would be
to assert the existence somewhere in time of an utterly
indescribable event, which is precisely what nobody can
assert of the world of time, since this world is nothing
unless in so far as it is describable. For the same
reason no will, infinite or finite, ever, by any temporal
interference, turned aside a single atom in its flight.
The physical world shows us, indeed, a plan, but only in
so far as the space and time phenomena symbolize and
very poorly translate an unity, that, as it is in itself, is an
unity of will, of self-consciousness, of a divine interest in
truth, of an equally divine self-possession, of an eternal
rest in the fullness of perfected being. In this will, the
finite wills themselves share, and of it they are a part,
since this unity includes, knows, and justifies the organized relationships of the whole universe of finite appreciations. The physical world, then, *expresses* such a world-
will, but is not subject to the interference of this will.

Turning to the other aspect of the natural order — to
the aspect in which this seems to be a world of evolution,
— we now see something of what that point of view also
means. The world is for us human observers a world
that contains processes of evolution, in so far as, in this
or that portion of it, we detect temporal series of phenomena that are not merely describable, but that, regarded as
wholes, suggest to us something significant, — a tale, an

appreciable form of some lengthy sequence, — an ideal realized, a bit of a plan embodied. The first question of a philosophy of evolution is, Have we a right thus to look for the suggestion of plans symbolized by the most rigid and necessary causal sequences of nature? The answer is, Certainly. For, as we now see, all describable truth is an outward symbol of an appreciable truth. Of this one central principle our doctrine of the Logos assures us; and to look for a plan embodied in a physical sequence is not to look for a designing Dæmon in nature, interfering with rigid causation. On the contrary, thus to look is simply to watch for signs and hints of the appreciable aspect that, as we already know, is there. To believe that my friend lives as a conscious being, is not to doubt that in the physical world his only representative is a nervous mechanism, whose physiological processes are as rigidly necessary and purely material as the flight of a planet or the fall of a stone. My friend's physical life is, indeed, merely a series of reflexes, with which his will never interferes, any more than the concave side of the curve interferes with the convex. Regarded physiologically, his consciousness is a superfluous extra accompaniment, or as it has been called, an "epiphenomenon," that does nothing with his brain-molecules, but merely runs parallel to them; but regarded more deeply, his will, his appreciative inner life, is really his bit of the truth of the Logos, and is the only real truth present. It is the physiological view, after all, that has to do only with seemings. His brain is the phenomenal outer aspect of this deeper truth. Well, even so in nature the truth present is once more the mind of the Logos. Of this mind the laws of matter are the show. When we search for a hint of the significance of things, we do not doubt the absolute validity and unchangeableness of physical laws in their own sphere. We look for signs of the truth that is behind them, interfering not with them, but speaking through the mask of them. Such signs appear to us as processes of evolution. As I often misread my friend's mind, so every such interpretation of nature's facts is tentative, and may be wrong. In this sphere we can but guess.

We have, however, now mentioned a somewhat novel contrast between our descriptive and our appreciative attitude towards a temporal series of events, a contrast at which it is necessary still to glance a moment. When, namely, I physically describe, that is, explain events by their causes, I first seize upon some one instant of time, some one event, and ask: What *is* the configuration of the world *now?* Having found in a measure this description of one moment of the world, this cross section of the temporal series of events, I ask myself: How did this condition result from the previous state of the world? Descriptively, or contemplatively, then, I study the world *from* one moment to another. But when I view a physical series appreciatively, when I estimate the world, or any part of it, say a kind action, or the inner life of my friend, or a process of evolution, I don't thus dwell on the momentary description or configuration of things, but I, as it were, take in at one glance a whole series of moments. I treat some portion of the world as a story. I look before and after until I have grasped the whole of it. So (to take a case that already illustrates our attitude towards all evolution), as I follow a melody, I don't dwell so much on the single note, but on the whole sequence, and on the sequence as a whole. Or, once more, to estimate such an act as that of the good Samaritan in the parable is not to study his single attitudes, as configurations of the molecules of his body. Now indeed he comes, now he stops, now he kneels, now he rises. And all these conditions might be causally explained as a series of described configurations of his molecules. But not thus does one estimate the good Samaritan ideally. One rather looks at the whole story of his deed *as one* whole story, just as one considers a melody, or a progression of chords, or a drama, or any such sequence of events.

To appreciate the world in historical terms, then, to find processes of evolution in it, we must in some measure forsake the purely temporal and limited point of view to which we naturally find ourselves confined, and to which every scientific explanation of nature is always confined. To appreciate even hypothetically the meaning of a process in time, we must in some measure transcend time. And this once more suggests how the ideal interests that the processes of nature seem to serve wherever we find evolution cannot themselves be viewed as physical factors in these processes. An evolution is a series of events that in itself as series is purely physical, — a set of necessary occurrences in the world of space and time. An egg develops into a chick; a poet grows up from infancy; a nation emerges from barbarism; a planet condenses from the fluid state, and develops the life that for millions of years makes it so wondrous a place. Look upon all these things descriptively, and you shall see nothing but matter moving instant after instant, each instant containing in its full description the necessity of passing over into the next. Nowhere will there be, for descriptive science, any genuine novelty or any discontinuity admissible. But look at the whole appreciatively, historically, synthetically, as a musician listens to a symphony, as a spectator watches a drama. Now you shall seem to have seen, in phenomenal form, a story. Passionate interests will have been realized. The will of the growing animal, the ideals of the poet, the history of the evolving races, these will have passed before you. In taking such a view are you likely to be coming nearer to the inner truth of things? Yes; for the consciousness of the Logos must be one that essentially transcends our own natural time-limitations; and in so far as we view sequences in their wholeness, we are therefore likely to be approaching the unity of his world-possessing insight. In doing all this, however, we are not learning how ideals have interfered with nature's mechanism, but how nature's mechanism, in its temporal sequences, symbolizes, as it must, a world of ideals. The student of evolution finds the world mechanical, because he is watching describable processes. But he finds the world also teleological, because he is viewing not merely the sequences as such, but the wholes of sequence ; is listening not merely for the notes of nature's music (the passing events of instant after instant), but for the melody (the appreciable total of the life that is made up of many successive instants). And as the appreciable is deeper and truer than the describable, as the insight into the whole of what we mortals call time is logically prior, in the unity of the eternal Logos, to the isolation of our own finite lives, so the student of evolution, in thus viewing the world of history, the world of interests that in the world of appreciation contend for the mastery, of ideals that long for realization, is coming nearer to the truth of things than is he who merely describes the necessary sequence of time. It is true that every such interpretation of nature is fragmentary and hypothetical ; since we dwell not at the centre of the truth of the Logos, but in our finite isolation of half-conscious temporal insights. It is also true that every interpretation which I make of my friend's inner life is fragmentary and hypothetical. It is nevertheless true that in both cases interpretation in appreciative terms is deeper than mere description of phenomena, and is more likely to get at the truth of things.

And now, surely, we may see how vain are the anxieties of those who wonder how conscious life could ever have been evolved on our planet under purely physical conditions, and what will become of all such life when the energy of the stars runs down. For at the present stage of our argument we know that there is no real

process of nature that must not have, known or unknown
to us, its inner, its appreciable aspect. Otherwise it could
not be real; since in so far as it is merely describable, it
is also merely show, is merely abstract, like the numbers
and the geometrical figures, and has no true fullness of
being.[1] The difference between living and inanimate nature is for us now merely the difference between the nature that like the face of a friend is near enough to our
own for us to get a sympathetic suggestion of what appreciative truth it probably embodies, and the nature that
like the infinitely complex ether waves which fill the inter-
planetary spaces is too remote from our own to be appreciable from our point of view. But the power of nature
to embody divine appreciations is not in this fashion limited. Even so, processes of evolution are for us such
series of events as are near enough to our human interests
to suggest their probable interpretation as stories. And
so what we call life appeared on our globe as soon as nature's products were such as can at present come within
the range of our appreciative insight. The "miracle"
of the beginning of life is merely the subjective miracle
of our own human point of view. Beyond that beginning
we have no appreciative insight. This side of it we have.
The "discontinuity" exists in us, not in the truth.

"Animism," to be sure, the tendency that we formerly
also called "anthropomorphism," the tendency by mere
analogy to endow stones or planets with a quasi-human
life, remains a misleading tendency. For it is not ours
to speculate *what* appreciative inner life is hidden behind the describable but seemingly lifeless things of the
world. But what we know is that it must be what it is
in so far as the self-consciousness of the Logos finds a
place for it; and this place must be, like that of our own
finite consciousness, a place in the world of appreciation.
The rest is to us mortals as yet wholly unknown. But this

[1] Or, as Hegel would say, *Wirklichkeit.*

consideration sets aside the anxious question as to the rise of consciousness in general. The world has always had its appreciable aspect. We mortals ourselves stand on the shore of this boundless world of appreciation, and describing this or that pebble, or looking at this or that breaking wave, seem to understand a little of their meaning. We know that the whole limitless ocean is full of an infinite meaning, since otherwise its throbbing billows and innumerable currents, its depths and unexplored solitudes, its resistless tides and its divinely mighty storms, would not be real. If we ask what this meaning is, we see again only wave after wave approaching, curving, gleaming, and breaking on the beach; and we hear only the eternal thunder of this restless life. Each new wave we men call a process of evolution. The world of what appears to us as endless time seems in our neighborhood to be filled with such processes. And herewith our empirical knowledge ends. Do we doubt whether there is truth and clear insight behind all this imperfect experience of ours? The very question, as we have already seen, involves its own answer. The problem can exist only as transcended by the insight of the Solver of problems.

IX.

The third and last of our concluding considerations relates to the problem of freedom.

If one asks as to the world of appreciation in its wholeness, What efficient power caused it to exist? the question is for the first meaningless. For cause, as usually understood, relates to the world of description, and to the explanation of temporal sequences. The only cause that you can seek in the world of appreciation is in a very different sense a cause. It is, namely, a justification for this as against any other fashion of will and of self-consciousness. The world in its wholeness appears to us in space and time as a describable system of phenomena, bound together by rigid law. That, however, just *this* system of phenomena, these atoms, these physical laws, this order of nature should be there, rather than some other equally describable system, with other atoms and other types of motion, — this seems to us the mere fact, the gigantic caprice of nature. Viewing this same caprice in its other aspect, namely, as a system of appreciable truth and of the inner ideals of the Logos, we do not indeed get rid of the aspect of what Hegel called *Unmittelbarkeit* or " immediacy" about the world. It is what it is. So the Logos, from eternity, and in one organic all-embracing act, constitutes his system of appreciative truth. If we still ask why? we must answer, not with Schopenhauer, " For no reason," but with all the rational idealists, " Freely, and solely for the reason most pleasing to himself, but not without reason." For such is the necessary consequence of the conception of an untrammeled and fully self-possessed Self, who solves all his own problems, including the problem, Why this eternal choice? The element of caprice is there, in so far as none but the Self can fathom his own will. The World-Will is so far like a fair maiden, " in her silence eloquent," who chooses because such is her choice. Yet the caprice is, in the case of the completely self-conscious Will, a necessary element of its reason. The highest Reason has no reason beyond it, and in so far it is capricious. But it includes all lower reasons, and all finite points of view, and so as against them is infinitely less capricious, in the baser sense of the word, than they, since they are infinitely less aware of their own meaning ; and it lacks their blindness.

It is for this reason that we have called the world of appreciation one of freedom. But how are our finite wills related to this freedom? Are we predestined to our place in the world-order? Are we "impotent pieces of the game he plays?" The answer, as I conceive, is this: In so far as we are clearly conscious of our own

choices, we ourselves are part of the world of appreciation. We are then, ourselves, conscious bits of the Self.
Our wills are part of his freedom. And hereby we too are
free. Only in so far, however, as we are *not* conscious of
our choices, but only find in ourselves blind and unconscious impulses, mere facts of hereditary temperament, or
of momentary mood, we do not enter into his freedom.
Some one else, we know not who, some ancestor, some
good or evil angel, may then have chosen these things for
us, not we. But our conscious volition is a fragment of
the freedom of the World-Will.

But how, one may ask, can I be in any sense thus free?
After all, is not my consciousness, viewed as a fact in
time, tied hopelessly to this describable nervous mechanism
of mine? The world, in its divinely free capriciousness,
involves a physical order that necessarily contains just
this organism. What the organism itself will do in given
circumstances, is therefore physiologically determined by
the whole order of nature and by the whole of past time.
And my will moves no atom of this mechanism aside from
its predestined course. And yet I, whose will is just
so much of the world of appreciation as constitutes the
inner aspect of this describable mechanism, — I shall in
some sense be free? How explain such a paradox?

In answer I appeal afresh to that double aspect which
the world of time has already presented to us as we spoke
of the facts of evolution. Whatever the true facts about
what we call time may be, as they are known to the Self,
we are sure that the order of nature, from what we are
obliged to call the infinite past to the infinite future, just
because it does all of it express one law, just *because* it
must all be absolutely foreknown, is present in one time-
transcending instant to the insight of the Logos. It is
present, I insist, because it is all one truth, and because
the infinite Self is there to know all truth. But how all
the world of time can and must thus form to the infinite

Self a single instant of time-transcending knowledge is after all not so very hard to conceive, at least in general. You all the while, in your finite capacity, in so far as you are self-conscious, *do* transcend time, yes, you yourself. A sequence of chords is not a mere series of events to you, whose earlier moments are non-existent when the later are there. The whole series is one artistic moment to you. Reflection continually transcends time. Your life is a "looking before and after." This time-transcendence bears precisely the relation to the single events of your life that consciousness in general bears to your brain-states. This transcending of a time-series, and estimating it as one whole, is in fact what one might call the soul of the natural order. For the ideal or appreciable order is thus in fact linked to the natural order precisely as mind in the finite sense is linked to body. Without time to reflect upon and transcend, there would indeed be no finite consciousness of an ideal or appreciable value in things. But this consciousness of the appreciable aspect of the events of time views the temporal world as the musical hearer views the whole symphony, seeing the end in the beginning, and the beginning in the end, not explaining, not describing in causal terms, but making an appreciable synthesis of time in one glance.

This being the case, our own consciousness, at a moment of choice, is itself twofold. Our organism passes through a series of states, constituting what we call an act. This act fills up a considerable time. Of the successive states we are aware. So far we ourselves live in time, and follow the series, perceiving nothing but what must be describable and necessary. On the other hand, if we are truly self-conscious, we are aware of some significance, of some ideal value, in the series of states as a whole. The melody (to return to that figure) — the melody of conduct interests us, far more than the notes of our momentary physical reaction. But in just so far we actually seem to ourselves to be choosing the conduct as such, since we are approving this whole series of physical events. On this side of our twofold consciousness, then, we are all the while truly transcending time, yes, are taking hold upon and forming spiritually part of that absolutely time-transcending appreciation that the Self possesses in view of the whole physical order. Such an inclusive moment of conscious choice, in fact, does possess in one act a past and a future, does estimate whole series of events, and, although, in its finite capacity, it is dependent on a brain state, still, in its significance, in this its ideal comment, it takes hold upon the distant in time. Such consciousness, therefore, being always a time-transcending estimate of physical series as wholes, may be indeed dependent on brain-states, but in significance it is already, in its measure, a part of the eternal world-estimate, which, as we have learned, is a far deeper reality than the world of physical nature itself, and as a whole is no event in time at all, but a transcendent spiritual estimate of all time.

But if you have followed me thus far into this rather breathless region of speculation you may now finally ask, "But does all this make us morally free?" I answer, in a very profound sense, it does. For gather once more into one the threads of our argument. The Self, we say, regards its world in a twofold way: (1) As a time series of events in which the earlier events fatally cause the later; (2) As an eternally complete world total, whose significance it ideally estimates and chooses. And we, in so far as we are morally judging beings, in so far as we too make ideal estimates, are a part of the Self in this second sense, living not merely in time, but also above time, beyond time. In so far as we are temporal facts, we are indeed mere descendants of an animal ancestry, mere creatures of nerves. But we are far more than temporal. And now remember: this temporal order, rigid and necessary in itself, is it not after all only one of infinitely numerous possible world-orders, any one of which *could* be conceived by the Self, but all of which, from the eternal point of view, are deliberately left unconceived, unreal, because of the ideal estimate which the Self makes in choosing *this* world? What then, though we are bound in the temporal world, may we not indeed be free, — yes, and in a non-temporal and transcendent sense effective too in the eternal world? May we not in fact, as parts of an eternal order, be choosing not indeed this or that thing in time, *but helping to choose out and out what world this fatal temporal world shall eternally be and have been?* This, as some of you know, was Kant's famous doctrine of what he called the transcendental or extra-temporal freedom and the temporal necessity of all our actions. From this point of view, as you may already in part see, the natural and the spiritual orders, the physical and the moral orders, the divine and the human, the fatal and the free, may be finally reconciled. If this be so, then indeed we shall no longer fear fate, no longer dread the facts of nervous physiology, no longer be appalled by nature, no longer appeal to temporal miracles to save the ideals. God and Cæsar will indeed become reconciled. Is such an hypothesis after all impossible? I think not. I hold it rather to be the deepest truth.

But all this, I once more admit, must still seem, when thus presented, very unpersuasive. The limits of a relatively untechnical discussion permit as I thus close only this dim suggestion of one of the deepest insights of modern philosophy. If it is right, your acts are at once from the temporal point of view absolutely bound, and from the eternal point of view absolutely free. For you enter into the divine order in two ways. In this world you are a fact in time, descended from the animals, a creature with just this brain, doomed for countless ages to precisely this conduct. But the whole temporal order is for the absolute Self, of whom you are a part, only

one way of looking at truth. All eternity is before
him at a glance. He has chosen not temporally, but in
an act above all time, yet an act in which you yourself
share, to conceive this world which contains you. He has
chosen this world for the sake of its worth. And in the
estimate that eternally chooses, your will, your time-transcending personality, your consciousness has its part also.
You are not morally free to change laws in *this* world.
But you are moral and free because you are in the eternal sense a part of the eternal World-Creator, who never
made the world at any moment of time, but whose choice
of this describable world of time in its wholeness is what
constitutes the world of appreciation, which is the world
of truth.

LECTURE XIII.

OPTIMISM, PESSIMISM, AND THE MORAL ORDER.

Too long I have detained you, in the previous lecture, with the discussion of the intricate speculative problems suggested to us by the physical world. This evening I return to more practical issues. During the course of our historical discussions, we have had occasion to study the idealistic doctrines of earlier thinkers from two points of view. They appeared as efforts to explain the nature of human knowledge, and as attempts to give form to the spiritual interests of humanity. It is, of course, in the latter sense that idealism usually seems most attractive to the general reader. Other theories of the world may or may not be influenced by ethical considerations. A doctrine which defines reality in terms of the absolute Self seems bound to make prominent the spiritual. In fact this is, to many minds, a defect of idealism, in that the doctrine appears to them rather the outcome of a moral enthusiasm than an embodiment of a cool and critical scrutiny of the world as it is. We have already tried, so far as our limited time permitted, to remove from idealism something of this reproach of being a mere poem of moral enthusiasm. We do not believe in the world of the absolute Self because we merely long for something spiritual in our world. The doctrine, such as I conceive it to be, seems to me rather the outcome of a rigid logical analysis, whose nature indeed I could only sketch in these brief lectures, but whose value for philosophy is indicated by the whole history of modern thought. Yet now that the theoretical question has been considered, we have a right

in conclusion to draw what advantage we can for our spiritual interests from the truths that theory has taught us.

I.

You are aware already how much and how little this
idealism pretends to know about the world. The world
has inevitably the moment of relatively capricious will
about it. Its existence is a fact, chosen from eternity by
the Self. We cannot fathom this choice, we cannot be
clear as to the precise meaning of this decree, except in
so far as we men too share in the choice, that is, in so far
as we too, in our own active life, are conscious of our own
purposes. In choosing for ourselves, we enter into and
partake of the Self who chooses this from the infinity of
possible worlds. No abstract " descriptive " reason can
deduce what it is about the world which makes it good, that
is, worth choosing. We can for the first only say, So it
is. We can comprehend the significance of this world-
estimate, of this appreciative aspect of things, only in so
far as we too are appreciative, are more than theoretical,
are will as well as thought.

From the purely theoretical or " descriptive " point of
view all will, all appreciation, is capricious ; for in vain
do you try to show by merely describing the laws and
contents of things why they should possess this or that
value. Deduction only proves ideal values when such
values have already been presupposed. Yet this capriciousness of the will is not, as Schopenhauer thought,
irrationality. The rational will is one that to complete
self-consciousness adds self-justification, and that is, accordingly, its own judge and its own vindicator. Is the
choice that wills the world of this nature ? Regarded
from the purely theoretical side it must appear as capricious, for there can be no merely theoretical, or, as we are
accustomed to say, logical reason, why it might not have
chosen otherwise. But regarded as the choice of an eternal

World-Self, the world cannot, so to speak, be the choice of a dissatisfied and peevish Logos, who eternally sorrows that he does not choose some other world instead. For dissatisfaction is due to either one of two causes: (1) That the dissatisfied will is not the only one concerned, but finds itself defeated by a foreign opponent; or (2) That the dissatisfied will is foolish, and knows not what it really wants. We finite bits of the Self are well acquainted with both these sources of grief; and since the World-Self is simply the self-conscious organism of all of us, he too is inevitably well acquainted with the *nature* of these our woes, and in so far shares them. But his acquaintance with our griefs need not be, cannot be, the sense of the entire failure of the whole organism of his timeless choice. That choice includes all the time events, and it is of the essence of temporal moments of consciousness to be discontented. But Hegel has already suggested to us how above the endless conflict victory may live. It is the purpose of this final lecture to give to that thought further illustration.

Two principles must be propounded at the start. Their reconciliation may be difficult. They form in fact the opposing members of the great " antinomy " of the spiritual world. They are, that is, in sharp apparent conflict with each other. Yet they must both be true, for they are both demonstrable.

One of them is the principle that there must be some sort of evil present wherever there is a finite will. It is not joyous to be finite, in so far as one *is* finite. One longs always to know more, and to possess more; and one lives in all sorts of paradoxical relations to other finite life. One lives in time, or in some such imperfect form of appreciative consciousness, and one preserves one's finitude, and so one's endless cares, by wondering and striving with some sort of reference to the other moments of time, to the other appreciations that lie beyond one. To be sure all this has too its joyous side, in so far, namely, as there is more about our finite life than its mere finitude. Most of us had rather be finite than nothing, although even that is not necessarily our opinion. But to be bounded in a nut-shell and to have bad dreams as well is of the essence of temporality and finitude in so far as they are regarded as such.

In view of this truth one can well say that, speaking in temporal terms, there just now *is* in the world nobody who is content with it. The Omar Khayyám stanzas of Fitzgerald are so far philosophically right, and forever true : —

> " Up from Earth's Centre through the Seventh Gate
> I rose, and on the Throne of Saturn sate,
> And many a Knot unravel'd by the Road ;
> But not the Master-Knot of Human Fate.

> " There was the Door to which I found no Key ;
> There was the Veil through which I might not see :
> Some little talk awhile of Me and Thee
> There was — and then no more of Thee and Me.

> " Earth could not answer ; nor the Seas that mourn
> In flowing Purple, of their Lord forlorn ;
> Nor rolling Heaven with all his Signs revealed
> And hidden by the sleeve of Night and Morn."

No better account could be given of the temporal order as it appears, when viewed appreciatively, at any finite moment, or of the inevitable result of seeking the divine or the satisfying therein. So viewed the seas are indeed of their Lord forlorn. As Lord he is found in no temporal moment, whether one passes through the " seventh gate " or not to look for him. If one is speaking of the complete God, the true Logos, and if one is using the temporal and not the eternal sense of *is*, it is perfectly accurate to say that God *is not*, say in the year 1892, just as he was not in Elijah's fire and earthquake. He is no affair of contemporary history. No reporter of even a celestial news-paper could discover, by any watching, items of current interest concerning him. His omnipresence is the presence of time and of space in him, not of his completeness in any part of them. He is their universal, they are not his prison. Therefore search the world as you might at this moment, with the well-known astronomer's telescope that very truthfully showed no God, or with the eyes of men and angels; you would doubtless find only discontented worms and seraphs, and other such finite toilers, — the whole creation groaning and travailing in pain, and cry-ing, Lord, how long! For time is in fact very long, nor does one get to the end of sorrow in the whole of it. Some of these finite creatures would indeed be calling this or that temporal joy good, but all of them, however amused they were, would be in the act of striving for the next moment of time to come. For to do that seems to be of the very essence of temporal consciousness. Not one of them all who knew what he was saying would be uttering the fatal cry that Faust was to avoid : " Oh moment, stay, thou art so fair ! " The best of their joyous moments would be under the illusion that the next mo-ment was likely to be a little better; and they would be hoping for that, as one hopes continually, while one listens to music, for the next phrase, and colors one's joy with this longing.

The other principle mentioned above is the thought that, notwithstanding all this, the Logos in his wholeness must find his choice of this universe rational, and so, in and through all this imperfection, must find a total per-fection. Were it a problem how to have a better world, the Self, as complete, would have solved the problem. Were it a question of a wiser choice, the Self in his wis-dom would have executed from eternity this wiser choice. Were it a matter of foreign necessity that inflicted evil, the Self would, in existing, have eternally absorbed this foreign element into his own organic nature.[1] The world that is, is then indeed, as Leibnitz said, the best of possible worlds. The problem is, How can this be, without interfering with the foregoing principle of the essential evil of finite existence?

II.

Let us begin our discussion of this ancient problem with its most immediately obvious illustration, the problem of moral evil. One who first sees the truth that the world of the Self must be, in its wholeness, a good world, is likely to rejoice even too easily in the notion that through this insight he has come indeed very near to the goal that all the religions have sought. Yet one who finds himself thus close, as it were, to the gate of the celestial city and to a glimpse of the golden glories within it, nigh to the palace of the king, does, after all, well to tremble, nevertheless, when he considers how easy it is to say such things about the perfection of God's world, and how hard it is to give concreteness and weight to the mere abstractions of the religious consciousness. God's world, in being good, can surely be nothing less serious than a moral order. And a moral order, regarded from a temporal point of view, is so grave and stern a thing! Remember the fate of poor Ignorance, in Bunyan's "Pilgrim's Progress," the fate that we mentioned when we were studying Schopenhauer's pessimism. Poor Ignorance reached the very gate of the celestial city, yet the angels carried him

---

[1] Here, of course, Von Hartmann's doctrine of the twofold nature of his unconscious, as Will and Wisdom, these two being essentially foreign to each other, will suggest itself to some. The former lecture has suggested my own reason for holding that these two are inseparable. The parallelism and at the same time the opposition of my own views to those of Von Hartmann will be obvious to many readers. Like him I am endeavoring to draw a synthetic conclusion from the post-Kantian idealists, from Schopenhauer, and from modern science. I have worked, for the most part, quite independently of his influence. I must acknowledge his great value and his priority.

away to the bottomless pit. Those who view the perfection of God's world merely in this first abstract fashion run indeed the risk of a similar fate. Pessimism and despair are not so far away from them as they think. It is not until they shall have learned somehow the seriousness of the moral aspect of the divine order; it is not until they have faced the tragedy of life, as well as its divine consummation; it is not until they have learned to recognize the moral order as essentially a hard master, and the misery of the finite world as a necessary element of the essentially severe significance of the universe; it is not until all this has come home to them that they will have any real right to the comfort that idealism offers. I want to make this fact plain.

All popular religious faith usually begins, as we saw in an earlier lecture, by assuring a man after far too light and easy a fashion that everything will be well in this world for those who do God's will, and that the moral order secures at once the triumph of the good cause, and the joy of all who serve this cause with a pure heart. Just at the present moment, curiously enough, despite all the skepticism of the day, such easy religious optimism as this chances to be in great popular favor; and for all my idealism, I regret this popularity of optimism. During these controversies concerning creed-revisions and other forms of religious progress which have been before the public during the past few years, I have noticed not only that it has been customary to frown upon all attempts to defend stern old dogmas, such as the depravity of man and the universal condemnation of all our race in its unsaved condition, but that the reason given as an axiomatic justification for this disapproval has usually been a very optimistic reason. People who pretend at other times to be very agnostic, become here of a sudden very confident. It would be melancholy, they say, to live in a world where the heathen had not as fair a chance for salvation as anybody else. It would be atrocious if the consequences of sin were to prove too grave. If we cannot reconcile a given supposition with the mercy of God, then the supposition must be false. And all this reasoning, when more fully analyzed, usually proves to mean, in the minds of those who use it, a sense that if there is any spiritual order in this universe it must be an order that does not permit very many ills, and that, above all, does reward, quickly, all good efforts. Thus reasoning, the religious optimist of the day finds his comfort in an assurance of the kindliness of God, of the early triumph of morality and of the general peacefulness of the universe, an assurance, I say, which, on the whole, I cannot share. I believe, indeed, that all the evil is part of a good order. I believe in the supremacy of the spiritual; and yet often during those popular controversies of recent years, I have found myself, as a relatively dispassionate metaphysical observer, sympathizing rather with the advocates of the sterner old creeds, not, to be sure, because I have accepted the sometimes irrational form which tradition had given to this or that dogma, but because I regretted the loss of moral rigidity which our fathers knew how to conceive as the very essence of the truly spiritual. But, not to weary you with the details of too well-known and unfruitful theological controversies, I may as well at once remind you of a modern poem which confesses in a most interesting fashion just such a religious optimism as I now have in mind, and as I do *not* accept. I am undertaking at this point a study and criticism of such a fashion of conceiving the world of spiritual concerns; I am glad to be able to let it express itself so fervently and skillfully. The poem which I refer to is one of the few really strong productions of the interesting Southern poet, Sidney Lanier, whose death a few years since deprived our country of a promising, but so far comparatively undeveloped man. The poem, entitled " How Love looked for Hell," is in-

tended to describe the world where all evil is purely illusory, and where the spirit triumphs by simply denying
the existence of all its opponents.   Many people, and for
that matter many idealists, conceive their world in these
terms.   And I therefore let Lanier state their case : —

> " To heal his heart of long-time pain
>   One day Prince Love for to travel was fain
>   With Ministers Mind and Sense.
> ' Now what to thee most strange may be ? '
>   Quoth Mind and Sense.   ' All things above,
>   One curious thing I first would see, —
>   Hell,' quoth Love.
>
> " Then Mind rode in and Sense rode out :
>   They searched the ways of man about.
>   First frightfully groaneth Sense,
> ' 'T is here, 't is here,' and spurreth in fear
>   To the top of the hill that hangeth above
>   And plucketh the Prince : ' Come, come, 't is here.'
>   ' Where ? ' quoth Love."

Accordingly, as Lanier proceeds to describe, Love follows his minister Sense to the place where, according to
the latter, there is a very black stream flowing, and where
a very cold wind blows, while beyond the stream one can
see lost souls struggling in burning lakes.   Love goes
very curiously to the place, hunting somewhat skeptically,
as if, to borrow a certain modern and possibly too crudely
optimistic comparison that I have sometimes found in use,
he were an electric light engaged in the search for a
shadow ; and lo ! when he reaches the spot in question,
somehow the scene has become transformed.   The black
stream has changed to a living rill, and instead of the
flaming lake beyond there are only lilies growing.

Sense is of course somewhat disconcerted by this change
of the scene.

> " For lakes of pain, yon pleasant plain
>   Of woods and grass and yellow grain
>   Doth ravish the soul and sense ;

> And never a sigh beneath the sky,
> And folk that smile and gaze above."

Such a transformation Love has wrought by his mere coming, and in his unconsciousness he also wonders.

> "Then Love rode round, and searched the ground,
> The caves below, the hills above ;
> ' But I cannot find where thou hast found —
> Hell !' quoth Love."

Hereupon, however, Sense having failed, the other minister is appealed to : —

> " There, while they stood in a green wood
> And marveled still on Ill and Good,
> Came suddenly Minister Mind.
> 'In the heart of sin doth hell begin :
> 'T is not below, 't is not above,
> It lieth within, it lieth within :'
> (' Where ? ' quoth Love.)

> " ' I saw a man sit by a corse ;
> *Hell's in the murderer's breast: remorse !* '
> Thus clamored his mind to his mind ;
> Not fleshly dole is the sinner's goal,
> ' Hell 's not below, nor yet above,
> 'T is fixed in the ever damnëd soul ' —
> ' Fixed ? ' quoth Love.

> " ' Fixed : follow me, would'st thou but see
> He weepeth under yon willow tree,
> Fast chained to his corse !' quoth Mind.
> Full soon they passed, for they rode fast,
> Where the piteous willow bent above.
> ' Now shall I see at last, at last,
> Hell,' quoth Love.

> " There when they came Mind suffered shame :
> ' These be the same and not the same ;'
> A-wondering whispered Mind.
> Lo, face by face two spirits pace
> Where the blissful willow waves abóve :
> One saith : ' Do me a friendly grace —'
> (' Grace ! ' quoth Love.)

"' Read me two dreams that linger long,
    Dim as returns of old-time song,
        That flicker about the mind.
    I dreamed (how deep in mortal sleep !)
    I struck thee dead, then stood above
    With tears that none but dreamers weep ; '
        ' Dreams,' quoth Love.

"' In dreams, again, I plucked a flower
    That clung with pain and stung with power,
        Yea, nettled me, body and mind.
    'T was the nettle of sin, 't was medicine ;
    No need nor seed of it here Above ;
    In dreams of Hate true Loves begin.'
        ' True,' quoth Love.

"' Now strange,' quoth Sense, and ' Strange,' quoth Mind ;
    ' We saw it, and yet 't is hard to find,
        — But we saw it,' quoth Sense and Mind.
    ' Stretched on the ground, beautiful crowned
    Of the piteous willow that wreathed above,'
    ' But I cannot find where ye have found
        Hell,' quoth Love."

Once more, then, Love fails, you see, since even as he approached Remorse, too, has fled. Thus Lanier depicted Love as wandering in his own universe. Mind and Sense find all sorts of mischief there, but they cannot show such things to their master. Abiding is only the ideal ; evil is but the illusion.

Here, then, is an embodiment, — in extreme form to be sure, but in a form that you will recognize, — of that modern faith which, in curious contrast to the prevalent agnosticism of our age, defends the spiritual in the world by denying the very existence of evil. I need hardly tell you more at length how to many minds such a doctrine contains the very deepest essence of religion. In such a world, think they, we can make easy work of demonstrating the immortality of the soul, the final restoration of all things, the unreality of Satan, the triumph of every good cause, in short, the gracious perfection which is hidden behind every apparent and illusory evil of life. To such persons thus to deny ill is to have spiritual insight, and Love is indeed ignorant of hell just because Love knows all things. I do not know how far Lanier regarded this as a final doctrine. But let us for the moment treat it as such, and draw further conclusions for which he is indeed not responsible.

Extremely characteristic of the mood of such religious optimism is in many minds a dread of the natural order as science knows it. Your optimist of this type, if he devotes himself to political theorizing, has a peculiarly violent dislike for economic facts. To his mind there are no evils in society except competition and poverty, which will both cease so soon as we by chance fall to loving one another, and to owning the property of the nation in common. Crime is not a result of anything deep in human nature ; selfishness is a mere incident of a defective social system. With fewer hours of labor, we should have many times the spirituality that we now have. Sin is not only mere ignorance; it is something still more limited; it is mere ignorance of the proper theory of the functions of government. Satan is mainly an invention of false theories in political economy. A single tax system, or a nationalized labor army, would end the sorrows of mankind, and make us all artists and patriots. The end of human woe is n't far off ; the day of the Lord is at hand.

The day of the Lord is in fact, in one form or another, the favorite hope of these romantic optimists. Evil being only an illusion, the spiritual powers being in complete ownership of the entire world, there is no reason why any day the scene of our sorrow should not be entirely transformed. In the hope of such transformation the faithful wait and trust. Meanwhile they expect little help from mere science, which once for all deals with the world of mind and of sense in a lower sphere. The truth of the spirit is not plain to the natural man ; the faithful rather pray to the Lord that such an one's eyes may be opened, so that he may see the chariots of the Lord all about him. Then he will believe in his immortal destiny, he will forsake remorse, gloom, dread, yes, even strenuousness itself. Spirituality, after all, is n't a very strenuous thing. That is n't its true quality. It rather blesseth him that gives and him that takes. In the world of the divine love all is well.

III.

But now is this, after all, a truly spiritual doctrine of the world ? Is this the notion of life and its problems to which a genuine idealism leads us ? I confess that I do not think so ; I hold rather that Love, in Sidney Lanier's vision, was rather the deluded one, or, if you like, the deceiver ; I hold that good is the final goal of ill in a wholly different sense, and that the gravity of the issues of the spiritual world is one which no one is fitted to understand until he has once fairly comprehended the sense and the bitterness of such a pessimism as even that of Schopenhauer himself. For a true pessimism, not as the last word of wisdom, but as an element of the true doctrine, is as much a moment in genuine spirituality as tragedy is a part of the fortune of true love. Even in Lanier's poem Love had felt heart-pain, and needed healing. Evil is not a dream, but a bitter truth, which we make spiritual by conquering it. And as for the day of the Lord, as for the moment when the divinely grave meaning, the genuine spirituality, of the world dawns upon man's comprehension, the first of the great prophets whose literary remains have come down to us from the days of ancient Israel fully expressed the essential fact concerning that experience when he said to the optimists of his time : " Woe unto you that desire the day of the Lord ! To what end is it for you ? The day of the Lord is darkness, and not light. As if a man did flee from a lion, and a bear met him; or went into the house, and leaned his hand on the wall, and a serpent bit him."

I assure you in all earnestness, speaking as an idealist, as one who longs to have men recognize the spiritual order, to believe in the supremacy of the good in this our world, to rise above sense, and to feel secure of the rationality of the universe, — speaking thus, I still regard as one of the most lamentable and disheartening features in our modern life the dreary opposition between those who, studying the order of nature as science shows it, remain agnostic about the spiritual realities of the world, and those who, on the other hand, believing, as they say, in a divine order, remain gently optimistic, and refuse to look at the woes and horrors of the world of Darwin and of science, because forsooth, since the Lord reigns, all must be right with the world. Thus on the one hand we have a romantic idealism that loves, with false liberalism, to cheapen religious faith by ignoring all the graver dogmas of the traditional creeds, that invents, meanwhile, social utopias, that denies the profound waywardness and wickedness of human nature, and that refuses to grapple by the throat the real ills of life; while on the other hand we have an agnosticism that refuses to believe in the spiritual, because once for all there is so much mischief in the phenomenal order of nature. A genuine synthesis of this optimism and its opposing pessimism, a spiritual idealism that does not deny the reality and the gravity of evil, a religion that looks forward to the day of the Lord as to something very great and therefore very serious, and that accepts life as something valuable enough to be tragic — this is what we need.

In human history the schoolmaster to bring us to the higher sense of what a genuine idealism means has always been just that bitter sense of the unreality and vanity of religious optimism which Amos so fervently expressed, and which for other thinkers, for a Voltaire or for a Swift, has frequently taken either the form of a skeptical assault upon all faith in the supremacy of the good in the universe, or else the shape of a cynical despair which, at all events in man's nature, could find no encouraging feature. The difficulties of religious optimism are indeed manifold enough. If all is ordered for the best in the best of possible worlds, if, in the presence of the divine love, even the hell of remorse itself ceases to exist, if what is called sin is a mere medicine of the soul, a nettle that stings a trifle, in order that we may be the better spiritually for the experience, if in a higher state we shall see that there was positively nothing to lament in this mortal life, then indeed the whole universe of action loses its gravity and its earnestness. Why should I not sin, since sin also is an illusion? Why not experience the sting of the nettle of crime, since that also is a medicine? If all is well, what is there to resist, to conquer, to change, to meet courageously, to regret, to avoid? If divine wisdom is present equally in the highest and the lowest, equally in the good and in the ill, then why resist the unreal evil? Whatever I am God chooses me, and surely not as a vessel of wrath, for there is no wrath in him at all, only gentleness, love, peace.

I need not dwell on such difficulties of the optimistic scheme. In its spirituality, as you see, it is in danger of becoming out and out immoral. Nor need I point out how, along with the study of the empirical facts which show us the world full of apparent ills all about us, these fundamental difficulties of optimism have led many to abandon altogether the hope of vindicating for any spiritual order a supremacy in our world. And, in fact, for those who, like myself, accept a general idealistic scheme of things there would seem at first sight to be no resource open, but either a resigned acceptance of the divine order as something to be conceived only in mystical terms, or else a consent to such a pessimism as Schopenhauer's.

The first resource here, to wit, mystical resignation, which once for all accepts the divine order as real and supreme, which still admits that the finite world is full of evil, and which then solves its problem by simply refusing to face it, and by surrendering all clear thought in favor of a rapt and helpless adoration of God, — this resource is already known to us from our study of Spinoza, and, still better, of the "Imitation." Your mystic is never an optimist of the type suggested in Sidney Lanier's poem. He rather loves to dwell on the miseries of the finite life. These are for him perfectly real miseries. The source of them, however, is simply our own absorption in our finitude. Why the divine order permits us to become thus absorbed is never clear, nor can it be made clear for the mystic. It is God who knows, not I, why I am thus imprisoned in the fatal misery of my finite ignorance. What he means by letting me become finite is utterly mysterious. I submit to this, as to everything else: —

> "The Ball no question makes of Ayes and Noes,
> But Here or There as strikes the Player goes ;
> And he that toss'd you down into the Field,
> He knows about it all — *He* knows — *He* knows."

The divine wisdom is existent for itself, not for me. It is remote, foreign, impenetrable, so long indeed as I remain finite. If I consent to lose myself indeed, there may come moments of ecstasy, when I shall, as it were at the moment of my vanishing, seem to catch a glimpse of God's meaning. But the glimpse will mean little; it will be inexpressible, a divine suggestion, with no bearings upon practical life in this world.

Are we now, as idealists, condemned to such a mysticism as this? If we are, is not the way indeed a short one to Schopenhauer's pessimism? In fact, all the three views of life that we have just been considering are not so remote from one another in their oppositions as might seem at first sight to be the case. The fact is that the finite world is full of at least apparent evils. Religious optimism of the simple-minded sort simply denies their actual existence. God's perfection, it says, excludes them. They are n't anything positive. They are essentially unreal. All is light and clear when viewed from above. The ills of life, including even the crimes of the world of sense, vanish from God's point of view. Mystical resignation, on the contrary, while asserting that the evils of life have a genuine existence, deprives them of any significant place in the divine order as such. The evils are, for the mystic, once more illusions, only so long as you remain in the finite world they are necessary illusions. God, too, knows them to be here in our finite world, doubtless even wills them to be here, so long as we remain remote from absorption in him. The sins inseparable from our finite existence are imposed upon us as the penalties of our consenting to remain apart from him. The difference between these two views is, that, on the one hand, for the believer in Sidney Lanier's conquest of divine Love, the higher insight brings with it to the finite beings a certain joy in their very finitude, a delight in their own past sins, in these experiences that have proved a medicine to them. This joy seems to make them content with the flowers and caresses of their world. On the other hand, the mystical resignation never sees in the finite world anything but dust and ashes, and to the end turns from it scornfully to God, who is the only good. Yet the two views agree in this, that they both alike deprive the finite world of all gravity and of all deeper ethical significance. What we do here, our work, our purposes, our problems, our doubts, our battles, all these things have for the mystic as for the optimist no essential meaning. There are no issues in the finite world for either view. And this idea, that just because there are no true issues in the finite world, just because

there is no gravity about it, nothing stern, nothing worthy
of a good fight, no salvation that may be lost, and is hard
to win, no significant toil that ought to be entered upon
and that is calling for us with the voice of a positive duty
— that just because of all this our life is essentially vain ;
what is such an idea but the very essence of pessimism
itself ? Pessimism, then, the sense of the utter vanity of
life, is the necessary outcome of every half-hearted scheme
of the moral order, of every scheme which says you can
escape the evils of finitude, if at all, only in case you can
find some way to deny their existence. For the fact is
that from every such half-hearted scheme of the moral
order we return to the facts of life themselves. There
they are, our ills and our sins — denying does not destroy
them, calling them illusions does not remove them, declaring them utterly insignificant only makes all the more
hollow and empty the life of which they are an organic
part. If, then, the only escape of our philosophy from the
individual ills of life lies in denying their significance, and
so the significance of this whole seeming world whereof
they are a part, then indeed are we of all men most miserable. For our life is *in* this world. And if the world
of experience is *only* a vain show, then the last word is a
sense of the utter illusoriness and insignificance of the
issues of life which is the very essence of pessimism.

Or once more, to put the matter more concretely : If
one who had long been toiling courageously up the steep
and narrow path of virtue, fighting sin after sin, doing
good as it was given him, aiming in his little way for the
victory of righteousness in the finite world, if such an
one, I say, has suddenly revealed to him as a truth the
substance of Lanier's vision of all-conquering Love, who
wins not by warfare with ill, but by a simple ignoring of
ill, in whose presence crimes become the medicine of the
soul, and hatreds the germs of the glorified friendships of
free spirits — will not your moral hero of the finite world,

scarred with his long warfare, worn with toils and sorrows, a patient servant of the good cause which as he
fondly had hoped needed him — will he not see the cheat
and delusion of all his warfare? What vainer than the
conflict with all the powers of hell, when there are no
such powers? Will he not say of us all in a new and
bitter sense : —

> " 'T is we who wrapt in gloomy visions keep
> With phantoms an unprofitable strife " ?

Nay, what shall it profit us that after the manner of men
we have fought wild beasts at Ephesus? There are no
wild beasts, you see. It was all a dream, our morality.
This optimistic awakening, — could any irony of fate
seem to us more bitter? We have offered our little all to
virtue, and the offering was vain; for in the world of
truth there was no offering to bring to virtue. Thus the
whole moral conduct of finite beings proves to be based
upon as irrational a striving as that which makes Schopenhauer call the blind world-will so worthless a thing. If
the mystical interpretation of life be the right one, if the
finite world is indeed simply banished from God, and has
no share in him except at the moment when it denies
itself, the pessimistic result is once more the plain one.
All these half-hearted views, in their endless dialectic,
resolve themselves into the same vanity.

And yet they are not without worth — these partial
insights — as approaches to the truth. When religious
optimism declares the joyous divine love to be all-conquering and omnipresent, it is trying to express a truth. Dissatisfied with his eternal world the divine Self cannot be.
It is only in the temporal world that from moment to
moment, as the drama changes, there is of necessity restlessness, evil, strife, and therefore a serious business involved. That the evil also, however real to the finite
being, however lamentable or hateful from the finite point

of view, has its place in the perfection of the Self, this is what optimism means, and in so far it is right. The truth in fact will lie somehow in a synthesis of all these points of view, for all three have a certain relative validity. The genuine moral order must contain that "perfection in imperfection" which Browning, in his best and most vital poems, was always striving to describe to us. Thus constituted it must be indeed problematic, even as the mystics make it, and tragic, even as the pessimists declare it, but also somehow perfect just as optimism dreams.

IV.

Can we now suggest, from an idealistic point of view, how the world of the one Self can be thus at once a world of moral issues, and a world of moral completeness ; a world of goodness, and yet a world where evil has its genuine place ; a world of restless spirituality, where at every moment of time there is something for moral agents to do, and a world of supreme triumph, where the spirit eternally rests from his labors? All these things, apparently, a moral order which is to be at once divine in its perfection so that we can worship it, and great in its needs so that our life may not be vain as we try to serve the good — all these paradoxically opposed qualities a moral order must contain. Is it conceivable that they should be reconciled? Is not the very attempt an absurdity? I answer that, on the contrary, if you look at the matter fairly, and from the point of view of an idealist's interpretation of life, nothing is more possible than just such an union of the apparently conflicting requirements of the religious conception of the world.

Consider, then, that more familiar problem of practical and daily life with whose philosophical bearings our historical study of Hegel and of Schopenhauer has now made us acquainted. All living, in the first place, however commonplace its aims, however accidental its ideals,

involves a deep paradox. We long to live. Very well,
then, we long to be active. For life means activity; and
activity, that again means longing, striving, suffering
lack, hoping for the end of the activity in which we are
immediately engaged. This is the essence of living, just
as Schopenhauer said. Life is will; and every will aims
at its own completion, that is, at its own cessation. I will
to be wiser than I am. Well, then, I will that my present
foolishness shall cease. I will to get somebody's love;
and that means that I will the cessation of my unloved
condition. Every will aims at the attainment of its
desire; and attainment is the death of just this desire,
and so of just this act of will. And yet, on the whole, I
will to live. I will then that which will always be in one
sense a longing for its own cessation; I will to suffer
lack; I desire to be always desiring. My highest good,
then, whatever my life, will always have this tinge of bitterness about it, will always be a restless, longing, suffering good. Hegel saw this paradox, declared it to be the
very essence of spirituality, gloried in it, and founded his
whole system on the paradoxical logic of passion. Schopenhauer saw the same truth in another light, and abandoned hope in life because of the universality of this
truth. As for us, we have found reason to side in this
one respect rather with Hegel. The life that we seek in
this world cannot be colorlessly perfect. At the very lowest estimate of its seriousness it has the worth and the
risk of the game about it. We win only by risking defeat; we have our courage only by conquering our fear;
we can triumph in life only by transcending the pains of
risk and of conflict even while they are in us and part
of us. Well, if this be so in other sorts of life, may it
not also be so in the moral life? Sin is moral defeat,
and is therefore indeed a part of a world where there is
serious moral effort, just as lost games are part of the
world of every earnest player. Imagine, then, that the

infinite Self, in the unity of his eternal life, wills a complete moral consciousness. Must not this consciousness express itself in a world of finite persons, each one of whom is limited enough not merely to strive and suffer, but also to be in danger of sin? Many of these moral agents, then, *will* sin, *will* fail in the conflict of life. Their errors will not be unreal ; their remorse will not be an illusion. But in the spiritual tragedy of the world as known to the divine perfection their failure will have the share that bitterness and sorrow always have in the life of the stern and earnest will. Or, once again, to make this notion of the moral world clearer, remember that, as we saw at the last time, the infinite Self, looking at the world in its entirety, must contain, must include, must consciously possess its whole spiritual world, as the musical consciousness, in its estimate of the succession of sounds, contains not merely the single notes, not merely the chords as they come singly in time, but the whole symphony, whose dissonances may thus be moments in the eternal perfection of the whole. Regarded temporally, music, which, as Schopenhauer suggested, does in this respect resemble the whole life of the will, is restless, insatiable, unable to give you any perfection at any single moment of its progress. Everything it gets only to flee from its own attainment. And even the final chords which its striving reaches in any composition would be worthless if alone. Yet this finite and temporal imperfection, this restless flight from every note, every melody, every chord, every chord-sequence, constitutes the indwelling perfection of the whole work. Mozart, as you may know, used to say, in words which the German philosopher Von Hartmann has very significantly quoted, that the blessedest moment of his artistic production was the one wherein this significance of his whole composition came home to him in one instant, wherein as it were he transcended time, and possessed all the succession of rest-

less musical strivings in one artistic glance. " My ideas,"
says, in substance, Mozart, in a letter to a friend, " come
as they will, I don't know how, all in a stream. If I like
them I keep them in my head, and people say that I often
hum them over to myself. Well, if I can hold on to them,
they begin to join on to one another, as if they were bits
that a pastry cook should joint together in his pantry.
And now my soul gets heated, and if nothing disturbs me
the piece grows larger and brighter until, however long it
is, it is all finished at once in my mind, so that I can see
it at a glance as if it were a pretty picture or a pleasing
person. Then I don't hear the notes one after another,
as they are hereafter to be played, but it is as if in my
fancy they were all at once. And that *is* a revel (*das ist
nun ein Schmaus*). While I'm inventing, it all seems to
me like a fine vivid dream ; but that hearing it all at once
(when the invention is done), that's the best. What I
have once so heard I forget not again, and perhaps this is
the best gift that God has granted me."

Well, such non-temporal grasping of the significance of
a restless temporal progress, we must indeed attribute, as
we have seen, to the Self in whom our logical analysis
found the realization of all truth. The truth of time
must be seen by the absolute Knower, as Mozart saw his
whole compositions. For that is, not the dream, but the
technically defensible result which our idealism has forced
upon us. If what we have to call the infinite past and
future have even at this instant a genuine truth, so that
of any moment in the past or in the future there is only
one of two contradictory assertions now true, then the infinite Self to whom I appeal when I talk of past and future
must, in the eternal sense, grasp and possess the whole of
time. After this fashion, then, the very paradox may be
realized by his consciousness which we are now seeking
to explain, the paradox of a world where, in the individual moments of life, there is indeed evil, dissonance,

tragedy, restlessness, imperfection, where the struggle
with these things is not illusory, and where the value of
the whole does not come, as in Sidney Lanier's dream,
through an abolition of the knowledge of individual ills,
through an ignoring of evil, whether physical or moral,
but rather through an eternal insight into the value of
the entire restless life of the whole temporal world.

But perhaps you may say that such a vindication as this
of the perfection of the divine order does not, after all,
sufficiently do justice to the gravity of the moral world.
The moral world, as experience shows it to us, is not
a symphony, nor anything else artistic, but either it is a
world of moral agony, of crime, of darkness, as Amos
said, and not of light, or else our conscience, in condemn-
ing sin as absolutely hateful, is wrong. Conscience declares that moral evil simply ought not to exist. Moral
evil is n't a mere dissonance in the world-symphony, any
more than it is, as Sidney Lanier's optimistic dream made
it, a gentle medicine for the soul. Sin is through and
through regrettable, diabolical. It ought not to exist.
No contrast of temporal and eternal will save us here.
So, in its stern hatred of the wrong, our moral consciousness seems to declare. Can our idealism aid us in reconciling the divine perfection with such dissonances, with
such paradoxes as these of the moral world?

Well, I admit, indeed, that it is very hard to formulate
the truth as to this problem without giving it the false
accent. Yet, after all, we have now in our hands all the
elements that are necessary for a genuine solution of the
problem of the existence of sin, in so far, at least, as it
is related to the consciousness of the sinner himself.
Spiritual evil has, to be sure, other aspects that will need
yet more study.

Sin, says our moral consciousness, is utterly hateful,
and ought not to exist in a perfect world. If our moral
consciousness is wrong in asserting this, then one appar-

ently returns to Lanier's superficial optimism. Evil is
only illusory. But in that case, as we saw, the world
utterly loses deeper significance. If, however, moral evil,
as it exists in the sinner's soul, is *not* illusory, then how
can the divine order be at once good and triumphant, in a
world where there is so much sin ? The answer is suggested to us by a consideration not now of sin as such,
but of latent sin, namely, of temptation. In the world of
our own acts we have an experience which is very enlight-
ening as to the paradoxical constitution of the whole
moral world. Only the tempted, as we saw when we
studied Hegel's doctrine, — only the tempted can be holy.
For instance, if I find in myself an evil impulse, I find
what in itself considered is, indeed, something hateful,
lamentable, possibly horrible, something which regarded
for itself can apparently form no part of a good order.
If I tolerate the impulse, if I declare it to be just the nettle
of sin, if I call its evil illusory, then my moral optimism
is indeed open to the condemnation of Amos, who cries
woe upon all such vindications of the divine order. But
suppose I resist the evil impulse, hate it, hold it down,
overcome it, then, in this moment of hating and condemn-
ing it *I make it a part of my larger moral goodness.*
The justification of the existence of my evil impulse comes
just at the instant when I hate and condemn it. Con-
demning and conquering the evil will makes it part of a
good will. Here is the paradox of all will stated not now
in artistic but in moral terms. There are elements in a
good world which, individually regarded, ought not to be
there, which are in themselves hateful, regrettable, the just
object of wrath. Yet they become part of the world of
the good will just in so far as they are in fact hated, condemned, subdued, overcome. The good world is not innocent. It does not ignore evil ; it possesses and still conquers evil.

Well, then, if this is true of our latent sins, of our

resisted temptations, if they are permissible parts of a
moral order, in so far as they are condemned and hated
by our larger moral consciousness, then, I ask, may not
the same be true of our actual sins, only in a yet graver
and more tragic sense ? Is n't there a deep truth after
all in the stern theology that said that even sin exists for
the glory of God, but that God's glory is vindicated not
through an ignoring, but through a hating and a triumphing over sin ? " I," a sinner may say, " am in all my
wickedness a part of the divine order, which is perfect.
Therefore my sin is illusory." We answer, not illusory
is this sin. Only, just because our idealism makes of the
divine Self one transcendent person, in whom and for
whom are all things, persons, and acts, just for this reason
there is open to us a vindication of the moral order of
God, which will insist at once upon the gravity of sin and
upon the perfection of the divine morality. In God, so
we say to the willful sinner, you are a part of a good will,
which bears just such organic relation to your sinfulness
as, in a good man, his virtue bears to the evil impulse
that forms a part of his goodness. *The hatred and condemnation of just your life and character makes God
holy.* God loves you, indeed, in so far as you are in any
wise worthy; but just in so far as you are a rebel, you
enter into the perfect moral order, not because your evil
is illusory, but because God knows you to hate you and to
triumph over you. Your evil will bears to his the relation that a brave man's fears bear to his triumphant
courage, just the relation that a good man's weaknesses
bear to the scorn which his conscience feels towards such
weaknesses. Just because of that unity of the infinite
Self which idealism teaches, God's organic perfection vin-
dicates sin by scorning it, makes it a part of his moral
order only by hating it, binds in the chains of his hatred
all the countless ills of the finite world, and rests in his
eternal perfection beyond the moral dissonances of the

temporal world, just because everywhere in this temporal world each dissonance is resolved, is condemned, is restlessly transcended. Whatever we are, we are, indeed, a part of God's perfection. But the question is, what sort of part? Are we there to be scorned, despised, condemned by the organic Self, whose perfection will be vindicated in such case through the very courage and emphasis of its scorn and hatred for us? If so, whatever our sin, it is part of the moral order, only the moral order exists by conquering us, and we live only to be despised by the very Self that includes us. God's holiness we, then, assist, but only as the evil impulse serves the saint's triumphant higher self. God's glory we then, in our way, also serve, but only as vessels of his wrath. But do we ourselves choose the good? Then once more we enter into the divine order, but this time as vessels of honor, as ministers of the good, as servants and not as enemies, as co-workers and not as rebels, as beloved and not as scorned.

Thus I have tried to show you how idealism, by its very definition of the divine Self as the one organic personality, in whom and for whom we all exist, is able to suggest a solution of this one amongst the religious problems of the ages, and a synthesis of the truths that are at the heart both of moral optimism and of moral pessimism, both of the mystical and of the morally active religious piety, both of the faith in God's eternal perfection and of the desire to do right in the temporal world. All this, you remember, is true, so far as to the explanation of the existence of sin as it exists within the evil-doer's soul. There is another aspect of the problem of evil that is much darker from our finite point of view than this one; and to this other aspect I must pass as I close.

v.

For I do not feel that I have yet quite expressed the full force of the deepest argument for pessimism, or the full seriousness of the eternal problem of evil.   In fact, when, in the past, I have gone over these considerations in company with those of my fellows who have experienced widely and deeply, I have always found that whether they were themselves naturally disposed to be pessimists or not, they declined to recognize this way of looking at our question about evil as really exhausting the meaning of it.   The mood that genuinely questions the value of life is after all a very gloomily ingenious mood.   Its dialectic is endless ; it turns its reflection from sorrow to sorrow, with a remorselessly industrious scrutiny ; it refuses easy comfort; it readily finds the philosopher's formulas pedantic and unspiritual; and in fact no lighter experience of grief, no superficial disappointment, no mere wounded sentiment, nor yet even a transient remorse, can give you a true sense of what the problem of evil is.   Even that remorse which Lanier's poem depicts is ill-adapted to express whether hell has its seat in this universe.   In fact, to see where the worst problems of life lie is a very black experience.   And yet, so much does human reason love insight, that I have never met a man who was alive to these deepest problems, and who still repented him of his insight.   The strong and hearty beings who know not the clear bitterness of all higher truth often wonder how men can doubt as to the worth of life, and often condemn as mere morbidness every such scrutiny as that in which we are now engaged.   Many persons I know, and honor, too, — men of cheerful souls and well-knit purposes, high-minded men and strenuous, to whom every ultimate, above all every philosophical inquiry as to this matter of the meaning and the final justification of life, seems essentially either vain or dangerous.   Why we live, they say, and what our duty is, and why it is a worthy thing to do our duty, and how evil is to be explained, — to ask this *why ?* is to hesitate, to dream, to speculate, to poison life. The best thing is to work and not to inquire.

Yet there is another way of viewing life, and that is just the way upon which we have been dwelling. It is the way of men who demand ultimate answers, and who, if they can't get them, prefer doubt, even if doubt means despair. Pessimism, in the true sense, is n't the doctrine of the merely peevish man, but of the man who, to borrow a word of Hegel's, "has once feared not for this moment or for that in his life, but who has feared with all his nature; so that he has trembled through and through, and all that was most fixed in him has become shaken." There are experiences in life that do just this for us. And when the fountains of the great deep are once thus broken up, and the floods have come, it is n't over this or that lost spot of our green earth that we sorrow; it is because of all that endless waste of tossing waves which now rolls cubits deep above the top of what were our highest mountains. In our natural state, you see, we desire many things, some more, and some less; life has its strange mingling of joys and of pangs; but there is nothing in it absolute, nothing whose place could n't be taken by another. We are, then, cheerful and reasonably content, just because everything in our world has its price, and can conceivably be gained by finite labor; nor is there for us anything this side death that might not, with good fortune, turn out well for us. This is the mood that, of course, with an inaccurate use of the superlative, and so with a very characteristic exaggeration of speech, common sense calls optimism. The mood which really opposes it, however, is just the mood that has learned to demand absolute standards, and that finds none; the mood that refuses to be comforted with such good things as can be brought, because it longs for the priceless goods of the spirit. This opposing mood, then, this true pessimism, is in its very nature the mood of the painfully awakened, who cry for God's truth, and who so far find it not. It is the despair of those who want a plan in life, and who see how our ordinary and natural life is planless, accidental, a mere creature of fortune. This despair is the first voice, in many hearts, of the truly devout spirit. He who has never felt it does not know what the deepest religious experience must involve. And he who has once become possessed of this longing for a deeper meaning in life than natural experience can give or can find there, would not for worlds exchange his insight, gloomy as he may find it, for the vain cheerfulness of unchastened optimism. Better, to his mind, this waste of dark tossing waves than the blind and misbelieving world before the flood; better to be broken in spirit, than to be vainly puffed up with miserable finite conceits.

Well, it is just this absolutely inquiring mood, just this thorough-going doubt, that we shall not yet have shaken by all the foregoing. Easy it is, such doubt will say, easy it is to refute the religious optimists of Lanier's type; easy it is to get past the stately resignation of the mystical mood; easy, too, if you will, for an idealist, to justify the existence of countless evils in the finite world, if only they have the less tragic type. Only there are still doors to which we have found no key. The eternal insight of the All-knower may look in lofty peace upon the restless flight of our time-moments. Everywhere in his world there will be change and dissatisfaction; yet in his completeness he may judge it all as good. But there is still one condition that must be met by the struggles of the finite world, if they are obviously to conform to this solution of our problem. They must, namely, be significant conflicts. If they are, then, so far, the difference of the eternal and the temporal aspects does, indeed, aid us. As for the willing sinner and his just remorse, it is n't in his case that one need feel deeply concerned. He has played the game of sin; he is only exemplifying the rules of the game. The awakened sinner may sometimes banish himself almost cheerfully to that hell, bearing, with a stern contempt for his own sorrow, the bitterness of his moral defeat.

No, the worst tragedy of the world is the tragedy of the brute chance to which everything spiritual seems to be subject amongst us — the tragedy of the diabolical irrationality of so many among the foes of whatever is significant. An open enemy you can face. The temptation to do evil is indeed a necessity for spirituality. But one's own foolishness, one's ignorance, the cruel accidents of disease, the fatal misunderstandings that part friends and lovers, the chance mistakes that wreck nations: — these things we lament most bitterly, not because they are painful, but because they are farcical, distracting, — not foemen worthy of the sword of the spirit, nor yet mere pangs of our finitude that we can easily learn to face courageously, as one can be indifferent to physical pain. No, these things do not make life merely painful to us; they make it hideously petty. They are like the "mean knights" that beat down Lancelot during his hopeless wandering in search of the Grail.

Some of you may know a little poem called "The Fool's Prayer," a bit of verse that was first printed some years ago, and that has more recently been rather often quoted by the author's growing circle of readers and admirers. The author himself, a man of not altogether happy destiny, is now dead. I knew him well; he was first a valued teacher and adviser of my own, and afterwards an intimate friend. The words sprang so earnestly from his heart, and they suggest our problem here so thoughtfully, that I may venture to repeat the most of them : —

> "The royal feast was done ; the king
> Sought out some new sport to banish care,
> And to his jester cried : 'Sir Fool,
> Kneel now, and make for us a prayer.'

" The jester doffed his cap and bells
  And stood the mocking court before ;
They could not see the bitter smile
  Behind the painted grin he wore.

" He bowed his head, and bent his knee
  Upon the monarch's silken stool ;
His pleading voice arose : ' O Lord,
  Be merciful to me, a fool !

" ' No pity, Lord, could change the heart
  From red with wrong to white as wool ;
The rod must heal the sin ; but Lord,
  Be merciful to me, a fool !

" ' Tis not by guilt the onward sweep
  Of truth and right, O Lord, we stay ;
'T is by our follies that so long
  We hold the earth from heaven away·

" ' These clumsy feet, still in the mire,
  Go crushing blossoms without end ;
These hard, well-meaning hands we thrust
  Among the heart-strings of a friend

" ' The ill-timed truth we might have kept —
  Who knows how sharp it pierced and stung ?
The word we had not sense to say —
  Who knows how grandly it had rung ?

" ' Our faults no tenderness should ask,
  The chastening stripes must cleanse them all ;
But for our blunders — oh, in shame
  Before the eyes of heaven we fall.

" ' Earth bears no balsam for mistakes ;
  Men crown the knave, and scourge the tool
That did his will ; but thou, O Lord,
  Be merciful to me, a fool.' "

I think that you will see how my old friend here suggested where the burden of the problem of evil lies much
more wisely than Lanier did. For my friend, who wrote

these words, thus touched upon one element of that caprice of life which does prove the cruelest note in all its tragedies. As I knew him, the poet of these verses was peculiarly sensitive to the presence in the world of that willfulness both of fortune and of our fellows, which not because of conscious sinfulness, nor yet because of any obviously necessary discord of motives, but because of mere brute accident or stupidity, tears to pieces whatever is spiritual, kills our infant children, leaves our unrecognized heroes to die neglected and ineffective, sunders the wounded hearts of faithful lovers, makes brother war with brother, plunges society into bitter confusions, defeats over and over the most sacred ideals. My friend sometimes even used this fateful fact of defeat, I remember, as a sort of test of the spirituality of things. Were they good, he said, willfulness would assail them the more surely. Once, when he was a little weary because of the hatred that he had met with during some of his undertakings in a very good cause, I said to him, by way of a sort of conventional comfort and of friendly admonition at once, " Why do you work so hard as you do for the good of people who only misunderstand you after all? They don't deserve the good things that you offer, for they are people who won't and can't appreciate your trouble. Why cast pearls before swine ? They only turn and rend you." " Ah, Royce," replied my friend, " but one does n't quite surely know that they were pearls that he cast until he feels the tusks."

But perhaps you will say that, thus put, the problem of the stupidity of our human nature and of our fortune seems a rather sentimental problem, after all. Is not this capriciousness of life simply part of its painfulness ? Is it manly to lament just this woe so deeply ? I answer, to the enlightened soul it is n't ever so much the painfulness as the blind irrationality of fortune that seems to drive God out of our thoughts when we look at our world.

Mere pain can be borne, for cause, very fairly.   One may whine, but one can still hold out to the end and not lament it when it is once over.   But this capriciousness of life is what really makes it seem like an evil dream. Consider once more that horror involved in hereditary disease, and in the fatal and unearned baseness which often goes therewith.   Consider the way in which the wrong-doing of one person often entails not the physical pain, but the utter and inevitable corruption and endless moral degradation of another.   Consider how not mere disloyalty, but a transient mistake, may wreck the most spiritual of causes, after years of devotion have built up its fortunes nearly to the heights of success. These, alas! are the mere commonplaces of our temporal order.   Is it easy to say that these things are needed as a part of the gravity of the spiritual world?   No, for they don't make the world spiritually grave!   They make it rather insane and contemptible.   Moral evil in the willful sinner himself, you can look in the face and defy, and that too even if you are yourself the sinner.   Here, you can say, is my natural foe; I know what he is and wherefore he is.   I condemn him, and I rejoice in defeating him. But the hopeless and helpless degradation of the sinner's passive victim, how shall you speak comfortably or even defiantly after that?   Here is the place only for pity; and in a world that is full of such things, and that always will be full of such things, so long as its order is the prey of the mechanical accidents of nature, where is there room for anything but pity for its worthlessness?

Well, here indeed we find the enemy of whose works Shakespeare wrote in the sonnet that begins

" Tired of all these, for restful death I cry."

And this will always be the cry of our darker moments so long as the tragedies of our world decline to appear to us as mainly moral tragedies.   Nay, if it were only our sin that kept us from God, might men not often hope to see his face? The true devil is n't crime, then, but brute chance. For *this* devil teaches us to doubt and grow cold of heart; he denies God everywhere and in all his creatures, makes our world of action, that was to be a spiritual tragedy, too often a mere farce before our eyes. And to see this farcical aspect of the universe is for the first time to come to a sense of the true gloom of life.

VI.

Well, then, if this is the final and deepest truth of pessimism, what comfort still remains for one who in hopeless affliction, or in the chaos of defeated spirituality, still looks to the truth for aid? Surely concerning this sort of doubt one can only speak in the tenderest and most respectful of terms. Cowards shrink from the petty pains of fortune; sinners and sentimentalists want to get rid of the penalties of sin; but they who most lament and wonder over this capricious irrationality of the world are just the noblest and gentlest of souls, who would pause at no heroism were its warfare only a significant one, who would shrink from no pang, if only by enduring it one served God; but who cannot endure this weary dwelling cheek by jowl with the mocking demons of chance and absurdity. Well, can one still plausibly insist that somehow, in fashions unknown to us, the infinite Self is strong enough to make the facing and the endurance of even these demons somehow significant? Can our chance be by any possibility his rationality; our chaos his order, our farce his tragedy, our horror his spirituality? Yes, even this may come home to us if we remember that he at least, in his absoluteness, does not find these things as foreign facts, forced upon him from without. He endures them, as we do; he condemns them as we must; but he *knows* them, as we in our finitude cannot. And so, if knowing them he wills these horrors for himself, must he

not know wherefore? In our strength we cannot walk
when we face them. Can we not walk in his strength? He
who solves all problems, shall he not solve this one also?
And thus, indeed, if in our finitude we have but one comfort, surely we have that. From our finite point of view
there is no remotely discoverable justification for this
caprice. This is to our eyes no embodiment of a stern
moral order. It is Satan's own irresistible and mocking
presence in our life. He ought not to be here; yet no
thing that we can do will have any chance to remove
him. And so, indeed, *were* our insight into the truth of
the Logos based upon any sort of empirical assurance, it
would surely fail us here. But now, as it is, if we have
the true insight of deeper idealism, we can turn from
our chaos to him, who is our own true and divine self, and
can hear from him with absolute assurance this one word:
"O ye who despair, I grieve with you. Yes, it is I who
grieve in you. Your sorrow is mine. No pang of your
finitude but is mine too. I suffer it all, for all things are
mine; I bear it, and *yet* I triumph." This word of the
Self, I say, we can be sure of, for it is the one final word
of our whole idealistic insight. It is this thought of the
suffering God, who is just our own true self, who actually
and in our flesh bears the sins of the world, and whose
natural body is pierced by the capricious wounds that hateful fools inflict upon him — it is this thought, I say, that
traditional Christianity has in its deep symbolism first
taught the world, but that, in its fullness, only an idealistic interpretation can really and rationally express.
Were not the Logos our own fulfillment, were he other
than our own very flesh, were he a remote god, were he not
our own selves in unity, were he foreign to the horror and
to the foolishness of our chaotic lives, we should indeed
look to him in vain ; for *then* his eternal peace would be
indifference and cruelty, his perfection would be our despair, his loftiness would be our remote and dismal help-

lessness. But he is ours, and we are his. He is pierced
and wounded for us and in us. Our defeats are his;
and yet, above time, triumphant in the sacred glory of
an insight that looks before and after through the endless
ages and the innumerable worlds, he somehow finds
amidst all these horrors of time his peace, and so ours.
"My peace," he says, " I give unto you; not as the world
giveth, give I unto you." This, then, at last, is the true
realization of the rapt wonder that the mystics sought.
What in time is hopelessly lost, is attained for him in his
eternity.

I know not that I have persuaded you of all this.
True philosophical persuasion would rest upon something
much more elaborate than I have had time to present. I
have only sketched. What I do know is that of such
truth philosophy must yet some day persuade those who
are ready to listen and apt to comprehend. Herein, too,
as I think, are woven into one cord the strands of partial
knowledge that in our history we have been finding. Spinoza and Schopenhauer, Berkeley and Fichte, Kant and
Hegel, join in suggesting to us our result. Like the predecessors of Childe Roland, they stand at the close of our
day, ranged along the hillsides to view the end of our
quest. For herewith, indeed, the task of these lectures is
ended. We have found in a world of doubt but one assurance — but one, and yet how rich! All else is hypothesis.
The Logos alone is sure. The brief and seemingly so
abstract creed of philosophy: " *This world is the world
of the Logos,*" has answered our questions in the one
sense in which we can dare to hope for an answer. The
rest is silence — and, here on the earth, endless labor in
the might of the spirit, for whom and in whom is all sorrow and bitterness, and all light and life — and peace.

APPENDIX A.

———◆———

ANYTHING resembling an exhaustive bibliography of the topics treated in the present book is excluded by the plan of the work. A syllabus, with notes, containing a few suggestions for the further study of the problems and thinkers considered in the course of these lectures, was prepared, was printed in a series of broadsides, and was then put into the hands of the hearers on some of the occasions of the delivery of the lectures. This syllabus, much revised, here follows as an appendix. For its fragmentariness, the nature of the present undertaking may be some explanation. It extends to the historical lectures of the course. Of the doctrinal lectures it gives only a brief suggestion in a single summary statement.

SYLLABUS.

The general purposes of this course are : —

1. To give personal characterizations of some of the more noteworthy modern thinkers.

2. To suggest, as clearly as may be possible without technical details, something of the nature of their various attitudes towards the great concerns and issues of humanity.

3. To illustrate, in the light of such a study, certain significant spiritual problems of our own day.

LECTURE I.

INTRODUCTION.

I. The general business of philosophy.

II. The variety and seeming failure of the philosophers.

III. The positive significance of philosophy.

IV. The many-sidedness of truth.

V. The skeptical element in philosophy in its relation to the positive purpose of the study.

VI. The limitations of the present undertaking.

LECTURE II.

NOTES. The periods of modern philosophy, as distinguished for the
present purpose, are : —

1. Period of Naturalism and of Rationalism : From Galileo to Spinoza.
[Its specially noteworthy characteristics are, in addition to its general
interest in outer nature : (1) Its belief that the whole order of nature is
subject to rigid laws of a mechanical type ; (2) Its faith in the power of
the human reason to know absolute truth ; and (3) Its fondness for mathematical methods in philosophy.]

II. Period of the study of the Inner Life : From Locke to Kant.
[Its general characteristics are : (1) A critical analysis of the powers of
man's mind ; (2) A growing skepticism; (3) In the end a tendency towards
revolutionary reconstructions of all doctrine].

III. Period of recent philosophy : From Kant to the present time.
[Beginning at the culmination of the previous critical period, the third
period is at first devoted to the study of the inner life, but is later led to
fresh efforts to comprehend outer nature. It is throughout much influenced by natural science and by the newer study of history. In consequence it develops the idea of evolution. Its problem is the synthesis and
reconciliation of our knowledge of outer nature with our understanding of
the inner life of man.]

The principal dates of Spinoza's life are as follows : birth, 1632 ; excommunication from synagogue, 1656 ; first philosophic work (*Principles
of Cartesian Philosophy*) published, 1663 ; Theologico-Political Tractate

published 1670; refusal of a call to a professorship in Heidelberg, 1673; death, 1677. Spinoza's principal treatise is the *Ethics*, published posthumously in 1677. He lived first in Amsterdam, then in various minor Dutch towns, and died at the Hague.

His principal works have been recently translated into English in Bohn's Philosophical Library, in two volumes. The best accounts and commentaries in English are those of Pollock (*Spinoza's Life and Philosophy*, London, 1880), Martineau (*Study of Spinoza*), and John Caird (*Spinoza*, Edinburgh, 1888). The best complete edition is that of Van Vloten and Land (The Hague, 1882–83, 2 vols.).

For comparison are added the dates of several other early modern thinkers.

Montaigne	1533–1592	Jakob Boehme	1575–1624
Giordano Bruno	1548–1600	Hobbes	1588–1679
Bacon	1561–1626	Descartes	1596–1650
Galileo	1564–1641	Pascal	1623–1662
Campanella	1568–1639	Locke	1632–1704
Kepler	1571–1630	Malebranche	1638–1715

LECTURE III.

THE REDISCOVERY OF THE INNER LIFE; — FROM SPINOZA TO KANT.

Introductory characterization of this period as one of analysis. skepticism, and study of the Inner Life.

I. Value of skepticism in philosophy.

II. The problem concerning Innate Ideas; its origin and early stages in modern discussion.

III. Locke's treatment of the question : historical consequences of the controversy, direct and indirect; its value for the study of the Inner Life.

IV. Berkeley's idealism.

V. Hume's skepticism.

VI. The transition of Kant.

Locke (1632–1704) has been often edited. A good edition of his *Essay on the Human Understanding*, for purposes of actual study, is the one in Bohn's Philosophical Library, in the edition of his *Philosophical Works*. The best life is that by H. R. Fox Bourne, London and New York, 1876, 2 vols.

Berkeley was born 1684, died 1753. He matriculated at Trinity College, Dublin, in 1700, took his Master's degree in 1707, published his *Essay towards a New Theory of Vision* in 1709, and his *Treatise concerning the Principles of Human Knowledge* in 1710. From 1729 to 1731 he lived

in Rhode Island, planning his university, which was to be established in
the Bermudas. The plan came to nothing. In 1732, returned to England, he published his *Alciphron*. He became bishop of Cloyne in 1734.
The best recent edition of his works is that of Fraser (Oxford, 1871). The
same editor has also written his life, published at the same time as the
works.

Hume was born in Edinburgh, 1711, died 1776. His *History of England*
appeared in 1754–1762. His first philosophical treatise, the *Treatise on
Human Nature*, was written between 1734 and 1737. His *Essays* appeared
in 1748. The philosophical works have been edited in four volumes by
Green and Grose, London, 1874–75. On this whole period one may read
Leslie Stephen's *History of English Thought in the Eighteenth Century*.

LECTURE IV.

KANT.

  I. Difficulties of the study of Kant.
 II. Kant's person and character.
III. Kant's religious views, and his early philosophical develop-
       ment, in outline.
 IV. His doctrine of Space and of Time.
  V. His doctrine as to the Laws of Nature.
 VI. The Moral Law as the central truth in Kant's world.

Kant was born in 1724; received his appointment as professor in the
university of his native city, Königsberg (in far eastern Prussia), in 1770;
published the *Critique of Pure Reason* in 1781; published his own prin-
cipal works between this year and 1798; and died in 1804. The best
English translation of the *Critique* is that of Max Müller. The transla-
tion in Bohn's Library, by Meiklejohn, is now regarded as superseded.
Watson's *Selections from Kant* (Macmillans, 1886), Wallace's *Kant*, in
Blackwood's Philosophical Library (Edinburgh and Philadelphia, 1882),
Edward Caird's *Critical Philosophy of Immanuel Kant* (2d ed., New York,
Macmillans, 1889, 2 vols.), and J. H. Stirling's *Text-Book to Kant* (New
York, Putnams, 1882), are the best aids to the study of Kant in English.
The German literature on the subject is enormous, embracing some hun-
dreds of works.

BRIEF OUTLINE SUMMARY OF KANT'S DOCTRINE.

1. The origin of Kant's philosophy is the problem of human reason as
the eighteenth century had developed this problem. The problem was,
How can the truth which not only theology, but also common sense and
natural science, pretend to know about our world, be defended against
skepticism ? Our human powers being once for all so limited, how can any
genuine truth of any sort be known ?

2. Kant's first answer is : Things in themselves are of necessity unknown

to us. We can know in a theoretical sense only the things that appear to our senses, that is, the Phenomena of the World of Show. Neither common sense, nor science, nor theology, can, with theoretical assurance, carry us beyond the world as it *seems* to our human powers of observation and experience.

3. In particular, Space and Time can be shown to be mere forms of our human sense-consciousness, and to have no relation to things in themselves. The unknowable real world without us exists, therefore, neither in space nor in time. We know not *how* this world exists at all; we only recognize *that* it exists.

4. But we can nevertheless be sure that our world of seeming things in space and time must conform to rigid laws, such as the law of causation. For our active understanding, in thinking our world, is bound by its own nature, in order to preserve, as it were, our very sanity (or, as Kant would say, the Unity of our Self-Consciousness), to regard all observed facts as conforming to laws. Yet these laws of Nature, which science studies, are the very creation of our own understanding acting upon the data of our senses. Such laws are not the laws of the unknowable real world at all. They hold only for the show-world of our experience. Our own understanding is, therefore, the source for us of all knowable rational truth.

5. Yet, ignorant as we are of all absolute truth, confined as we are for all theoretical knowledge to the seeming world of sense and understanding in space and time, we are yet morally bound to postulate that the real world of the things in themselves is a Divine Moral Order; that is, we are bound to act as if such a real and absolute moral order were known to us to exist.

6. In this way we are theoretically certain that the seeming world is a world of orderly law, such as common sense and science believe in; and we are practically certain that the unknown *real* world is a divine and moral world, because it is our duty to treat that unknown world as if it were divine and moral.

LECTURE V.

FICHTE.

I. Restatement of Kant's general significance in modern thought.
II. A possible transformation of Kant's world : First statement of the Idealism common to Fichte, Schelling, and Hegel, and of its relations to Christianity.
III. Fichte's fortunes and character.
IV. and V. Fichte's Subjective Idealism.
VI. His book on the "Vocation of Man."

Johann Gottlieb Fichte was born in 1762, was a student in Leipzig and Jena from 1780 to 1784, was private tutor thereafter, and lived in great poverty, until 1794, when he was called to a professorship in Jena, as a result of his first book, published in 1792. In 1799 he was removed from his professorship on a charge of atheism, but was later active, as professor, at the new University of Berlin, until his death in 1814. His publications were numerous. Of his best works the most popular, translated by William Smith, have been published in several editions by Trübner & Co. (3d ed., London, 1873, in one vol.). On this whole period, in its general aspects, a very useful book, is the German, is the *History of Literature* by Julian Schmidt.

LECTURE VI.

THE ROMANTIC SCHOOL IN PHILOSOPHY.

Introductory summary of Kant and Fichte : —

I. The arbitrary element in Fichte's doctrine, and the relation of this arbitrariness to the Romantic School and to the doctrines of our day.

II. The place of the Romantic School in German literature. Wider and narrower use of the term Romantic School. Characteristics of the principal members of the Romantic School proper.

III. Illustrations of the Romantic view of life : Friedrich Schlegel and Novalis.

IV. Schelling and Caroline. Sketch of some of Schelling's views.

Concerning the Romantic School, on the literary side, the reader must be referred to the bibliographies of German literature. The well-known early essays of Carlyle form here an introduction which has not yet lost its value for English readers ; and his translations are of permanent worth. Heine's sketches of the History of German Thought and Literature are as suggestive as they are charming and untrustworthy. Schelling's voluminous writings are still for the most part accessible only in the original. The best recent technical and critical exposition of a portion of his doctrine is that by Professor John Watson, *Schelling's Transcendental Idealism* (Chicago, 1882).

For comparison are added a number of biographical dates, in both German and English Literature : —

	BORN			BORN
Herder	1744		Tieck	1773
Goethe	1749		Schelling	1775
Schiller	1759		Schopenhauer	1788
Fichte	1762		Wordsworth	1770
A. W. Schlegel	1767		Scott	1771
Schleiermacher	1768		Coleridge	1772
Hegel	1770		Southey	1774
Friedrich Schlegel	1772		Byron	1788
Novalis	1772		Shelley	1792

LECTURE VII.

HEGEL.

I. Schelling's doctrine of Identity.
II. Hegel's character and attitude.
III. The paradox of Self-consciousness.
IV. Systematic application of the paradox.

Hegel was born in 1770 at Stuttgart, studied at the University of Tübingen, was private tutor from 1793 to 1800, was docent at Jena from 1801 until after the battle of Jena, was gymnasium director at Nürnberg from 1808 until 1816, was then made professor at Heidelberg, and from 1818 until his death, in 1831, was professor at Berlin. His works, including many very unevenly edited notes of his academic lectures, were published by his pupils in eighteen volumes (1832–45), and his son has recently added as nineteenth volume his letters. His life was written admiringly by Karl Rosenkranz (1844), and reviewed, together with his system, with much severity of criticism, by Haym (*Hegel und seine Zeit*, 1857). Since Haym's book and Trendelenburg's keen criticism of the dialectic method in his *Logische Studien* (2d ed., 1862, 3d ed., 1870), the Hegelian doctrine has received less and less attention in Germany, although its indirect and unconsciously effective influence has been great. On the other hand, in Great Britain, Dr. Hutchinson Stirling's *Secret of Hegel* (London, 1865), one of the most waywardly constructed of remarkable philosophical books, began (through its very skillful exposition of some features of Hegel's thought) a movement that has given Hegel first-class importance for recent speculation. Wallace's *Logic of Hegel*, and Caird's *Life of Hegel*, in Blackwood's Philosophical Series, are important introductions to the study of the philosopher. Mr. W. T. Harris's *Hegel's Logic*, in Grigg's Philosophical Classics, is a scholarly exposition of a highly technical sort.

LECTURE VIII.

SCHOPENHAUER.

I. The significance of Pessimism.
II. The general character of Schopenhauer's system.
III. Schopenhauer's person, fortunes, and quality.
IV. Summary of his principal treatise.
V. Estimate of Schopenhauer's doctrine.

Arthur Schopenhauer was born in 1788, published the first volume of his principal work in 1818, made in 1820 an effort to succeed as docent at Berlin, but failing here, lived as wanderer and recluse until his death at Frankfort in 1860. The recent expiration of the copyright upon his works (published in six volumes by Brockhaus) has led to many reprints of part or all of his writings. His philosophy is best expounded by himself, and so fine a master of style should be read in his own tongue, although he is now extremely accessible in English translations. His two biographers, Frauenstädt and Gwinner (the latter's *Schopenhauer's Leben*, published in 1878, is the best), have told the story of his eccentric career with much detail. Very useful is Wallace's *Life of Arthur Schopenhauer* (London, Great Writers series, 1890).

LECTURE IX.

THE RISE OF THE DOCTRINE OF EVOLUTION.

I. The return to the outer order initiated by Schopenhauer.

II. The Romantic School in its relation to historical science.

III. The Historical School and the idea of evolution.

IV. The problems of the doctrine of Evolution.

V. Empiricism, skepticism, and philosophy.

VI. The position of Mr. Herbert Spencer.

VII. The Monistic movement.

VIII. Outlook towards a positive creed.

LECTURES X. TO XIII.

GENERAL SUMMARY OF THE POSITIVE LECTURES OF THE COURSE.

I. The positive lectures discuss : (1) The general cosmological problems connected with certain aspects of the doctrine of Evolution (Lecture X.) ; (2) The general doctrine of Idealism as the result of the historical movement that the previous lectures have traced, and as the fundamental doctrine of philosophy (Lecture XI.) ; (3) The application of the doctrine of idealism to the explanation of the fundamental problems of science, in so far as they concern the relations between natural law and moral freedom, and between the inner life and the external world (Lecture XII.) ; and (4) The concluding discussion of the moral and religious issues that centre about the problem of optimism and pessimism (Lecture XIII.).

II. The doctrine of idealism itself has two portions, here called respectively Analytic Idealism (the doctrine with which the name of Berkeley is especially associated), and Synthetic Idealism (or the doctrine of the universal self as the world thinker).

III. It is the province of analytic idealism to show, by a study of the elements whereof all our beliefs consist, that, in case the real world is to be knowable at all, it must be, in its deepest nature, a world of ideas, that is, of facts that can only exist for minds. In other words, the knowable world *is*, only in so far as beings with minds actually *know it to be*.

IV. There remains the alternative, however, that the real world is existent as something essentially unknowable (as, for instance, Mr. Herbert Spencer asserts). This doctrine is considered in Lecture XI. and is there set aside.

V. A final objection to the whole foregoing argument for idealism appears, in case one asserts that, after all, nobody ever does truly *know* any reality beyond his own self, so that our previous discussion is helpless as against a stubborn skepticism, which doubts every possible assertion about reality.

VI. To this it is finally answered that the objection is in one sense as well founded as it is imperfectly understood by those who regard it as a truly skeptical objection. Properly regarded, this very assertion, that beyond the self no truth is knowable, brings to fulfillment our synthetic idealism, by showing us that there is but one self in the world, namely, the Logos or world-mind. The *finite* self knows truth beyond its own limitations, just because it is an organic part of the complete Self.

VII. The doctrine of idealism once thus discussed in its abstractness, the remaining argument depends throughout on the thought that only experience can give us any clue to the contents and the actual world of this world-mind, and that idealism is in no sense a doctrine of illusion, or one which leaves finite selves to their own caprices. Idealism demands (1) That we should interpret experience in terms of the doctrine of the world-mind ; but that (2) We should depend upon experience for the revelation of that truth which, for us finite beings, must remain a fast " outer " truth, just because it is the content of other mind than our own bits of selfhood, and is universally true for all intelligences.

VIII. The problem of the philosophy of experience is, then, to distinguish between what is really " outer " and what is " inner " about our finite experience, that is, between " facts," and our private point of view about the facts.

IX. The world of outer experience is then the world of FACTS. But what is a fact ? It appears to be something, in the first place, that one must *describe*, in some sort of universal terms, in order to get at the truth of it. The principle of ordinary realism is, that you must not be sentimental or otherwise emotional in your account of the truth of things, but rather *exact in your descriptions of what things are*. And this principle has a thoroughly idealistic justification. Not APPRECIATION, then, but DESCRIPTION shall give you outer truth. This is the characteristic presupposition of all natural science. And descriptive thinking is such as seizes on *universal* aspects of things, as opposed to momentary and transient aspects.

X. But what does this presupposition involve ? In the first place, as developed in the work of science, the presupposition involves the assumption that the world is *essentially describable*. But one can only describe, in general terms, the *well-knit*, the *orderly*, that which conforms to LAW. Hence science assumes the universality and rigidity of the laws of nature. And because the most exact descriptions are possible only in case of processes of a mechanical type, such as go on in SPACE and in TIME, science assumes that all things are a part of nature's mechanism. Man too, from this point of view is a thing amongst things, a product of nature, with a nervous mechanism, but without free will.

XI. Yet this point of view is as inadequate as it is partially true. For a closer analysis shows that one can only *describe* what has first been *appreciated*, that there therefore must be universal types of appreciation, and that in consequence IDEALS must be deeper than MECHANISM, so that, in order to be relatively describable, nature must embody purposes, and so be possessed of worth.

XII. With this result we return to our idealism, which is now enriched by the thought that the NATURAL ORDER must also be a MORAL ORDER, that the world of the absolute Self must appear to us as having two aspects, one a temporal, the other an eternal aspect, one of LAW and one of WORTH. Man then turns out to be at once a part of nature's mechanism, and a part of the Moral Order ; at once temporally determined and morally free.

XIII. It is this consideration that in the concluding lecture leads to special suggestions as to the problem of evil.

APPENDIX B.

ON KANT'S TRANSCENDENTAL DEDUCTION OF THE CATEGORIES.

THE statement of the spirit of the Deduction in my text, page 126 sqq., is confessedly a paraphrase of only a few of the central thoughts of this extremely intricate doctrine. A recent editor of the "Kritik," Erich Adickes,[1] has shown, in a fashion which I find on the whole very convincing, that the very difficult deduction of the first edition is in fact a piecemeal combination of a number of independent lines of argument which Kant must have written down at decidedly different times during the years 1772-80.[2] As to what, notwithstanding the variety and the diverse origin of Kant's different trains of thought in this deduction, is the most important outcome of the whole, opinions have of course differed widely. But Falckenberg, in his "Geschichte d. neueren Philosophie,"[3] has stated the general and ultimate

---

[1] *Immanuel Kant's "Kritik der reinen Vernunft," mit einer Einleitung und Anmerkungen, hrsg. v. Dr. Erich Adickes.* Berlin, 1889.

[2] *Op. cit.* page 683, *note:* "Im vorhergehenden habe ich nachzuweisen versucht, dass was man bisher im allgemeinen für eine einheitliche grossartige Konception hielt, vielmehr als eine mosaikartige Zusammenstellung und Verschlingung verschiedener Gedanken aus verschiedenen Zeiten anzusehen ist." The view here carried out by Adickes with very great critical ingenuity, was suggested in a general way as early as 1878 by Benno Erdmann, in his book, *Kant's Kriticismus in der ersten und in der zweiten Auflage der "Kritik der reinen Vernunft,"* on page 25. The notion is to-day rendered an inevitable one by a combination of the internal evidence of the text of the first edition with the evidence as to Kant's method of work presented in Erdmann's edition of the *Reflexionen,* and in Reicke's *Lose Blätter.* As to some of the special results of Adickes, opinions will of course differ.

[3] Pages 268, 269, 272, note 3. "Ein doppeltes ist was nach Kant ausserhalb der Vorstellung des Individuums existiert. (1) Die unbekannten Dinge an sich. . . . (2) Die Erscheinungen selbst, mit ihren erkennbaren immanenten Gesetzen. . . . Die Dinge u. Ereignisse der Erscheinungswelt

result of the Kantian argument as to the reality and the constitution of the world of the objects of our human knowledge, in a
fashion that, as I hold, correctly represents what is, for the fully
developed Kant, the most important thing to be proved in the
Deduction and in its related arguments.   According to Falckenberg, namely, the final view of Kant is that one must distinguish
between my subjective, or momentary consciousness, and my
ueberindividuelles transcendentales Bewusstsein, which is equivalent to *die menschliche Gattungsvernunft*.[1]   This latter it is
which gets its sense data from the unknown *Dinge an sich*,
which applies the categories to these sense-data, which gives the
"laws" to "nature," which constitutes the world of "objects,"
which makes these objects independent of my momentary consciousness, which distinguishes them from the *subjektive Vorstellungen* of the *empirisches Bewusstsein*, and which at the same
time secures a complete agreement between the *subjektive Vorstellungen* and the *eine Erfahrung*, or the universal experience
wherein all sane human beings agree.   This then is the outcome of the completed Kantian doctrine, separated from all the
dross of imperfect and frequently inconsistent comments, expla-
nations, and proofs, with which, especially in the first edition,
he confused it.   This it is which the Deduction is above all to
prove.   This is that notion of the one Self, constitutive of the
one true experience, which Kant introduced to philosophy, and
which only the peculiar limitations of his personal point of view
prevented him from developing further in the direction in which
the post-Kantian thinkers continued the progress of thought.
While, as I have said, this seems to me, in the light of the most
recent results of " Kant-philology," indubitably the true outcome
of Kant's study concerning the nature and objectivity of truth for

existieren sowohl vor als nach meiner Wahrnehmung, sind etwas von meiner subjektiven und momentanen Vorstellung derselben verschiedenes."
" Was ausserhalb meines gegenwärtigen Bewusstseins ist, ist deshalb noch
nicht ausser allem menschlichen Bewusstsein."

[1] *Op. cit.* page 269. *Die Erscheinung*, says Falckenberg, is for Kant
something that stands between the *absolute* object, the *Ding an sich*, and
the *Subjekt, deren gemeinschaftliches Product es ist*, as a sort of *relatives
Ding an sich.* On p. 139 of my text I myself have pointed out how much
Kant's *unity of self-consciousness* tended towards the later interpretation of
Fichte and others.

us men, the fact of course remains that in the " Kritik " there
are very many passages which not only bear but require a less
developed and less consistent, as well as a more subjective interpretation. These passages content themselves with saying that,
while the *Dinge an sich* are and remain unknowable, we, limited to our *Vorstellungen* as we are, actually do apply our categories to the world of the *Vorstellungen*, because it is our nature
to do so ; [1] and so we build up the world of the *Erscheinungen*
by a process of binding *Empfindungen* together through the
instrumentality of the categories, thus creating objects which
are themselves nothing but our own private *Vorstellungen*.
From this less advanced and subjective point of view the dif-
erence between my *empirisches* or *subjektives Bewusstsein* and
my *transcendentales Bewusstsein*, that is, my total self, would
become at best merely a quantitative, not a qualitative difference. For, from *this* point of view, at each moment I apply
my categories. My *Gemüth* is of such a nature that I must do
so. By this application I get, in the world of each moment,
a categorized object. The object thus gained is itself nothing
but my *Vorstellung*, existent here and now. My whole experience consists of the numerous moments of my life ; and since
each moment is categorized, the whole series must be. If one
asks why I have a *right* thus to categorize my moments of experience, the only answer is that my experiences are my own, and
may be treated as my own nature determines. If one asks
why I thus categorize in each moment the experiences thereof,
the only answer is, that otherwise I could not *think* them. If
one still asks why could I not think otherwise, the only reply
is that such is the nature of *my* thought. The product of the
moment thus remains subjective ; there is nothing objective but
the *Dinge an sich*, and they are unknowable.

Kant's doctrine, stated in this *second* and purely subjective
fashion, is the doctrine that many interpreters have found in
his book, as the main outcome of the *Analytik*. If, as I have
stated, it is *not* his final view, why, one may ask, does it often
seem so prominent in the Deduction and elsewhere, especially in

---

[1] Falckenberg recognizes and briefly summarizes these inconsistent passages on p. 270 and 271, *op. cit.*

the first edition? Why, again, if this was the case, and Kant's true doctrine was *not* this second one, did he fail to perceive the consequences of the assumption of the difference between the *empirisches* and the *transcendentales Bewusstsein*? Why did he leave the inconsistent passages standing? Why did he not proceed further on the road towards the later idealism?

These questions can only be answered by a reference to the now so well-known but peculiarly complex conditions of Kant's own development. He took no definite step forwards until he was forced to do so. He unconsciously preferred inconsistency to any dangerous symmetry and dogmatism of statement. His own doctrine of an *objektive Einheit des Bewusstseins*, equivalent substantially to what Falckenberg calls *die menschliche Gattungsvernunft*, was of extremely slow and consequently imperfect growth in his mind. There was a stage of his critical philosophy in which he certainly did *not* yet hold it. He worked with wonderful patience and conscientiousness. He builded far better than he knew. An unconsciousness as to his own consequences remained to the end a peculiar characteristic of his mind and his method. Therefore, although it is indeed our privilege to-day to understand Kant (if one may borrow again his own often quoted words) *besser als er sich selber verstand*, a brief popular summary of his Deduction must limit itself to a comparatively neutral statement of his views.

The present is no place for any lengthy discussion of Kant-philology. I must confine myself, therefore, to a few mere references and statements concerning the real outcome and the gradual development of the Kantian doctrine.

The best recent discussion of the whole matter of the relation of *empirisches* and *transcendentales Bewusstsein* is, so far as I can see, the admirable study by Vaihinger, *Zu Kant's Widerlegung des Idealismus*,[1] a paper wholly free from any effort to read a falsely consistent meaning into Kant's complex doctrine of the nature of "objectivity," but still seriously devoted to demonstrating what was the actual tendency of Kant's growing thought. Vaihinger stands side by side with Benno Erdmann

---

[1] Published in the *Strassburger Abhandlungen zur Philosophie* (Freiburg u. Tübingen, 1884), pp. 87–164.

as one of the two highest authorities at present concerning Kant's growth and teaching. Both these scholars are thorough philologists, cautious, elaborate, patient, and at the same time capable of broad outlooks and wide generalizations. This present paper of Vaihinger's is in his best mood. His principal result is the statement and explanation of the remarkable thesis:[1] "From Kant's fundamental assumptions follows necessarily the existence of a physical world independent of our [subjective] ideas." Surprising as this notion must seem to those who interpret their Kant in a purely subjective fashion, it is not only true that Kant stated this thesis in so many words in the famous Refutation of Idealism, of the second edition, but it is also true, as Vaihinger shows, and as all intelligent readers of the "Kritik" must in the end come to recognize, that this doctrine is, despite all of Kant's hesitancy and inconsistencies, the deepest expression of the genuine spirit of the whole "Kritik." Nor is this principle of the real objectivity of Kant's physical world at all opposed to the other equally fundamental thesis of Kant, namely, the thesis that, as I have stated the matter on page 34 of my text, "Man's nature is the real creator of man's world," so that "it is the inner structure of the human spirit which merely expresses itself in the visible nature about us." For Kant's most important metaphysical deed lies precisely in his distinction of the private or subjective personality proper from the universally human and therefore genuine selfhood, and in his reference of the phenomena and laws of outer nature in space and time to the constructive and objectively categorizing activity of the latter, that is, to the relatively universal Unity of Apperception. Hereby he prepared the way for the further universalizing of this human selfhood into the notion of the World-Self of objective idealism, — the highest and deepest result of all modern philosophy. "I" exist, for Kant, in a twofold sense. I am here and now in the world as this succession of flying moments, this *empirisches Bewusstsein*. But I also exist in another way; I have *objektive Einheit der Apperception*, and to this *objektive Einheit* I, as empirical subject,

---

[1] *Op. cit.* p. 140: "Aus Kant's fundamentalen Annahmen folget nothwendig die Existenz einer von der Vorstellung unabhängigen Körperwelt."

must submit. Now this *objektive Einheit* is something essentially human. "We" possess it together. "*Es gibt nur eine Erfahrung.*" [1] It is the *objektives Subjekt* of this higher experience who is affected somehow by the unknowable *Dinge an sich*, who applies the categories to his *Empfindungen*, and who thus gives laws to nature. For me, as private subject, these laws are outer, these categorized things are objective and unchangeable. Meanwhile, I, as private subject, can still know these outer things because, *although* they are independent of my momentary caprice, they are not independent of my deeper, of my genuinely human personality. I, even in the privacy of the moment, *share* in the nature of the *objektive Einheit*, repeat its activity, reconstruct its original constructions, join my transient to my deeper selfhood, and am thus, by implication, *more* than my purely subjective self.

Vaihinger's philological demonstration of the foregoing interpretation of Kant's outcome will be all the more convincing to the reader in view of the fact that Vaihinger himself is quite free from all suspicion of any predisposition to force an " Hegelian" interpretation, or any absolutely idealistic tendencies upon Kant. His strictly objective discussion of the fact is, therefore, extremely persuasive. I can here only refer to it in this general fashion, and must leave the technically skilled reader to study it for himself.

Apart from Vaihinger's paper, the careful reader of the "Kritik" will often have pondered over such phrases as refer to the difference between the *objektive Einheit* and the *subjektive Einheit der Apperception*, and over such statements as those in the deduction of the principle of causation, in the second Analogy of Experience, where repeatedly the distinction is drawn

[1] In one of the *Reflexionen* of Benno Erdmann's edition, vol. ii. p. 285, Kant himself gives this thought an expression that is almost startingly near the later formulas of constructive idealism. I refer to *Refl.* 989 of Erdmann's arrangement : — " Dinge werden vorgestellt als Erscheinungen, weil es Wesen gibt, die Sinne haben. Dieselben Wesen haben aber auch Verstand, unter dessen Gesetzen die Erscheinungen stehen, sofern ihr mögliches Bewusstsein nothwendig zu einem allgemeingiltigen Bewusstsein stimmen muss, d. i., sie haben eine Natur." Yet this note doubtless belongs to a time before 1781.

between "subjective succession" in *me*, and "objective sequence" *im Gegenstande*. The reader will have observed that over this distinction Kant himself struggles with an almost pathetic earnestness of reflection, that he again and again seeks to give it final articulation, and again and again fails, his clearest assertions being after all those which approach nearest to Vaihinger's formulation as above, and to the wording of the Refutation of Idealism in the second edition. Slowly it will dawn upon the reader that Kant is in the birth-throes of bringing forth a new and wonderful reflective notion, whose correspondent in the spiritual faith of humanity is very old, but whose existence as a reflective doctrine is highly novel. This notion is that of the *objectively subjective self*, — objective to me in my private capacity, but subjectively constructive of the world of the standard human experience, in so far as this is the true or normal self. Kant does not himself fully know what he is producing. He feels the birth throes; he gives forth all sorts of uncertain sounds; he often seems to deny, and in fact does deny his own offspring. But none the less is it truly his offspring.

But the best view of Kant's relation to the new doctrine we get as we read the notes now accessible in Benno Erdmann's "Reflexionen," and in Reicke's "Lose Blätter." Here Kant's endlessly patient efforts to deduce ever afresh the categories, his wavering between a subjective and an objective interpretation of their application, the gradual and for a long time very dim appearance of the *transcendentale Einheit*, Kant's own final obscurity as to whether it really is a conscious and wholly actual or complete self at all, his own unconscious hints at the coming objective idealism, — all these things are depicted in a fashion that makes intelligible to us as never before the piecemeal structure of the text of the "Kritik," the inevitable inconsistencies of that great work, and the beautifully conscientious self-restraint of the patient Kant himself, who stood on the border of the promised land of modern idealism, and could not enter. In the light of all this we understand how the thesis of the Refutation of Idealism in the second edition, a thesis which has been a stone of stumbling and a rock of offense to numberless readers, is in fact one of the most genuinely consistent and

idealistic of Kant's propositions, so that, as Vaihinger declares:[1]
" Die Anerkennung einer von unseren empirischen Vorstellungen unabhängigen Körperwelt im Raume, ist eine nothwendige
und unabweisliche logische Consequenz aus den fundamentalen
Positionen Kants.   Diese Consequenz hat Kant auch gezogen."

Yet, of course, there remains the conflict between the consistent Kant who drew his own final conclusions, and the hesitant Kant whose language is often so narrowly subjective.   The
historical fact of this conflict has led me, in my general statement of Kant's results in my text, to prefer, as I have said, a
more neutral formulation, which points towards the deeper consequences, but does not expressly embody them.

It remains, of course, all the while sure that Kant's *ursprüng-
liche* or *objektive Einheit der Apperception* was at its deepest
never the unity of a true World-Self in any absolute or complete sense.   The argument of the Dialectic forbade Kant to
look for *absolute Vollständigkeit* in any direction.   Kant's
highest principle was at its best, therefore, limited to what
Falckenberg calls a *menschliche Gattungsvernunft*.   This limitation, meanwhile, was precisely what later thinkers were bound
to transcend.

As a fact, therefore, one would give an unhistorical impression of the true Kant, in all his admirable cautiousness of phraseology, if one took his doctrine of the *transcendentales Bewusstsein*, as he stated in his most advanced and suggestive discussions, out of its characteristically obscure environment, and set it
down as not only Kant's final, but as his *whole* doctrine.   Unable in my text to present all the aspects of the argument of the
Deduction, I have therefore deemed it least misleading to lay
stress on the relatively neutral and therefore somewhat equivo-
cal statement of his views.   I have pointed out how he appealed to the *transcendentale Einheit der Apperception;* I
have pointed out how this *Einheit* is, for each of us, our true
self, and how the appeal is constantly made to it by every one
of us, in so far as he is rational.   This notion is so far unquestionably Kantian.   What I have not pointed out, except inciden-
tally, as in the passage on page 139 of the text, is that the *tran-*

[1] *Op. cit.* p. 164.

scendentale Einheit der Apperception is in effect what Falckenberg calls it, a *menschliche Gattungsvernunft*, and is so already,
by implication, identical with the Self of later idealists, a Self
which is only Kant's *transcendentale Einheit* writ large. I
have deliberately left doubtful, in the text, how far Kant's categorized world of physical nature is genuinely objective for the
individual consciousness. The Kant of the final stage of the
critical philosophy knew that this world is objective for the
individual, is no product of his *empirisches Bewusstsein*, is *not*
set in order, nor categorized, nor objectified by his momentary
thinking, but is properly accepted by him as a world of fact.
The Kant of an earlier stage, while the critical philosophy was
forming, did not yet hold this view. The Kant of the final
stage attributed the application of the categories to an *ursprüng-
liche Einheit der Apperception*, with which the *empirisches
Bewusstsein* is simply bound to agree. The Kant of the earlier
stage made no clear distinction between *empirisches* or *subjektives*, and *objektives* or *transcendentales Bewusstsein* at all.
But, by reason of that curious fashion of composition which
Adickes has so well demonstrated in the text of his own edition,
various stages of the growing critical philosophy are represented
in the book as it comes before us. And the actual Kant, by
reason of all the complexity of his marvelous investigation, was
himself never wholly aware of his own inconsistencies, nor of
the extent to which they obscured his true thought.

APPENDIX C.

THE HEGELIAN THEORY OF UNIVERSALS.

In the text, pp. 222–226, I have briefly set forth Hegel's theory as to the reality of the " concrete " universal. The one true Genus, according to him, is the divine *Idee*, *in* which, according to Hegel, every genuine individual reality has its organic place. This theory of the Organic Universal as the *Totalität* containing and determining all the interrelated and true Individuals, which latter have genuine being only as members of the organized body of their Universal, has been shown in the text to be a necessary result of the Hegelian metaphysics of Self-consciousness. The historical importance of the matter justifies here the addition of a few citations and references for the use of the more technical student.

The Hegelian theory of Universals is intended, of course, as the text has also shown, to offer a solution of the ancient question as to the reality of universals. What objective validity have our general concepts ? " They *must* have validity, they *must* correspond to objective truth," so some thinkers have said, " because all science is of the general, and all science is also of the truth." " They *cannot* have, *as* general ideas, objective validity," so other thinkers have said, " because all that truly exists in the world is individual. For there is no such thing as dog in general. There are in the world only individual dogs. The universal, therefore, exists only as realized in the single individual."

In view of this antinomy of traditional discussion, Hegel offers his characteristic solution. The real world is the world of the Absolute Self. His truth is organic, is *allumfassend*, is a *Totalität*, and is, in logical formulation, the universal *Idee*. Now the *Idee* is not an " abstract universal," nor a general idea that is merely *exemplified* by the individual objects of the world.

On the contrary, they are *in it ;* for in it they live and move and have their being ; and it, on the other hand, is in them only in so far forth as they are first in it.   No finite individual, in its isolation, embodies the *Idee*, or corresponds to this true Universal.   Only the organic totality of the finite embodies the Universal.   And in *this* sense the Genus is real.   Hegel's theory, expressed in his own words, is : —

"Alles Wirkliche, in sofern es ein Wahres ist, ist die Idee, und hat seine Wahrheit allein durch und kraft der Idee.   Das einzelne Seyn ist irgend eine Seite der Idee; für dieses bedarf es daher noch anderer Wirklichkeiten, die gleichfalls als besonders für sich bestehende erscheinen ; in ihnen zusammen und in ihrer Beziehung ist allein der Begriff realisirt.   Das Einzelne für sich entspricht seinem Begriffe nicht ; diese Beschränktheit seines Daseyns macht seine Endlichkeit und seinen Untergang aus." [1]

To the illustration of this theory it is worth while, however, to devote some further space.   With his customary manysidedness of treatment, Hegel, of course, endeavors to show how previous theories of the universal have a relative and historical justification as stages on the way to the true insight, and as embodiments of lower and partly untrue forms of the universal forms, which are presented to us in the phenomenal appearances of the finite world.

To these lower forms of the universal, Hegel devotes a patient and extended attention; and we must first briefly refer to the principal one amongst them.

I.

In particular, then, Hegel's theory of Universals cannot be understood without a clear distinction between the lower form of what he calls *Verstandes-Allgemeinheit*, and the true or higher form of the *Vernunft-Allgemeinheit* or *Allgemeinheit des Begriffes*.   The Understanding, according to Hegel, is the first form of the activity of thought.[2]   As such it produces, not *Begriffe* in the proper sense at all, but what Hegel technically

---

[1] The passage here given in full is referred to and in larger part translated in the text, p. 224.

[2] *Encycloped.* § 467, *Werke*, vol. vii. 2, p. 355.

calls *Gedanken*.[1] *Gedanken* of this first sort are the universals
of the understanding, such ideas as *man* or *house* or *animal*.
These are often called *Begriffe*, but wrongly.[2] On this stage
they are the product of analysis and abstraction ; and abstraction is as necessary in the beginning of our thinking as it is
untrue from the higher point of view. It is the very business
of philosophy to transform *Gedanken* into *Begriffe*.[3] The *Gedanke*, as it is first reached, embodies the universal qualities or
characteristics present in each of many individuals. Out of
such individuals it thus makes an abstractly defined class or
Gattung. This class, or genus of the understanding, is related
to the sub-classes and individuals that fall within its *Umfang* in
the fashion that the Aristotelian logic originally defined.[4] The
Gattung, namely, has species or *Arten*, which as subordinate
classes are *subsumed* under it, forming each a part of its *Umfang*, while the individuals are in their turn subsumed under the
various *Arten*. Both *Gattung* and *Art*, for this stage of thinking,
express only *das Gemeinsame* found in each and all of many
individuals. In experience, meanwhile, only the individuals can
be shown, not the *Gattung*. For the *Gattung* is not yet the
Begriff, which will turn out to be much more than *ein Gemeinschaftliches*. This *Gattung* of the understanding has no
Existenz. For it is thus far, on its subjective side, the *Gedanke*
of the observer, which, being formal, does not explain either

---

[1] *Phänomenol., Werke*, vol. ii. pp. 24–25.

[2] *Encyclop., Werke*, vol. vi. p. 324.

[3] *Phänomenol., Werke*, vol. ii. p. 26. On the definition of the *Verstand*,
see, also, *Werke*, vol. vii. 2, p. 356. The understanding is there "formal."
Its activity depends upon *Abstrahiren*. " Trennt er das Zufällige vom Wesentlichen ab, so ist er durchaus in seinem Rechte und erscheint als Das
was er in Wahrheit seyn soll." *Das Wesentliche*, so abstracted, the understanding uses to define its universals.

[4] "Aristoteles," says Hegel, in his *Gesch. d. Philos., Werke*, vol. xiv. p.
368, " ist der Urheber der *verständigen* Logik ; ihre Formen betreffen nur
das Verhältniss von Endlichen zu einander, und in ihnen kann das Wahre
nicht gefasst werden." This observation occurs in connection with a discussion of the Aristotelian theory of universals, which is there said to involve the method used "in den endlichen Wissenschaften," namely, "*das
Subsumiren des Besondern unter das Allgemeine.*" It is just this sort of
universality and this kind of subsumption that Hegel's theory is intended
to supersede.

the content of the individual thing, or the totality of the actual
relations of this individual thing to others in the real world.[1]
Speaking in objective terms we can indeed already say that the
Gedanke corresponds to an *allgemeine Natur*, present as *das
Wesentliche*, or as *die bestimmte Wesentlichkeit* of the finite individuals that belong to the *Gattung*. For the thoughts even of
the understanding have a lower sort of truth. Whatever is in
the world is the embodiment of thought; and in so far as the
Gedanken of the understanding are also the product of thought,
they do correspond to the inner nature of things. Only, the
universals of the understanding tell but a portion of the real
truth about the objects present in experience. And in just so
far these universals are untrue. The *Begriff*, or the truly objective thought of the whole nature of things, will be " mehr als nur
die Angabe der wesentlichen Bestimmtheiten, d. i., der Ver-
standesbestimmungen einer Sache." [2] The universal of the
understanding, applying to a nature which is only exemplified
by each individual, and which exists nowhere but in such individual examples (as *animality* exists only in individual *animals*), tells us nothing about the interrelationship of the individuals themselves, gives us therefore no *Einheit des Begriffes*.

Of this universal of the understanding Hegel gives us many
accounts. No intelligent student of his works can confound *this*
sort of universality with the true *Vernunft-Allgemeinheit*, whose
exposition forms Hegel's peculiar contribution to the theory of
universals. To sum up so far: The universal of the under-

---

[1] It is of this stage of thought that Hegel is speaking when, in the *Encyclop.*, *Werke*, vol. vi. p. 46, he says : " Das Thier als solches ist nicht zu
zeigen, sondern immer nur ein Bestimmtes. Das Thier existirt nicht, sondern ist die allgemeine Natur der einzelnen Thiere." *Thier* is, so far, no
Begriff, no true universal at all. And *Existenz*, with its verb *existiren*,
has a special meaning in Hegel's logic. The *Begriff*, when we get to it,
will have a higher sort of reality, namely, what Hegel calls *Objektivität*,
something much more than bare *Existenz*.

[2] *Logik*, *Werke*, vol. iii. p. 274. Compare *Encyclop.*, *Werke*, vol. vi. p.
65, where the business of the understanding in grasping the *wesentlichen
Inhalt* of finite things, in classifying abstractly, and in applying predicates
accordingly, is further illustrated. The technical phrases *wesentliche Bestimmtheit*, *bestimmte Wesentlichkeit*, etc., refer, then, only to universality as
conceived by the understanding.

standing is the *first* discovery of our thought when the latter
is applied to things. Of this universal it was that Aristotle's
logic gave the traditional theory. Aristotle himself, to be sure,
in his *metaphysical* theory, really transcended the limitations of
his *logical* theory, and implied the existence of a deeper and
truer sort of universality in the nature of things. But he did
this haltingly.[1] His metaphysical instinct is truer than his logic.
He uses the higher universal, but has a logical theory only of
the lower. And as for this lower, it appears to the understanding as objectively existent only *in each individual*, as constituting the essence or *wesentliche Bestimmtheit* thereof. Subjectively it is represented by the *Gedanke*, which is the thought of
some abstractly defined class-essence. And such class-essences
appear to the understanding to have no *Existenz* as such, apart
from the individuals in which they are exemplified. This is
why we are accustomed to say, from the point of view of ordinary thought, that general ideas do not represent concrete realities, and that only the individual is real.

II.

Principal Caird, in his "Philosophy of Religion,"[2] after describing the foregoing lower sort of universality, and pointing
out its inadequacy to the expression of the truth of the real
world, proceeds, in a confessedly Hegelian spirit, to set forth
the nature of the *Vernunft-Allgemeinheit*, and its application to
the comprehension of the relations of God and the world, as
follows : —

" But thought is capable of another and deeper movement.
It can rise to a universality which is not foreign to, but the very
inward nature of things in themselves, not the universal of an
abstraction from the particular and different, but the unity
which is immanent in them and finds in them its own necessary

---

[1] *Gesch. d. Phil., Werke*, vol. xiv. p. 283 : " Hat Aristoteles aber auch . . .
die allgemeine Idee nicht logisch herausgehoben, (denn sonst wäre seine
sogenannt Logik, die etwas Anderes ist, für die Methode als der eine Begriff
in Allem zu erkennen), so erscheint doch andererseits bei Aristoteles die
Idee Gottes, selbst auch als ein Besonderes an ihrer Stelle neben den Andern,
obzwar sie alle Wahrheit ist."

[2] Page 229, sqq.

expression; not an arbitrary invention of the observing and classifying mind, . . . but an idea which expresses the inner dialectic, the movement or process towards unity, which exists in and constitutes the being of the objects themselves. This deeper and truer universality is that which may be designated *ideal or organic universality.* The idea of a living organism . . . is not a common element which can be got at by abstraction and generalization, by taking the various parts and members, stripping away their differences, and forming a notion of that which they have in common. That in which they differ is rather just that out of which their unity arises and in which is the very life and being of the organism; that which they have in common they have, not as members of a living organism, but as dead matter, and what you have to abstract in order to get it is the very life itself. Moreover, the universal, in this case, is not last but first. We do not reach it by first thinking the particulars, but conversely, we get at the true notions of the particulars only through the universal. What the parts or members of an organism are, — their form, place, structure, proportion, functions, relations, their whole nature and being, is determined by the idea of the organism which they are to compose. It is it which produces them, not they it. In it lies their reason and ground. They are its manifestations or specifications. It realizes itself in them, fulfills itself in their diversity and harmony. . . . You cannot determine the particular member or organ save by reference to that which is its limit or negation. It does not exist in and by itself, but in and through what is other than itself, — through the other members and organs which are at once outside of and within it, beyond it, and yet part and portion of its being. . . . Here, then, we have a kind of universality which is altogether different from the barren and formal universality of generalization, and the indication of a movement of thought corresponding to an inner relation of things which the abstracting, generalizing understanding is altogether inadequate to grasp."

Applying the notion of universality thus reached to the relations of our own thought to the reality about which we think, Principal Caird next proceeds, on p. 233, sqq., to "a brief consideration of the relation of Nature to Finite Mind." He dwells upon the well-known opposition between matter and mind, which, for the understanding, are two separate and opposed realities. He states the familiar problem as to how mind can know the natural order outside of our minds, shows that this problem is the same in principle with the problem about the relation between finite mind and God, and suggests, as a solution of both problems, the thought, the "Nature," the finite mind, and God or the infinite mind, are not discordant or irreconcilable ideas, but ideas which belong to one organic whole or system of knowledge. After devoting considerable space to the illustration of this view, and dwelling further on the "principle of Organic Unity" (p. 238), he points out (p. 239) that the problem of knowledge is to be solved on the basis of the theory of the organic universal itself. "It is but a spurious idealism which makes the world without only the illusory creation of the individual mind. Rather the truth is that the individual mind must renounce its own isolated independence, must cease to assert itself, must lose itself in the object, before it can attain to any true knowledge of Nature. . . . In order, therefore, to attain to the universal life of reason that is in the world, it is an indispensable condition that I renounce my own individuality, my particular thought and opinion, and find the true realization of my own reason in that absolute reason or truth which Nature manifests. . . . The principle in fine that solves the difference between Nature and Finite Mind is, that their isolated reality and exclusiveness is a figment, and that the organic life of reason is the truth or reality of both."

On page 240, Principal Caird continues his discussion by applying the same principle to "the solution of the higher problem of Religion, or of the relation of the Finite Mind to God." "Here, too, it will be seen that the understanding, which clings to the hard independent identity of either side . . . renders any true solution impossible. . . . A true solution can be reached only by apprehending the Divine and the Human, the Infinite and the Finite, as the moments or members of an organic whole, in which both exist, at once in their distinction and their unity." Principal Caird then gives as a further illustration of the true theory of universals, and as an aid in comprehending the organic unity first mentioned, "the relation of the individual to other individuals" in the "case of our social relations." "The ordinary conception of self-identity isolates the individual from his fellow-men." But this, says our author, is wrong. "The abstract individual is not truly man, but only a fragment of humanity, a being as devoid of the moral and spiritual elements which are of the essence of the man's life, as the amputated limb of participation in the vital existence of the organism. The social relations are a necessary part of the being of the individual. . . . It is not by supposing in the first place a number of individual human beings, each complete in himself, and then combining these individuals, that we reach the idea of the Family; rather must we first think the Family in order to know the individual. . . . Here, as elsewhere, the universal is the *prius* of the particular. Yet the universal must not be conceived as having any reality apart from the particulars, any more than the body apart from its members. The true idea is reached only by holding both together in that higher unity which at once comprehends and transcends them, that organic unity, whether of the Family or the State, which is the living integration of the individual members which compose it." "In the same fashion," continues Principal Caird, "the true Infinite is not the negation of the Finite, but that which is the organic unity of the Infinite and Finite."

III.

The foregoing quotations from Principal Caird will serve, both to give an excellent summary of certain aspects of the Hegelian theory of universals, and to show that the theory itself is no novelty to English readers.[1] It has become a commonplace of discussion for one whole school of neo-Hegelians.

To pass, however, to Hegel's own account of the matter. "Thought," says Hegel, "is in the first place thought after the fashion of the understanding; but thought does not remain on this stage, and the *Begriff* is not a mere *Verstandesbestim-*

---

[1] Cf. also Professor Edward Caird's *Social Philosophy of Auguste Comte,* p. 199: "The universal of science and philosophy is . . . not merely a generic name, *under* which things are brought together, but a principle which unites them and determines their relation to each other."

mung." [1]   The higher movement of the *Vernunft* depends on the well-known *Dialektik* of thought, which takes the abstract facts and qualities that the understanding has sundered, the *Bestimmungen*, or *Seiten*, or *Individuen* of the finite world, and discovers " die Einheit der Bestimmungen in ihrer Entgegensetzung." [2]   This *Dialektik* has a "positive result," namely, the discovery of *das Vernünftige*, which is not merely *ein Abstraktes*, but "zugleich ein Konkretes,[3] weil es nicht einfache, formelle Einheit, sondern Einheit unterschiedener Bestimmungen ist.   Mit blossen Abstraktionen oder formellen Gedanken hat es darum überhaupt die Philosophie ganz und gar nicht zu thun, sondern allein mit konkreten Gedanken."

The *Allgemeinheit des Verstandes* is, therefore, transformed into the *Begriff* whenever *two* related processes have been carried out : (1) When the formal abstractions or *wesentliche Bestimmungen*, which the understanding separates from one another, and opposes to one another, — such abstractions as *right* and *left*, *inner* and *outer*, *substance* and *accident*, — have been united once more by organic ties, and shown to be interrelated and inseparable [4] ; and (2) When, by the same means, the things of the finite world have been shown to be members of one organic total.   The intimate relationship of these two processes for Hegel is one of the prominent characteristics of his whole method.   *Das Wahre ist konkret* means for him equally, "The truth is an organic union of interrelated aspects, characters, qualities," and "The truth is the Universal in which the particulars and individuals are organically joined." [5]   For example,

---

[1] *Encycl., Werke*, vol. vi. p. 147.   The following pages contain a repetition of the account given above of the nature and limitations of the *Verstandes-Allgemeinheit*.

[2] *Loc. cit.*, p. 157.

[3] On the Hegelian use of *konkret*, see the excellent definition of Falckenberg's *Gesch. d. neueren Philosophie*, p. 478 : "The concrete *Begriff* of Hegel is an Universal that has the Particular *in itself*, and that produces its own particulars (*sich besondert*)."

[4] *Logik, Werke*, vol. iv. pp. 63, 64.

[5] "Das einzelne Seyn ist irgend eine Seite der Idee," Hegel has said in the passage quoted above.   In various passages he identifies *Seite* with *Bestimmung;* so, for instance, in the *Religionsphilosophie, Werke*, vol. xii. p. 422, where he speaks of the *Zusammenhang zweier Seiten oder Bestimmungen*.   From these and many other passages it easily becomes evident

in the case of any man such as Caius or Titus, Hegel says : [1]
" Was der einzelne Mensch im Besonderen ist, das ist er nur in
sofern, als er vor allen Dingen Mensch als solcher ist und im
Allgemeinen ist, und diess Allgemeine ist nicht nur etwas ausser
und neben andern abstrakten Qualitäten . . . sondern vielmehr das alles Besondere Durchdringende und in sich Beschlies-
sende." Moreover, as he tells us, *das Allgemeine* is here, in
case of humanity, and in its deepest truth, something more than
all men.[2] It does more than include in an indifferent way the
individuals. It is for them all not " bloss etwas *denselben
Gemeinschaftliches*," it is their *Grund*, their *Boden*, their *Substanz*. Now here is humanity regarded as something universal
and *konkret*. As such it is at once *all men*, and it is more. It
is something pervading and determining all the characteristics
of each man, and binding together all his *besondere Qualitäten*.
It is thus *konkret* in two senses, namely, in so far as in it all
men are together, and in so far as through it all *Qualitäten* of
each man are united. Yet not even in this passage is Hegel
expounding the completely organic universal, but only a form on
the way towards the realization of it. It will be noticed, however, that here he distinctly declares that the individual is *im
Allgemeinen*, " *in the Universal*," which is, *therefore*, the inclusive *Substanz* of the individuals.

The notion of the *Vernunft-Allgemeinheit* thus introduced receives a lengthy development in the " Logik." The way for this
Allgemeinheit des Begriffes is prepared, in the larger " Logik,"
by elaborate discussions under the head of *Wesen* (that is, in Part
Second of the work). In the second division of *Wesen*, in dis-

that for Hegel both abstract *characters* and abstract *individuals* are to be
treated alike, in so far as they have their truth only in the organic whole
of which they are elements. Compare once more Falckenberg's definition
of Hegel's use of " concrete," as given above. That the Individual is contained *in* the Universal is also expressly asserted by Hegel (*Werke*, vol. vi.
p. 323 ; compare p. 316).

[1] *Encyclop.*, *Werke*, vol. vi. p. 340.

[2] *Id.*, p. 339. In case of the form of logical judgment which Hegel is
discussing in the passage now cited, he is laying special stress upon the fact
that here already, although the true *Vernunft-Allgemeinheit* has not been
fully reached, the individual stands in relation to others, and is not conceived by himself, or apart from his relations.

cussing the *Erscheinung*, Hegel shows, in a fashion which he
was elsewhere fond of dwelling upon, and illustrating, that the
qualities or *Eigenschaften* of every finite thing are its *Weisen
des Verhaltens zu Andern ;* [1] so that all the things of the finite
world are what they are by virtue of their relations to one another.   They are in *Wechselwirkung,*[2] and it is their nature to
be so.   Hence the world of these finite things is a world of a
Gesetz, or all-embracing law, of which the things and qualities
are the *appearance,* while this *Gesetz* or *Reich der Gesetze* is a
self-determined *Totalität.*   As the law at the basis of the finite
world is, however, *fully* expressed, but *only* expressed in the
phenomena themselves, the result here is an *Einheit des Innern
und des Aeussern* wherein, as Hegel tells us, the *Begriff* is
already present in a latent form ; for our world of finite things
is thus *a totality of interrelated individuals that embody a
law and make it manifest.*   It is, however, just this *Totalität*
that *im Begriffe als solchem* appears as *das Allgemeine.*[8]   In
the world of *Wesen* this unity of inner and outer is so far called
die Wirklichkeit.[4]   The true nature of *Wirklichkeit* appears
in the exposition of the category of *Substanz* at the end of
Wesen, where finally *die absolute Substanz,* or general nature
of things, appears as a " Totality " that is as a " simple Whole,"
which determines itself " and contains its self-determinations in
itself."   This Totality is *das Allgemeine,* which, together with
its correlated categories, *das Einzelne* and *das Besondere,* makes
up the *Begriff,* to which Hegel herewith passes.

The intricate exposition of the *Begriff,* in the third part of
the " Logik," is rendered somewhat clearer by the lecture notes
which were added by Hegel's editors to the corresponding paragraphs of the " Encyklopädie."   From these one or two quotations have been made in the text.   It is perhaps enough to point
out here that one best and most easily sees what the *Begriff* is
meant to be if one passes forthwith to the place where its nature
is " writ large " in the world of *Objektivität,*[5] into which it

---

[1] *Logik, Werke,* vol. iv. p. 125.

[2] *Id.,* p. 128.

[8] *Logik, Werke,* vol. iv. p. 174.

[4] *Id.,* p. 178.   *Die Wirklichkeit* appears first as *das Absolute,* which corresponds (*loc. cit.* pp. 187–190) to Spinoza's *Substance.*

[5] *Logik, Werke,* vol. v., pp. 167–228 ; *Encyclop., Werke,* vol. vi. pp. 365–384.

" passes over," and in which it expresses itself. Here one has a repetition on a higher stage of what took place in *Wesen.* Once more one deals with a world of objects, only now they are known to embody the *Begriff*, whose true universality they show in three ascending phases, *mechanism, chemism*, and *teleology.* The world of mechanism, or, as one might say, the world at " Machine," is the world whose parts have indeed interrelationships, but only those of abstract law. In the world of " affinities " or of " Chemism," the individuals exist only as interrelated, and only by virtue of their affinities and the results of these. In the still truer and more inclusive world of " Teleology," or, as one might say, in the world as " Organism," the interrelatedness of the individual objects and their coöperation as instruments of one immanent purpose, which is their true universal, prepares the way for that complete union of *Begriff* and *Objekt* which is given us in the *Idee.* The *Idee*, in fact, is the world as " Person " so far as the categories of the " Logik " enable the notion of personality to be introduced. The full notion of personality is developed, later in the system, in the philosophy of spirit.

These Hegelian formulations of the theory of universals have no doubt many antiquated features. Their presence and importance in the system is indubitable. As pointed out in my text, the most interesting expressions of the whole doctrine occur in Hegel's ethical and theological works. A full collection of passages is impossible in the present space. A few more may yet be given. It is an explicit and deliberate application of the theory of the organic universal when Hegel says, in his " Rechtsphilosophie," that the individual man is no person " ohne Relation zu anderen Personen." [1] This notion, closely related to that of the *Allgemeinheit des Bewusstseins* mentioned in the text, appears very prominently in the whole structure of the " Rechtsphilosophie." It is another application of this same theory when Hegel says, in the " Religionsphilosophie," in describing the life of the church, that the subjective religious consciousness has to be realized by *eine Vielheit von Subjekten und Individuen*, but that, since this consciousness is to be *universal* in the deeper

---

[1] *Werke*, vol. viii., p. 417. Cf. p. 110 : " Es ist durch die Vernunft ebenso nothwendig dass die Menschen in Vertrags-Verhältnisse eingehen als dass sie Eigenthum besitzen."

sense, " so ist die Vielheit der Individuen durchaus zu setzen als
nur ein Schein, und eben dieses, dass sie sich selbst als diesen
Schein setzt, ist die Einheit des Glaubens. . . . Das ist die
Liebe der Gemeinde, die aus vielen Subjekten zu bestehen
scheint, welche Vielheit aber nur ein Schein ist." [1] " Many members," then, but only one body, one Lord, one faith. Further
on Hegel discusses in the same spirit the relation of the individuals to their universal as illustrated by the relation of the faithful to the person of Christ. The application of the same theory
of universals to the general problem of the relation of God to
the world appears at the close of the " Encyklopädie." The "Naturphilosophie" is also full of applications : so, for instance, the
explanation of the relations of the sexes, and of the struggle of
the various species of animals for existence, as in both cases due
to the fact that the universal can nowhere completely realize itself
in any one individual, or in any group of individuals. [2] Since, according to Hegel, the *Idee* cannot come to *full* expression in outer
nature, the Universal is in all these cases displayed to us only
imperfectly, as an endless series of efforts towards the completely
organic, which is perfectly realized only in the world as spirit.

To return, finally, for one moment, to the logical theory itself : It is the immanently organic nature of the true universal
that in the doctrine of the *subjektiven Begriff* forces the *Begriff*
to develop its various *Seiten* in the *Urtheil*, since only by virtue of the relation of apparently divided, but really and organically inseparable, aspects or individuals can any universality
be realized. Of *Urtheile* the highest sort, before the class in
the *Urtheile des Begriffes* proper is reached, is the *disjunctive judgments*, just because they represent the *Unterschiede*
or *Besonderungen* of their subjects as in every case an interrelated group of species or of individuals. [3] For " das Allgemeine ist das Einfache welches ebensosehr das Reichste in sich

[1] *Werke*, vol. xii., pp. 313, 314. The important thing here is that Hegel
expressly regards this as an application of his logical theory. Compare
p. 309.
    [2] *Werke*, vol. vii., 1, pp. 640, 641, 643, 645, 648, 649. In particular, p.
648, " Die Gattung existirt in einer Reihe von einzelnen Lebendigen," —
not in any single individual.
    [3] *Werke*, vol. v., pp. 102–107.

selbst ist," [1] and this wealth of the universal gets *unfolded* in the disjunctive judgment. The universal is *die Negativität überhaupt*; [2] and this self-differentiation gets an expression in the disjunctive judgment. It is the *Begriff* itself that *sich disjungirt* in the true disjunctive judgment. [3] But the genuine *Urtheil des Begriffes* is something still higher, since not only the fact, but the inner necessity and self-determination of this differentiation must be made evident, a thing which can only be done by forms of judgment that carry us on to the *Schluss*. [4] The *Schluss* passes through a number of successive forms whose highest is the *disjunctive conclusion*, [5] wherein once more the reason for the result reached by the conclusion lies in the relation of one included member or *Moment* of some universal to the universal itself, and to the other members or *Momente* of the same organic and self-differentiated whole. With the disjunctive conclusion the transition is made to the world of *Objektivität*, where, as before shown, the universal is realized in explicitly organic form as the totality of the related individuals or *Momente*, whose perfection and truth is the *Idee*.

One word still in conclusion as to the relation of the lower or Aristotelian form of the "universal of the understanding," to Hegel's own "universal of the reason." Hegel himself says: [6] "The logic of the mere understanding is contained in the logic of reason, and can be made at once therefrom. Nothing is needed for this purpose but the omission from the latter of the dialectical and so distinctively rational element." It is well to observe that, as Hegel himself has confessed, in one of his letters to Niethammer, [7] it was according to this method that he felt himself obliged to proceed in the exposition of his logic,

[1] *Id.*, p. 36.

[2] *Id.*, p. 39. Readers of the discussion of *Negativität* in the text will see the significance of this consideration.

[3] *Id.*, p. 105.   [4] *Id.*, p. 115, sqq.

[5] *Id.*, p. 162, sqq.

[6] *Encyclop.*, *Werke*, vol. vi. p. 158 : "In der spekulativen Logik ist die blosse Verstandes-Logik enthalten, und kann aus jener sogleich gemacht werden ; es bedarf dazu Nichts als daraus das Dialektische und Vernünftige wegzulassen."

[7] See the recently issued vol. xix. of the *Werke*, edited by Karl Hegel (Leipzig, 1887), part i. p. 340.

which he undertook for the boys in the Nürnberg gymnasium. Only *die verständige Logik*, he tells Niethammer, is suited to gymnasial instruction. Youth at this time needs purely *positiven Inhalt* and is not ripe for *das Spekulative*. The dialectical can be only here and there suggested, and never correctly presented in such elementary work. Hence it happens that in the so-called *Propaedeutik*, which Rosenkranz edited from Hegel's posthumous MSS and published in 1840 as the eighteenth volume of the "Werke," and which contains the gist of Hegel's instruction to the boys at Nürnberg, one finds but few hints of the Hegelian theory of Universals. If this little volume, in fact, were our only record of Hegel, all his peculiar theories, whether as to Idealism in general or as to the nature of Self-consciousness, or as to Universals, would remain almost wholly unknown to us ; and such theories must not be sought there, but in Hegel's own deliberate expressions of them, and above all in the works which he himself published during his life.

INDEX.

A CATALOGUE OF
SELECTED DOVER BOOKS
IN ALL FIELDS OF INTEREST

A CATALOGUE OF SELECTED DOVER
BOOKS IN ALL FIELDS OF INTEREST

RACKHAM'S COLOR ILLUSTRATIONS FOR WAGNER'S RING. Rackham's finest mature work—all 64 full-color watercolors in a faithful and lush interpretation of the *Ring*. Full-sized plates on coated stock of the paintings used by opera companies for authentic staging of Wagner. Captions aid in following complete Ring cycle. Introduction. 64 illustrations plus vignettes. 72pp. 8⅝ x 11¼. 23779-6 Pa. $6.00

CONTEMPORARY POLISH POSTERS IN FULL COLOR, edited by Joseph Czestochowski. 46 full-color examples of brilliant school of Polish graphic design, selected from world's first museum (near Warsaw) dedicated to poster art. Posters on circuses, films, plays, concerts all show cosmopolitan influences, free imagination. Introduction. 48pp. 9⅜ x 12¼. 23780-X Pa. $6.00

GRAPHIC WORKS OF EDVARD MUNCH, Edvard Munch. 90 haunting, evocative prints by first major Expressionist artist and one of the greatest graphic artists of his time: *The Scream, Anxiety, Death Chamber, The Kiss, Madonna,* etc. Introduction by Alfred Werner. 90pp. 9 x 12. 23765-6 Pa. $5.00

THE GOLDEN AGE OF THE POSTER, Hayward and Blanche Cirker. 70 extraordinary posters in full colors, from Maitres de l'Affiche, Mucha, Lautrec, Bradley, Cheret, Beardsley, many others. Total of 78pp. 9⅜ x 12¼. 22753-7 Pa. $5.95

THE NOTEBOOKS OF LEONARDO DA VINCI, edited by J. P. Richter. Extracts from manuscripts reveal great genius; on painting, sculpture, anatomy, sciences, geography, etc. Both Italian and English. 186 ms. pages reproduced, plus 500 additional drawings, including studies for *Last Supper,* Sforza monument, etc. 860pp. 7⅞ x 10¾. (Available in U.S. only) 22572-0, 22573-9 Pa., Two-vol. set $15.90

THE CODEX NUTTALL, as first edited by Zelia Nuttall. Only inexpensive edition, in full color, of a pre-Columbian Mexican (Mixtec) book. 88 color plates show kings, gods, heroes, temples, sacrifices. New explanatory, historical introduction by Arthur G. Miller. 96pp. 11⅜ x 8½. (Available in U.S. only) 23168-2 Pa. $7.95

UNE SEMAINE DE BONTÉ, A SURREALISTIC NOVEL IN COLLAGE, Max Ernst. Masterpiece created out of 19th-century periodical illustrations, explores worlds of terror and surprise. Some consider this Ernst's greatest work. 208pp. 8⅛ x 11. 23252-2 Pa. $6.00

DRAWINGS OF WILLIAM BLAKE, William Blake. 92 plates from Book of Job, *Divine Comedy, Paradise Lost*, visionary heads, mythological figures, Laocoon, etc. Selection, introduction, commentary by Sir Geoffrey Keynes. 178pp. 8⅛ x 11.   22303-5 Pa. $4.00

ENGRAVINGS OF HOGARTH, William Hogarth. 101 of Hogarth's greatest works: *Rake's Progress, Harlot's Progress, Illustrations for Hudibras, Before and After, Beer Street and Gin Lane*, many more. Full commentary. 256pp. 11 x 13¾.   22479-1 Pa. $12.95

DAUMIER: 120 GREAT LITHOGRAPHS, Honore Daumier. Wide-ranging collection of lithographs by the greatest caricaturist of the 19th century. Concentrates on eternally popular series on lawyers, on married life, on liberated women, etc. Selection, introduction, and notes on plates by Charles F. Ramus. Total of 158pp. 9⅜ x 12¼.   23512-2 Pa. $6.00

DRAWINGS OF MUCHA, Alphonse Maria Mucha. Work reveals drafts-man of highest caliber: studies for famous posters and paintings, render-ings for book illustrations and ads, etc. 70 works, 9 in color; including 6 items not drawings. Introduction. List of illustrations. 72pp. 9⅜ x 12¼. (Available in U.S. only)   23672-2 Pa. $4.00

GIOVANNI BATTISTA PIRANESI: DRAWINGS IN THE PIERPONT MORGAN LIBRARY, Giovanni Battista Piranesi. For first time ever all of Morgan Library's collection, world's largest. 167 illustrations of rare Piranesi drawings—archeological, architectural, decorative and visionary. Essay, detailed list of drawings, chronology, captions. Edited by Felice Stampfle. 144pp. 9⅜ x 12¼.   23714-1 Pa. $7.50

NEW YORK ETCHINGS (1905-1949), John Sloan. All of important American artist's N.Y. life etchings. 67 works include some of his best art; also lively historical record—Greenwich Village, tenement scenes. Edited by Sloan's widow. Introduction and captions. 79pp. 8⅜ x 11¼.
                                                23651-X Pa. $4.00

CHINESE PAINTING AND CALLIGRAPHY: A PICTORIAL SURVEY, Wan-go Weng. 69 fine examples from John M. Crawford's matchless private collection: landscapes, birds, flowers, human figures, etc., plus calligraphy. Every basic form included: hanging scrolls, handscrolls, album leaves, fans, etc. 109 illustrations. Introduction. Captions. 192pp. 8⅞ x 11¾.
                                                23707-9 Pa. $7.95

DRAWINGS OF REMBRANDT, edited by Seymour Slive. Updated Lipp-mann, Hofstede de Groot edition, with definitive scholarly apparatus. All portraits, biblical sketches, landscapes, nudes, Oriental figures, classical studies, together with selection of work by followers. 550 illustrations. Total of 630pp. 9⅛ x 12¼. 21485-0, 21486-9 Pa., Two-vol. set $15.00

THE DISASTERS OF WAR, Francisco Goya. 83 etchings record horrors of Napoleonic wars in Spain and war in general. Reprint of 1st edition, plus 3 additional plates. Introduction by Philip Hofer. 97pp. 9⅜ x 8¼.
                                                21872-4 Pa. $4.00

THE EARLY WORK OF AUBREY BEARDSLEY, Aubrey Beardsley. 157 plates, 2 in color: *Manon Lescaut, Madame Bovary, Morte Darthur, Salome,* other. Introduction by H. Marillier. 182pp. 8⅛ x 11. 21816-3 Pa. $4.50

THE LATER WORK OF AUBREY BEARDSLEY, Aubrey Beardsley. Exotic masterpieces of full maturity: *Venus and Tannhauser, Lysistrata, Rape of the Lock, Volpone,* Savoy material, etc. 174 plates, 2 in color. 186pp. 8⅛ x 11. 21817-1 Pa. $5.95

THOMAS NAST'S CHRISTMAS DRAWINGS, Thomas Nast. Almost all Christmas drawings by creator of image of Santa Claus as we know it, and one of America's foremost illustrators and political cartoonists. 66 illustrations. 3 illustrations in color on covers. 96pp. 8⅜ x 11¼. 23660-9 Pa. $3.50

THE DORÉ ILLUSTRATIONS FOR DANTE'S DIVINE COMEDY, Gustave Doré. All 135 plates from Inferno, Purgatory, Paradise; fantastic tortures, infernal landscapes, celestial wonders. Each plate with appropriate (translated) verses. 141pp. 9 x 12. 23231-X Pa. $4.50

DORÉ'S ILLUSTRATIONS FOR RABELAIS, Gustave Doré. 252 striking illustrations of *Gargantua and Pantagruel* books by foremost 19th-century illustrator. Including 60 plates, 192 delightful smaller illustrations. 153pp. 9 x 12. 23656-0 Pa. $5.00

LONDON: A PILGRIMAGE, Gustave Doré, Blanchard Jerrold. Squalor, riches, misery, beauty of mid-Victorian metropolis; 55 wonderful plates, 125 other illustrations, full social, cultural text by Jerrold. 191pp. of text. 9⅜ x 12¼. 22306-X Pa. $7.00

THE RIME OF THE ANCIENT MARINER, Gustave Doré, S. T. Coleridge. Dore's finest work, 34 plates capture moods, subtleties of poem. Full text. Introduction by Millicent Rose. 77pp. 9¼ x 12. 22305-1 Pa. $3.50

THE DORE BIBLE ILLUSTRATIONS, Gustave Doré. All wonderful, detailed plates: Adam and Eve, Flood, Babylon, Life of Jesus, etc. Brief King James text with each plate. Introduction by Millicent Rose. 241 plates. 241pp. 9 x 12. 23004-X Pa. $6.00

THE COMPLETE ENGRAVINGS, ETCHINGS AND DRYPOINTS OF ALBRECHT DURER. "Knight, Death and Devil"; "Melencolia," and more—all Dürer's known works in all three media, including 6 works formerly attributed to him. 120 plates. 235pp. 8⅜ x 11¼. 22851-7 Pa. $6.50

MECHANICK EXERCISES ON THE WHOLE ART OF PRINTING, Joseph Moxon. First complete book (1683-4) ever written about typography, a compendium of everything known about printing at the latter part of 17th century. Reprint of 2nd (1962) Oxford Univ. Press edition. 74 illustrations. Total of 550pp. 6⅛ x 9¼. 23617-X Pa. $7.95

THE COMPLETE WOODCUTS OF ALBRECHT DURER, edited by Dr. W. Kurth. 346 in all: "Old Testament," "St. Jerome," "Passion," "Life of Virgin," Apocalypse," many others. Introduction by Campbell Dodgson. 285pp. 8½ x 12¼. 21097-9 Pa. $7.50

DRAWINGS OF ALBRECHT DURER, edited by Heinrich Wolfflin. 81 plates show development from youth to full style. Many favorites; many new. Introduction by Alfred Werner. 96pp. 8⅛ x 11. 22352-3 Pa. $5.00

THE HUMAN FIGURE, Albrecht Dürer. Experiments in various techniques—stereometric, progressive proportional, and others. Also life studies that rank among finest ever done. Complete reprinting of *Dresden Sketchbook*. 170 plates. 355pp. 8⅜ x 11¼. 21042-1 Pa. $7.95

OF THE JUST SHAPING OF LETTERS, Albrecht Dürer. Renaissance artist explains design of Roman majuscules by geometry, also Gothic lower and capitals. Grolier Club edition. 43pp. 7⅞ x 10¾ 21306-4 Pa. $3.00

TEN BOOKS ON ARCHITECTURE, Vitruvius. The most important book ever written on architecture. Early Roman aesthetics, technology, classical orders, site selection, all other aspects. Stands behind everything since. Morgan translation. 331pp. 5⅜ x 8½. 20645-9 Pa. $4.50

THE FOUR BOOKS OF ARCHITECTURE, Andrea Palladio. 16th-century classic responsible for Palladian movement and style. Covers classical architectural remains, Renaissance revivals, classical orders, etc. 1738 Ware English edition. Introduction by A. Placzek. 216 plates. 110pp. of text. 9½ x 12¾. 21308-0 Pa. $10.00

HORIZONS, Norman Bel Geddes. Great industrialist stage designer, "father of streamlining," on application of aesthetics to transportation, amusement, architecture, etc. 1932 prophetic account; function, theory, specific projects. 222 illustrations. 312pp. 7⅞ x 10¾. 23514-9 Pa. $6.95

FRANK LLOYD WRIGHT'S FALLINGWATER, Donald Hoffmann. Full, illustrated story of conception and building of Wright's masterwork at Bear Run, Pa. 100 photographs of site, construction, and details of completed structure. 112pp. 9¼ x 10. 23671-4 Pa. $5.50

THE ELEMENTS OF DRAWING, John Ruskin. Timeless classic by great Viltorian; starts with basic ideas, works through more difficult. Many practical exercises. 48 illustrations. Introduction by Lawrence Campbell. 228pp. 5⅜ x 8½. 22730-8 Pa. $3.75

GIST OF ART, John Sloan. Greatest modern American teacher, Art Students League, offers innumerable hints, instructions, guided comments to help you in painting. Not a formal course. 46 illustrations. Introduction by Helen Sloan. 200pp. 5⅜ x 8½. 23435-5 Pa. $4.00

THE ANATOMY OF THE HORSE, George Stubbs. Often considered the great masterpiece of animal anatomy. Full reproduction of 1766 edition, plus prospectus; original text and modernized text. 36 plates. Introduction by Eleanor Garvey. 121pp. 11 x 14¾. 23402-9 Pa. $6.00

BRIDGMAN'S LIFE DRAWING, George B. Bridgman. More than 500 illustrative drawings and text teach you to abstract the body into its major masses, use light and shade, proportion; as well as specific areas of anatomy, of which Bridgman is master. 192pp. 6½ x 9¼. (Available in U.S. only) 22710-3 Pa. $3.50

ART NOUVEAU DESIGNS IN COLOR, Alphonse Mucha, Maurice Verneuil, Georges Auriol. Full-color reproduction of *Combinaisons ornementales* (c. 1900) by Art Nouveau masters. Floral, animal, geometric, interlacings, swashes—borders, frames, spots—all incredibly beautiful. 60 plates, hundreds of designs. 9⅜ x 8-1/16. 22885-1 Pa. $4.00

FULL-COLOR FLORAL DESIGNS IN THE ART NOUVEAU STYLE, E. A. Seguy. 166 motifs, on 40 plates, from *Les fleurs et leurs applications decoratives* (1902): borders, circular designs, repeats, allovers, "spots." All in authentic Art Nouveau colors. 48pp. 9⅜ x 12¼. 23439-8 Pa. $5.00

A DIDEROT PICTORIAL ENCYCLOPEDIA OF TRADES AND IN- DUSTRY, edited by Charles C. Gillispie. 485 most interesting plates from the great French Encyclopedia of the 18th century show hundreds of working figures, artifacts, process, land and cityscapes; glassmaking, paper- making, metal extraction, construction, weaving, making furniture, clothing, wigs, dozens of other activities. Plates fully explained. 920pp. 9 x 12. 22284-5, 22285-3 Clothbd., Two-vol. set $40.00

HANDBOOK OF EARLY ADVERTISING ART, Clarence P. Hornung. Largest collection of copyright-free early and antique advertising art ever compiled. Over 6,000 illustrations, from Franklin's time to the 1890's for special effects, novelty. Valuable source, almost inexhaustible.
Pictorial Volume. Agriculture, the zodiac, animals, autos, birds, Christmas, fire engines, flowers, trees, musical instruments, ships, games and sports, much more. Arranged by subject matter and use. 237 plates. 288pp. 9 x 12. 20122-8 Clothbd. $14.50

Typographical Volume. Roman and Gothic faces ranging from 10 point to 300 point, "Barnum," German and Old English faces, script, logotypes, scrolls and flourishes, 1115 ornamental initials, 67 complete alphabets, more. 310 plates. 320pp. 9 x 12. 20123-6 Clothbd. $15.00

CALLIGRAPHY (CALLIGRAPHIA LATINA), J. G. Schwandner. High point of 18th-century ornamental calligraphy. Very ornate initials, scrolls, borders, cherubs, birds, lettered examples. 172pp. 9 x 13. 20475-8 Pa. $7.00

ART FORMS IN NATURE, Ernst Haeckel. Multitude of strangely beautiful natural forms: Radiolaria, Foraminifera, jellyfishes, fungi, turtles, bats, etc. All 100 plates of the 19th-century evolutionist's *Kunstformen der Natur* (1904). 100pp. 9⅜ x 12¼.   22987-4 Pa. $5.00

CHILDREN: A PICTORIAL ARCHIVE FROM NINETEENTH-CENTURY SOURCES, edited by Carol Belanger Grafton. 242 rare, copyright-free wood engravings for artists and designers. Widest such selection available. All illustrations in line. 119pp. 8⅜ x 11¼.
        23694-3 Pa. $4.00

WOMEN: A PICTORIAL ARCHIVE FROM NINETEENTH-CENTURY SOURCES, edited by Jim Harter. 391 copyright-free wood engravings for artists and designers selected from rare periodicals. Most extensive such collection available. All illustrations in line. 128pp. 9 x 12.
        23703-6 Pa. $4.50

ARABIC ART IN COLOR, Prisse d'Avennes. From the greatest ornamentalists of all time—50 plates in color, rarely seen outside the Near East, rich in suggestion and stimulus. Includes 4 plates on covers. 46pp. 9⅜ x 12¼.   23658-7 Pa. $6.00

AUTHENTIC ALGERIAN CARPET DESIGNS AND MOTIFS, edited by June Beveridge. Algerian carpets are world famous. Dozens of geometrical motifs are charted on grids, color-coded, for weavers, needleworkers, craftsmen, designers. 53 illustrations plus 4 in color. 48pp. 8¼ x 11. (Available in U.S. only)   23650-1 Pa. $1.75

DICTIONARY OF AMERICAN PORTRAITS, edited by Hayward and Blanche Cirker. 4000 important Americans, earliest times to 1905, mostly in clear line. Politicians, writers, soldiers, scientists, inventors, industrialists, Indians, Blacks, women, outlaws, etc. Identificatory information. 756pp. 9¼ x 12¾.   21823-6 Clothbd. $40.00

HOW THE OTHER HALF LIVES, Jacob A. Riis. Journalistic record of filth, degradation, upward drive in New York immigrant slums, shops, around 1900. New edition includes 100 original Riis photos, monuments of early photography. 233pp. 10 x 7⅞.   22012-5 Pa. $7.00

NEW YORK IN THE THIRTIES, Berenice Abbott. Noted photographer's fascinating study of city shows new buildings that have become famous and old sights that have disappeared forever. Insightful commentary. 97 photographs. 97pp. 11⅜ x 10.   22967-X Pa. $5.00

MEN AT WORK, Lewis W. Hine. Famous photographic studies of construction workers, railroad men, factory workers and coal miners. New supplement of 18 photos on Empire State building construction. New introduction by Jonathan L. Doherty. Total of 69 photos. 63pp. 8 x 10¾.
        23475-4 Pa. $3.00

THE DEPRESSION YEARS AS PHOTOGRAPHED BY ARTHUR ROTH-STEIN, Arthur Rothstein. First collection devoted entirely to the work of outstanding 1930s photographer: famous dust storm photo, ragged children, unemployed, etc. 120 photographs. Captions. 119pp. 9¼ x 10¾.
23590-4 Pa. $5.00

CAMERA WORK: A PICTORIAL GUIDE, Alfred Stieglitz. All 559 illustrations and plates from the most important periodical in the history of art photography, *Camera Work* (1903-17). Presented four to a page, reduced in size but still clear, in strict chronological order, with complete captions. Three indexes. Glossary. Bibliography. 176pp. 8⅜ x 11¼.
23591-2 Pa. $6.95

ALVIN LANGDON COBURN, PHOTOGRAPHER, Alvin L. Coburn. Revealing autobiography by one of greatest photographers of 20th century gives insider's version of Photo-Secession, plus comments on his own work. 77 photographs by Coburn. Edited by Helmut and Alison Gernsheim. 160pp. 8⅛ x 11.
23685-4 Pa. $6.00

NEW YORK IN THE FORTIES, Andreas Feininger. 162 brilliant photographs by the well-known photographer, formerly with *Life* magazine, show commuters, shoppers, Times Square at night, Harlem nightclub, Lower East Side, etc. Introduction and full captions by John von Hartz. 181pp. 9¼ x 10¾.
23585-8 Pa. $6.95

GREAT NEWS PHOTOS AND THE STORIES BEHIND THEM, John Faber. Dramatic volume of 140 great news photos, 1855 through 1976, and revealing stories behind them, with both historical and technical information. Hindenburg disaster, shooting of Oswald, nomination of Jimmy Carter, etc. 160pp. 8¼ x 11.
23667-6 Pa. $5.00

THE ART OF THE CINEMATOGRAPHER, Leonard Maltin. Survey of American cinematography history and anecdotal interviews with 5 masters—Arthur Miller, Hal Mohr, Hal Rosson, Lucien Ballard, and Conrad Hall. Very large selection of behind-the-scenes production photos. 105 photographs. Filmographies. Index. Originally *Behind the Camera.* 144pp. 8¼ x 11.
23686-2 Pa. $5.00

DESIGNS FOR THE THREE-CORNERED HAT (LE TRICORNE), Pablo Picasso. 32 fabulously rare drawings—including 31 color illustrations of costumes and accessories—for 1919 production of famous ballet. Edited by Parmenia Migel, who has written new introduction. 48pp. 9⅜ x 12¼. (Available in U.S. only)
23709-5 Pa. $5.00

NOTES OF A FILM DIRECTOR, Sergei Eisenstein. Greatest Russian filmmaker explains montage, making of *Alexander Nevsky,* aesthetics; comments on self, associates, great rivals (Chaplin), similar material. 78 illustrations. 240pp. 5⅜ x 8½.
22392-2 Pa. $4.50

HOLLYWOOD GLAMOUR PORTRAITS, edited by John Kobal. 145 photos capture the stars from 1926-49, the high point in portrait photography. Gable, Harlow, Bogart, Bacall, Hedy Lamarr, Marlene Dietrich, Robert Montgomery, Marlon Brando, Veronica Lake; 94 stars in all. Full background on photographers, technical aspects, much more. Total of 160pp. 8⅜ x 11¼. 23352-9 Pa. $6.00

THE NEW YORK STAGE: FAMOUS PRODUCTIONS IN PHOTO-GRAPHS, edited by Stanley Appelbaum. 148 photographs from Museum of City of New York show 142 plays, 1883-1939. *Peter Pan, The Front Page, Dead End, Our Town,* O'Neill, hundreds of actors and actresses, etc. Full indexes. 154pp. 9½ x 10. 23241-7 Pa. $6.00

DIALOGUES CONCERNING TWO NEW SCIENCES, Galileo Galilei. Encompassing 30 years of experiment and thought, these dialogues deal with geometric demonstrations of fracture of solid bodies, cohesion, leverage, speed of light and sound, pendulums, falling bodies, accelerated motion, etc. 300pp. 5⅜ x 8½. 60099-8 Pa. $4.00

THE GREAT OPERA STARS IN HISTORIC PHOTOGRAPHS, edited by James Camner. 343 portraits from the 1850s to the 1940s: Tamburini, Mario, Caliapin, Jeritza, Melchior, Melba, Patti, Pinza, Schipa, Caruso, Farrar, Steber, Gobbi, and many more—270 performers in all. Index. 199pp. 8⅜ x 11¼. 23575-0 Pa. $7.50

J. S. BACH, Albert Schweitzer. Great full-length study of Bach, life, background to music, music, by foremost modern scholar. Ernest Newman translation. 650 musical examples. Total of 928pp. 5⅜ x 8½. (Available in U.S. only) 21631-4, 21632-2 Pa., Two-vol. set $11.00

COMPLETE PIANO SONATAS, Ludwig van Beethoven. All sonatas in the fine Schenker edition, with fingering, analytical material. One of best modern editions. Total of 615pp. 9 x 12. (Available in U.S. only) 23134-8, 23135-6 Pa., Two-vol. set $15.50

KEYBOARD MUSIC, J. S. Bach. Bach-Gesellschaft edition. For harpsichord, piano, other keyboard instruments. English Suites, French Suites, Six Partitas, Goldberg Variations, Two-Part Inventions, Three-Part Sinfonias. 312pp. 8⅛ x 11. (Available in U.S. only) 22360-4 Pa. $6.95

FOUR SYMPHONIES IN FULL SCORE, Franz Schubert. Schubert's four most popular symphonies: No. 4 in C Minor ("Tragic"); No. 5 in B-flat Major; No. 8 in B Minor ("Unfinished"); No. 9 in C Major ("Great"). Breitkopf & Hartel edition. Study score. 261pp. 9⅜ x 12¼. 23681-1 Pa. $6.50

THE AUTHENTIC GILBERT & SULLIVAN SONGBOOK, W. S. Gilbert, A. S. Sullivan. Largest selection available; 92 songs, uncut, original keys, in piano rendering approved by Sullivan. Favorites and lesser-known fine numbers. Edited with plot synopses by James Spero. 3 illustrations. 399pp. 9 x 12. 23482-7 Pa. $9.95

PRINCIPLES OF ORCHESTRATION, Nikolay Rimsky-Korsakov. Great classical orchestrator provides fundamentals of tonal resonance, progression of parts, voice and orchestra, tutti effects, much else in major document. 330pp. of musical excerpts. 489pp. 6½ x 9¼.   21266-1 Pa. $7.50

TRISTAN UND ISOLDE, Richard Wagner. Full orchestral score with complete instrumentation. Do not confuse with piano reduction. Commentary by Felix Mottl, great Wagnerian conductor and scholar. Study score. 655pp. 8⅛ x 11.   22915-7 Pa. $13.95

REQUIEM IN FULL SCORE, Giuseppe Verdi. Immensely popular with choral groups and music lovers. Republication of edition published by C. F. Peters, Leipzig, n. d. German frontmaker in English translation. Glossary. Text in Latin. Study score. 204pp. 9⅜ x 12¼.
23682-X Pa. $6.00

COMPLETE CHAMBER MUSIC FOR STRINGS, Felix Mendelssohn. All of Mendelssohn's chamber music: Octet, 2 Quintets, 6 Quartets, and Four Pieces for String Quartet. (Nothing with piano is included). Complete works edition (1874-7). Study score. 283 pp. 9⅜ x 12¼.
23679-X Pa. $7.50

POPULAR SONGS OF NINETEENTH-CENTURY AMERICA, edited by Richard Jackson. 64 most important songs: "Old Oaken Bucket," "Arkansas Traveler," "Yellow Rose of Texas," etc. Authentic original sheet music, full introduction and commentaries. 290pp. 9 x 12.   23270-0 Pa. $7.95

COLLECTED PIANO WORKS, Scott Joplin. Edited by Vera Brodsky Lawrence. Practically all of Joplin's piano works—rags, two-steps, marches, waltzes, etc., 51 works in all. Extensive introduction by Rudi Blesh. Total of 345pp. 9 x 12.   23106-2 Pa. $14.95

BASIC PRINCIPLES OF CLASSICAL BALLET, Agrippina Vaganova. Great Russian theoretician, teacher explains methods for teaching classical ballet; incorporates best from French, Italian, Russian schools. 118 illustrations. 175pp. 5⅜ x 8½.   22036-2 Pa. $2.50

CHINESE CHARACTERS, L. Wieger. Rich analysis of 2300 characters according to traditional systems into primitives. Historical-semantic analysis to phonetics (Classical Mandarin) and radicals. 820pp. 6⅛ x 9¼.
21321-8 Pa. $10.00

EGYPTIAN LANGUAGE: EASY LESSONS IN EGYPTIAN HIERO-GLYPHICS, E. A. Wallis Budge. Foremost Egyptologist offers Egyptian grammar, explanation of hieroglyphics, many reading texts, dictionary of symbols. 246pp. 5 x 7½. (Available in U.S. only)
21394-3 Clothbd. $7.50

AN ETYMOLOGICAL DICTIONARY OF MODERN ENGLISH, Ernest Weekley. Richest, fullest work, by foremost British lexicographer. Detailed word histories. Inexhaustible. Do not confuse this with *Concise Etymological Dictionary*, which is abridged. Total of 856pp. 6½ x 9¼.
21873-2, 21874-0 Pa., Two-vol. set $12.00

A MAYA GRAMMAR, Alfred M. Tozzer. Practical, useful English-language grammar by the Harvard anthropologist who was one of the three greatest American scholars in the area of Maya culture. Phonetics, grammatical processes, syntax, more. 301pp. 5⅜ x 8½.   23465-7 Pa. $4.00

THE JOURNAL OF HENRY D. THOREAU, edited by Bradford Torrey, F. H. Allen. Complete reprinting of 14 volumes, 1837-61, over two million words; the sourcebooks for *Walden*, etc. Definitive. All original sketches, plus 75 photographs. Introduction by Walter Harding. Total of 1804pp. 8½ x 12¼.   20312-3, 20313-1 Clothbd., Two-vol. set $70.00

CLASSIC GHOST STORIES, Charles Dickens and others. 18 wonderful stories you've wanted to reread: "The Monkey's Paw," "The House and the Brain," "The Upper Berth," "The Signalman," "Dracula's Guest," "The Tapestried Chamber," etc. Dickens, Scott, Mary Shelley, Stoker, etc. 330pp. 5⅜ x 8½.   20735-8 Pa. **$4.50**

SEVEN SCIENCE FICTION NOVELS, H. G. Wells. Full novels. *First Men in the Moon, Island of Dr. Moreau, War of the Worlds, Food of the Gods, Invisible Man, Time Machine, In the Days of the Comet.* A basic science-fiction library. 1015pp. 5⅜ x 8½. (Available in U.S. only)
20264-X Clothbd. $8.95

ARMADALE, Wilkie Collins. Third great mystery novel by the author of *The Woman in White* and *The Moonstone.* Ingeniously plotted narrative shows an exceptional command of character, incident and mood. Original magazine version with 40 illustrations. 597pp. 5⅜ x 8½.
23429-0 Pa. $6.00

MASTERS OF MYSTERY, H. Douglas Thomson. The first book in English (1931) devoted to history and aesthetics of detective story. Poe, Doyle, LeFanu, Dickens, many others, up to 1930. New introduction and notes by E. F. Bleiler. 288pp. 5⅜ x 8½. (Available in U.S. only)
23606-4 Pa. $4.00

FLATLAND, E. A. Abbott. Science-fiction classic explores life of 2-D being in 3-D world. Read also as introduction to thought about hyperspace. Introduction by Banesh Hoffmann. 16 illustrations. 103pp. 5⅜ x 8½.
20001-9 Pa. $2.00

THREE SUPERNATURAL NOVELS OF THE VICTORIAN PERIOD, edited, with an introduction, by E. F. Bleiler. Reprinted complete and unabridged, three great classics of the supernatural: *The Haunted Hotel* by Wilkie Collins, *The Haunted House at Latchford* by Mrs. J. H. Riddell, and *The Lost Stradivarius* by J. Meade Falkner. 325pp. 5⅜ x 8½.
22571-2 Pa. $4.00

AYESHA: THE RETURN OF "SHE," H. Rider Haggard. Virtuoso sequel featuring the great mythic creation, Ayesha, in an adventure that is fully as good as the first book, *She.* Original magazine version, with 47 original illustrations by Maurice Greiffenhagen. 189pp. 6½ x 9¼.
23649-8 Pa. $3.50

UNCLE SILAS, J. Sheridan LeFanu. Victorian Gothic mystery novel, considered by many best of period, even better than Collins or Dickens. Wonderful psychological terror. Introduction by Frederick Shroyer. 436pp. 5⅜ x 8½. 21715-9 Pa. $6.00

JURGEN, James Branch Cabell. The great erotic fantasy of the 1920's that delighted thousands, shocked thousands more. Full final text, Lane edition with 13 plates by Frank Pape. 346pp. 5⅜ x 8½.
23507-6 Pa. $4.50

THE CLAVERINGS, Anthony Trollope. Major novel, chronicling aspects of British Victorian society, personalities. Reprint of Cornhill serialization, 16 plates by M. Edwards; first reprint of full text. Introduction by Norman Donaldson. 412pp. 5⅜ x 8½. 23464-9 Pa. $5.00

KEPT IN THE DARK, Anthony Trollope. Unusual short novel about Victorian morality and abnormal psychology by the great English author. Probably the first American publication. Frontispiece by Sir John Millais. 92pp. 6½ x 9¼. 23609-9 Pa. $2.50

RALPH THE HEIR, Anthony Trollope. Forgotten tale of illegitimacy, inheritance. Master novel of Trollope's later years. Victorian country estates, clubs, Parliament, fox hunting, world of fully realized characters. Reprint of 1871 edition. 12 illustrations by F. A. Faser. 434pp. of text. 5⅜ x 8½. 23642-0 Pa. $5.00

YEKL and THE IMPORTED BRIDEGROOM AND OTHER STORIES OF THE NEW YORK GHETTO, Abraham Cahan. Film *Hester Street* based on *Yekl* (1896). Novel, other stories among first about Jewish immigrants of N.Y.'s East Side. Highly praised by W. D. Howells—Cahan "a new star of realism." New introduction by Bernard G. Richards. 240pp. 5⅜ x 8½. 22427-9 Pa. $3.50

THE HIGH PLACE, James Branch Cabell. Great fantasy writer's enchanting comedy of disenchantment set in 18th-century France. Considered by some critics to be even better than his famous *Jurgen*. 10 illustrations and numerous vignettes by noted fantasy artist Frank C. Pape. 320pp. 5⅜ x 8½. 23670-6 Pa. $4.00

ALICE'S ADVENTURES UNDER GROUND, Lewis Carroll. Facsimile of ms. Carroll gave Alice Liddell in 1864. Different in many ways from final Alice. Handlettered, illustrated by Carroll. Introduction by Martin Gardner. 128pp. 5⅜ x 8½. 21482-6 Pa. $2.50

FAVORITE ANDREW LANG FAIRY TALE BOOKS IN MANY COLORS, Andrew Lang. The four Lang favorites in a boxed set—the complete *Red, Green, Yellow* and *Blue* Fairy Books. 164 stories; 439 illustrations by Lancelot Speed, Henry Ford and G. P. Jacomb Hood. Total of about 1500pp. 5⅜ x 8½. 23407-X Boxed set, Pa. $15.95

HOUSEHOLD STORIES BY THE BROTHERS GRIMM. All the great Grimm stories: "Rumpelstiltskin," "Snow White," "Hansel and Gretel," etc., with 114 illustrations by Walter Crane. 269pp. 5⅜ x 8½.
21080-4 Pa. $3.50

SLEEPING BEAUTY, illustrated by Arthur Rackham. Perhaps the fullest, most delightful version ever, told by C. S. Evans. Rackham's best work. 49 illustrations. 110pp. 7⅞ x 10¾. 22756-1 Pa. $2.50

AMERICAN FAIRY TALES, L. Frank Baum. Young cowboy lassoes Father Time; dummy in Mr. Floman's department store window comes to life; and 10 other fairy tales. 41 illustrations by N. P. Hall, Harry Kennedy, Ike Morgan, and Ralph Gardner. 209pp. 5⅜ x 8½. 23643-9 Pa. $3.00

THE WONDERFUL WIZARD OF OZ, L. Frank Baum. Facsimile in full color of America's finest children's classic. Introduction by Martin Gardner. 143 illustrations by W. W. Denslow. 267pp. 5⅜ x 8½.
20691-2 Pa. $3.50

THE TALE OF PETER RABBIT, Beatrix Potter. The inimitable Peter's terrifying adventure in Mr. McGregor's garden, with all 27 wonderful, full-color Potter illustrations. 55pp. 4¼ x 5½. (Available in U.S. only)
22827-4 Pa. $1.25

THE STORY OF KING ARTHUR AND HIS KNIGHTS, Howard Pyle. Finest children's version of life of King Arthur. 48 illustrations by Pyle. 131pp. 6⅛ x 9¼. 21445-1 Pa. $4.95

CARUSO'S CARICATURES, Enrico Caruso. Great tenor's remarkable caricatures of self, fellow musicians, composers, others. Toscanini, Puccini, Farrar, etc. Impish, cutting, insightful. 473 illustrations. Preface by M. Sisca. 217pp. 8⅜ x 11¼. 23528-9 Pa. $6.95

PERSONAL NARRATIVE OF A PILGRIMAGE TO ALMADINAH AND MECCAH, Richard Burton. Great travel classic by remarkably colorful personality. Burton, disguised as a Moroccan, visited sacred shrines of Islam, narrowly escaping death. Wonderful observations of Islamic life, customs, personalities. 47 illustrations. Total of 959pp. 5⅜ x 8½.
21217-3, 21218-1 Pa., Two-vol. set $12.00

INCIDENTS OF TRAVEL IN YUCATAN, John L. Stephens. Classic (1843) exploration of jungles of Yucatan, looking for evidences of Maya civilization. Travel adventures, Mexican and Indian culture, etc. Total of 669pp. 5⅜ x 8½. 20926-1, 20927-X Pa., Two-vol. set $7.90

AMERICAN LITERARY AUTOGRAPHS FROM WASHINGTON IRVING TO HENRY JAMES, Herbert Cahoon, et al. Letters, poems, manuscripts of Hawthorne, Thoreau, Twain, Alcott, Whitman, 67 other prominent American authors. Reproductions, full transcripts and commentary. Plus checklist of all American Literary Autographs in The Pierpont Morgan Library. Printed on exceptionally high-quality paper. 136 illustrations. 212pp. 9⅛ x 12¼. 23548-3 Pa. $12.50

AN AUTOBIOGRAPHY, Margaret Sanger. Exciting personal account of hard-fought battle for woman's right to birth control, against prejudice, church, law. Foremost feminist document. 504pp. 5⅜ x 8½.
20470-7 Pa. $5.50

MY BONDAGE AND MY FREEDOM, Frederick Douglass. Born as a slave, Douglass became outspoken force in antislavery movement. The best of Douglass's autobiographies. Graphic description of slave life. Introduction by P. Foner. 464pp. 5⅜ x 8½. 22457-0 Pa. $5.50

LIVING MY LIFE, Emma Goldman. Candid, no holds barred account by foremost American anarchist: her own life, anarchist movement, famous contemporaries, ideas and their impact. Struggles and confrontations in America, plus deportation to U.S.S.R. Shocking inside account of persecution of anarchists under Lenin. 13 plates. Total of 944pp. 5⅜ x 8½.
22543-7, 22544-5 Pa., Two-vol. set $12.00

LETTERS AND NOTES ON THE MANNERS, CUSTOMS AND CONDITIONS OF THE NORTH AMERICAN INDIANS, George Catlin. Classic account of life among Plains Indians: ceremonies, hunt, warfare, etc. Dover edition reproduces for first time all original paintings. 312 plates. 572pp. of text. 6⅛ x 9¼. 22118-0, 22119-9 Pa.. Two-vol. set $12.00

THE MAYA AND THEIR NEIGHBORS, edited by Clarence L. Hay, others. Synoptic view of Maya civilization in broadest sense, together with Northern, Southern neighbors. Integrates much background, valuable detail not elsewhere. Prepared by greatest scholars: Kroeber, Morley, Thompson, Spinden, Vaillant, many others. Sometimes called Tozzer Memorial Volume. 60 illustrations, linguistic map. 634pp. 5⅜ x 8½.
23510-6 Pa. $10.00

HANDBOOK OF THE INDIANS OF CALIFORNIA, A. L. Kroeber. Foremost American anthropologist offers complete ethnographic study of each group. Monumental classic. 459 illustrations, maps. 995pp. 5⅜ x 8½.
23368-5 Pa. $13.00

SHAKTI AND SHAKTA, Arthur Avalon. First book to give clear, cohesive analysis of Shakta doctrine, Shakta ritual and Kundalini Shakti (yoga). Important work by one of world's foremost students of Shaktic and Tantric thought. 732pp. 5⅜ x 8½. (Available in U.S. only)
23645-5 Pa. $7.95

AN INTRODUCTION TO THE STUDY OF THE MAYA HIEROGLYPHS, Syvanus Griswold Morley. Classic study by one of the truly great figures in hieroglyph research. Still the best introduction for the student for reading Maya hieroglyphs. New introduction by J. Eric S. Thompson. 117 illustrations. 284pp. 5⅜ x 8½. 23108-9 Pa. $4.00

A STUDY OF MAYA ART, Herbert J. Spinden. Landmark classic interprets Maya symbolism, estimates styles, covers ceramics, architecture, murals, stone carvings as artforms. Still a basic book in area. New introduction by J. Eric Thompson. Over 750 illustrations. 341pp. 8⅜ x 11¼.
21235-1 Pa. $6.95

GEOMETRY, RELATIVITY AND THE FOURTH DIMENSION, Rudolf Rucker. Exposition of fourth dimension, means of visualization, concepts of relativity as Flatland characters continue adventures. Popular, easily followed yet accurate, profound. 141 illustrations. 133pp. 5⅜ x 8½.
23400-2 Pa. $2.75

THE ORIGIN OF LIFE, A. I. Oparin. Modern classic in biochemistry, the first rigorous examination of possible evolution of life from nitrocarbon compounds. Non-technical, easily followed. Total of 295pp. 5⅜ x 8½.
60213-3 Pa. $4.00

PLANETS, STARS AND GALAXIES, A. E. Fanning. Comprehensive introductory survey: the sun, solar system, stars, galaxies, universe, cosmology; quasars, radio stars, etc. 24pp. of photographs. 189pp. 5⅜ x 8½. (Available in U.S. only)
21680-2 Pa. $3.75

THE THIRTEEN BOOKS OF EUCLID'S ELEMENTS, translated with introduction and commentary by Sir Thomas L. Heath. Definitive edition. Textual and linguistic notes, mathematical analysis, 2500 years of critical commentary. Do not confuse with abridged school editions. Total of 1414pp. 5⅜ x 8½.   60088-2, 60089-0, 60090-4 Pa., Three-vol. set $18.50

Prices subject to change without notice.

Available at your book dealer or write for free catalogue to Dept. GI, Dover Publications, Inc., 180 Varick St., N.Y., N.Y. 10014. Dover publishes more than 175 books each year on science, elementary and advanced mathematics, biology, music, art, literary history, social sciences and other areas.